EUCALYPTS

Golden Gleams, a c. 1908 carbon photograph by John Kauffmann (1864–1942), who used eucalypts as a subject for his soft-focus artistic works. His exhibitions influenced later photographers such as Harold Cazneaux.

EUCALYPTS

A CELEBRATION

John Wrigley and Murray Fagg

ALLEN&UNWIN

Contents

INTRODUCTION vi

PART 1

THE BIOLOGY OF EUCALYPTS 1

1 Evolution and Distribution 3
2 Where Eucalypts Occur 9
3 Growth Characteristics 15
4 Reaction to Fire and Drought 27
5 Eucalypts as Wildlife Habitat 35
6 Plant Parasites of Eucalypts 45

PART 2

CLASSIFYING EUCALYPTS 51

7 The Three Genera 53
8 Naming Eucalypt Species 59
9 Botanists Who Named Eucalypts 63
10 Identifying Eucalypts 71

PART 3

A SOCIAL HISTORY OF EUCALYPTS 75

11 Traditional Aboriginal Society 77
12 European Settlement 91
13 A Brief History of Forestry 107
14 Eucalypts in Wartime 117

PART 4

UTILISING EUCALYPTS TODAY 121

15 Propagation and Cultivation 123
16 Managing Pests and Diseases 127
17 Hybrids and Cultivars 131
18 Landscaping and Planting 135
19 Eucalypt Arboreta 147
20 Timber Production 155

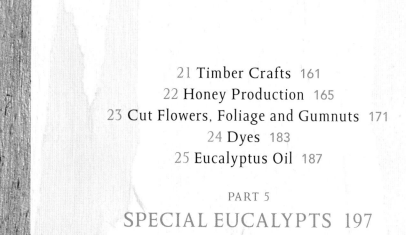

21 Timber Crafts 161
22 Honey Production 165
23 Cut Flowers, Foliage and Gumnuts 171
24 Dyes 183
25 Eucalyptus Oil 187

PART 5

SPECIAL EUCALYPTS 197

26 Iconic Groups of Eucalypts 199
27 Endangered Eucalypts 207
28 Significant Individual Eucalypts 215
29 Eucalypts Overseas 229

PART 6

EUCALYPTS IN ART AND CULTURE 241

30 Painting Gum Trees 243
31 Photographing Gum Trees 251
32 Flower Painters and Illustrators 257
33 Eucalypts in Applied Art 267
34 Eucalypts in Advertising 275
35 Australiana and Collectables 279
36 Music, Stage and Screen 287
37 Eucalypts and Children 293
38 Eucalypts in Australian Literature 298

ACKNOWLEDGEMENTS 304

ABBREVIATIONS FOR PHOTO CREDITS 306

REFERENCES 306

CHECKLIST OF SPECIES 313

INDEX 338

Introduction

This is a book about a tree, a land and a nation, a celebration of all the things that link this tree to the landscape and to the national psyche. No other country's vegetation is so dominated by a single group of plants. About 95 per cent of the forest trees of Australia belong to this group. Is it any wonder that when Australians see eucalypts growing overseas, they feel homesick?

Charles Darwin wrote in *The Voyage of the Beagle* in 1836:

> The extreme uniformity of the vegetation is the most remarkable feature of the landscape of the greater part of New South Wales. Everywhere we have an open woodland . . . The trees nearly all belong to the one family, and mostly have their leaves placed in a vertical, instead of, as in Europe, in a nearly horizontal position; the foliage is scanty, and of a peculiar pale green tint, without any gloss.

What is a eucalypt? To the modern botanist it is a name for plants in three closely related genera: *Eucalyptus*, *Corymbia* and *Angophora*; to the average Australian they are 'gum trees'. The term 'gum tree' was first used by Captain James Cook in his journal in 1770, referring to northern Australian 'eucalypti' and following comments by Joseph Banks about the gum exuding from trees at Botany Bay:

> Here are but few sorts of Trees besides the Gum Tree, which is most numerous, and is the same that we found on the Southern Part of the Coast, only here they do not grow near so large.
> The Woods do not produce any great variety of Trees; there are only two or three sorts that can be called Timber, the largest is the gum Tree, which grows all over the country; the wood of this Tree is too hard and ponderous for most common uses.

From the forest giants of moist coastal areas to the shrub-like, slender-trunked mallees of our arid interior, eucalypts dominate our landscapes. The Aboriginals recognised their value for shelter, medicine, food, spear-making and canoe building. Subsequently, we have used them for timber, honey production, amenity planting, firewood, oils and erosion control. We have exported them to many other countries where they have formed important forestry plantations and been useful shade trees.

Tracks fringed by eucalypts are a common Australian scene.

Their performance in such a variety of climates and soil types has earned them a reputation for hardiness unrivalled by any other group of trees. Absent only from dense rainforests and our waterless deserts and with more than 850 species, there is one for almost any location. They withstand our severe bushfires by adopting ingenious survival methods. Some have huge masses of tissue at or below ground level called lignotubers that reshoot after the fire has passed. Others have dormant buds below the thick bark and these are able to sprout into new branches.

Eucalypts provide food and shelter for our wildlife. Nectar from the flowers is food for parrots and honeyeaters as well as small mammals; leaves of several species are the staple food for Koalas; hollows in their trunks are used as nesting sites for birds, mammals and reptiles.

Eucalypts are part of the Australian landscape—both the natural landscape and the modified landscape. The country track through farmland with its fringe of eucalypts, or the stately isolated trees left in the middle of wheat fields—these are images that give us a sense of identity.

Our relationship with eucalypts has changed with time. Where once the trees were seen as obstacles to our exploitation of the land, we now form landcare groups to replant the land our forefathers fought so hard to clear.

Eucalypts have been a source of inspiration for art, literature and music. We have sung about 'a home among the gum trees'; we have read stories of gumnut babies to our children; we have admired paintings of beautiful ghost gums by Albert Namatjira; and a novel called *Eucalyptus*, littered with botanical names, has won the highest literary awards of the country.

Travellers across our great land appreciate the majesty of River Red Gums (*Eucalyptus camaldulensis*) lining our rivers, the colourful flowers of the sandplain mallees and the grandeur of the immense Karri (*E. diversicolor*) trees of the south-west.

Let's celebrate these wonderful plants by learning a little more about them.

Magnificent isolated eucalypts in the middle of agricultural land are a familiar part of the Australian landscape.

PART 1

THE BIOLOGY
OF EUCALYPTS

Arillastrum gummiferum, from New Caledonia, is thought to be related to the ancestor of the eucalypts. PHOTO: DANIEL LETOCART.

1 Evolution and Distribution

SOME 208 MILLION YEARS AGO THE GREAT SUPERCONTINENT PANGAEA, which connected all land masses, began to separate into two parts—Laurasia and Gondwana. Gondwana consisted of what we now know as Africa, South America, Australia, India, New Zealand, New Caledonia and Antarctica. Fossil records indicate that vegetation at this time consisted of ferns, horsetails, cycads and conifers living in a hot, wet environment. The origin of the first flowering plants (Angiosperms) is still being debated, but those that evolved in the western part of Gondwana radiated throughout the southern continents, forming tropical forests.

Between 120 and 100 million years ago, Gondwana gradually broke up with the separation of Africa, South America and India. About 80 million years ago New Zealand and New Caledonia separated from the remaining Gondwana landmass and, eventually, about 50 million years ago, Australia left Antarctica and drifted north. As this happened, Australia's climate changed—it became drier, fires were more frequent and the soil became more impoverished.

The broad-leaved plants of the tropical forests could not cope with such changes and plants began to evolve to adapt to these new conditions by the development of small hard leaves set close together and other features that aided in survival. Tropical forests still existed in favourable areas and it is thought that *Arillastrum*, a genus now only found in New Caledonia, is probably the most likely progenitor of the eucalypts as it shares a number of features with *Angophora*. Other genera still existing in the tropical rainforest of northern Australia are also thought to have some affinity to the eucalypt group. These are *Stockwellia quadrifida* a monotypic genus from the Atherton tableland and *Allosyncarpia ternata* from Arnhem Land.

Gondwana and its fragmentation
Gondwana when the continents were joined and the vegetation consisted of ferns, horsetails, cycads and conifers.

Between 120 and 100 million years ago, Gondwana gradually broke up, with the separation of Africa, South America and India.

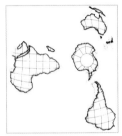

After New Zealand and New Caledonia separated from the remaining Gondwana landmass, Australia left Antarctica and drifted north into its present position.

A third genus, *Eucalyptopsis*, with two species from Papua New Guinea, is also related. The precise relationship of these species with the eucalypts is still being argued by academics.

There is fossil evidence of eucalypts in Australia at least as far back as 45 million years ago from rocks near Lake Eyre in South Australia. Fossils in the company of these eucalypts include tree ferns, Kurrajongs (*Brachychiton*) and Araucaria-like trees, while ripple marks suggest water was abundant. In other parts of Australia there are pollen deposits from 34 million years ago. More recent fossil examples include leaves and fruit from 20 million years ago and a tree stump dated 22 million years ago found in the Lachlan Valley, New South Wales.

Thought to be a close relative of the eucalypts, this *Allosyncarpia ternata* grows in protected pockets among the eucalypt woodlands of Kakadu National Park.

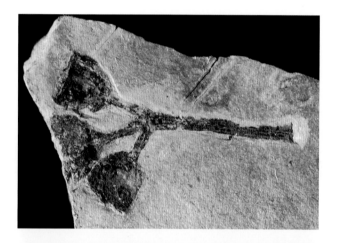

Top left: Fossil gumnuts from Berwick Quarry, Victoria, found in rocks which also contain fossil eucalypt and Southern Beech (*Nothofagus*) leaves. These rocks are dated about 20 million years ago. PHOTO: COURTESY MARY WHITE, FROM HER BOOK *THE GREENING OF GONDWANA*.

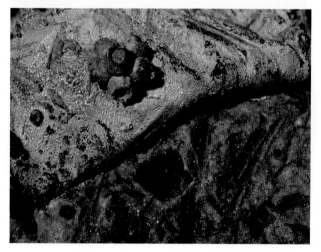

Left: Fossil gumnuts from near Lake Eyre, South Australia, dated about 45 million years ago. The top part of this photo shows a piece of latex removed from the fossil cavity in the rock beneath. The cast allows botanists to examine in fine detail the shape of the plant fragment, which has rotted away leaving a different material to that which formed the hard silcrete of today's rock. PHOTO: COURTESY MARY WHITE, FROM HER BOOK *AFTER THE GREENING: THE BROWNING OF AUSTRALIA*.

Distribution

Eucalypts are found in almost every vegetation type in Australia, with the exception of the highest peaks of the Snowy Mountains and most rainforest communities. In arid districts they are confined to areas where some residual moisture is available. All but four species and one variety are native to Australia with several other species spilling over into Papua New Guinea and nearby islands. The four non-native species are *Eucalyptus deglupta*, the only species to occur naturally in the northern hemisphere, found in Papua New Guinea and as far north as Mindanao in the Philippines; *E. urophylla*, found on Timor and six nearby Indonesian islands; *E. wetarensis* from Wetar Island near Timor; and *E. orophila* from East Timor, both closely related to *E. urophylla*. *E. alba* var. *alba* only occurs on East Timor, while the other variety, var. *australasica*, is widespread in the Northern Territory and the northern Kimberley.

Two of the most widely distributed eucalypts in Australia are the River Red Gum (*E. camaldulensis*), absent only from Tasmania and the southern coastal regions of the mainland, and the famous Coolabah (*E. coolabah*), which is found over much of the arid and semi-arid parts of the mainland. Many other species have very restricted distributions. *Eucalyptus recurva*, a mallee from near Mongarlowe in the Southern Highlands of New South Wales is known from only five plants. *Eucalyptus copulans*, a smooth-barked tree from the Blue Mountains which grows up to 20 metres, is known from only one tree, and the Meelup Mallee (*E. phylacis*) a small tree or mallee with coarse, non-fibrous bark, is only known

Trees of *Eucalyptus urophylla* near the village of Fatum Nasi, north of So'e, West Timor. These trees are growing at an altitude of about 1530 metres. PHOTO: B. HADLOW.

from a single population of about 25 trees in the Cape Naturaliste area of south-west Western Australia.

Of the species that only occur naturally outside Australia, the Rainbow Gum (*E. deglupta*) is the best known and most widely grown. Its common name derives from its multi-coloured trunk, on which the bark peels sporadically, revealing the green fresh bark beneath. The new bark then gradually changes to blue, purple, orange and maroon. It occurs on Mindanao in the Philippines as well as New Britain, New Guinea and Sulawesi, and is the only eucalypt to thus be found naturally in the northern hemisphere. As a fast-growing tree to 60 metres, it is now widely grown in plantations

The Rainbow Gum (*Eucalyptus deglupta*) does not occur in Australia. It is aptly named for the colours of its bark. PHOTO: A. LEUBSCHER.

River Red Gums (*Eucalyptus camaldulensis*) on backwaters of the River Murray, northern Victoria. They can withstand seasonal flooding.

The Mongarlowe Mallee (*Eucalyptus recurva*), a rare species discovered in 1985. PHOTO: M. CRISP/APII.

in Brazil, Africa, Taiwan and Malaysia, where its timber is used as pulpwood for paper manufacture.

The Timor Mountain Gum (*E. urophylla*) is another species that has found a place in world forestry. Although endemic to Timor, it is now grown in plantations in Brazil, Africa, China, Papua New Guinea and Malaysia. Its timber is used for firewood, heavy construction work and paper manufacture, and the oil distilled from the leaves is a good source of paracymene, used in perfumery and disinfectants. It forms a tree to 45 metres.

In 1995, Timor Mountain Gum was closely examined by Lindsay Pryor and foresters from the CSIRO and was considered to consist of three separate species, *E. urophylla*, *E. wetarensis* and *E. orophila*. *Eucalyptus orophila*, confined to the mountain districts of central East Timor, is a smaller tree to 14 metres with broader leaves, and *E. wetarensis,* a narrow-leaved species growing to 17 metres, is endemic to Wetar Island off the north coast of Timor.

The fourth extra-Australian species is the White Gum (*E. alba* var. *alba*), native to Timor. It is closely related to the Australian subspecies (var. *australasica*), differing mainly in having larger gumnuts. Its timber is used for fuel and heavy construction work.

Natural distribution of eucalypts outside Australia

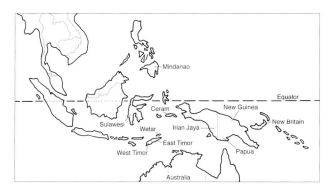

SPECIES	DISTRIBUTION
Corymbia disjuncta	Papua (PNG) Australia
C. latifolia	Papua (PNG) Australia
C. novoguinensis	Irian Jaya (Indonesia) Papua (PNG) Australia
C. papuana	Irian Jaya (Indonesia) Papua (PNG) Australia
Eucalyptus alba var. *alba*	East Timor
E. brassiana	Papua (PNG) Australia
E. deglupta	New Britain (PNG) New Guinea (PNG) Ceram (Indonesia) Sulawesi (Indonesia) Mindanao (Philippines)
E. orophila	East Timor
E. pellita	Papua (PNG) Australia
E. tereticornis	Papua (PNG) Australia
E. urophylla	East Timor West Timor (Indonesia) and nearby islands
E. wetarensis	Wetar Island (Indonesia)

WHITE GUM
(*Eucalyptus alba* var. *australasica*)

While var. *alba* occurs only in Papua New Guinea and East Timor, this handsome tree is found in the Kimberley and the Top End of the Northern Territory where it favours seasonally wet situations. It will reach 20 metres high and may become completely deciduous in the dry season. White Gum is closely related to the Northern Salmon Gum (*E. bigalerita*), differing in the shape of the leaves, which are broader and almost round. They occupy similar situations. The main feature of both species is their smooth trunks, which may be orange, pale pink or yellow, maturing to white and then grey before they shed their bark. The fragrant white flowers may be borne prolifically and have been used for honey production.

This photograph shows the beautiful orange-coloured bark of *E. alba* var. *australasica*.

Salt Gum (*Eucalyptus salicola*), growing here on the very edge of Lake Harvey, a salt lake in Western Australia. It is very tolerant of salty soils.
PHOTO: BROOKER & KLEINIG/APII.

2 Where Eucalypts Occur

AUSTRALIA'S ISOLATION SINCE THE BREAK-UP OF THE SUPERCONTINENT GONDWANA HAS contributed greatly to the distinctiveness of its vegetation. About 75 per cent of Australia's woody plants are described as 'endemic', meaning they occur only in Australia. What makes our vegetation unique is that most of the continent is dominated by two plant groups—the eucalypts and the acacias.

Our current vegetation was mostly shaped over the last 65 million years. During the early part of this period, Australia had a uniformly humid and warm, seasonally wet climate. The continent was already very old and weathered with soils of low fertility and these humid conditions further reduced the fertility by the formation of soils that bind nutrients such as phosphorus into insoluble iron and aluminium compounds. Apart from a few places with volcanic activity, the continent became dominated by infertile soils and sands.

The northern drift of the continent resulted in much drier conditions, especially in the last 15 million years. In the last 3 million years there was considerable climate variation, with glaciation and sea level changes. With climatic fluctuations plant communities expand and contract, often leaving relicts scattered in specialised habitats, encouraging the formation of distinct species.

Many Australian plants have special adaptations that suggest fire has been a major influence on their evolution over a long period of time. There is strong evidence that the use of fire by Aboriginal people over the last 40,000 years probably resulted in more frequent and less intense fires than in pre-Aboriginal times, and that this has contributed to the dominance of eucalypts and other fire-adapted plants in the vegetation.

The long period of aridity in Australia has led to the formation of wide areas of saline soils and wetlands. At least 21 species of eucalypt are known to occur in saline soils over part of their natural distribution. Examples include Swamp Mahogany (*Eucalyptus robusta*) in swampy estuarine sites along the central east coast, and *E. halophila* and Salt Gum (*E. salicola*) on the margins of salt lakes in south-western Australia.

There have been several attempts over the years to develop a classification system for the vegetation of Australia. This has resulted in a range of terminology, with various botanists and ecologists using different categories. Thus the term 'closed forest' has a similar meaning to 'rainforest', which is often popularly known as 'jungle' when it occurs in the tropics. This has also resulted in vegetation maps showing distinct straight-line edges to vegetation types at state borders when different definitions and systems have been used by adjacent states.

In most of these systems a key element is the per cent cover of the uppermost plant layer—this attempts to quantify the amount of foliage compared with sky you see when looking directly upwards. Other considerations are the height of the dominant plants and the plant groups that make up the various layers within the vegetation.

In 2001 the Commonwealth government adopted the National Vegetation Information System (NVIS) in an attempt to standardise classification and vegetation mapping. To avoid confusion, this is the system we use in discussing vegetation types in this chapter, mainly those dominated by eucalypts. The full NVIS classification divides each of these broad groups into many sub-groups.

Rainforest and vine thickets

Often called 'closed forests' and defined as having more than 70 per cent cover (i.e. you could see less than 30 per cent sky if you looked straight up) this vegetation can occur from the tropics down to Tasmania. We don't expect to find eucalypts in these forests, and in a broad sense we define Australian rainforests by the absence of eucalypts.

Eucalypt tall open forests

These occur only in the wetter areas of eastern Australia from north Queensland to Tasmania, and in the south-west of Western Australia. Tall open forests are defined by having dominant eucalypt trees from 30 to 100 metres tall, with 30–70 per cent cover. They

Eucalypt tall open forest. Messmate Stringybark (*Eucalyptus obliqua*) dominate this forest fringing the Picton River in Tasmania.

have a well-developed, often broad-leaved shrubby understorey sometimes including tree ferns. They are often adjacent to rainforests. The above-ground biomass in these forests—the weight of all the living material in a given area—is considered to be among the highest in the world. Large areas of eucalypt tall open forest were extensively logged following European settlement, and the remaining forests are mostly 'secondary', having had the larger trees removed. Approximately 33 per cent of the pre-European extent has been cleared, accounting for about 1.5 per cent of the total clearing in Australia. Tall open forests are sometimes found in the islands north of Australia, where Rainbow Gum (*E. deglupta*) occurs on deep, moist, well-aerated soils of high fertility.

Eucalypt open forests

One of the most widespread vegetation types, these forests are defined by the eucalypts, varying from 10 to 30 metres in height, with 30–70 per cent cover. They occur along the plains, foothills and ranges of the Great Dividing Range, the subcoastal ranges of south-west Western Australia and around the Top End. In general they occur in areas of moderate temperature and rainfall where the phosphorus level in the soil is also relatively moderate by Australian standards. Eucalypt open forests are considered 'species rich', with a mixture of several eucalypts growing in combination, rather than one species being dominant in an area. They generally have a shrubby understorey, but in drier sites it might be grassy with scattered shrubs or cycads. This vegetation has been extensively cleared for agriculture or grazing. Approximately 30 per cent of the pre-European extent has been cleared, accounting for just over 10 per cent of the total clearing in Australia.

Eucalypt low open forests

These forests are defined as having trees from 5 to 10 metres in height with 30–70 per cent cover, and they occur on less favourable sites where extreme cold, dryness or poor soils limit growth. The eucalypt species might be the same as those growing in adjacent open forest under better conditions. Most of this vegetation was

Eucalypt low open forest. Messmate Stringybark (*Eucalyptus obliqua*) and the grass-tree (*Xanthorrhoea* sp.) dominate this forest near Myponga in South Australia.

Eucalypt open forest. Brittle Gum (*Eucalyptus mannifera*) dominates this forest near the Shoalhaven River in New South Wales.

not suitable for agriculture and there was less clearing. Approximately 14 per cent of the pre-European extent has been cleared, accounting for about 0.2 per cent of the total clearing in Australia.

Eucalypt woodlands

Woodlands in general are defined as having 10–30 per cent cover, which usually means that the canopies of the trees do not touch each other. It is the spacing of the trees rather than their height that is important. They can be single trunked, or occasionally tall mallees. The understorey can be shrubby or grassy. They occur from the tropics to Tasmania and the goldfield regions of Western Australia, usually in a transition zone between the open forests and the arid or mallee regions. Sometimes the trees can be quite tall, as with the River Red Gums (*E. camaldulensis*) on riverine flats. Approximately 31 per cent of the pre-European extent has been cleared, accounting for about 33 per cent of the total clearing in Australia.

Eucalypt open woodlands

Open woodlands are characterised by broad spacing between trees, with less than 10 per cent cover. The trees can be single trunked or mallee-like, tall or quite stunted. Such open woodlands occur in lower rainfall areas fringing forested areas, or where moisture or nutrients may limit tree growth. The largest areas are now in Queensland and the Northern Territory, but they once covered vast areas of south-eastern and Western Australia in what we now know as the 'wheatbelt'. In the south the understorey tends to be a shrubby layer, but in the north the ground layer is often hummock grasses such as *Triodia* or tussock grasses such as *Sorghum* or *Themeda*. Sometimes the eucalypt trees are scattered with acacias, banksias or native pines. Approximately 25 per cent of the pre-European extent has been cleared, accounting for about 13 per cent of the total clearing in Australia.

Eucalypt woodland. Merrit (*Eucalyptus urna*) and rough-barked Black Morrell (*E. melanoxylon*) with an understorey of salt bushes (chenopods) dominate this woodland near Peak Charles in Western Australia.

Eucalypt open woodland. Blakely's Red Gum (*Eucalyptus blakelyi*) is one of several eucalypt species living in this grassy woodland in the Australian Capital Territory.

Tropical eucalypt woodland/grassland. A range of trees, including the Darwin Stringybark (*Eucalyptus tetrodonta*) with scattered cycads and palms and a grass understorey, is typical of this woodland in the Northern Territory's Top End.

Mallee shrubland. Slender mallee eucalypts with a *Triodia* sp. understorey dominate this low shrubland near Norseman in Western Australia.

Madura Mallee Ash (*Eucalyptus diversifolia* subsp. *hesperia*), growing as a spreading shrub only 50 centimetres tall on the windswept cliff tops of the Great Australian Bight.

Tropical eucalypt woodland/grassland

This vegetation group contains the so-called tall bunch-grass savannas and the associated eucalypt woodland of the far north of Western Australia, the Top End and parts of Cape York Peninsula. Typified by the presence of tall annual grasses, often *Sorghum* species, they usually occur in monsoonal regions with a marked wet and dry season. Some of these are deciduous or semi-deciduous woodlands, where eucalypts such as *E. alba* and *E. confertifolia* can lose most of their leaves by the end of the dry season. About 9 per cent of pre-European extent has been cleared, accounting for about 0.2 per cent of total clearing in Australia.

Mallee woodlands and shrublands

Mallee eucalypts are multi-trunked trees or shrubs which grow from a swollen, underground woody structure called a lignotuber. The number of stems or branches might be influenced by the frequency of bushfires or soil type and their height is usually determined by soil nutrients. The lignotuber or 'mallee root' contains food reserves, enabling the plant to regenerate quickly after all the above-ground parts have been destroyed by fire. About a quarter of the eucalypts can exhibit a mallee form in some situations. The trees rarely exceed 10 metres in height but can be quite stunted. The understorey can range from woody shrubs to hummock grasses such as *Triodia*. Approximately 35 per cent of the pre-European extent has been cleared, accounting for about 14 per cent of the total clearing in Australia.

Other habitats

Eucalypts will occur from time to time in other Australian vegetation types. Occasionally a eucalypt will tower above a fairly uniform stand of *Callitris* pines or a bloodwood will stand alone in a red desert sandplain. On the windswept Nullarbor cliffs above the Great Australian Bight there are spreading eucalypts only 50 centimetres tall that don't fit neatly into the groups above. It must be kept in mind that these vegetation classifications are human constructs in our effort to put order into the infinite combinations of our biological diversity.

Typical mallee growth habit can be seen in these White Mallee (*Eucalyptus dumosa*), with clusters of stems arising from each underground lignotuber.

3 Growth Characteristics

Eucalypts may assume several growth forms. As trees, they may be enormous forest giants such as the Mountain Ash (*Eucalyptus regnans*) from the ranges of eastern Victoria and Tasmania, the tallest hardwood tree in the world. A fallen tree was measured at 132 metres but the tallest existing tree is said to be 99.6 metres high. Another giant, the Karri (*E. diversicolor*) from south-west Western Australia, has been recorded at 90 metres tall. More frequently, where eucalypts are a dominant component of woodland areas, they adopt a spreading form with trunks that may be straight and relatively unbranched, or with a spreading crown that may derive from branches beginning closer to the ground. The common name 'Apple' was applied to a number of eucalypts by the early settlers as it was thought that their growth habit resembled an apple tree.

Some hint of the massive mallee lignotuber can be seen in this Red Mallee (*Eucalyptus socialis*), although the bulk of it is below the ground.

As well as the conventional tree form, eucalypts may adopt a multi-trunked form referred to as a mallee. Seedlings develop a woody structure known as a lignotuber at or near ground level which contains dormant buds. This swells as the plant grows and several slender trunks arise from it. Mallees are more commonly found in drier areas, but can also occur near the coast. They rarely exceed 10 metres and at times are much smaller, resembling a shrub. The Bell-fruited Mallee (*E. preissiana*) may only reach 2.5 metres high. The formation of lignotubers also occurs in species other than mallees. The giant Jarrah (*E. marginata*) from Western Australia, reaching 35 metres high, has a lignotuber from which new shoots will develop if the tree is damaged by fire or chopped to ground level.

Two other terms may be found to describe some Western Australian eucalypts. These are 'mallet' and 'marlock'. A mallet is a small tree lacking a lignotuber and with branches steeply angled to the trunk. It also lacks epicormic buds (see Chapter 4). The Fuchsia Gum (*E. dolichorhyncha*) is a mallet with red, pendulous fruits and yellow anthers and is often used as an ornamental. A marlock is also a small tree with a single trunk and mostly without a lignotuber but with spreading, leafy branches often borne close to the ground. The Moort (*E. platypus*) is an example that is often seen in cultivation and it is useful as a screen for salt-laden winds. These terms tend to be confusing as some individual trees may adopt a mallee habit. It is probably safer to simply recognise the terms 'tree' and 'mallee'.

Bark form

The bark characteristics of a eucalypt can help in the identification of a species. For convenience, we have divided bark form into smooth and rough barks. It is necessary to be careful, however, as the appearance of the bark may vary between individuals of the same species. All but one *Angophora* are rough barks.

Smooth barks

The term 'gum tree' has generally been applied to those species with smooth bark. They shed their bark annually in strips or flakes or slabs, often revealing a colourful fresh bark beneath. The only smooth bark *Angophora*—Sydney Red Gum (*A. costata*), commonly seen around Sydney—is characterised by its beautiful salmon-coloured new bark.

In several Western Australian species, the peeling bark is reddish and curls off in strips to reveal a bright green, shiny bark below. This is called minnirichi bark, a name more frequently applied to the peeling bark of some *Acacia* species. It can be seen in the Southern Cross Silver Mallee (*E. crucis*) and the well-known Caesia (*E. caesia*).

Some of these smooth-barked species, such as the eastern Candlebark (*E. rubida*) or the western Powder-bark Wandoo (*E. accedens*) have a white powder on their surface.

Those that shed their bark in long strips are known as ribbon gums, the strips often tangling in branches prior to falling. The Manna Gum or Ribbon Gum (*E. viminalis*), a tall forest tree of the New South Wales tablelands, Victoria and Tasmania, is often left with a stocking of permanent bark for a few metres at the base, with ribbons of peeling bark left among the upper branches.

In some species this newly exposed bark is marked with scribble-like tracks caused by the larvae of a group of small moths, *Ogmograptis* spp, and are thus known as scribbly gums. Two species, *E. racemosa* and *E. haemastoma*, are widely distributed on the east coast; others, such as Snow Gums, occur on the tablelands.

Some smooth-bark gums tend to lose their bark irregularly, resulting in a mottled appearance to the bark as the trunk weathers at different rates. The Spotted Gum (*Corymbia maculata*) is a common example.

The Sydney Red Gum (*Angophora costata*) is the only *Angophora* with smooth bark. The outer layer of bark is shed annually.

Southern Cross Silver Mallee (*Eucalyptus crucis*) is one of the minnirichi-barked eucalypts whose bark splits and flakes off in small strips, sometimes curling, to show contrasting colours beneath.

Top left: The powdery-white surface of the Powder-bark Wandoo (*Eucalypus accedens*) will come off on your fingers.

Top right: Weeping Snow Gum (*Eucalyptus lacrimans*), one of several scribbly gums, is host to one of the minute moths of the genus *Ogmograptis*, whose larvae leave a scribbly trail scar after each year's bark has been shed.

Left: Araluen Gum (*Eucalyptus kartzoffiana*) shows the ribbons of bark, shed every year, that get caught in the branches. These can act as flying firebrands during bushfires.

Above: Spotted Gum is an apt name for *Corymbia maculata*. It is common and easily recognised in the eastern coastal forests.

Rough barks

About half of the eucalypts are considered rough barks. In this group the bark is not shed but the dead bark remains on the tree. In some species the rough bark extends to the small branches; in others it is shed from the upper branches. The form of this permanent bark varies between species.

In the Stringybarks, the bark remains in longitudinal interlaced fibres forming spongy greyish or brown layers. There are about 28 species of Stringybarks and one of the most common is the Red Stringybark (*E. macrorhyncha*), which occurs on the tablelands and western slopes of New South Wales and in Victoria.

Ironbarks develop a hard dark bark that is usually deeply furrowed and impregnated with kino, a reddish-brown gum exuded from the trunk. They are mostly found in the eastern states, with one species in the Kimberley. The Narrow-leaved Ironbark (*E. crebra*) occurs from just south of Sydney to Cape York in the north.

Some eucalypts develop a tessellated bark, which may be seen for a short way up the trunk or may reach up into the branches. The Morton Bay Ash (*C. tessellaris*), widespread in Queensland, is a good example of the bark forming a stocking which covers the lower section of the trunk for 1–4 metres. In this case the dead bark forms hard squares and abruptly changes to smooth, powdery-white bark above. Many of the bloodwoods exhibit tessellated bark—the Yellow Bloodwood (*C. eximia*) from coastal New South Wales has flaky, yellowish-brown papery bark, which may be seen into the young branches. The Large-fruited Yellowjacket (*C. watsoniana*) from central Queensland has yellow, papery bark.

Box bark is more difficult to define. The dead, flaky bark is usually retained on the trunk for a period before eventually falling, leaving patches of paler bark. The appearance varies considerably between species and even between individuals of the same species. The common eastern species Poplar Box (*E. populnea*) retains its bark into the small branches.

In summary, while bark characteristics may be a guide to identification, they are not reliable due to the variability between species and individuals and the imprecise descriptions of bark types.

Opposite top: Dunn's White Gum (*Eucalyptus dunnii*) shows a clear distinction between the rough bark at the base of the tree and the smooth bark above.

Opposite bottom: Tindal's Stringybark (*Eucalyptus tindaliae*) has bark typical of this group of eucalypts.

Above left: This *Eucalyptus sideroxylon*, known as Red Ironbark, clearly shows the characteristics of this easily recognised bark group.

Above centre: Moreton Bay Ash (*Corymbia tessellaris*) has lower bark fissured into squares, then an abrupt change to smooth bark at about shoulder height. PHOTO: BROOKER & KLEINIG/APII.

Above right: The flaky papery bark of the Large-fruited Yellowjacket (*Corymbia watsoniana*) is a bark type not often encountered in southern Australia.

The term 'box' bark is broad in scope, being applied to the Yellow Box (*Eucalyptus melliodora*, left) and the Grey Box (*E. moluccana*, right).

Leaf form

The leaf form of eucalypts changes as they progress from seedlings to maturity. Even the cotyledons or seed leaves vary considerably from species to species and were considered by Joseph Maiden in 1934 to be a possible means for their identification. The first true leaves of a seedling are known as their juvenile foliage. As the plant develops, these leaves change through intermediate foliage to the adult leaves and their shape and form may be used to assist in the identification of a species. Juvenile foliage may persist in some species to maturity with flowers and fruits being borne while in this state. The Argyle Apple (*E. cinerea*) flowers with a high percentage of juvenile and intermediate foliage mixed with some adult leaves.

These juvenile leaves may appear from a growing point when a tree is injured through wind damage or even chopped down.

The first few leaves of most seedlings are borne in opposite pairs on a square stem, with each pair being at right angles to the preceding pair. They may adopt a variety of form and colour. They are often grey and may be linear, round, stalkless, stem-clasping or have a pointed or rounded tip. The adult leaves are borne alternately in *Eucalyptus* and *Corymbia* and form as the plant grows. In *Angophora* the adult leaves are opposite each other. It is thought that each leaf remains on the tree for two to three years. In several tropical species that are partially deciduous in the dry season, this is obviously not so.

An interesting feature of the young leaves of the genera *Corymbia* and *Angophora* is the rubbery covering of the new leaves. In the developing leaf bud, the leaves tend to stick together and as they emerge they remain shiny until after the leaf is fully developed. At this stage the leaf may be carefully pulled apart to expose a transparent membrane of natural rubber (caoutchouc). Children may become practised at this and are able to blow it up like a small balloon. Apparently this rubbery cuticle is not present in most members of the *Eucalyptus* genus. The adult leaves also bear oil glands giving eucalypts their characteristic aroma when crushed. The arrangement of the oil glands and the leaf venation can help to identify the species.

Some eucalypts show a dramatic change in their foliage from broad opposite juvenile leaves to typical long alternate leaves as they mature. Both can be seen in this young Tenterfield Woollybutt (*Eucalyptus banksii*).

Young shoots can arise from epicormic, or dormant, buds when a tree is injured or cut. They often display juvenile leaf shapes and can have unusual colours.

BELL-FRUITED MALLEE
(*Eucalyptus preissiana*)

Bell-fruited Mallee is a wonderfully ornamental small shrub rarely exceeding 2 metres high and spreading to 4 metres. With a sprawling habit and smooth, greyish stems, it has grey-green oval leaves to 12 centimetres long and bright-yellow flowers up to 5 centimetres across in spring. The large, bell-shaped fruits are up to 3.5 centimetres across. Its flowers and fruits are valued for floristry and are often exported or sent interstate. They also produce ample nectar attracting birds and small mammals. The shrub is commonly cultivated and performs well in areas of low humidity. Good drainage is preferred and shrubs may be heavily pruned to maintain a good shape. Overseas, it is grown in mild climates and is often used as a potted specimen. A second subspecies, subsp. *lobata*, grows on sand dunes, is much more compact, and has larger gumnuts to 3.5 centimetres in diameter. Both subspecies occur on the south coast of Western Australia, between the Fitzgerald River National Park and the Stirling Ranges.

The flat top of the bell-shaped fruit can be seen on the right.

KARRI (*Eucalyptus diversicolor*)

A giant forest tree from the moist forests of south-west Western Australia, Karri may reach 80 metres high and is the second-tallest hardwood tree in the world, behind the Mountain Ash of Tasmania and Victoria. The bark is smooth and grey, with mottled patches of yellow and orange, shedding in irregular flakes. After shedding, the trunks have a delightful orange appearance. The leaves are paler on the underside and the small white flowers are seen in summer and autumn. The Karri's fine, hard, reddish timber is used for building material and plywood production and is particularly valued for the long, knot-free lengths of timber derived from the straight trunk. The Gloucester Tree, near Pemberton (see p. 226) is famous for its fire tower, which is 58 metres above the ground and reached by venturesome tourists using a series of pegs drilled into the trunk to form a ladder.

An old growth Karri forest near Pemberton in southern Western Australia.

Flowers and fruits (gumnuts)

The flowers of most eucalypts are creamy-white and often not conspicuous, but there are a few species with brightly coloured flowers. With the exception of the Red Ironbark (*E. sideroxylon*) and the Yellow Gum (*E. leucoxylon*), both of which may have white, pink or red flowers, the most colourful species occur in the south-west of Western Australia and in the tropical north, where several orange- or red-flowered species occur.

Most species hold their flower buds in the leaf axils, either singly or in threes or sevens. The bloodwoods and some boxes and ironbarks hold their flowers in clusters at the end of branchlets, resulting in a more conspicuous floral display. In a few species, such as the Jingymia Mallee (*E. synandra*), the flowers have evolved a shape that might not at first glance look like a eucalypt.

The flowers of *Angophora* are readily distinguished by the presence of tiny greenish petals and the hard, woody, green sepals (see p. 23). All *Corymbia* species and most *Eucalyptus* do not have separate sepals and, where they are present in *Eucalyptus*, they are often difficult to detect. In most *Eucalyptus* and *Corymbia*, the sepals are united to form the bud cap or outer operculum and the petals form the inner operculum. In many species the two opercula are fused and are shed when the flower develops. The anthers of eucalypts adopt many forms and were used by William Blakely as an important character in distinguishing species. As this pursuit requires great patience, persistence and a little imagination, no further amplification will be attempted here.

The fruits of eucalypts, generally called gumnuts, offer a further means of assisting identification.

In *Angophora* the gumnuts are ribbed and the buds lack an operculum but sepals and petals are present. The petals usually fall when or soon after the flower opens, while the woody sepals persist.

In *Eucalyptus* and *Corymbia*, when the flower dies the anthers fall off and the base of the flower expands to form the fruit or gumnut, known as a capsule. The nature of this structure varies greatly between species. As the gumnut matures, the top of the capsule dries and

A few of the bloodwoods, such as this Long-fruited Bloodwood (*Corymbia polycarpa*), have very dense clusters of flowers.

The flattened flower base and partially united filaments of the Jingymia Mallee (*Eucalyptus synandra*) give it an unusual appearance.

splits, usually into three or four sections, forming valves which open to allow the seed to be released. These valves may be sunken into the cup-like capsule or level with the rim or exserted—protruding from it—to become a conspicuous part of the gumnut. These then become important diagnostic features for the species.

The shape and size of the gumnut are also variable. The bloodwoods and ghost gums generally have urn-shaped gumnuts. In others, such as the Bushy Yate (*E. lehmannii*), the capsules may be fused into a large, woody cluster. Other species may have minute gumnuts, like the Tropical Red Box (*E. brachyandra*), with hemispherical fruits 2–3 millimetres across, or massive ones like the Mottlecah (*E. macrocarpa*) with shallow, cup-like gumnuts up to 6.5 centimetres in diameter.

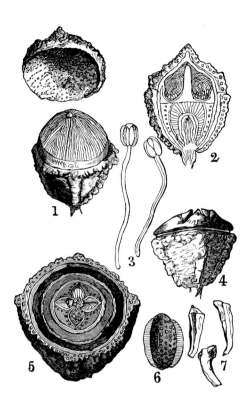

Ferdinand von Mueller's illustration for an 1887 schoolbook uses the Tasmanian Blue Gum (*Eucalyptus globulus*) to explain the parts of the eucalypt flower and fruit.

1. A bud prior to opening, with bud cap removed.
2. Cross-section through a bud with cap intact.
3. Anthers, the shape of which Blakely used as an aid to identification.
4. A gumnut.
5. Cross-section through a gumnut.
6. A seed.
7. The chaff that accompanies the seed.

The fruit of the Sydney Red Gum (*Angophora costata*) show the typical ribs of *Angophora* fruit and the hard woody sepals on the rim.

Two clusters of eucalypt fruit—Sydney Blue Gum (*Eucalyptus saligna*), with valves sunken into the cup-like capsule (far left) and Cabbage Gum (*Eucalyptus amplifolia*) with valves exserted (left).

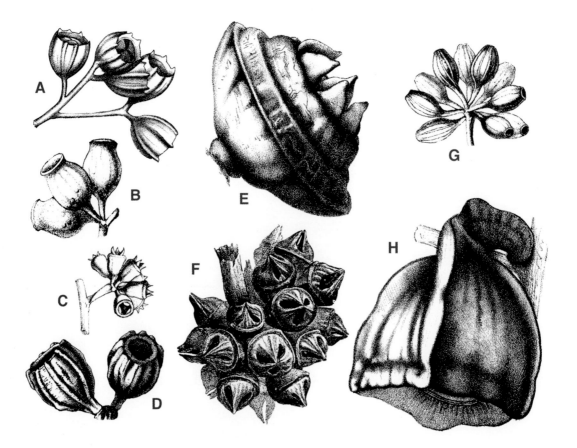

Early lithographs of a variety of eucalypt gumnuts illustrating the differences in size and form.

A Sydney Red Gum (*Angophora costata*). The small teeth around the rim are the residual sepals typical of *Angophora*.

B Yellowjack (*Corymbia bloxsomei*). The gumnuts of most *Corymbia* species are urn-shaped.

C Brown Mallet (*Eucalyptus astringens*). The exserted valves are obvious on these gumnuts.

D Ridge-fruited Mallee (*E. angulosa*). Both the common name and the botanic name indicate the angled grooves on the gumnut.

E Mottlecah (*E. macrocarpa*). This species has the largest gumnuts, which may reach 6.5 centimetres across.

F Bushy Yate (*E. lehmannii*). The clustered gumnuts remain fused even after the seeds are shed.

G Sugar Gum (*E. cladocalyx*). The valves on these barrel-shaped gumnuts remain deeply enclosed at maturity.

H Square-fruited Mallee (*E. tetraptera*). The unique shape and size of the gumnuts make it readily recognisable.

Seeds

The shape of eucalypt seeds varies greatly between species but is constant within a species and, once the collector is experienced, the shape is a reliable means of helping with identification. The release of seeds also varies with the species as some species hold their seed on the tree for some years and others release it on maturity. When the released seed is examined, it appears to be in two forms—larger, usually darker particles (the actual seeds) and narrower, paler material called chaff, which is of no consequence.

Close-up of the seeds of the Black Gum (*Eucalyptus aggregata*). The larger, dark-grey, flattened ovoid particles are the fertile seeds and the small light-brown particles are the chaff. PHOTO: *EUCLID*.

CARBEEN (*Corymbia tessellaris*)

This well-known tree, often known as Morton Bay Ash, forms a tall, handsome tree reaching 25–30 metres high. It is related to the ghost gums but is distinguished by a skirt of tessellated bark reaching 1–4 metres up the trunk. It is widespread on a variety of soils, from north-west of Narrabri in New South Wales to the tip of Cape York and into Papua New Guinea. The dark-brown timber is resistant to termites and is used in wharf and bridge construction as well as internal and external flooring, landscaping and fencing. The tree is commonly used in parks and public landscaping, where it is tolerant of light frosts only.

Tree showing the clear 'skirt' of dark tessellated bark part-way up the trunk. PHOTO: BROOKER & KLEINIG/APII.

A forest fire with flames rising to the crown of the eucalypts. The fire-front
of this fire near Margaret River in Western Australia in 1983 was travelling at
800–1000 metres per hour just one hour after it started. PHOTO: CSIRO.

4 Reaction to Fire and Drought

FIRE AND EUCALYPTS ARE INTEGRAL TO THE AUSTRALIAN ENVIRONMENT. EUCALYPTS EVOLVED in a regime of fire as Australia became warmer and lightning became more frequent. As soils became more impoverished due to excessive leaching, eucalypts became proficient at scavenging and storing nutrients. They developed extensive root systems that were able to extract phosphorus by using biochemical methods and also soil fungi known as mycorrhiza. Most species stored these nutrients in lignotubers—huge, swollen organs, rich in dormant buds that begin to develop in seedlings and form at ground level or just below the surface. Nutrients were also stored in the heartwood of the trunks, beneath the thickened bark. All of these functions helped the eucalypt to survive, and even thrive, on fire. As one commentator has said, 'For most eucalypts, fire was not a destroyer but a liberator.'

Eucalypts in forests or woodlands appear to have adapted to not only survive fire, but to promote it by providing the ideal fuel. The leaves of many eucalypts contain oils and waxes, which have a high heat content and burst into flame rapidly. Their presence encourages burning even when foliage is green. This accounts for the often reported 'exploding canopies' in extreme fires. But tree foliage does not usually ignite without heat from combustion at ground level. Eucalypts shed about a third to half of their leaves annually, many species shed their bark, and most drop branches. This fallen material dries rapidly in our climate, but decomposes slowly. The flammability of the litter is helped by its low mineral content. On average, it takes three to five years for litter to build up sufficiently to sustain a fire.

Having created the ideal fire environment, how does the eucalypt cope with fire? It must be remembered that for the average forest fire less than 5 per cent of the biomass is consumed as fuel. There is much of the tree left to resume the fight for survival. The spreading root system is well insulated below the soil surface. Tests have shown that quite severe fires are required to significantly heat the soil to a depth greater than 2.5 centimetres.

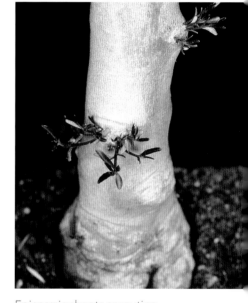

Epicormic shoots sprouting from the base of a Brittle Gum (*Eucalyptus mannifera*) two weeks after a fire.

Epicormic shoots nine months after fire on *Eucalyptus viminalis* (left) and *E. bridgesiana* (right), showing their distinctive and different reversion to juvenile foliage.

Apple Box (*Eucalyptus bridgesiana*) clothed in a mantle of epicormic foliage, nine months after a fire.

Mature trees are protected by their bark, and the bark types determine the impact of fire. The insulation properties of the different barks are similar, so it is their thickness that determines how much protection they provide the tree. It has been suggested that the presence of kino gum in the bark adds to its insulation. However, some barks in themselves are flammable and in severe fires can burn away to permanently damage the tree. Those that annually shed their bark can build up an added fuel load at the base of the tree, increasing the fire intensity and leading to the characteristic fire scars.

Most eucalypts have a 'secret weapon' hidden beneath their bark that gives them a fire advantage over many other trees. After the fire, under the insulating bark, growth centres known as epicormic buds begin to emerge. They can send out clumps of shoots over most parts of the surviving tree. These form a green mantle over the bare trunk and branches, and with rain and sunlight they extend to form new branches. These clumps of new shoots often take the form of immature foliage, displaying opposite leaves of a different shape to the mature leaves that might have been burnt. With time, they revert to the mature foliage form.

All but a few species also develop lignotubers. These are most obvious in mallees, which may develop massive growths, the largest of which has been measured at 20 metres across, with more than 300 stems emerging from it. Mallees exist in an environment which is particularly fire-prone, as its associated vegetation can include resinous spinifex and other flammable grasses and shrubs. After a fire, the mallee's lignotuber resprouts at an astonishing rate. Many of these sprouts become the woody stems that give the mallee its characteristic appearance.

Lignotubers exist in forest trees as well as in mallees. Even the mighty Jarrah (*Eucalyptus marginata*) is capable of reshooting from the base if its above-ground parts are damaged.

Some eucalypts that lack lignotubers rely on seed dispersal to overcome the ravages of fire. The towering Mountain Ash (*E. regnans*) forests of Victoria and Tasmania are fire sensitive as this species has no insulating bark, no lignotuber and no epicormic buds.

The Western Australian mallee known as Tallerack (*Eucalyptus pleurocarpa*), sprouting blue-grey leafy shoots from its lignotuber after a fire.

A forest of skeletons, mostly Alpine Ash (*Eucalyptus delegatensis*), two years after a fire. Alpine Ash is one of the eucalypts that does not have a lignotuber and rarely survives a severe fire. The next generation will rely on seed germination.

In fact, *E. regnans* possesses features that seem likely to encourage fire—a heavy fall of flammable leaf litter (twice as much as other species), an open canopy and streamers of hanging bark that take the flames up to the canopy as well as acting as firebrands to be blown well ahead of the fire-front to start new fires. As a result, the whole community is destroyed by a fire storm. But the speed of the fire through the canopy is just enough to burn the leaves but not completely burn through the small woody seed capsules. The rapid drying of these causes their valves to open and release a rain of seed to the ash beds below. With appropriate rain, the nutrients from the ash and the increased sunlight, up to 2.5 million seedlings per hectare have been recorded in the weeks following a fire.

But there is a price to pay for such a fire strategy. These forests tend to occur as even-aged stands, all arising after the same fire event. As it takes about twenty years before the trees are mature enough to flower and produce seed, any fire interval shorter than that can exterminate the species locally.

Fire may act to allow seed germination in a variety of ways: by the release of seed from the canopy as mentioned with Mountain Ash (*E. regnans*) above; by altering the environment to provide better conditions for germination, such as added light and reduced competition; and through the release of nutrients into the seedbed which makes scarce resources available.

For mallee eucalypts, soil moisture is often the limiting factor for seed germination. After a fire, the mature mallee trees are leafless, and their lack of transpiration allows the soil to retain more moisture for longer after rain. This is often enough to trigger germination, resulting in 5000–10,000 seedlings per hectare.

In some vegetation types there seem to be few seedling eucalypts in the absence of fire. It has been shown that Wandoo (*Eucalyptus wandoo*) regenerated in ash beds following fires, but rarely otherwise. Similarly, another study showed no regeneration of Salmon Gum (*E. salmonophloia*) in mature woodlands, but abundant seedlings in recently burnt areas.

In some instances there is a third party involved. Many eucalypt species release small quantities of seed

A forest of Brown Stringybark (*Eucalyptus baxteri*) with advanced epicormic shoots, two years after a fire. Most seedlings will not receive enough light to survive as the canopy thickens.

more or less continually. However, most of that seed is rapidly consumed by ants. It is only when there is a massive seed release triggered by fire that 'predator satiation' occurs and reasonable amounts of seed remain to germinate.

Some seedlings might be sitting in the surface layer in a semi-dormant state, but fire will allow them to 'wake up' and delve into their lignotubers for the energy to sprout and flourish into new trees.

No discussion of eucalypts and fire would be complete without mentioning fire frequency and the history of fires in Australia. This is influenced by changing climate and the interference of man, both Aboriginal and European. Based on current evidence, most scientists believe that fire activity has been relatively constant over the last 10,000 years, with the greatest increase occurring during the period of early European settlement. This was followed by a reduction of burning to present-day levels which are, on average, lower than at any time in that 10,000-year period.

However, average figures do not take into account the different fire frequencies that each vegetation type is best adapted to. Changes to the frequency of burning will change the composition of the vegetation. Long periods without fire will cause some vegetation to degenerate, and the difference in growth and vigour between plants in a recently burnt area compared with those in a long-unburnt area is obvious and often spectacular. In some cases these changes can be measured. For example, Jarrah (*E. marginata*) has been shown to increase its girth following fire and the scorch of its foliage.

It is estimated that the natural fire frequency for some of our eucalypt vegetation would be:

Mountain Ash forests: 75–150 years
Eucalypt open woodlands: 7–25 years
Mallee shrubland: 5–10 years

Eucalypts and their relationship to fire is a complex topic, and a multitude of books and scientific papers have been written about it. Stephen Pine sums it up well in his book, *Burning Bush: A Fire History of Australia*:

Eucalyptus is not only the universal Australian, it is the ideal Australian—versatile, tough, sardonic, contrary, self-mocking, with a deceptive complexity amid the appearance of massive homogeneity; an occupier of disturbed environment; a fire creature.

Reaction to drought

Many of the methods that eucalypts have evolved to cope with fire also function as a means to overcome drought. While the word drought is used to describe a long period without rain, it is also used in biology to describe any stressful shortage of water. In fact, eucalypts have been accused of 'creating drought' in countries where they have been planted. Their spreading and often deep root systems extract maximum moisture from the surrounding environment, frequently resulting in poor health or death for species which have not evolved to live with them.

The very efficient root growth of the eucalypt is shown dramatically in the accompanying diagram of the root system of the Jarrah (*Eucalyptus marginata*) in Western Australia.

In the 1860s, Trappist monks planted the Tasmanian Blue Gum (*E. globulus*) in the malaria-ridden Pontine

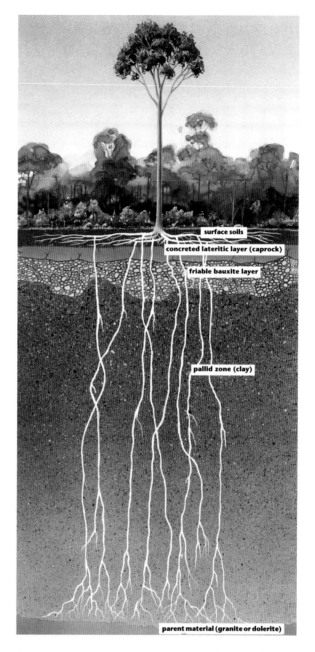

surface soils
concreted lateritic layer (caprock)
friable bauxite layer
pallid zone (clay)
parent material (granite or dolerite)

A section through a typical soil profile in a Jarrah forest (*Eucalyptus marginata*) illustrates how some eucalypt roots are capable of searching for moisture. The Jarrah roots tend to grow in two layers. The surface roots stretch out, often to four times the width of the tree canopy. The second layer, searching for fissures in the rocky lateritic soil, pierces the clay subsoils, eventually reaching the water table in the quest for nutrients and moisture. These extensive roots may reach a depth of 40 metres.
ILLUSTRATION: IAN DICKINSON, *LANDSCOPE MAGAZINE*, WESTERN AUSTRALIAN DEPARTMENT OF ENVIRONMENT AND CONSERVATION.

By the end of 2008 the prolonged drought in south-eastern Australia had resulted in patches of almost leafless woodland. It is likely that many of these trees near Cooma will not recover.

Marshes, near Rome, in order to drain them. The seed was sent from Australia by Ferdinand von Mueller and the success of the project earned him a papal knighthood.

Lignotubers serve as the eucalypts' major insurance against drought as they store water as well as nutrients. Eucalypt leaves are toughened and conserve moisture by closing the leaf pores (stomata) and hanging vertically to avoid maximum exposure to the sun. They also tend to turn their leaves so that the edge faces the sun, minimising the heating of their flat surfaces.

In dry periods, flowering is usually reduced and leaves are shed to reduce water loss. In extreme circumstances such as those experienced in southern Australia in the early years of the 21st century, some eucalypts have not been able to cope with drought. They first shed their leaves, and if the drought continues patches of dead trees will start to appear on some hillsides.

In parts of tropical Australia there is an annual period of drought called the dry season. Some tropical eucalypt species such as the Northern Salmon Gum (*E. bigalerita*) and the White Gum (*E. alba* var. *australasica*) become deciduous, or almost so, during this season. The new flush of leaves emerging at the start of the wet season can be bright red.

An interesting insight into the water regime of eucalypts under the effect of climate change is seen in a field trial experiment being carried out at the University of Western Sydney. Here, a number of huge structures have been built to house mature plants of Sydney Blue Gum (*E. saligna*). Carbon dioxide has been fed into the houses at high concentrations equivalent to what can be expected in our atmosphere in 50 years if we don't reduce our carbon emissions. The trees are monitored every fifteen minutes to determine the amount of

CO$_2$ absorbed and the amount of water used. The increased CO$_2$ stimulates photosynthetic activity and thus increases plant growth rate and reduces stomatal apertures, resulting in less water use.

Although it is still early days, the results so far indicate that similar-sized trees use about 25 per cent less water under high CO$_2$ conditions. Thus, eucalypt forests could become more productive and allow more water to be available for other uses. Perhaps there might be some positive aspects of climate change!

At the end of the dry season in northern Australia it is common to see leafless eucalypts. These trees will burst into leaf at the start of the wet.

Deciduous eucalypts in northern Australia often have a red flush of new leaves at the start of the wet season.

Striated Pardalotes can nest in small hollows in trees,
or in tunnels in creek banks. PHOTO: GERARD SATHERLEY.

5 Eucalypts as Wildlife Habitat

IN EUCALYPTS, TREE HOLLOWS DEVELOP IN A NUMBER OF WAYS. THEY MAY BEGIN WHEN A branch is lost in a wind storm, or when a tree is struck by lightning or damaged by fire. These occurrences expose the tree's heartwood, which is more vulnerable to decay than the outer sapwood. It may be attacked by fungus or termites, which will excavate the heartwood. Water may enter the hole and accelerate the decomposition. This, however, is a very slow process and it has been shown that large hollows may take up to 200 years to develop and be large enough to be used by birds and mammals as shelters and nesting sites.

While hollows will develop in non-eucalypt species, the dominance of eucalypts in all forests other than rainforests and *Callitris* forests makes them a most important wildlife habitat. It has been estimated that more than 300 species of native vertebrates use hollows for either shelter or nesting. From the tiny Thornbills to the massive Powerful Owl, 14 per cent of Australia's bird population (111 species) has been recorded using eucalypt tree hollows. Mammals also use them regularly. Possums, gliders and microbats use them for shelter and raising their young. About 32 per cent of Australia's mammal population (86 species) are known to shelter in tree hollows. The microbats often use small cracks not much bigger than themselves. Some mammals also use free water in hollows as a drinking source to save them venturing to the ground. Even reptiles and amphibians are known hollow users, with 78 species of reptiles and 29 species of amphibians recorded as users. Reptiles may use hollows for seeking food, such as bird eggs or small invertebrates—or, in the case of the Large Lace Monitor, the young of small mammals—but some species such as the arboreal Brown Tree Snake use them as a nest site. Invertebrates such as feral and native bees frequently use tree hollows to build their nests.

Many of the larger species of eucalypts will develop hollows, but the River Red Gum (*E. camaldulensis*) in inland areas and the Manna Gum (*E. viminalis*) are particularly important in this regard.

Many eucalypts are hollowed by termites from within, and it is only when a branch breaks that access is available to wildlife.

This native bee colony lives within a eucalypt hollow. The entrance is a small crack with wax coating the edges.

Nocturnal animals, such as these Western Pygmy Possums, play a significant role in pollinating some eucalypts—flecks of pollen can be seen on the fur surrounding their faces. Here they are seeking nectar from the flowers of Yarldarlba (*Eucalyptus youngiana*) in the Great Victoria Desert. PHOTO: JIRI LOCHMAN.

As so much of our fauna depends on eucalypt tree hollows, their importance to wildlife conservation cannot be overestimated and even dead trees should be regarded as significant wildlife habitats.

Nectar

Nectar from eucalypt flowers provides the main food resource for many wildlife species offering them one of their major sources of protein. Eucalypt flowers produce huge quantities of nectar, and honeyeaters and parrots are frequent visitors. Flocks have been seen to follow the mass flowering of eucalypts as different species flower in different seasons. The nectar also attracts many insects, which birds such as wattle birds use to supplement their diet. Sugar Gliders, Squirrel Gliders and Pygmy Possums also regularly forage for nectar. In return, these birds and mammals serve as pollinators carrying pollen from tree to tree.

Seeds

The seeds of many species of eucalypt are voraciously devoured by a number of species of parrots. In south-eastern Australia small flocks of Gang-gang Cockatoos will target a particular eucalypt until all the seeds have been consumed. They break off a small branch and hold it in one foot while they eat and then release the unwanted branchlet to the ground. King Parrots, Crimson Rosellas and Eastern Rosellas are other parrot species that are fond of eucalypt seeds.

Ants, too, are important consumers of eucalypt seed, much of which rains down onto the floor of the forest as the gumnuts dry out and open.

Seeds within the gumnuts are an important food source for the Gang-gang Cockatoo. With their tongue and beak they can carefully separate the seeds from the chaff, scattering some seeds in the process. By breaking off twigs containing gumnuts they ensure these will soon dry out and release further seed. PHOTO: JIRI LOCHMAN.

Australia's iconic Koala is one of the few mammals to specialise in eating the low-nutrient leaves of eucalypts. Here the leaf blades have been eaten, leaving only the stems. PHOTO: JIRI LOCHMAN.

Koalas

Most animals find eucalypt leaves fibrous and unpleasant to eat or, in many cases, quite poisonous. Koalas, however, are equipped with a specialised digestive system which retains the leaves and allows them to be metabolised very slowly, extracting the maximum food value from this low-nutrient foliage. Due to this slow metabolic activity, the Koala is generally sluggish and may sleep up to 18 hours a day.

While eucalypts are their staple food, Koalas have been known to eat other species such as Brush Box (*Lophostemon confertus*) and species of *Acacia* and *Melaleuca* that may occur in their home region. The natural distribution of Koalas is from south-eastern South Australia, through Victoria to Cape York. Some breeding populations have been introduced to areas outside this range, such as Kangaroo Island off the coast of South Australia. Their favourite trees vary depending on their home range. Some 40 to 50 eucalypt species have been recorded as being eaten, but some of the Koala's main target species include the Tallowwood (*E. microcorys*), Manna Gum (*E. viminalis*), Forest Red Gum (*E. tereticornis*), the Grey Gums (*E. propinqua* and *E. punctata*), Scribbly Gum (*E. racemosa*), and the River Red Gum (*E. camaldulensis*). Koalas eat 200–500 grams of leaves each day.

SOME KOALA FOOD TREES

COMMON NAME	BOTANIC NAME
Lemon-scented Gum	*Corymbia citriodora*
Blue-leaved Stringybark	*Eucalyptus agglomerata*
Bancroft's Red Gum	*E. bancroftii*
Brown Stringybark	*E. baxteri*
River Red Gum	*E. camaldulensis*
Red Gum	*E. chloroclada*
Mountain Grey Gum	*E. cypellocarpa*
Broad-leaved Ironbark	*E. fibrosa*
White Stringybark	*E. globoidea*
Woollybutt	*E. longifolia*
Yellow Box	*E. melliodora*
Tallowwood	*E. microcorys*
Yellow Stringybark	*E. muelleriana*
Narrow-leaved Peppermint	*E. nicholii*
Messmate Stringybark	*E. obliqua*
Parramatta Red Gum	*E. parramattensis*
Poplar Box	*E. populnea*
Grey Gum	*E. propinqua*
Grey Gum	*E. punctata*
Scribbly Gum	*E. racemosa*
Red Stringybark	*E. resinifera*
Swamp Mahogany	*E. robusta*
Grey Ironbark	*E. siderophloia*
Forest Red Gum	*E. tereticornis*
Tindal's Stringybark	*E. tindaliae*
Manna Gum	*E. viminalis*
Narrow-leaved Grey Box	*E. woollsiana*

The larvae of cup moths have bizarre markings and stinging hairs. *Doratifera vulnerans*, shown here, feeds on a range of eucalypt leaves.

This Brown Barrel (*Eucalyptus fastigata*) has been damaged by cockatoos as they rip away the bark in their search for wood-boring grubs.

Invertebrates

Innumerable insects and spiders inhabit eucalypts, some using them as shelter, others as food. Many invertebrates provide food for birds, mammals and reptiles, as we have mentioned. The larvae of butterflies and moths are particularly prevalent feeders on eucalypt foliage, although in summer the well-known Christmas Beetles and other scarabs may cause considerable damage to the growing tips.

The larvae of the beautiful Emperor Gum Moth feed mainly on eucalypts, but have been known to eat Brush Box and Water Gum (*Tristaniopsis laurina*). The colourful caterpillars of this moth are mostly bright green, often with yellow, red or purple tubercles. Several species of cup moth larvae also feed on eucalypts. The larvae are commonly known as Chinese Junks because of their unusual shape. They are mainly green, with red stinging hairs that can deliver a painful sting if touched. The cup-like pupa, which is deposited on a twig, resembles a gumnut.

The larvae of some beetle species bore into the heartwood of eucalypts, and in the case of stringybarks one may find the bark shredded by cockatoos in search of these succulent caterpillars.

Of special interest is the group of insects known as scribbly gum moths (*Ogmograptis* spp.), the larvae of which burrow under the bark of several smooth-barked gums, and when the bark falls their conspicuous tracks are revealed on the fresh bark. Around Sydney, *E. haemastoma* is commonly seen on the Hawkesbury sandstone and *E. racemosa* occurs on the coastal plains from Nowra to Bundaberg with *E. rossii* found on the tablelands. All these species, as well as the widespread Snow Gum (*E. pauciflora*), are frequently seen with scribbles.

In Western Australia, the Jarrah Leafminer, a tiny moth about 6 millimetres long, lays its eggs under the surface of the leaves of Jarrah (*E. marginata*) and several other eucalypts. The grub causes severe damage to the leaves, which resembles fire scorch, and may result in defoliation.

Sap suckers are also associated with eucalypts. Lerps belong to the psyllid family and make intricate shelters on the leaves where they remain sedentary, frequently exuding a sugary substance enjoyed by birds and often harvested by ants. When their populations are great, serious defoliation may occur. The Spotted Gum Lerp (*Eucalyptolyma maideni*), which infests Spotted Gums (*Corymbia maculata*) and Lemon-scented Gums (*C. citriodora*), has been accidentally introduced into

One of the minute moths of the genus *Ogmograptis*, whose larvae cause the marks on several species of scribbly gums. This moth has yet to be given a species name—it causes scribbles on *Eucalyptus racemosa*.
PHOTO: NATALIE BARNETT/CSIRO ENTOMOLOGY.

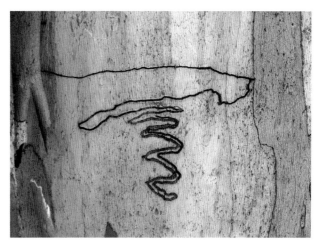

A scribble caused by an *Ogmograptis* moth larvae, this one on Snow Gum (*E. pauciflora*).

A leaf covered with galls, and a single gall split open to show the grub inside (top right). Galls of this kind are most likely to be caused by wasps.

Top left: Ants (*Rhytidoponera tasmaniensis*) attending lerp (*Glycaspis* sp.) on the immature leaf of a eucalypt. The ants harvest the sugary secretion of the lerp.

California, where it has become a pest. Related to lerps is the Gum Tree Scale (*Eriococcus coriaceus*), which is found on the leaves and stems of many species and is kept under control in Australia by a parasitic wasp which lays its eggs in the scale.

Some species of termites build their colonies in the branch stubs or burnt-out hollows in eucalypts and feed on the surrounding rotting wood. Others build earth mounds, sometimes up to 3 or 4 metres high, from where they construct protective tunnels to their feeding locations. They frequently feed on eucalypt wood and their tunnels are often seen on the tree trunks leading to a broken limb, from where they can access the heartwood of the tree.

A diverse array of wasps, flies, beetles, coccids, moths, mites, and even bacteria and fungi, may cause swellings known as galls on the leaves, stems or roots of eucalypts. Little is known about the way these galls are formed and often the facts are further confused by the insect that finally emerges from the gall, which may be a parasite on the original insect that formed the gall.

Some galls on eucalypt leaves result from a very strange animal relationship between a fly and a nematode. A microscopic, worm-like organism, this nematode lives inside a tiny fly (*Fergusonina* sp.), which deposits it on the leaf of a eucalypt as the fly lays its eggs. The resulting gall houses both the larvae of the fly and the nematodes, both of which feed inside the gall. As the fly larvae mature, the nematodes enter the body of the emerging fly and it flies off to mate and repeat the cycle. Species of *Eucalyptus*, *Angophora* and *Corymbia* are involved in this symbiotic relationship.

A termite mound incorporating fallen dead timber but probably also accessing the heartwood of the living tree by some small access tunnel.

Nesting material

Strands of the fibrous bark of stringybark eucalypts are often gathered by birds for use as nesting material. The Red Stringybark (*E. macrorhyncha*) and the White Stringybark (*E. globoidea*) are two widespread species used in this way. The bark disturbed by cockatoos in search of food may also be used for nesting material.

In California, where eucalypts have become naturalised, bird fanciers recommend the use of eucalypt leaves, fresh or dried, as nesting material for parrots. The leaves are said to be a natural deterrent for pests in nest boxes. Dried leaves are even sold in 4 oz bags for hobbyists who don't live in areas where eucalypts are found.

Fallen timber in creeks and rivers

The widespread River Red Gum borders many inland creeks and rivers, where it is frequently a victim of floods and winds and loses its hold on the fragile banks. The trees end up totally or partially submerged in the water, forming a snag. These snags slow down the speed of flow and are important fish and invertebrate habitats. Shrimps use them for shelter and thus provide food for fish. Many native fish use snags as breeding sites and smaller native fish use them as a refuge from predation. It is not uncommon to see shoals of small fish schooling around these sites. The endangered Murray Cod uses snags for spawning and their fry use them for shelter.

Snags caused by fallen eucalypts in the Lachlan River, New South Wales, provide excellent breeding places for fish.

RIBBON GUM OR MANNA GUM (*Eucalyptus viminalis*)

Four subspecies are recognised for this plant but subspecies *viminalis* is the most widespread and the tallest of them all. It commonly reaches 60 metres high, but the tallest tree has been recorded in Tasmania at 88 metres high. Ribbon Gum is found from south-eastern South Australia through well-watered parts of Tasmania, Victoria and north to Inverell in New South Wales. It is characterised by its smooth, white to cream, powdery bark, with sometimes an extensive stocking of rough, fibrous bark at its base. The bark exudes a sweet, crumbly white manna after the leaves have been damaged by psyllid insects, and this gives the tree its other common name of Manna Gum. These gummy nodules are sweet and were relished by Aboriginals. The bark sheds in long ribbons, which are frequently seen hanging in the canopy of the tree.

The Ribbon Gum is a most important Koala food tree and its flowers, held in groups of three, are an excellent source of nectar and pollen for apiarists and food for the tiny Sugar Gliders that inhabit the forests. The honey is particularly sweet. The pale-pink timber is used in the building industry for flooring and joinery as well as pulp. This species is resistant to frosts and makes a fine shade tree for rural properties and parks, but is too large for the average garden. The other three subspecies are much smaller trees. Subspecies *cygnetensis*, known as the Rough-barked Manna Gum, is a tree of about 10 metres high, occurring from south-east South Australia to the Grampians in Victoria. It has rough bark to the larger limbs and mostly seven buds in the flower clusters. Subspecies *hentyensis*, known as the Western Tasmanian Sand Gum, only reaches 6 metres high on the poor white sands north of Strahan. It has virtually no rough bark and has broader juvenile leaves. Subspecies *pryoriana* is a small tree to 15 metres high from the infertile coastal sands of southern Victoria. This subspecies has rough bark over most of its trunk and buds in groups of three.

Far left: Long ribbons of bark hang from the branches of the aptly named Ribbon Gum.

Left: Granules of manna collected beneath a Ribbon Gum near Braidwood, New South Wales. They have a sugary, sweet taste.

Mistletoes are usually recognised as a denser clump of foliage among the more open foliage of the eucalypt. They often have a more yellowish-green colour. The mistletoe at the centre of this photo is *Muellerina celastroides*.

6 Plant Parasites of Eucalypts

ORGANISMS THAT LIVE ON OR IN ANOTHER ORGANISM AND DERIVE ALL OR PART OF THEIR nutrient from their host, usually to the detriment of the host, are called 'parasites'. While people are quite familiar with the insects, nematodes, fungi and bacteria that attack plants, and many of these pests are in fact parasites, there is less familiarity with flowering plant parasites on hosts such as eucalypts. In fact, one group of these parasitic plants, the mistletoes, are so intricately associated with eucalypts that no discussion of eucalypt biology would be complete without mention of them.

There are three broad categories: mistletoes, dodders and root parasites. Correctly, these plants should be called 'hemi-parasites' because they do have chlorophyll in their foliage and thus undertake photosynthesis to produce their own food from the energy of sunlight. However, they cannot exist without a host to supplement what they can produce themselves.

The Mistletoebird (*Dicaeum hirundinaceum*) has a unique role in dispersing mistletoes in Australia. PHOTO: NEVIL LAZARUS.

Mistletoes

Mistletoes found on eucalypts in Australia belong to the families Loranthaceae and Viscaceae. They are woody flowering plants which start life when their seed germinates on the surface of the host. Both their moisture needs and their nutrient needs are supplied by the host plant, so they must quickly establish a link to the tissues conducting nutrients and water. They are then dependent on their living host.

Mistletoe fruit are usually fleshy and often brightly coloured to attract birds, for without the birds mistletoes are doomed. The mistletoe fruit is a single-seeded berry and within its outer coat is a sticky layer of a material called viscin, which is rich in glucose. The birds that feed on mistletoes have specialised eating behaviour, swallowing the seed in its sticky layer after extracting it from the coat.

In Australia there is one bird so specialised in its association with these plants that it is called the Mistletoebird (*Dicaeum hirundinaceum*), but the task of spreading the mistletoe seeds has also been taken up by some honeyeaters. The Mistletoebird has a very simple digestive system and the seed passes through the bird quite quickly, usually being defecated about four to twelve minutes after being eaten, with some sticky viscin still undigested.

A look at the anatomy of a normal bird would indicate that when perched on a branch its droppings would mostly miss the branch and fall to the ground. The Mistletoebird, in an amazing quirk of evolution, has developed the habit of twisting its body around at the time of defecation so that there is a fair chance that the dropping will land and stick to the branch on which it is perched.

It is interesting to note that there are no mistletoes in Tasmania, and that Mistletoebirds are also absent from that island.

With the mistletoe seed in its dropping glued to the branch of a eucalypt or other tree, it starts to germinate. A root is the first to emerge, but in this case the tip of the root is modified to form a 'haustorial pad', which

looks a bit like a suction cap. It slowly waves around until it makes contact with the eucalypt branch. Enzymes in the haustorial pad allow it to penetrate the host's tissue and form 'roots' within the host, mostly in the water-conducting tissue just beneath the bark, where it forms a connection called a 'haustorium' which swells as the plant grows. From this point on, the mistletoe grows like most other plants, producing leaves and eventually flowers and, of course, those essential bird-attracting fruits.

As discussed earlier in this book, eucalypts have evolved strategies to minimise water loss in times of drought. The 'breathing holes' or stomates on the eucalypt leaf surface close up when under water stress to reduce moisture loss. The mistletoes parasitising the tree have no such water-saving strategies, leaving their stomates wide open like a tap and draining the tree's valuable moisture by evaporation. When trees have only minor mistletoe infestations they can cope with this water loss, but in times of drought a heavily infested tree is under far more stress than its neighbours and often dies.

This isolated Yellow Box (*Eucalyptus melliodora*) on the left is heavily infested with mistletoes, seen here as pendulous clumps of foliage. The tree on the right has died and the dead mistletoes can be seen among its skeleton branches.

This mistletoe seed has been deposited on the host branch in a bird dropping. Its green 'root' has grown and a fat haustorial pad is attaching itself to the branch. Secreted enzymes will now allow it to penetrate and connect to the host's tissue.

Amyema pendula shows the typical Loranthaceae mistletoe flower structure. Its leaves are similar in shape to those of its eucalypt host.

Fire can be a great 'cleansing agent' for trees infested with mistletoes. Most eucalypts have developed strategies for regeneration after fire, but the mistletoes that infested them have no such fire resistance and are usually killed.

In man-made landscapes of scattered trees with grazing pasture beneath, the cycle of periodic fires reaching the canopy has been broken. Individual trees, isolated from crown fires, can become covered with an ever-increasing load of mistletoes, often leading to the tree's death. The skeletons of such trees are a common sight in semi-cleared landscapes.

Loranthaceae

The most easily noticed mistletoes are those of the family Loranthaceae, sometimes called 'loranths'. They are most conspicuous as denser clumps of foliage on the outer branches of eucalypts, often with a slightly darker or more reddish-yellow colour to their leaves. They are not confined to eucalypts and can be found on other plant groups.

An interesting aspect of their biology is the apparent mimicry of some species to the foliage of the host tree. Loranths growing on eucalypts usually have leaf shapes that resemble eucalypt leaves, but those growing on she-oaks, for example, often have more needle-like leaves.

Of the Australian loranths, about 33 are known to grow on eucalypts while 31 have never been recorded on eucalypts. Just three species have been recorded only on eucalypts and this probably reflects a lack of host data.

The larger genera of loranths are *Amyema*, *Lysiana*, *Decaisnina*, *Dendrophthoe* and *Muellerina*. Some species are recorded as growing on a wide range of eucalypts. *Amyema melaleucae*, for example, is recorded as having at least 110 different eucalypt species as its host, despite its misleading name.

Viscaceae

The family Viscaceae includes the mistletoes of Europe, most conspicuously the genus *Viscum* about which so much folklore has arisen. The mistletoe clumps stay green and leafy throughout the northern winter when many host trees lose their leaves, perhaps leading the Druids and other nature worshippers to believe that the mistletoe was the 'heart' of the tree, keeping it alive through its deciduous phase. The belief in the sacred and magical properties of mistletoe included its role in fertility rites, and from there it is not hard to see how it became an excuse for less sacred romantic activities at the various festivals and, eventually, the office Christmas party.

Australia has only fifteen species in the Viscaceae family and, of those, only three are recorded as growing on eucalypts, which certainly would not be considered their preferred host.

Dodders

Dodder is the common name given to two totally unrelated plants that have evolved independently to have a very similar appearance and growth habits. The first is the genus *Cuscuta* in the family Convolvulaceae, which does not attack eucalypts. The second is the genus *Cassytha* in the family Lauraceae, although it looks nothing like the noble Laurel tree.

Both of these plants are almost-leafless parasitic twiners with minute flowers, tapping into their host plants by way of haustoria. But unlike the mistletoes their haustoria are only about the size of a pinhead.

Cassytha germinates on the ground from hard long-lived seeds, developing a root and shoot system like most plants. Seedlings then start searching for a plant to climb upon, but unlike other twiners they send small suction-cap-like haustoria into the stems or leaves of their host and draw out moisture and nutrients. They have some chlorophyll in their stems, so can produce some of their food from the energy of sunlight, but without their host they cannot survive.

With time the *Cassytha* no longer requires its link with the soil and can survive as a tangled mass of leafless stems from the nutrients and moisture it draws from

its host. It can kill its host and the part of the dodder attached to that host will also die, but as long as a few stems can link up with a new host and develop haustoria, the plant will survive and proliferate in the new plant.

Australia has about twenty species of *Cassytha* and they do not appear to discriminate in their range of hosts. Most *Cassytha* species are slender and parasitise low, shrubby plants. But *Cassytha melantha*, sometimes called Coarse Dodder-laurel, is a much more robust plant that can smother eucalypts up to 8 metres tall, certainly enough to overpower mallee eucalypts or kill young saplings.

While mistletoes are dependent on birds and aerial transfer of their seeds, *Cassytha* germinates on the ground from long-lived seeds encased in fleshy fruit. There appears to be evidence that wallabies, and now the introduced rabbit, are important carriers, as viable seed has been found in their droppings.

Coarse Dodder-laurel (*Cassytha melantha*), with its tangled twining stems, can overcome eucalypt saplings and mallees.

Root parasites

Flowering plants that parasitise eucalypts underground via their roots are much more difficult to study. In Australia there are several of these woody flowering plants, such as Native Cherry (*Exocarpos cupressiformis*), Quandongs (*Santalum* spp.) and the Western Australian Christmas Tree (*Nuytsia floribunda*), in the family Loranthaceae.

The latter is the most spectacular. It is often considered a mistletoe that just happens to form its haustoria on roots rather than aerial branches. It is certainly not selective of the roots of eucalypts; in fact, it forms haustoria with any plant it can find, and not just plants—it has been known to try to unite with underground electricity cables. It slices off the root of the plant it parasitises and connects its own root to the end, drawing out moisture and nutrients.

Most other woody root parasites are in the family Santalaceae. Those on eucalypts are in the genera *Santalum* and *Exocarpos*. The genus *Santalum* includes the fragrant Sandalwood and the arid Quandong. The genus *Exocarpos* is most conspicuous in eastern Australia as the Native Cherry, with its bright-green pine-like appearance, but there are arid and northern species too. The root system produced by these plants is like a branching taproot, with a shallow system of fine, fragile laterals which form haustoria when they contact host roots. It is thought that they are not very specific in their choice of hosts but would certainly attach themselves to eucalypt roots when available.

Other underground examples of parasitism are more complex and, of course, difficult to study. Some orchids, such as the Hyacinth Orchids (*Dipodium* spp.), are hemi-parasites, using a fungus as the link with their host. They often grow in the litter beneath eucalypts. Fungi themselves could be considered parasites, as they sometimes grow on living trees. Parasites demonstrate the complex web of life that links any one group of plants, such as eucalypts, with others in the environment.

Western Australian Christmas Tree (*Nuytsia floribunda*) in full flower, next to the eucalypt it is parasitising.

A Native Cherry (*Exocarpos cupressiformis*), with its pine-like appearance, stands out from its surrounding eucalypt hosts. Usually bright green, the foliage turns reddish during winter in cold regions.

PART 2

CLASSIFYING EUCALYPTS

7 The Three Genera

THE GENUS *EUCALYPTUS* WAS NAMED BY THE FRENCH BOTANIST CHARLES LOUIS L'HÉRITIER de Brutelles in 1792 from a specimen collected by David Nelson, a botanist on one of the ships during Captain Cook's third voyage to the Pacific in 1777. *Eucalyptus* is derived from two Greek words, *eu* meaning 'well' and *kalyptos* meaning 'covered', referring to the cap that protects the flower before it opens. Although Joseph Banks and Daniel Solander collected eucalypts from Botany Bay and the Endeavour River in north Queensland in 1770, it was Nelson's specimen of a Messmate (*Eucalyptus obliqua*), collected from Bruny Island, Tasmania, that was the first described and became the 'type species' (the species nominated to best define the characteristics of the genus) of the great genus. Interestingly, some eucalypt fruits from Banks and Solander's collection had been given to the German botanist Joseph Gaertner in 1787 and illustrated under the name *Metrosideros* in 1788.

Botanists have since determined that the genus should be further divided and today the term covers three genera: *Eucalyptus*, *Angophora* and *Corymbia*. As at 2010, *Eucalyptus* is by far the largest genus, with about 757 species; *Corymbia* has 93 species and *Angophora* has ten.

The genus *Angophora* was described as being distinct from *Eucalyptus* in 1797 by the Spaniard Antonio José Cavanilles, who recognised the opposite mature leaves, the absence of a cap over the developing flowers, small greenish sepals and the distinctly ribbed capsules. He named *Angophora* from the Greek *angos*, meaning 'goblet', and *phoros,* meaning 'bearing', in reference to the vase-like fruits. The type species was *A. cordifolia*, now known as *A. hispida*. There are ten recognised species and two subspecies.

Opposite: This red-flowered form of the Water Gum (*Eucalyptus petiolaris*) shows the bud with its cap firmly in place (top right); below that is a bud with the protective cap splitting off, and two open flowers showing the absence of petals.

The herbarium specimen designated as the 'type' for the species *Eucalyptus obliqua* is held in the Natural History Museum, London. L'Héritier had this specimen in front of him when he formulated his concept for the genus. It was collected in Tasmania by David Nelson on Captain Cook's third voyage. PHOTO: NHM.

The illustration by artist Joseph Redouté that accompanied the description of *Eucalyptus obliqua* by L'Héritier in his work *Sertum Anglicum* in 1792. It is basically the mirror image of the central part of the type herbarium specimen, with open flowers replacing the buds.

DWARF APPLE (*Angophora hispida*)

The Dwarf Apple occurs near the coast of New South Wales, from Sydney to Gosford, and is the type species of the genus *Angophora*. It is a tall shrub or small tree, rarely exceeding 8 metres in height, and sometimes adopting a mallee habit. Its juvenile, stem-clasping, roughish leaves are retained throughout the tree. Large bunches of creamy-white flowers are seen from spring through summer and these attract a range of beetles and other insects, which in turn encourage birds. It is a hardy plant in cultivation, preferring a well-drained, sunny site and tolerating frosts. Its somewhat informal habit is suited to the native garden. A closely related species, *A. robur*, occurs further north, near Coffs Harbour.

The name 'Apple' for these eucalypts was in use by at least 1820, when explorer John Oxley (1785–1828) used it in his journal, supposedly because the colonists saw some resemblance to English apple trees.

Flowers showing the opposite leaves of *Angophora* clearly in the background.

Angophora hispida growing as a shrub in a recently burnt area of the Royal National Park, south of Sydney, New South Wales.
PHOTO: D. GREIG/APII.

Marri (*Corymbia calophylla*) has large, urn-shaped gumnuts whose shape is characteristic of the genus *Corymbia*.

Almost 200 years later, in 1995, a further separation was made with the naming of the genus *Corymbia* by Ken Hill and Lawrence Johnson of the Royal Botanic Gardens, Sydney. *Corymbia* is derived from the Latin *corymbium*, meaning 'corymb', a botanical term describing the way the head of flowers is arranged. *Corymbia* consists of two main groups—the Bloodwoods and the Ghost Gums—both groups tending to occur in tropical and subtropical regions of the country, although there are some exceptions to this. *Corymbia* species may be readily recognised by their urn-shaped fruits, which in many species are quite large. The type species of this genus is *C. gummifera*, the Red Bloodwood, which is widely distributed on the east coast, from the Victorian border to south-east Queensland.

There has been much controversy over the above classification. In 1971, Lindsay Pryor and Lawrence Johnson, while accepting *Angophora* as distinct, had proposed seven subgenera for the remaining species. These were *Symphyomyrtus*, *Monacalyptus*, *Idiogenes*, *Corymbia*, *Blakella*, *Gaubaea* and *Eudesmia*. Two of these subgenera, *Corymbia* (the Bloodwoods) and *Blakella* (the Ghost Gums), were then combined and raised to genus level by Hill and Johnson in 1995 to form the genus *Corymbia*. Some botanists were still not comfortable with this arrangement and in 2000 Ian Brooker published a paper dividing *Eucalyptus* into seven subgenera, but including *Angophora* as one of those subgenera. This did not gain general acceptance and the above division of the eucalypts into three genera—*Angophora*, *Eucalyptus* and *Corymbia*—is likely to remain.

RED BLOODWOOD (*Corymbia gummifera*)

The Red Bloodwood is a common tree of the east coast seen from eastern Victoria to south-east Queensland. It is the type species of the genus *Corymbia*. It has rough bark and its spreading crown is covered with masses of cream blossoms from December to May, attracting nectar-feeding birds. The large, urn-shaped gumnuts are often used by children to make pipes. The durable timber from the Red Bloodwood is resistant to termites, making it useful for fencing posts. In cultivation it is hardy in most well-drained soils and it is tolerant to frosts and salt-laden winds. It is also possibly the inspiration behind the popular 'Gumnut Babies' created by May Gibbs. It is closely related to the Pink Bloodwood (*C. intermedia*), which differs in having winged seeds and gumnuts that are not flared at the rim.

The prominent cream flowers of the Red Bloodwood are popular with birds.

A roadside tree in full flower on the south coast of New South Wales.

The unusual leaf tips of Hook-leaved Mallee (*Eucalyptus uncinata*), are
responsible for its name, as the adjective 'uncinate' means 'shaped like a hook'.

8 Naming Eucalypt Species

THERE ARE RULES FOR ASSIGNING CORRECT SCIENTIFIC NAMES TO PLANTS AND THESE ARE SET out in the *International Code for Botanical Nomenclature*, originally composed in 1905 and updated about every six years. These rules provide botanists with guidelines to describe a new species and publish their reasons in a recognised journal. The basic description is written in Latin with a more detailed description following in English or another modern language. The plant is given a Latinised genus and a species name, for example, *Eucalyptus viminalis*. This name is formally followed by the name of the botanist who described the plant (called the author, and often abbreviated), for example, *Eucalyptus viminalis* Labill. In this case the description was written by the Frenchman Jacques J.H. de Labillardière.

When botanists name new species, they also designate one herbarium specimen as the 'type' for each species and indicate the herbarium in which it is held. This enables other botanists to gain an insight into their concept of the species, and to compare other specimens with the 'type'. The species name is derived from either Latin or Greek and usually either describes some distinctive feature of the plant, or honours a person who in some way was connected with its discovery or assisted the author, or indicates the place or habitat where the species occurs.

The epithet *'viminalis'* in the name *Eucalyptus viminalis* refers to its flexible ribbons of bark.

In the case of *E. viminalis*, the species name is derived from the Latin word *vimineus* meaning 'having long, flexible shoots' and refers to the long ribbons of peeling bark held in the tree as the bark is shed. The Woollybutt (*E. longifolia*), from southern New South Wales, has leaves up to 25 centimetres long and its specific name describes this feature. Another leaf characteristic is reflected in the name *E. uncinata*, which refers to the curved tip of the leaf, alluded to also in its common name of Hook-leaved Mallee.

The species name of the Bristle-leaved Bloodwood (*Corymbia dunlopiana*) honours Clyde Dunlop, who was curator of the Northern Territory Herbarium when the species was described by Sydney botanists Ken Hill and Lawrie Johnson in 1995. Plants can be named after people (living or deceased) based on their surname, or even a nickname. About 20 per cent of eucalypts are named after people.

Burracoppin Mallee (*Eucalyptus burracoppinensis*) is named for the town in Western Australia near to where it occurs.

BRISTLE-LEAVED BLOODWOOD
(*Corymbia dunlopiana*)

A small, often twisted tree to 7 metres high with rough, grey-brown bark to the small branches, this tree is found in savannah grassland in the Top End of the Northern Territory. Its bristly, stem-clasping, juvenile leaves are held into the top branches. Its main features are its prominent pink flowers and large, urn-shaped gumnuts. Due to its small size and ornamental appearance, *C. dunlopiana* is an ideal specimen for home gardens, where it performs well even in subtropical areas. Previously, this species was included in *C. setosa*, which has white flowers and occurs further south in the Northern Territory and in tropical Queensland.

The bristles on the stems and leaves give this plant its common name.

In some cases, the name chosen by the author is much more obscure, particularly with plants that have been described in earlier days when the reason for the name was not always explained in the publication. The famous Jarrah (*E. marginata*), described in 1802 by the English botanist James Donn, is a case in point. His species name is based on the Latin *marginatus* which means 'with a margin', apparently referring to the leaves, but they do not have a particularly conspicuous edge or margin compared with other species.

If you browse the Checklist of Species at the end of this book, you will find a few exceptions to the above methods of applying names.

For instance, Tony Bean may have had his tongue in his cheek when he named *Eucalyptus taurina* (*taurina* = of bulls). He apparently was chased by a bull when he first found this species. The Mt Misery Mallee (*E. dolorosa*) is an endangered species occurring north of Perth on the slopes of Mt Misery. *Dolorosa* is Latin for 'sad' and the species name is thus an oblique reference to the locality where it is found.

Eucalyptus praetermissa is a mallet occurring fairly commonly in the Fitzgerald River National Park, Western Australia. Surprisingly enough, it was not noticed by botanists until 1991 so Ian Brooker and Steve Hopper used the Latin *praetermissus*, which means 'overlooked', when they described the species.

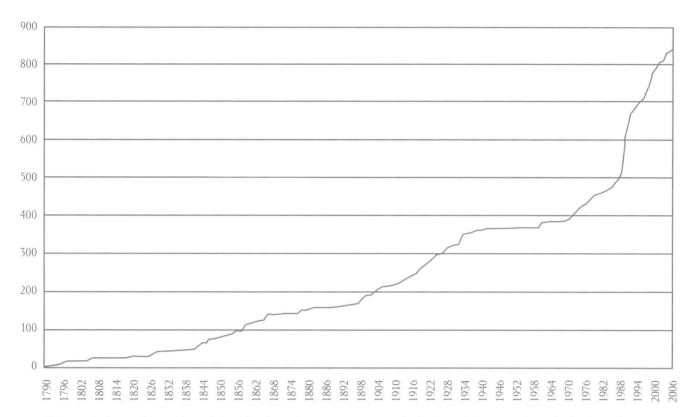

This graph shows the number of described eucalypt taxa on the vertical axis and the years along the horizontal axis.

Finally *Corymbia serendipita* was given its name, an anglicised version of 'serendipity', because the botanists were so happy when they discovered the species.

In this book we most often use the term species, but occasionally we use the term 'taxon' (plural taxa) to describe a group of plants that are recognised as being distinct and have been given a name. The name can apply to a genus, species, subspecies (subsp.) or variety (var.). The latter terms apply when a species is divided further into distinct forms.

Each botanist who names a species or taxon provides added information for those who come after them. Our knowledge of the identity of eucalypts has increased exponentially over time with more accurate descriptions of their morphology and easier access to remote areas for more collecting. In recent years new tools, in the form of molecular DNA analysis, have become available to help botanists make judgements about what is a valid species and how species are related to each other.

Having established how eucalypt species are named, we can look at the rate at which new species, or taxa,

have been named. The graph above shows that the latter years of the twentieth century and the first years of the 21st century have resulted in an almost 100 per cent increase in the number of taxa now recognised.

Inevitably readers of botanical or horticultural books ask why plants change their names from time to time. We have already explained that some *Eucalyptus* species have been changed to *Corymbia* species, but name changes can also happen within the same genus. For example, the Ghost Gum of central Australia was known for many years as *Eucalyptus papuana*. In 1995, the generic name was changed to *Corymbia*, but when botanists looked closely at the group known generally as Ghost Gums, they found there were even more differences than earlier botanists had realised; in fact, 24 species and subspecies were named. The original *E. papuana*, named and described by Ferdinand Mueller in 1875, occurred only on the tip of Cape York and in Papua New Guinea, so a new name had to be applied to the central Australian species. It is now called *C. aparrerinja*, a name derived from the Aboriginal name for the tree.

9 Botanists Who Named Eucalypts

WITH SUCH A LARGE GROUP OF PLANTS, VERY MANY BOTANISTS HAVE DABBLED IN THE taxonomy of eucalypts over the last 200 years. When we look at those botanists listed as an 'author' for a species, a few stand out as being particularly prolific.

The author is the botanist who gives the plant its scientific Latin name, and whose own name follows the Latin name in formal references to the plant. These botanists are said to have 'described' the plant. When later botanists redefine the use of that name using another concept, they keep the original author's name in the new author citation, crediting the original author's work, for example, *Eucalyptus caesia* Benth. and *Corymbia peltata* (Benth.) K.D.Hill & L.A.S.Johnson.

Of those who have authored a large number of species, there are a few who took a particular interest in the eucalypts, and there are those general botanists who had a large impact on the broad Australian flora because of their time and place. George Bentham and Ferdinand von Mueller described huge numbers of plants, and inevitably some of these were eucalypts. An interesting omission is Robert Brown (1773–1858), who left all the eucalypts for a second volume of his *Prodromus*, which was never published.

With databases such as the Australian Plant Name Index (APNI) it is possible to analyse the impact that particular botanists have had on a plant group. We could develop a 'top ten' for botanists whose names are attached to plants in a genus or family. We also have another listing of plants, the Australian Plant Census (APC), which indicates those names currently accepted by the botanical community. Thus, we have a means to assess which botanist's plant names have stood the test of time—those that are still considered valid species in the light of the knowledge and understanding that came later.

Some botanists tend to work in isolation, being the sole author of the scientific publications in which species are described; some form long-standing collaborations with a particular partner; and some are broadly collaborative, producing joint papers with a range of others. We have selected a few who have had a big impact on eucalypts, and listed them chronologically. We have used the term 'taxa' to describe any rank of name below the genus, whether it be a species, subspecies, variety or form.

Opposite: Yellow-top Mallee Ash (*Eucalyptus luehmanniana*), named by Ferdinand von Mueller in honour of Johann Georg Luehmann (1843–1904), his assistant.

George Bentham
(1800–84)

Bentham was an Englishman who never came to Australia. He studied law, but devoted his life to botany upon his inheritance following the deaths of his father and uncle (the famous political philosopher Jeremy Bentham) in 1833. In 1854 he donated his private herbarium of more than 100,000 specimens to the Royal Botanic Gardens in Kew, London, and from then on worked there in an honorary capacity at the herbarium. He was chosen by the directors of Kew to write the proposed *Flora Australiensis*, a decision that sparked some controversy as Ferdinand von Mueller in Australia had viewed the project as his own. Bentham published *Flora Australiensis* in seven volumes from 1863 to 1878, during which time he catalogued and described more than 7000 species.

Bentham described 89 taxa of *Eucalyptus*. Of those, twenty are still considered valid names in the APC, and his name still forms part of the authorship of 47 currently recognised eucalypts. His authorship is written as 'Benth.' when included in a plant's name. His name was honoured by Maiden and Cambage in 1915 when they described the Camden White Gum (*Eucalyptus benthamii*).

George Bentham (1800–84)

Ferdinand von Mueller
(1825–96)

Mueller was born at Rostock in Germany and orphaned at the age of fourteen after his parents died of tuberculosis. He became a qualified pharmacist and obtained a PhD from the University in Kiel in 1847. That same year, for the sake of his health, he set out on the five and a half month trip to Adelaide as an emigrant. He went to Victoria in 1852, and was appointed Government Botanist for that state in 1853. In his first decade there, he did a lot of field collecting, locally on horseback and as part of A.C. Gregory's expedition to northern Australia (1855–56). He was also appointed Director of the Royal Botanic Gardens, Melbourne, from 1857 to 1873 and made a hereditary baron by the king of Württemburg in 1871.

He was deeply disappointed at not being given the task of writing *Flora Australiensis*, but cooperated with Bentham in Kew by supplying specimens and keeping up a prodigious correspondence. He continued his scientific publications until his death, by which time he had made a huge impact on Australian botany.

Mueller had a fascination with eucalypts—not only with their size, which he continually boasted about, but also with distributing them around the world. He sent vast quantities of seed abroad, and at one time predicted that 'eucalypts are destined to play a prominent part for all times to come in the sylvan culture of vast tracts of the globe'. In 1879 he published the book *Eucalyptographia: A Descriptive Atlas of the Eucalypts of Australia*, the first of the beautifully illustrated folio book series to tackle the group.

Mueller described 135 taxa of *Eucalyptus* and another three jointly with others, plus one *Angophora* species. Of those, 62 are still considered valid names in the APC, and his name still forms part of the authorship of 96 currently recognised eucalypts. His authorship is abbreviated to 'F.Muell.' when included with a plant's name, although in some old publications you might see 'FvM'. His name was honoured in 1891 by Alfred Howitt when he described Yellow Stringybark as *Eucalyptus muelleriana*.

Ferdinand von Mueller (1825–96)   Richard Thomas Baker (1854–1941)   Joseph Maiden (1859–1925)

Richard Thomas Baker (1854–1941)

Baker was born in Woolwich, England, and emigrated to Australia in 1879. He soon joined the staff at Newington College, Sydney, as a science and art master. In 1888 he obtained an appointment at the Sydney Technological Museum, and in 1898 became curator and economic botanist. He was very interested in the practical uses of eucalypts, writing *A Research on the Eucalypts, Especially in Regard to Their Essential Oils* in 1902 in collaboration with H.G. Smith. Books on hardwoods, wood fibres and cabinet timbers followed. Baker retired from the museum in 1921, but continued to lecture in forestry at the University of Sydney until 1924.

Baker described 47 taxa of *Eucalyptus* on his own but was a strong collaborator, publishing another 25 taxa with joint authors, mostly his colleague at the museum, Henry Smith. He also published two *Angophora* species. Of all those, 28 are still considered valid names in the APC, and his name still forms part of the authorship of 38 currently recognised taxa. His authorship is written as 'R.T.Baker' when included with a plant's name. His name was honoured in 1913 by dermatologist Edwin Hall when he named the Small-leaved Apple as *Angophora bakeri*, and again in 1914 by Joseph Maiden when he described Baker's Mallee as *Eucalyptus bakeri*.

Joseph Maiden (1859–1925)

Maiden was born in London and abandoned his studies at London University to migrate to a warmer climate due to ill health. He arrived in Sydney in 1881 and was soon appointed curator of the newly formed Technological, Industrial and Sanitary Museum. He worked tirelessly to catalogue the very mixed collection that the museum had accumulated from the recent Sydney International Exhibition (1879–80). Unfortunately, the museum was associated with the Garden Palace, adjacent to the Botanic Gardens, and when the building was destroyed by fire in 1882 he lost most of his collection.

He laboured to rebuild the collection for the next ten years in what he called a 'wretched tin shed' before moving it into a new building at Ultimo, near the University of Sydney. (This eventually became the present Powerhouse Museum on a nearby site.) Under his leadership, that institution became a centre of phytochemical research and amassed a large herbarium. He was made Superintendent of Technical Education in 1894, and appointed Government Botanist and Director of the Botanic Gardens in 1896, retiring in 1924. During his time as director, he built up the herbarium and promoted botanical research.

By the age of 30, Maiden was already questioning

the eucalypt knowledge of the sage of Australian botany. In 1889 he wrote to William Baeuerlen, 'In reply to your query … in regard to Baron Mueller giving a Eucalypt a name which appears to us to be indefensible, I do not at present know what to advise.'

In 1896, the year of Mueller's death, he published his first eucalypt descriptions in a joint paper with the engineer Henry Deane, and it was not long before he was the pre-eminent eucalypt expert in Australia. By 1903 he had embarked on his *A Critical Revision of the Genus Eucalyptus*, a life's work that continued to be published in parts until 1933, eight years after his death.

Maiden described 155 taxa of *Eucalyptus*, but he was a collaborator and jointly described another 91, mostly in partnership with Deane or William Blakely. He also described one *Angophora* species. Of all the species he described, 145 are still considered valid names in the APC, and his name still forms part of the authorship of 175 currently recognised eucalypts. His authorship is written as 'Maiden' when included with a plant's name. His name was honoured in 1890 by Ferdinand von Mueller when he described Maiden's Gum as *Eucalyptus maidenii*, a name that was reduced in rank to *Eucalyptus globulus* subsp. *maidenii* in 1975.

Merrit (*Eucalyptus flocktoniae*), named in honour of botanical artist Margaret Flockton (1861–1953) by Joseph Maiden.

William Blakely (1875–1941)

William Blakely (1875–1941)

Blakely was the first of our major eucalypt botanists to be born in Australia, in Tenterfield, New South Wales. Because of his keen interest in plants he was appointed gardener at Jenolan Caves in 1898. Two years later he was transferred to the Botanic Gardens, Sydney, on probation, at seven shillings a day, because of his botanical knowledge. By 1907 he had impressed Maiden with his diligence in preparing interpretive material for guides in the Gardens, and by 1913 was transferred to the 'indoor staff', slow progress by today's standards! In 1925, the year of Maiden's death, Blakely was classified as Assistant Botanist.

Blakely worked closely with Maiden on *A Critical Revision of the Genus Eucalyptus* from 1913. When complete, the work did not include a key to the species. One year after the publication of the final part in 1933, Blakely produced, at his own expense, *A Key to the Eucalypts: With Descriptions of 500 Species and 138 Varieties and a Companion to J.H. Maiden's Critical Revision of the Genus Eucalyptus*. Unlike the large folios of Maiden's publication, this was a convenient-sized handbook that remained the mainstay for eucalypt identification for many years to come.

Blakely described 161 taxa of *Eucalyptus* but collaborated widely—jointly describing another 86. He

Maisie and Denis Carr with eucalypt seedlings, 1980. PHOTO: ANU.

Lawrie Johnson, photographed in 1993.
PHOTO: JAMIE PLAZA.

also described one *Angophora* species. Of all the species he described, 127 are still considered valid names in the APC, and his name still forms part of the authorship of 167 currently recognised eucalypts. His authorship is written as 'Blakely' when included with a plant's name. His name was honoured in 1917 when Maiden described Blakely's Red Gum as *Eucalyptus blakelyi*.

Stella Grace Maisie Carr (1912–88) and Denis John Carr (1915–2008)

Maisie Carr was born in Footscray, Victoria, and her early research was in ecology. Denis Carr was born in Stoke-on-Trent, England, and studied botany, leading to a PhD after discharge from the Royal Air Force after the Second World War. He migrated to Australia to take up a lectureship at the University of Melbourne in 1953. Maisie and Denis married in 1955 and most of their subsequent eucalypt research was published under joint authorship. They came to Canberra in 1967, when Denis was appointed professor at the newly formed Research School of Biological Science at the Australian National University. They undertook extensive studies of the floral morphology and taxonomy of the eucalypts, and self-published two books on these topics.

The Carrs described 57 taxa of *Eucalyptus* and collaborated only once, describing *Eucalyptus roycei* jointly with Alex George. Only ten are still considered valid names in the APC, partly because many of the taxa they concentrated on were later transferred to the genus *Corymbia*. Their names still form part of the authorship of 28 currently recognised eucalypts. Their author partnership is written as 'D.J.Carr & S.G.M.Carr' when included with a plant's name.

Lawrence (Lawrie) Alexander Sidney Johnson (1925–97)

Johnson was born in Cheltenham, New South Wales, and studied at the University of Sydney. He then joined the staff of the Royal Botanic Gardens, Sydney, where he spent the whole of his career. He was a herbarium botanist there from 1948 to 1972 and director from 1972 to 1985, after which time he was an Honorary Research Associate, active in that role until his death.

As well as having his name as author or co-author on more eucalypts than anyone else, he had a profound influence on the higher level classification of the eucalypts. His publication, *A Classification of the Eucalypts*, jointly written with Lindsay Pryor in 1971, set the framework for the three-genera arrangement of the group that is now accepted by all Australian herbaria.

Ian Brooker, photographed in 1998.   Ken Hill, photographed in 2004.   Dean Nicolle, photographed in 2009.
PHOTO: C. KNIGHT/DIGIFILM.

Johnson described only ten taxa of *Eucalyptus* and four taxa of *Corymbia* on his own, but it is his longstanding collaboration with colleague Ken Hill and their joint publication of 171 *Eucalypt* taxa and 62 *Corymbia* taxa that has had the most impact. He also described another twenty *Eucalyptus* taxa and three *Angophora* taxa jointly with other authors. Johnson and Hill were also responsible for transferring 84 previously described bloodwoods and ghost gums to the genus *Corymbia* when that genus was established.

Of those eucalypts Johnson authored or co-authored, 189 are still considered valid names in the APC, and his name still forms part of the authorship of 306 currently recognised eucalypts. His authorship is written as 'L.A.S.Johnson' when included with a plant's name. His name was honoured in 1978 when Ian Brooker and Don Blaxell named Johnson's Mallee as *Eucalyptus johnsoniana*.

Ian Brooker (b. 1934)

Brooker was born in Adelaide, South Australia, and graduated from the University of Adelaide. He started working in the soils area of the South Australian Department of Agriculture, later joining the Botany Department of the Australian National University, where he undertook further studies. Following this, he worked in Western Australia and later with the Forest Research Institute in Canberra, where he specialised in

eucalypts. Working for CSIRO, he eventually joined the Australian National Herbarium in Canberra, where his specialist eucalypt knowledge led to the production of the interactive computer key to the eucalypts, *EUCLID*, in ever more comprehensive editions from 1997 to 2006.

In a private capacity he published the popular *Field Guide to Eucalypts* (*Vol. 1* in 1983, *Vol. 2* in 1990, *Vol. 3* in 1994), in collaboration with David Kleinig, with whom he worked in the CSIRO Division of Forest Research.

Brooker described 44 taxa of *Eucalyptus* on his own, but collaborated widely and jointly described another 171, many of those with Steve Hopper, later Director of the Royal Botanic Gardens in Kew, London. Of all those, 179 are still considered valid names in the APC, and his name forms part of the authorship of 201 currently recognised eucalypts. His authorship is written as 'Brooker' when included with a plant's name. His name was honoured in 1979 when Alan Gray described Brooker's Gum as *Eucalyptus brookeriana*.

Kenneth (Ken) Hill (b. 1948)

Hill was born in Armidale, New South Wales, and worked as an exploration geologist before joining the staff of the herbarium at the Royal Botanic Gardens, Sydney, in 1983. His appointment was as research assistant on the eucalypts, although he also contributed greatly to the study of cycads and to the introduction of electronic computing tools to the herbarium's activities.

In the world of eucalypts his major contribution was his collaboration with Lawrie Johnson in jointly describing a large number of species and in establishing the genus *Corymbia* in 1995 and having it accepted by the botanical community.

Hill described only fourteen taxa of eucalypts on his own, plus another 236 which he described jointly with others, mostly Johnson. Of all those, 172 are still considered valid names in the APC, and his name still forms part of the authorship of 398 currently recognised eucalypts. His authorship is written as 'K.D.Hill' when included with a plant's name.

Dean Nicolle (b. 1974)

Nicolle was born in Adelaide, South Australia, and had an interest in eucalypts from his high school days. He completed his degree at the University of Adelaide and went on to do his PhD on a group of southern Australian mallees at Flinders University, South Australia, in 2008. With strong support from his father, he set up the Currency Creek Arboretum growing over 900 taxa of eucalypts. Most of the eucalypts in the plantation were grown from seed collected by Nicolle in the wild.

Nicolle started publishing on eucalypts in scientific literature in 1995, and has self-published reference books (*Eucalypts of South Australia* and *Eucalypts of Victoria and Tasmania*) as field guides, using his own photographs. He is self-employed as a consultant in the fields of botany, arboriculture and ecology.

At the time of printing, Nicolle had described 28 taxa of eucalypts on his own, plus another eighteen jointly with others. Interestingly, the APC recognises 48 names by Nicolle alone and another fifteen with joint authorship—this is because at the time of printing quite a few of his manuscript names were being recognised although they had not been formally published. His name forms part of the authorship of 68 currently recognised eucalypts. His authorship is written as 'D.Nicolle' when included with a plant's name.

Honoured in their names

The practice of naming plants after people has been around for a long time, certainly since 1753 when the modern system of naming plants with a genus name and a species name was initiated by Carl Linnaeus (1707–78). Indeed, Linnaeus himself had suggested in 1737 that there should be a link between the flower and the botanist for whom it was named. This link was not always positive—the vindictive Linnaeus named a stinking little weed '*Siegesbeckia*' after the German botanist Johann Georg Siegesbeck (1686–1755), who had criticised his system of classification. On the other hand, Linnaeus named the genus *Magnolia* after the French botanist Pierre Magnol (1638–1715) because 'it has very handsome leaves and flowers'.

In Australia, Ferdinand von Mueller was a master at naming plants after people he wanted to impress, often those who held the purse strings in the British colonial hierarchy. Thus, we have genera such as *Cardwellia*, named for Edward Cardwell (1813–86) who was Secretary for the Colonies from 1864 to 1866, and *Hollandaea* for Sir Henry Thurston Holland (1825–1914) who held positions in the Colonial Office and was later a politician and Secretary of State for the Colonies. Neither of these men ever came to Australia, nor had any great interest in botany.

Botanists rarely have the opportunity to describe a new genus and it is usually with a species name, correctly termed an 'epithet', that people are commemorated. Of the 860 or so species of eucalypts (not looking at subspecies and so on) about 170 are named after people, which is about 21 per cent. With such a large number of species it is not surprising that many of our prominent botanists have been honoured.

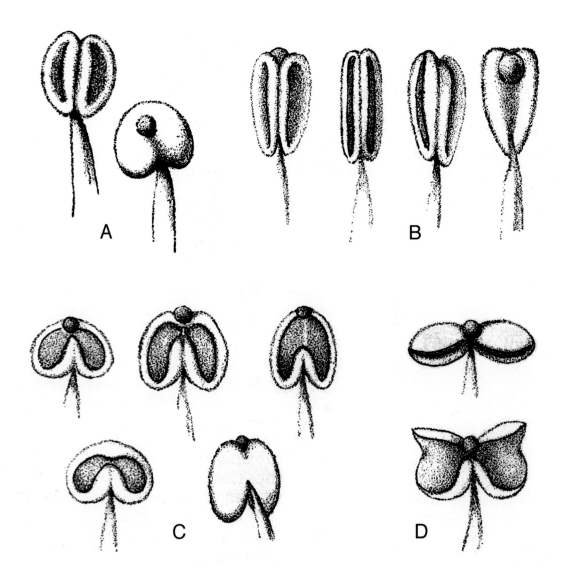

A few of the many different anther types illustrated in Blakely's key. Matching a specimen to these put it in a section or subsection, which was the starting point for keying out a plant. A: subsection Cordformes; B: subsection Longiores; C: section Renantherae; D: subsection Papilionantherae.

10 Identifying Eucalypts

'THE GENUS *EUCALYPTUS* IS ONE OF THE MOST PROTEAN IN THE PLANT KINGDOM.' SO SAID W.F. Blakely (1875–1941) in the preface to the first edition of *A Key to the Eucalypts* in 1934. Blakely's publication was the first comprehensive treatment of the genus. Second and third editions were published in 1955 and 1965 to include newly described species and to update other data which had become available.

Blakely worked closely with J.H. Maiden (1859–1925), Director of Sydney Botanic Gardens and New South Wales Government Botanist, whose eight-volume work *A Critical Revision of the Genus Eucalyptus* (1909–33) provided illustrations and descriptions of several hundred species, as well as detailed drawings of fruits, seed leaves, leaf form and so on. Maiden summarised the then present knowledge of classification, indicating the problems with using such characters as habit, bark, timber, gum exudates (kino), seed leaves, floral differences, leaf characters and fruits, all of which proved inconsistent. He concluded by saying:

> To sum up, for herbarium work the anthers and fruits are the best characters to
> go by, for the scientific forester, the bark and timber; but all characters display
> a puzzling amount of variation.

Blakely's key used anther structure, and while this method served taxonomists for many years, for the layman it was very complex and only the very astute and patient enthusiasts were able to cope with it. His key covered 522 species and provided detailed descriptions of each species together with common name, flowering time, distribution and uses. Many keys were developed for local regions by other botanists, but in most cases they were 'cut down' versions of Blakely's key, using similar characters but a reduced number of species.

In 1954 two foresters, Norman Hall and Doug Johnston, prepared a punch-card system using various characters of the eucalypts to aid in their identification. This included the 638 species and varieties then known. These cards were large

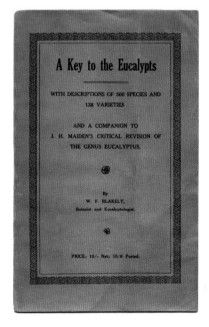

Blakely's *Key to the Eucalypts* (1934), covering what was then the genus *Eucalyptus*, was the only comprehensive Australia-wide reference for over 60 years.

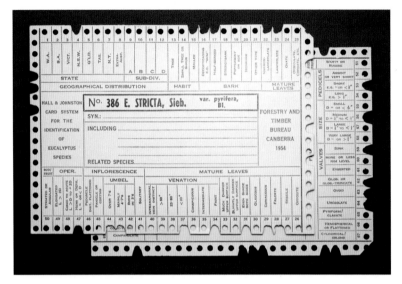

The third edition of the interactive computer key *EUCLID*, issued as a DVD in 2006.

Two cards from the first edition of Hall and Johnston's set of eucalypt identification punch cards issued in 1954, front and reverse. A rod inserted through a character's hole resulted in that card falling from the pack if the character was present.

index cards with 84 holes around the edge, each hole representing a character of the eucalypt. At the manufacturing stage these cards were cut to extend the hole to the edge of the card when the character was present. Inserting a rod such as a knitting needle through a hole representing a character allowed cards for species with that character to fall out of the pack. This process was continued with various characters until only a single card fell, identifying the species. A second edition of the system was released in 1964 with larger cards and 94 holes.

While punch-card keys were an improvement on Blakely's complex dichotomous key, they were bulky, expensive and fiddly to use, and certainly did not catch on with the general public. They did, however, enable the identification of eucalypts when one did not have anthers as a starting point—species could be eliminated based on the material at hand.

The concept of a series of 'character states', each one being present or absent, and a mechanism to sort these, paved the way for the next innovation in eucalypt identification. With the rise of personal computers, what could be done on punch cards could be done by computer. In the early years a range of different software programs vied with each other to be the platform for interactive plant identification keys. In the case of

eucalypts, it was a program called Lucid, developed in Queensland, that was eventually chosen.

EUCLID (which stands for EUCaLptus IDentification) was produced by the Centre for Plant Biodiversity Research, Canberra, run jointly by the CSIRO and the Australian National Botanic Gardens. The development of this program began in 1991 when Ian Brooker, a distinguished eucalyptologist, was asked to provide a list of characters that could be used as a basis for an interactive key. Many people were involved with compiling data, including photographs, drawings and distribution maps, and finally a first edition of *EUCLID* was produced in 1997 entitled *Eucalypts of South-eastern Australia*. This proved successful and further extensive field work was carried out over the whole of Australia with the collection of specimens, photographs of habit, bark, buds, seeds and juvenile foliage. The third edition, *EUCLID: Eucalypts of Australia* was published in 2006 for the whole country, describing 894 taxa and including over 10,000 images. It can be used by anyone with a minimal knowledge of botany and basic computer skills to identify eucalypt species from anywhere in Australia.

While identification of eucalypts may still appear to present a formidable obstacle for the average person to come to terms with, *EUCLID* has simplified the task and is fun to use.

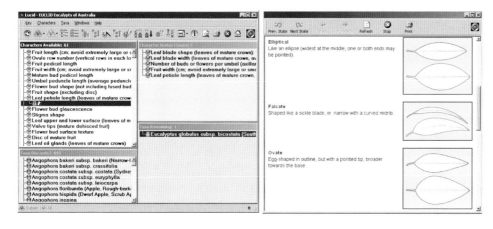

The *EUCLID* key. The right screen image shows the explanation of terms. The left screen image is the process of identifying your plant with the screen divided into four; *top left:* the character list; *top right:* characters chosen; *bottom left:* discarded species; *bottom right:* remaining species, in this case one, showing the name of the plant.

SILVER BOX (*Eucalyptus pruinosa*)

Widespread across the tropics of Australia, this distinctive small tree is a feature of savannah woodlands, where it is often the dominant member of the communities. On poorer soils trees often adopt a mallee form. Bark is grey and held on to the smaller branches. The silvery-grey, stalkless, juvenile leaves are borne on squarish stems and retained into the crown of the tree. They are broadly heart-shaped or elliptical and up to 14 centimetres long. The creamy-white to pale-yellow flowers are borne in sevens at the end of branches, where they make a fine display during the dry season. The decorative foliage and the bird-attracting flowers make it a suitable tree for parks and gardens in tropical areas. Flowering usually occurs in the second year from seed. A second subspecies, subsp. *tenuata*, has narrower gumnuts and occurs in the more northerly areas of the Northern Territory and across the Western Australian border. Some intergrading of these subspecies occurs.

The silver-grey leaves are opposite and have no stalk.

This tree has a single trunk, but others show more of a mallee form.

PART 3

A SOCIAL HISTORY
OF EUCALYPTS

Lerp, protective coverings that protect the soft body of psyllids, are sweet to taste. These psyllids are on the Brittle Gum (*Eucalyptus mannifera*).

11 Traditional Aboriginal Society

THE TRADITIONAL ABORIGINAL VIEW OF THE AUSTRALIAN ENVIRONMENT DIFFERED markedly from that of the Europeans, who took over Aboriginal land following settlement in 1788. The Aboriginal people saw themselves as part of the environment, intimately connected to the plants and animals and earth of the place where they lived, while the incoming Europeans saw the environment as something to be tamed, conquered and owned.

When considering Aboriginal plant use we must also consider the wide range of cultures spread over a vast continent with more than 200 language groups, and the diversity of vegetation and flora in the various areas inhabited by these groups. This makes generalisations and sweeping statements very difficult. In much of southern Australia we are reliant on the early written records of the colonists, who used a very different method of classifying plants, and had a very limited understanding of the practices of the indigenous people. While the Europeans classified plants based on the structure of their flowers, the Aboriginal people grouped and named plants depending on their usefulness or their importance to their culture. The more useful the plant, the more detailed its classification, sometimes resulting in a plant known to Western science as a single species being distinguished with different names for factors, such as edibility or where it grows, that most botanists would not take into account.

In looking at eucalypts in traditional Aboriginal culture we have considered them in terms of food, medicines, shelter, tools and ritual, even though these headings are very much a Western construct. Because plants distributed widely over the areas occupied by several Aboriginal language groups could have several names in different places, and any use of indigenous nomenclature would have to be qualified by which tribe or language group used that name, we have avoided such names in this book.

Bush coconuts on a Desert Bloodwood (*Corymbia terminalis*) in central Australia.
PHOTO: D. GREIG/APII.

Eucalypts as a food source

Given the ubiquity of eucalypts throughout most areas of Australia, except perhaps for the rainforests, the trees themselves provided rich hunting grounds for the Aboriginals. Indeed, some of the earliest European records relate to Aboriginals climbing eucalypts, even though they were not actually seen doing so. Abel Tasman noted in 1642 that his landing party in Van Diemen's Land (Tasmania) had seen large trees, about 5 metres in diameter with the lowest branch at a height of 19 metres, obviously eucalypts,

> Which . . . bore notches made with flint implements, the bark having been removed for the purpose. These notches, forming a kind of steps to enable persons to get up the trees and rob the bird's nests in their tops, were fully five feet apart, so that our men concluded that the natives here must be of very tall stature, or must be in the possession of some sort of artifice for getting up the said trees.

Tasman's party did not actually see any Aboriginals during their short stay in Australia, or solve the mystery of toe-holes 1.5 metres apart.

Later colonists were to become very familiar with the climbing skills of the Aboriginal people who used no other tools than plant-fibre rope and a stone axe. The eucalypt canopies provided a rich source of food, which included marsupials such as possums and Koalas, bird's eggs, honey and a range of insects. It has been suggested that these climbing skills enabled the hunting 'impact zone' to extend much higher above the ground than in most hunter-gatherer societies.

The eucalypts provided one special delicacy in both forested and arid parts of Australia in the form of the lerp coverings produced by psyllids, the sap-sucking insects that live on the surface of gumleaves (see p. 76). These insects exude a sugary substance which hardens as a protective covering over their soft bodies in an array of beautifully sculptured forms. The Aboriginals ate these with relish. When densely covering the surface of the leaf, the psyllids were stripped off by pulling the leaves

Aboriginal men extracting drinking water from the roots of Red Mallee (*Eucalyptus socialis*) in northern South Australia. PHOTO: J.C. NOBLE/NLA.

through the teeth. Psyllids also induced the production of edible 'manna' from trees such as the Manna Gum (*Eucalyptus viminalis*) (see p. 43).

Another food source from an insect–eucalypt partnership is the giant galls, sometimes called bush coconuts, which grow on a couple of desert bloodwoods, especially Tjuta (*Corymbia terminalis*). These galls are about the size of an apple, surrounding a grub about 4 centimetres in length. When the gall is broken open it has an outer rim of woody material surrounding an inner layer about 1 centimetre thick composed of white, edible flesh similar to a coconut. Aboriginal people ate both the grub and the fleshy gall.

In the arid parts of Australia the Aboriginals ground the seeds of some eucalypts between special stones to form an edible paste. Only a few species produced seeds that were eaten, including the central Australian Coolabah (*E. coolabah*) and the Warilu (*E. gamophylla*), whose paste is described by ethno-botanist Peter Latz as having 'a pleasant nutty flavour with only the faintest hint of eucalyptus oils'.

Eucalypts also provided a valuable source of liquid in areas devoid of water. Surface roots of some trees such as mallees could be dug up and broken into short lengths and left to stand vertically while they slowly dripped their precious watery liquid into a container. One long mallee root was able to satisfy the needs of

Above: Snappy Gum (*Eucalyptus leucophloia*) has bright-yellow inner bark used as an Aboriginal medicine when boiled with water.

Above right: Kino gum, commonly seen exuding from a range of eucalypts, had a variety of Aboriginal medicinal uses. This gum is on Yellow Box (*Eucalyptus melliodora*).

two or three thirsty men. Some eucalypts, such as the Yate (*E. cornuta*), produce a sweet sap when the bark is stripped from the tree. This is described as being a thick, purplish syrup with a taste like molasses, and Aboriginal people carried it around in bark containers for later consumption.

One Tasmanian eucalypt has a special place in Aboriginal ethno-botany as producing the only well-documented example of a traditional alcoholic beverage. *E. gunnii* is known as Cider Gum because it was later used by colonists for producing cider. Daniel Bunce, the Director of the Geelong Botanic Gardens from 1858, noted of this tree:

> The natives had also a method, at the proper season, of grinding holes in the trees, from which the sweet juice flowed plentifully, and was collected in a hole at the bottom, near the root of the tree. These holes were kept covered over with a flat stone, apparently for the purpose of preventing birds and animals coming to drink it. When allowed to remain any length of time, it ferments and settles into a coarse sort of wine or cider, rather intoxicating if drank to excess.

Eucalypts as medicines

A study of the use of traditional Aboriginal medicines requires an understanding of the concept of health and wellbeing in Aboriginal culture beyond the scope of this book. However, many maladies were attributed to supernatural forces and the 'healers' in Aboriginal society have been likened to a combination of the modern general practitioner and psychiatrist. In spite of the different beliefs surrounding the cause of illness, we know that many of the traditional medicines worked and medical scientists are today drawing on these ancient traditions.

In some places steam baths were used to treat respiratory ailments. A platform was built over a smouldering fire on which eucalypt leaves were placed and the patient was enveloped in a cloak made of animal skin.

In parts of central Australia the bright-yellow inner bark of the Snappy Gum (*E. leucophloia*) was boiled with water to make a medicinal wash for a wide range of ailments. The River Red Gum (*E. camaldulensis*) was also used to make a powerful antiseptic—the inner bark was boiled until the red gum came out and, when cooled, it could be used to treat a range of skin diseases.

The inner bark of the Darwin Stringybark (*E. tetrodonta*) was shredded and soaked in water to be used as a mouthwash to heal mouth sores. The very young red-coloured leaves of this tree were also crushed and mixed with water to treat skin sores. The 'kino' or gum that was responsible for Captain Cook coining the name 'gum tree' was used widely to make a drink for treating colds and fevers. Plugs of this reddish-yellow gum were also used to ease the pain of tooth decay.

The solid framework of eucalypt timber can be seen in this partly constructed dome-shaped shelter photographed by Herbert Basedow near Coopers Creek in northern South Australia at the turn of last century. The photo on the right shows a completed shelter, covered with clumps of *Triodia* and other herbage in central Australia. PHOTOS: H. BASEDOW/NMA.

Shelter

The shelters built by Aboriginals before European contact varied widely from place to place and between different vegetation types. They also varied according to the degree to which people settled in one place or were continually on the move. Many campsites were regularly used whenever the group was in the area, but the time spent in one location was determined by the food resources available.

In many cases a shelter consisted of little more than a windbreak of leafy eucalypt branches broken or cut from the surrounding trees. The frequent use of the same site over many years sometimes resulted in a coppiced effect for the surrounding eucalypts. In other areas more substantial structures were built, often using eucalypt timber to support a covering of thatched or layered leafy material, which varied greatly according to the available plants.

In northern Australia the availability of large sheets of bark removed from trees such as Darwin Stringybark (*E. tetrodonta*) provided the ideal building material. It could be used as roofing that could be draped over a framework of eucalypt poles, sometimes with a floor platform, or more simply as an A-frame.

Tools and implements

Aboriginal people had relatively few hand-crafted objects, as would be expected of people regularly on the move. Wooden implements could mostly be divided into those used for hunting or digging, those used as weapons, those used as containers or for food preparation, and those used to make water craft. Surveys of museum objects show that 35 per cent of woody species used to make artefacts were *Acacia* (most from only 49 different species). Next in importance are the eucalypts, comprising 30 per cent, and these were recorded from about 40 different species.

Aboriginals most often fashioned their implements from green wood because it was easier to work. Sometimes, if the job was not completed, the wood was soaked in water for a couple of days and if a partly completed item could not be finished it was buried in damp sand until work resumed. Most wooden implements were made with flaked stone tools and judicious use of fire. The hollow of a wooden bowl could be burned away and a wooden spear tip hardened by fire. Wedging was an important technique in getting a suitable piece of bark off a tree—the shape was marked out and wedges of wood or stone hammered in to prise the bark away from the parent tree.

Wooden tools are usually short-lived and we rely on museum collections for much of our information for southern Australia. The ethno-botanist Johan Kamminga has developed a considerable database of wood species used for Aboriginal artefacts. His list of eucalypts is far too extensive to reproduce in full, so only a few of the more versatile species will be mentioned here with the objects made from them.

- White Mallee (*E. dumosa*): spear, shield, boomerang, club, carrying container.
- Long-fruited Bloodwood (*C. polycarpa*): spear, spearthrower, peg, canoe paddle, clap sticks, didgeridoo.
- Darwin Stringybark (*E. tetrodonta*): spear point, grave post, canoe paddle, clap sticks, digeridoo, pipe, drum, coffin, bullroarer.

The bark from eucalypts was very useful in the making of canoes. The canoes themselves were relatively short-lived (not much more than two years), so most of our information about canoe-making comes from written reports and museum collections. However, in some cases the scar on the tree from which they were removed can last for more than 100 years, giving an insight into times past.

The type and design of eucalypt bark canoes varied around Australia. On the next few pages we look at three basic designs.

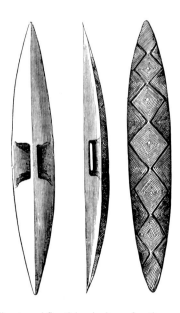

Above left: Sheets of bark from Darwin Stringybark (*Eucalyptus tetrodonta*) make excellent and flexible shelters for the warm climate of northern Australia. PHOTO: NTL.

Above right: A typical shield said to be made from Red Ironbark (*Eucalyptus sideroxylon*) or Yellow Gum (*E. leucoxylon*) and illustrated in Brough Smyth's *The Aborigines of Victoria* in 1876.

Part of a composed photo by noted photographer Charles Bayliss, taken in 1886 at Chowilla Station on the River Murray. The canoe, made from River Red Gum (*Eucalyptus camaldulensis*) easily supports three people in still water. PHOTO: NLA.

Murray–Darling canoes

The simplest were those from the Murray–Darling basin, made from a single piece of thick bark stripped from River Red Gum (*E. camaldulensis*) and shaped to form a simple boat while still pliable. These could be of a considerable size. The explorer Edward John Eyre, when he lived near Blanchetown in South Australia, wrote that they 'will hold seven or eight people easily; it is often over twenty feet long' (6 metres in today's measurements). He goes on to describe an 'ordinary' one used for fishing that was 4.5 metres long, nearly a metre wide and about 20 centimetres deep. It was

> formed out of a single sheet of bark, with one end a little narrower than the other and pointing upward. This end is paddled first; the bottom is nearly flat, and the canoe is so firm, that a person can take hold of one side, and climb into it from the water without upsetting it.

Making these canoes was no simple task and the tree was carefully chosen. Some were made from bark near the base of the tree, but occasionally bark was taken from many metres above the base. The shape was marked out and the outline etched through the bark to the hardwood using a much harder digging stick or similar instrument. A rope was passed around the tree trunk to stop the sheet falling and breaking. Short, sharp sticks were forced or hammered progressively between the bark and the tree's hardwood until the whole sheet was prised away from the trunk. The separated sheet of bark was then lowered to the ground—no mean feat for a 6-metre length of green bark.

The bark at the upper end was usually much thinner than that near the base of the tree. Props held the sheet in the desired shape and small fires were lit at regular intervals inside the sheet to dry out the moisture in the bark and cause it to curl upwards. As the rear end bark was too thick to curl upwards, a small barrier of clay mixed with grass was built across the back end to keep out

A typical 'canoe tree'—a large River Red Gum (*Eucalyptus camaldulensis*) on the banks of the River Murray near Morgan, South Australia, showing the scar where the bark was removed.

RIVER RED GUM (*Eucalyptus camaldulensis*)

This tree was named in 1832 by Frederick Dehnhardt (1787–1876), chief gardener of L'Hortus Camaldulensis di Napoli, a private garden owned by the Count of Camalduli, where the type specimen was growing. The River Red Gum may reach 35 metres high and is the most widely distributed eucalypt in Australia. It occurs along rivers and creeks and on seasonally wet land and is absent only from the south-west of Western Australia and Tasmania. The species has been revised in 2009 and seven subspecies have been described. The main differences will probably escape all but the most critical observer, as they involve shape of the bud cap, arrangement of stamens in the bud and the density of the vein pattern in the adult leaves. River Red Gum has been an iconic subject for artists and photographers as its gnarled form and smooth white bark dappled with grey or brown patches signify a typical Australian landscape. Its red timber is resistant to termites and is used for fencing, railway sleepers and construction work,

while old trees develop hollows providing nesting sites for birds and animals. Plantations are grown in many countries of the world, where River Red Gum is used for firewood and the production of charcoal for fuelling steel production. Fast-growing hybrids with Flooded Gum (*E. grandis*) and Tasmanian Blue Gum (*E. globulus*) have been developed and are now being produced in Australia to combat salinity. Nectar is produced prolifically and the subsequent honey is highly regarded. This eucalypt is widely planted as an ornamental in both Australia and California and grows quickly in most soils where underground water is available. Caution is required, however, as mature trees tend to drop large limbs.

Bottom left: Dry creek beds in arid Australia are often lined with River Red Gums.

Bottom right: Flowers provide a rich nectar source for birds in the drier regions.

the water. Canoes made this way were heavy, requiring several people to carry them to the water's edge.

These canoes were robust enough to have a fire burning on a bed of clay in the bottom of the craft, and could thus be used for fishing at night. The barrier of clay at the rear had to be renewed quite often, but the canoe itself could last a couple of years before it became too waterlogged to be manoeuvrable.

Southern coastal canoes

On the rivers and creeks of coastal New South Wales and eastern Victoria a second type of craft was built from large sheets of comparatively thin bark. These were areas where the River Red Gum did not grow, and the trees used tended to be stringybarks such as Messmate (*E. obliqua*). In these cases a complete cylinder of bark, 3–5 metres in length, was removed from the tree using a similar technique to that described above. The bark sheet was much thinner than that of River Red Gum. Once it was removed the stringy outer surface was stripped away and the sheet heated over fire to make it more pliable. When the moisture level in the bark was judged to be right, it was turned inside out and twine was wrapped around the two ends, bunching the pliable bark to form a high prow and stern. Sticks were inserted as struts and spreaders to form its shape and sometimes pliant branches were forced into the body of the craft to act as ribs (see p. 86).

Northern canoes

The third type of bark canoe was made in northern Australia and was more sophisticated. One style of these canoes featured in the award-winning 2006 Rolf de Heer movie *Ten Canoes*, set among the Yolngu people of Ramingining. The canoe design varied from place to place, as did the tree species, but the most likely species used was Darwin Stringybark (*E. tetrodonta*). The common factor in these canoes was the stitching of the bark.

In some cases a single sheet of bark was used, as in *Ten Canoes*, with the bow and stern sewn. An alternative was to have two strips of bark sewn together, one strip forming each side of the canoe, with stitching of plant fibre along the bow, stern and keel. The canoe was then caulked with various forms of gum. There is a record, from Spencer and Gillen's 1901 expedition, of one of these canoes measuring 5 metres in length and carrying eight Aboriginals crossing 32 kilometres of open sea, from the Pellew Islands to the mainland.

A fourth type of canoe was not made of bark, nor was it made from eucalypt. These were the dug-out canoes, for which a much softer wood was used. Interestingly, research suggests that the manufacture of these dug-out canoes by Aboriginals is quite recent, after the introduction of steel axes by Europeans, and that prior to this they were acquired via trade with Indonesian visitors to northern Australia.

A still from the movie *Ten Canoes*, showing one of the northern Australian methods of canoe construction. Darwin Stringybark (*Eucalyptus tetrodonta*) is the source of the bark and it is stitched with fibre at either end.
PHOTO: JAMES GEURTS/FANDANGO AUSTRALIA.

A carefully staged photograph by Thomas Dick in the early 1900s, probably taken near Port Macquarie on the north coast of New South Wales. The tied ends of the bark making up the canoe can be seen clearly. PHOTO: ANBG.

Ritual ceremonies

The trunks of living eucalypts provided a suitable surface for ritual decoration in much the same way as the walls of caves or large slabs of rock. Exposed to the weather, and subject to the growth and death of the trees, these decorations have not endured and we must turn to the records of early colonists for descriptions. There are several reports of painting on the trunks of eucalypts but these would have been very short-lived. Carvings on the other hand survived for much longer and were the topic of considerable research in the nineteenth century. These carvings were sometimes referred to as 'dendroglyphs', from the Greek words for wood and carving.

The intricate designs on the trunks of eucalypts appear to have served two purposes: the first as a marker for the graves of prominent Aboriginals, and the second as part of elaborate 'bora grounds', places for ceremony and perhaps corroborees. The custom of ritual carving of tree trunks (mostly eucalypts, but not always) seems most prevalent in inland New South Wales in an arc from Port Macquarie through Tamworth, Dubbo, and down to Griffith on today's maps—mostly the territories of the Kamilaroi and Wiradjuri Aboriginal peoples.

In most cases, the outer bark of the tree was removed from the area to be decorated, so the carving was done into the hard inner wood of the tree, a far more permanent marking than anything inscribed into the growing bark. There appears to be evidence that at least near Port Macquarie the growing bark was sometimes carved, but such work would grow over fairly quickly and leave little evidence a decade or so on.

Where the carved trees were associated with graves, there were usually only one or two such trees. One of the few documented examples is the grave of Yuranigh, the Aboriginal man who accompanied Sir Thomas Mitchell on his 1845 expedition into inland Queensland. Yuranigh's life bridged the old and the new Australian cultures in the period from about 1820 until his death in 1850. Mitchell wrote, 'his intelligence and his judgement rendered him so necessary to me that he was ever at my elbow. Nothing escaped his penetrating eye and quick ear.'

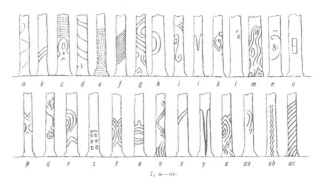

One of several drawings showing carved tree designs in *The Dendroglyphs or 'Carved Trees' of New South Wales* by R. Etheridge (1918).

Aboriginal carvings in the living bark, almost matching the scribbles on the bark of the Scribbly Gum (*Eucalyptus haemastoma*). The photo is by Thomas Dick and was taken in the early 1900s. Although Dick is known to have posed contemporary Aboriginals next to freshly made (with European axe) carvings, the fact that the bark has partly healed with age in this photo suggests it is likely to be genuine. PHOTO: ANBG.

Yuranigh returned to his own people when he died and five trees near his grave were carved as a sign of the respect in which he was held by his tribe. The trees were Yellow Box (*E. melliodora*) and, remarkably, three of them are still alive, albeit with many of the original carvings covered over by bark regrowth. The carving on one of the trees that has died is preserved under shelter at the grave. Mitchell, on learning of Yuranigh's death when he returned to Australia, paid a visit to the site out of respect. He obtained government authority to fence off the grave site, and commissioned and paid for a European-style headstone.

Information about the carved trees associated with ceremonial bora grounds is far more limited because those Europeans who might have documented such rituals were rarely in attendance. There are a few instances where the layout of the bora ground with up to 30 carved trees has been documented and their designs described. Today these carved trees are scattered through state or local museum collections in various states of preservation.

In northern Australia, especially on the Tiwi Islands, another ritual associated with death is the erection of grave posts, known as Pukumani poles, or tutini. Modern representations of these are now a prominent part of many museum and gallery exhibitions. Traditionally Tiwi used bloodwood trees (*Corymbia* spp.) for Pukumani poles, but cured Ironwood (*Erythrophleum chlorostachys*) is now the preferred timber for commercial carvings thanks to its durability. The current practice of carving Pukumani poles is an expression of the artist's cultural heritage through contemporary art. Traditionally, the

Above left: One of the carved tree trunks at Yuranigh's grave, now protected by a shelter roof, photographed near Molong, New South Wales in 2008. The trees were Yellow Box (*Eucalyptus melliodora*) and some at the site are still alive.

Above right: These hollowed logs of Darwin Stringybark (*Eucalyptus tetrodonta*) will hold the bones of deceased Aboriginals. Photographed by Ted Evans in 1946 at Gove Peninsula, Northern Territory. PHOTO: NTL.

poles were up to 4 metres tall and painted with elaborate designs. They were placed around the grave by the relatives of the deceased some time after the burial, during a public ceremony which provided a forum for artistic expression through song, dance, sculpture and body painting. The ceremony ensured the safe passage of the deceased's spirit to the afterworld.

Another example of eucalypts in mortuary ceremonies was the use of log bone-coffins in parts of Arnhem Land. These were usually Darwin Stringybark (*E. tetrodonta*) logs that had been hollowed out by termites. The ceremony took place some time after the death, when the bones of the deceased were retrieved from a burial platform. The selected hollow log was decorated with painted clan designs and totemic emblems. After the singing of sacred songs, the bone-coffin was placed in the ground, where it slowly decayed over many years. Full-size replicas are made and sold today as sculptures.

Pukumani poles made from Bloodwood (*Corymbia* spp.) play a part in a traditional funeral ceremony for the Tiwi people of Bathurst Island, Northern Territory. This photo is dated to the early 1900s. PHOTO: NTL.

DARWIN STRINGYBARK (*Eucalyptus tetrodonta*)

The Darwin Stringybark is common over the whole of the north, from the Kimberley, through the Top End to the Gulf and Cape York, Queensland, and is found in flat to undulating open forest and woodland. It forms a tree to 25 metres with fine stringy bark extending to the high branches. The large juvenile leaves are broadly lance-shaped and tend to hang down from the branchlets in a very characteristic fashion. The adult leaves are green to dull blue-green. The white to cream flowers present their stamens in groups of four and the buds show four prominent sepals, which persist as four teeth on the gumnuts. Flowering is seen from April to September. Aboriginals found many uses for the Darwin Stringybark. They made an extract from the inner bark to treat mouth sores and they removed sheets of the bark to construct shelters. The timber was also used for their day-to-day life in making canoes, coffins and musical instruments such as clap sticks and even digeridoos. Today it is the prime source of bark for the bark paintings sold to tourists.

A Darwin Stringybark growing at Bramwell near Cape York, Queensland.

This engraving by Walter Preston (1777–c. 1819), titled *View of Part of the Town of Parramatta, in New South Wales: Taken from the north side of the river* (1812), is one of the few illustrations to show tree stumps from land clearing. PHOTO: NGA.

12 European Settlement

In the first century or so of European settlement in Australia, eucalypts played a major part. They provided building materials for the colonists, had an impact on the way agriculture was conducted, became the centre of a thriving forestry industry, and proved essential to the building of mines, roads and bridges.

Settlement

When the first European settlers arrived, eucalypts were a major obstacle to transforming the environment to the preferred state—the ideal of an English rural landscape. In many references the comparison is drawn between what the settlers find in the Australian landscape and what they remember from England, the latter always being held up as the benchmark by which all else is measured.

On the arrival of the First Fleet in 1788 there was some initial enthusiasm for eucalypts—perhaps the sight of any trees after such a long voyage would have raised the spirits. The fact that eucalypts were evergreen was seen as positive. The fleet's surgeon, George Worgan, writing to his brother in England, noted, 'We *have*, and *shall* have all through the Winter green Trees in abundance to look at, that is more than you can say in your Winter.' Another surgeon, Arthur Bowes, commented, 'The tallest and most stately trees I ever saw in any nobleman's ground in England, cannot excel in beauty those which nature now presented to our view.'

But soon attitudes towards the eucalypts changed, perhaps as memories of England became fonder with the passing of time, perhaps as the trees were seen as obstacles to clearing and cultivating the land. A common element in this criticism of eucalypts is their comparison to English oaks, almost as if these too are the benchmark against which other trees should be measured. The eucalypts are repeatedly described as 'monotonous' or 'sombre'. This attitude was articulated by John Gould Veitch, a prominent English gardener and seed collector, when he visited Australia in 1864:

The first idea of a person coming from England is, that all the trees are dying, or that each specimen has been struck by lightning. The barren, desolate appearance this produces, deprives the country scenery of all beauty, or semblance of luxuriance.

Clearing the land

The imperative to make the new colony self-sufficient meant that preparing areas suitable for farming was a high priority. The land around Sydney Cove was dominated by eucalypts and their hard timber would have been a challenge for the new arrivals. The day after the landing of the First Fleet, all the tradesmen and 100 convicts were sent ashore with 'the necessary utensils for clearing the Ground and felling the Trees'. Surgeon Worgan, writing to his brother, comments that the main task for the first few months of the colony was 'the clearing of Land, cutting, Grubbing and burning down Trees, sawing up Timber & Plank for Building'.

It is often difficult to assess the appearance of the landscape that these early European settlers encountered. Our current views are influenced by what we see in the few remaining pockets of dense eucalypt-dominated land within the farming belt, but early descriptions give quite a different view. We find the colonists repeatedly describing the vegetation as 'like an English park'. This implies a rather open landscape with scattered large trees and a grassy understorey, probably the result of thousands of years of Aboriginal fire management, which ceased soon after settlement.

The words used by the early colonists must be treated with care, and we often forget how much the meaning of words can change. Today we use the word 'forest' for eucalypt vegetation where the canopies of the trees touch each other, usually with a shrubby understorey. In the early 1800s this was described as 'brush' while the word 'forest' was applied to open grassland with occasional scattered trees.

When the United States Exploring Expedition, led by Charles Wilkes, came to Australia in 1839, Wilkes had to explain to his American readers that 'forest' in New South Wales consisted of gum trees 'so widely scattered that a carriage may be driven rapidly through them without meeting any obstruction'. There is a similar description of the 'forest' between Hobart and Launceston, with Lieutenant Edward Lord explaining that 'forest land' in Tasmania had only one tree for every ten in the 'forests' of New South Wales.

With such open country in what became the prime agricultural land, at least in eastern Australia, it is not hard to see how the early settlers, known as 'squatters' because they just took possession of 'vacant' land, were able to move their flocks and initiate farms without having to do any intensive clearing. This open eucalypt country was quickly taken up by the first squatters, who were later able to purchase it as freehold. The more difficult, densely wooded forests were left for later squatters and then the 'selectors' to tackle. The selectors were those who purchased surveyed land when it was opened up for government sale in the middle of the nineteenth century (although the prime land was mostly purchased by those who had previously squatted on it).

Leading a party of squatters to take up land in what is now prime dairy country near Camperdown

RING BARKING.

An illustration of ringbarking in the Poplar Box (*Eucalyptus populnea*) country of inland New South Wales 'that had only lately been tried'. From *Australian Pictures: Drawn with Pen and Pencil* by Howard Willoughby in 1886. He states: 'It consists of cutting a notch round the tree through the bark and into the sap wood, to prevent the sap rising.'

A photo taken in 1993 near Womblebank in Queensland of a woodland opened up by ringbarking. Much of Australia must have looked something like this in the second half of the nineteenth century.

in western Victoria, the botanist Daniel Curdie wrote that 'the vegetation was so dense that we could scarcely reach the soil, and we walked on the ferns, grass, and other vines, from three to four feet from the ground'.

Strange as it might seem, it was not until 60 years after European settlement that the ringbarking of eucalypts was seen as a solution for the clearing of land. Until the 1850s, there appear to be few examples of large-scale ringbarking of eucalypts to open up the land. This soon changed. By the mid-1860s, ringbarking had taken off, with newspaper articles promoting the practice.

Debates in the newspapers and learned societies discussed the pros and cons of ringbarking. Those against it had several arguments: it was a waste of valuable timber, it would lead to land degradation and a change

in the climate, and it was aesthetically displeasing. The clergyman and scientist William Branwhite Clarke could not understand why educated gentleman farmers would 'deliberately leave acres of unfelled [ringbarked] timber, bare of foliage, barkless and broken by winds', and saw it as an insult to the 'All-wise Creator'. But others, such as wheat-breeder William Farrer, argued that it could quadruple the carrying capacity of 'ordinary bush'. There was, of course, a political aspect to this debate, as legislation decreed that squatters should be compensated for structural improvements to the land that they had occupied when this was later offered as freehold to selectors. Government inquiries were held into valuing the 'improvement' to land made by wholesale ringbarking. There were stories of squatters employing 'perfect armies of Chinamen' to ringbark their land so that it would become prohibitively expensive for any selector to apply for. The New South Wales legislature endorsed ringbarking and eventually settled on compensation of one shilling and threepence per acre of ringbarked trees.

There was some attempt in legislation in both New South Wales and Victoria to require ministerial permission for large-scale ringbarking, but it had little impact. The New South Wales Government had approved the ringbarking of almost four million acres by 1884, and another four million by 1888. The French colonist Edmund la Meslee compared the ringbarked eucalypt land near the River Murray in Victoria to Dante's *Inferno*, commenting:

> Nothing can give any idea of the infinitely sad and desolate air of these dead forests . . . the forest resembles a multitude of skeletons raising their long, fleshless arms to the sky.

Dwellings

While the eucalypts that dominated the land were often seen in a negative light, being referred to as 'gigantic weeds' by one New South Wales politician, they did provide everything the settlers needed for shelter in the bush. While grassy material for thatched roofs was the norm in many parts of Europe and the rest of the world at the time, in Australia it was the bark from eucalypt trees which provided for the basic human need for a roof over one's head.

Because eucalypt bark was widely used by the Aboriginals for both shelter and canoes, the settlers quickly realised its utility. Sheets of eucalypt bark were, for the early settlers, what sheets of galvanised iron and chipboard were to later house builders. In areas with suitable eucalypts, bark huts or 'humpies' could be knocked up in a few days, or at the very least a shady, waterproof annex to the canvas tent could be built.

Many eucalypts were suitable for harvesting bark sheets, a process that invariably resulted in the death of

the tree. The tree was left standing while two zigzag cuts about 2–3 metres apart were made with an axe, slicing through the bark and into the heartwood around the circumference of the tree. A vertical cut was made through the bark joining the two horizontal cuts and the bark could then be prised away from the tree as a flexible sheet. The best trees were those about one

The 'correct method of stripping bark to build a bush hut' from *Cassell's Picturesque Australasia* (1889). The zigzag cuts in the upper bark are from an axe wielded overhead. The bark has been removed from the tree on the left.

Removing bark from a felled Red Stringybark (*Eucalyptus macrorhyncha*) for a modern-day reconstruction of a bark hut. The bark can be readily prised away from the trunk.
PHOTO: BOB WOODHAMS.

Bark sheets in the foreground are weighed down with logs while they dry flat. In the background of this photo, taken in 1884, is the start of a bark wall for a hut. PHOTO: SLV.

The temporary St Paul's Church of England in Stanthorpe, Queensland, built from bark in 1872. PHOTO: SLQ.

metre in diameter, although often they were smaller. Records show that stringybarks, messmate, blackbutt and box trees were all used.

To flatten the sheets of bark without cracking them, the sappy side was dried in the sun or the heat of a campfire, then laid on flat ground either singly or in piles with logs over them to hold them flat for a few days.

To make the framework for the hut, smaller eucalypt trees about 20 centimetres in diameter were felled, stripped of bark, and set into the ground every metre or so. Long spars of smaller diameter were nailed horizontally to complete the frame. Heavier, longer posts were erected through the centre of the design to support the ridge pole which might be about 4 metres above the ground. A framework of smaller spars would support the bark roof. The bark sheets could be laid over this framework, usually with a 20-centimetre overlap. Detailed attention had to be given to the ridge-caps, which were also sheets of bark, laid lengthways and bent over the ridge. To avoid nail holes and leaks, these sheets of bark were usually weighed down with a framework of sapling spars, which were tied in place with wire or green-hide leather. A popular song of the day included the lines:

> Stringy bark and greenhide, that will never fail yer!
> Stringy bark and greenhide, the mainstay of
>   Australia.

While the roof of these dwellings was usually eucalypt bark until the widespread availability of galvanised iron, the walls reflected different levels of sophistication. The simplest and quickest walls were made from eucalypt bark, mostly stringybark as is evidenced by surviving photos.

The slab huts were slightly more upmarket. These required more time and skill to construct, and were far stronger and more solid. Large, straight eucalypt trees were felled to make the slabs. The settler sawed the tree into lengths, split it with wedges into quarters, and then split it again into slabs about 2 metres long, 30 centimetres wide and 5 centimetres thick. Because eucalypt wood shrinks so much on drying, the key was to lay these horizontally, one upon the other, freely resting between vertical supports fixed to the main solid vertical supporting timbers. As each slab shrank, the weight of the slabs above forced them down within their frame, ensuring the gaps between slabs were minimal. This ability to move with shrinkage gave rise to the term 'drop-log construction'. Slab walls could also be constructed using vertical slabs, but the gaps created by the shrinkage of the eucalypt timber had to be plugged up with clay or other material.

Stringybark roofs were even the norm on the 'wattle and daub' huts, which were made with mud or clay plastered between a network of flexible, straight interlaced sticks (usually these sticks were not eucalypts but acacias, giving rise to the popular name of 'wattles').

A modern reconstruction of a drop-log slab hut with a shingle roof (the gutter and downpipe are contemporary touches). The horizontal logs could drop with their weight to seal any cracks made by shrinkage of the timber on drying.

Jack Gardners's Stable in the Beech Forest, probably the base of a Mountain Ash (*Eucalyptus regnans*) c. 1930.

Opposite:

Top left: A vertical slab hut, the surgery and residence of a Dr Smith, photographed in Victoria around 1870. The roof and back wall are bark, and the chimney is constructed from timber, an ever-present fire hazard.
PHOTO: SLV.

Top right: The hollow base of a Mountain Ash (*Eucalyptus regnans*) provided a temporary home for the Davies family in Gippsland, Victoria (1880s).
PHOTO: NICHOLAS CAIRE/NLA.

Bottom: 'The Tree and the House Built Out of It' is the title given to this photo of Thomas Davies' house, made from a single Mountain Ash (*Eucalyptus regnans*).
PHOTO: NICHOLAS CAIRE/NLA.

As construction became more sophisticated, the stringybark roofs were replaced by shingles. This required a far greater level of skill, and the ability to use an adze. The ubiquitous eucalypt still provided the timber in most locations. The best shingles were the narrowest, about 8 centimetres wide and 40–45 centimetres long. Any wider and the wood was likely to curl or crack as it dried. This shrinkage on drying meant that each shingle should only be attached by a single nail to accommodate the movement, with the weight of surrounding shingles holding it in place.

The roof frame supporting the shingles was similar to that of the bark hut, though many more rafters and battens were required, and these had to be chipped flat with an adze so that they lined up when nailed.

Nearly all these huts had a stone fireplace, which used clay as a sort of cement to hold it together. The upper part of the chimney, high enough to direct the smoke away from the roof, was often made of eucalypt billets. Many of these fireplaces were huge, a metre and a half across, so that large logs could be burned without the effort of chopping them into smaller pieces. The interior of these settlers' huts also used sheets of stringybark to make beds or tables, the equivalent of today's sheets of chipboard. The twisted shapes of eucalypt branches became the frames for chairs and other furniture, often with kangaroo skins strung between them for comfort.

In the taller forests, only settled by selectors after the best and easiest land was occupied, occasionally giant eucalypts, hollowed out by fire and the ravages of time, were converted to living quarters. One of these was photographed by Nicholas Caire on the property of Thomas Davies in Gippsland in the 1880s. The family had felled a giant eucalypt, and roofed the hollow base to form a simple dwelling.

Caire also photographed the Davies' next dwelling, showing a small weatherboard cottage with shingle roof next to the stump of the giant Mountain Ash (*Eucalyptus regnans*) that provided the timber.

In South Australia a giant hollow River Red Gum (*E. camaldulensis*) was also used as a dwelling by Friedrich Herbig and his family near Springton, from 1855 to 1860. There are many other examples of hollow trees being used as stables and outhouses.

Agriculture

The squatters settling inland Australia in the first half of the nineteenth century were usually graziers wanting pasture for their cattle and sheep, but the main reason for selling land to selectors in the second half of the century was to provide smaller properties, on which it was anticipated that crops could be grown or dairies established. With the most open country already in the hands of grazier squatters, those seeking smaller blocks of land for intensive agriculture were left with densely timbered country, or the mallee.

Areas with fertile soil often supported the largest eucalypt trees. As mentioned earlier, ringbarking was one way to kill the trees if they were not felled by axe and saw. The timber then had to be burned. Either way, stumps or entire dead trees were dotted throughout the paddock and the farmers could pasture their cows after scattering grass seed or clover between the stumps.

If crops were to be grown, some farmers attempted to plough between the giant eucalypt stumps and waited for years, sometimes decades, for them to rot away. The alternative was to grub them out by digging huge holes around them, cutting through tap-roots, and then pulling out the stump using a bullock team. Occasionally, explosives were used.

For farmers coming from England, where the fields had been ploughed for centuries, this soil full of roots, fibres and stones was a nightmare. Bent and broken ploughshares were common.

At the other extreme was the mallee—a type of eucalypt vegetation that occupied about one-fifth of the continent. It was soon discovered that these multi-stemmed shrubs could be cleared using a heavy roller pulled by bullocks or horses. A primitive roller could be made from a very large, hollow eucalypt log through which a smaller tree trunk was inserted as an axle; others were made from disused metal boilers or other innovative bush contrivances. These rollers dislodged many shrubs from the sandy soil and flattened others. The material was then stacked up and burned.

In most cases the mallee roots, or lignotubers, remained in the ground. Shallow ploughing around these

roots, and the invention of the 'stump-jump plough' in around 1876, enabled crops to be planted in a patchwork throughout the paddock. When the stump-jump plough hit the obstacle of the solid root, the ploughshare moved up and over it rather than jamming or breaking.

Eucalypt lignotubers have evolved to regenerate by sending up new shoots after any disturbance. The

A farmhouse dwarfed by the stumps and stags of giant eucalypts that had been burnt or ringbarked. This photo was taken in Victoria in about 1900. PHOTO: SLV.

Top right: A typical mallee root. Even after rolling and clearing everything above ground, these huge lignotubers remained just below the soil surface, ready to send up new shoots.

ploughed paddock became a patchwork of growing wheat or other crop and tussocks of young eucalypt shoots emerging from each buried mallee root. The farmer had to hand trim the eucalypt shoots with a scythe or other implement at just the right time to allow the wheat heads to stick up higher at the time of harvesting. The horsedrawn harvesting machine could then traverse the paddock, removing wheat heads without contaminating the harvest with eucalypt shoots.

With such difficulties in removing eucalypt trees, it is a wonder that more were not left scattered throughout these farming lands. One explanation is hinted at in the words of Louisa Meredith when writing of the establishment of their farm in Tasmania. She pleads with her husband to leave some magnificent, isolated mature trees near the house, but goes on to say:

> the harbour which trees in the middle of the fields afford to the opossums, and the destructive, but most beautiful little parrots which abound here, was always used against me, and the death-doom rarely averted.

When each farm was struggling to grow its own vegetables and corn crops it becomes more understandable that an isolated tree supporting a family of possums could spell the end to a family's vegetable crops.

Louisa summed up the attitude to farming and 'the total destruction of every native tree' when writing of her first impressions of Australia in her 1844 book *Notes and Sketches of New South Wales*:

HOWARD'S AUSTRALIAN
STUMP-JUMPER PLOUGH.

Above: One of the many different models of the stump-jump plough available from agricultural catalogues in the 1880s.

Left: This, believe it or not, is a wheat field in the mallee, taken in 1920 near Sea Lake, northern Victoria. Here a father and son slash the regenerating mallee eucalypt shoots to keep them below the height of the growing wheat heads in order to harvest the crop.
PHOTO: BILL BOYD/MV.

In England we plant groves and woods, and think our country residences unfinished and incomplete without them; but here the exact contrary is the case, and unless a settler can see an expanse of bare, naked, unvaried, shadeless, dry, dusty land spread all around him, he fancies his dwelling 'wild and uncivilized'.

The mining industry

While today's mining practices might not seem very timber intensive, past mining booms had a huge impact on the surrounding eucalypt forests. Not only were mine shafts shored up with timber cut from the local forests, but huge immigrant camps required fuel for cooking and warmth. Once the industry in an area became mechanised, wood was needed for the steam-driven winders that hauled ore to the surface and ventilated the shafts. In the dry Western Australian goldfields, saline ground water had to be crudely distilled to make it drinkable, and this process also consumed large quantities of eucalypt timber fuel.

Around Kalgoorlie, in the early years of the twentieth century, the Salmon Gums (*E. salmonophloia*) and Gimlets (*E. salubris*) were quickly cleared by men with horses and carts, and a network of small railway tracks, known as 'woodlines', started fanning out. By 1903 there were several companies involved, and one, the W.A. Firewood Supply Company, had 60 kilometres of woodlines with two steam trains working around the clock. At their peak they were employing 1500 men and supplying over 500,000 tonnes of firewood per annum. By 1937 they were hauling timber from over 170 kilometres away.

In the first decades of the twentieth century, part of the refinement process for the Broken Hill mines relied on eucalyptus oil in a froth flotation process to separate the ore, resulting in a demand for huge quantities of oil from the distillers further south. The Broken Hill mines would also have consumed huge amounts of timber in an area of limited large trees. Much of the timber used remains deep below the ground in disused shafts, only a small proportion ever being visible in the headframes and other above-ground infrastructure.

Much of the eucalypt timber used in mining is hidden underground, used to shore up mine shafts. These timbers, deep underground at Kalgoorlie, Western Australia, are probably from Salmon Gums (*E. salmonophloia*) and Gimlets (*E. salubris*). PHOTO: CLIFF WINFIELD.

The four o'clock shift at the Sons of Gwalia mine in Leonora, Western Australia, in 1901. Not only did mines use considerable timber for the minehead and shafts, but having so many workers in often remote places required timber for fuel for cooking and water desalinisation. COURTESY SLWA, THE BATTYE LIBRARY (5409B).

The boom in mining in Australia in the 1980s and 1990s has unfortunately resulted in the loss of many of the old timber headframes and other mining structures. In Western Australia the Sons of Gwalia headframe has been reconstructed at Gwalia, and several others exist in various parts of Australia; thankfully they are heritage listed.

Infrastructure

If we look around today at the part played by eucalypts in the major infrastructure of the country, there are few examples. Ones that do come to mind for anyone travelling extensively in rural areas are bridges. Eucalypt timber bridges are still a major component of our minor road network and it will be a long time before these are all replaced with concrete.

When it comes to major structures made from eucalypts little changed between the latter part of the nineteenth century up until the Second World War. Indeed, major highway bridges were still being constructed from eucalypt timber well into the 1960s. Even for many existing structures built in the 1800s, gradual and continual replacement of timbers means that little of the original is still present today. It is estimated that the nineteenth-century jetties and wharves that are still in existence no longer contain any of their original timber.

Road bridges

In the early expansion of our road system, the abundance of strong and durable eucalypt hardwood made timber bridges a very cost-effective means of crossing creeks and rivers. Many of the bridges on minor roads are still the original timber bridges made from round timber logs. Today we think of bridges as public works, but in the early days of the colony many were private toll bridges, owners often charging whatever the market

Wooden road bridges, both large and small, are a mainstay of the country road system, a legacy of the days when most infrastructure relied on eucalypt timber. This bridge is near Nimmo, in the New South Wales high country.

could afford. A squatter could build a toll bridge across a creek on his property and pay for its cost within a month. Away from the big cities it was not until the 1850s that the governments initiated major bridge building; private and public punts on the larger rivers were the standard before that.

The legacy of timber bridges is most significant in Western Australia, the state with the most suitable eucalypts, with about 1500 still estimated to be in service in 1998 as part of the public road network.

Railway and tramway bridges

There seems to have arisen a distinction in terminology, with the word railway being applied to the public train system and the word tramway being applied to the private systems used by foresters to extract logs from the forest. In Western Australia, at the height of the railway system there were estimated to be about

7000 kilometres of public track, with another 6600 kilometres of tramway through the forests; steam locomotives would occasionally move from one system to the other. Both systems required bridges to span gullies and cross rivers; in southern Australia the timber used would mostly have been locally sourced eucalypts.

Railway surveyors had the luxury of navigating their track to avoid the steepest terrain, but this was not possible for the foresters. Their ability to improvise led to the construction of timber tramways into the heart of the tall timber. Wooden rails were laid on closely packed sleepers, and trolleys, drawn by horses, carried the logs and sawn timber to the nearest railway station or jetty. Horses were later replaced by steam-driven engines, and the wooden rails replaced by steel. These tracks and the elaborate trestle bridges that were built were often temporary, being dismantled and reconstructed elsewhere when the logging in one area was exhausted.

This trestle railway bridge was closed to traffic in 1987, but prior to that it was an important part of the Bairnsdale–Orbost line, near Nowa Nowa in eastern Victoria. It was erected in 1916 using local Red Ironbark (*Eucalyptus tricarpa*) and Coast Grey Box (*E. bosistoana*). It is 247 metres long and stands 20 metres above Stony Creek.

Railway sleepers

While not individually large structures, railway sleepers made from eucalypt timber played a big role in opening up the country. Eucalypt railway sleepers also formed a significant export trade, especially to South Africa. In Western Australia, Karri (*E. diversicolor*) and Jarrah (*E. marginata*) were the preferred timbers, while in eastern Australia the ironbarks were favoured. In the inland regions, River Red Gum was most commonly used.

Jetties

Jetties played a prominent role in the early development of the colonies, especially in South Australia and Western Australia with their long lengths of shallow coastline. The construction of jetties allowed ships to berth in the local regions and enabled settlers to get their products to markets. About 80 jetties were built in Western Australia and 111 in South Australia. Much of the timber

for these jetties would have been Karri, Jarrah and Tuart (*E. gomphocephala*) from Western Australia, also a major export for the construction of jetties and piers around the world due to its resistance to marine borers.

Today, few of the remaining wooden jetties are used commercially, but they form an important part of the recreational and tourism infrastructure for local communities.

Wharves

Wharves were built along the coast where deeper water was accessible close to shore, or near the mouth of the eastern Australian rivers. They were also built at regular intervals along the Murray–Darling river system, using River Red Gum timber. Paddle-steamers transported wool and other produce, and formed the backbone of our inland river transport system. While Karri and Jarrah would have been used in South and Western

Australia, Turpentine (*Syncarpia glomulifera*), a relative of the eucalypts, was preferred in eastern Australia due to its better resistance to marine borers.

Roads

One of the least-remembered infrastructure uses of eucalypt timber is that of road construction in our major cities in the late nineteenth century. Up until the 1880s, less than one-third of Sydney's 160 kilometres of roads had any formed surface. At that time a new surveyor with a passion for innovative road surfacing—Adrien Mountain—was appointed. He supervised the first woodblock surface to be laid in King Street, in 1880, using eleven different kinds of timber. The woodblocks were brick-shaped, 9 x 6 x 3 inches (22 x 15 x 7 centimetres) and coated with hot tar before being laid. The experimental laying in King Street was dug up in 1885 and measured for shrinkage and wear. Tallowwood (*E. microcorys*) was found to be the best timber for the task, followed by Spotted Gum (*Corymbia maculata*), Blackbutt (*E. pilularis*) and White Box (*E. albens*). As a result of this experiment numerous woodblock road pavements were laid in Sydney from 1886.

As was to be expected at the time, much of the work was manual. Cut woodblocks were piled by the side of the road under construction, which usually had a form of concrete foundation. Teams of men hand-passed the blocks towards a mobile hot tar machine, from which the blocks emerged dripping with tar. Men with leather gloves dropped the blocks into place, working in lines from each side of the road. Other men with sledge-hammers tapped the blocks so they fitted tightly together. As the rows met in the middle, a 'key man' carefully shaved the last block with a hatchet to ensure a tight fit and checked the row was straight.

Although softwood blocks had been used in America in the 1860s, Australia played a major role in developing pavements blocked with hardwood. For a number of years Australia exported eucalypt timber to England and Europe to be cut into blocks for road paving. Woodblocking was not confined to Sydney and was also used extensively in Melbourne and Brisbane.

In 1895 the American Consul in New South Wales,

The corner of Elizabeth and King Streets, Sydney, clearly showing the woodblock paving of the road surface, probably 1930s. PHOTO: MITCHELL LIBRARY, SLNSW.

G.W. Bell, wrote of Sydney's woodblock roads that, after visiting 'nearly every great city in the Christian world: 'It is safe to say that the streets of Sydney are better paved than those of any American city save Washington.' He goes on to say that the costs for this woodblock paving in Sydney is US$3.30 per yard, and that 'it will last twenty years with no expense for maintenance'.

By 1912 the city surveyor claimed that Sydney had 'the largest woodblocked area in the world owned by one municipality'. Although this method of roadbuilding was not used after 1932, repairing of woodblocked roads continued until after the Second World War.

Woodblocking Macquarie Street in Sydney in 1925.
Blocks can be seen piled on the pavement on the right.
PHOTO: MITCHELL LIBRARY, SLNSW.

Axemen felling a eucalypt in Tasmania in the early twentieth century. The technique changed little until the arrival of chainsaws after the Second World War. PHOTO: FRANK HURLEY/NLA.

13 A Brief History of Forestry

When Captain Cook arrived in Botany Bay, New South Wales, in 1770, he referred to the timber of the local trees as 'of a hard and ponderous nature'. A few years later, when he began to use them while establishing the new colony, Governor Phillip wrote:

> The timber of the site . . . has one very bad quality which puts us to very great inconvenience: I mean the large gum tree which splits and warps in such a manner when used green, to which necessity obliged us, that a storehouse boarded up with this wood is rendered useless.

These inauspicious beginnings to the Australian timber industry were soon resolved by understanding the need to season timber prior to use.

Before 1850, most eucalypt timber harvesting was manual, from the felling of the trees to sawing them into building products. Tree felling itself was little affected by technological change until after the Second World War. The essential tools were axes and crosscut saws. Eucalypts were generally cut above the butt—heights above the ground of 1–3 metres being common—but sometimes much higher, to avoid any defects. Cutters would have to build a platform on which to stand, or cut a notch into which were fitted saplings, or later a specially constructed springboard. These notches in old tree stumps can still be seen in some forests today.

Sawpits were a vital part of the process once the tree was felled. Sawing was so arduous that it was initially seen as punishment for convict offenders. The pits allowed one person to stand on the log while another held the end of the saw in the pit below, and was continually showered by sawdust. Pit saws were like other crosscut saws, with an extended 'T' handle to allow the blade to be pushed fully down to the surface of the log. They cut on the downstroke, so the person in the pit was there only to guide the blade.

Hewing and splitting were usually carried out near where the tree was felled, using a range of specialised tools. Splitting, a skill largely lost today, produced shingles,

Above: Hauling a log from the forest using a bullock team near Pemberton, Western Australia in 1928. Small log 'tracks' can be seen and rollers supporting the log keep it above the ground on these tracks. COURTESY OF SLWA, THE BATTYE LIBRARY (BA1913/1/13).

Top left: This coloured lithograph by S.T. Gill in 1865 is titled *Splitters*. While logs were cut through with a saw or axe, the timber was then usually split longitudinally by driving wedges into the end grain. PHOTO: NLA.

Top right: Waterwheels offered a source of power for timber mills in eastern and south-western Australia. This mill at Yallingup, Western Australia, was photographed in 1949. COURTESY OF SLWA, THE BATTYE LIBRARY (3881B/203).

palings and slabs from the careful fracture of the timber by hammering wedges into the end grain. The best railway sleepers were considered to be those manually split rather than sawn because only top-quality timber would split accurately.

After 1850, the sawmill became the central place to process timber. Better steel for saws, the use of waterwheels as a source of power, and then the availability of mass-produced steam engines made a huge impact on the industry.

With centralisation came the need to transport the logs from the forest to the mill. In the earliest days of settlement, the movement of timber had been by human hands. At Port Arthur in Tasmania large logs were carried out of the forests by convict 'centipedes' as part of their punishment. They consisted of up to 70 men on each side of a log which they supported on their shoulders, shuffling along like a giant centipede. With the rise of the sawmills, horse teams and bullock teams were most often used, right up until the Second World War. Bullocks were generally favoured because they were cheaper to buy, less fussy about what they ate, stronger on steep inclines, and did not require shoeing.

The simplest method was to drag the log behind the team, often with a 'shoe' on the front end to stop the log digging into the ground. Usually, however, some sort of wheeled device was used to raise the front end, or both ends, of the log above the ground. Sometimes wooden roads or tramways were constructed through the forest, often crossing steep gorges with trestle bridges. Initially these tramways used bullock teams, but steam engines soon replaced them.

Unlike other countries, Australia did not make extensive use of waterways to move its logs to the mills. There is an obvious lack of large rivers over much of the country, but another factor is that eucalypt wood is so dense that it usually will not float. River transport was undertaken for the non-eucalypt timbers such as Red Cedar (*Toona ciliata*) on the east coast, and Huon Pine (*Lagarostrobos franklinii*) in Tasmania because these timbers float. River Red Gum (*Eucalyptus camaldulensis*) logs were occasionally transported down the River Murray by barge, submerged and attached to outrigger-

floats; when freshly cut the logs are only slightly more dense than water.

Although caterpillar-tracked, petrol-driven vehicles started to replace some of the bullock teams after the First World War, it was not until the introduction of chainsaws following the Second World War that the industry saw really significant changes from the colonial period.

Fires have always been a constant threat to the eucalypt forests and it was not until the 1950s that a fuel-reduction program was introduced by scheduled control burning, a practice still causing some debate.

The historical development of the industry was different in each state as settlement proceeded across the country.

New South Wales

In the early days of the colony, after the need to season wood was realised, the local timber was soon used to repair ships damaged on the hazardous trips from England. Before long, the scarcity of timber in England prompted the British authorities to request shipments of timber for use in His Majesty's Dockyards. In 1803, about 160 pieces of timber were loaded on to HMS *Glatton*. The load consisted of Black Gum (*Eucalyptus aggregata*), Ironbark (probably *E. paniculata*), Mahogany (probably *E. resinifera* or *E. robusta*), Stringybark (probably *E. obliqua*) and Blue Gum (*E. saligna*).

The appetite for timber in the new colony was great and indiscriminate logging occurred until 1820, when timbergetters were licensed in an attempt to overcome the pillage of what had previously been thought to be an inexhaustible supply. Control of the regulations was ineffectual and the demand for land suitable for grazing and food production was so great the trees were still felled without thought for the future. In 1871, the first forestry reserves were created in the area near the Clarence River in northern New South Wales, and along the Murray River in the south to conserve the huge forests of River Red Gums (*E. camaldulensis*). By 1888, 2 million hectares were covered by about 1000 reserves in New South Wales. Loggers had to pay a registration fee as well as a royalty for any forest produce.

SYDNEY BLUE GUM (*Eucalyptus saligna*)

The name Sydney Blue Gum is something of a misnomer, as it occurs from Batemans Bay in southern New South Wales to south-east Queensland and inland to the Blackdown Tableland west of Rockhampton in Queensland. It is found in moist forests as a tall tree reaching 50 metres high and differs from the closely related Flooded Gum (*E. grandis*) by having a lignotuber and also by the structure of its gumnuts. It has rough, flaky bark at the base of its straight, smooth, bluish-grey to cream trunk. Sydney Blue Gum is a very important timber tree, where its pink to red wood is used in house construction and flooring. Many plantations have been planted in northern New South Wales and the timber is used in many overseas countries. This gum tree is fast growing in good loam and is an excellent tree for parks and rural properties. The flowers, seen in summer, are valued by apiarists for their nectar and pollen. Koalas will graze the leaves. In some seasons plantations may suffer severe psyllid attacks, which can cause serious defoliation but rarely the death of the tree.

This tree in the Australian National Botanic Gardens, Canberra, is 45 years old.

Sydney Blue Gum flowers are valued by apiarists.

Forests of River Red Gum (*Eucalyptus camaldulensis*) along the River Murray were some of the first forest reserves created in New South Wales.

door. Jarrah, in particular, was recognised as a superb timber for these purposes and was ruthlessly cut from the nearby Darling Ranges. It was also used for boat building as fishing, whaling and sealing were important sources of income and food for the community. The first sawmill was constructed at Mt Eliza in 1833 and in the 1830s and 1840s an export market was established, shipping Jarrah to England and South Africa. As timbergetters travelled further into the south-west, Karri (*E. diversicolor*) became their target, but it was not until 1882 that licences were issued to loggers. The construction of railways soon ensued and Jarrah was used for sleepers. It was also favoured for road-building blocks in England in the 1890s, leading to English financiers investing in the industry. By 1898 the

The creation of forest reserves in New South Wales was having little effect on the depletion of timber resources, despite the best efforts of the Chief Forester, R. Dalrymple Hay. A royal commission into the forestry industry was held in 1907 and after praising the work of Hay, who held the reins of the industry for 30 years, the Forestry Acts of 1914 and 1924 were passed. This allowed state forests to be designated and, by 1972, 1.3 million hectares of coastal eucalypt forest, 500,000 hectares of tableland eucalypt and 100,000 hectares of River Red Gum forest had been conserved in New South Wales state forests. Today ecologically sustainable forest management is the guiding philosophy for forest conservation and licences are issued to logging contractors, timber processors and sawmills in addition to the payment of royalties to the government for any timber taken from state forests. The amount of this royalty depends on the type of timber and its use.

Western Australia

Settlements were established on the Swan River in Western Australia in 1829 and timber was in great demand for construction work, bridges and homes. These settlers had the advantage of having Jarrah (*E. marginata*) and Wandoo (*E. wandoo*) at their back

Wandoo (*Eucalyptus wandoo*) was one of the first timber trees exploited by the Swan River colony when it was established in Western Australia.

JARRAH (*Eucalyptus marginata*)

Jarrah is one of Australia's best-known timber trees. It occurs, often in pure stands, on red loams in the wetter areas of south-west Western Australia, where it forms a tall tree to 35 metres high. In more northern areas, where the soils are sandy, it is seen as a mallee, rarely exceeding 4 metres. The bark is rough and fibrous and the leaves are darker on the top side. Unfortunately, many of the Jarrah forests have been stricken with the root fungus disease *Phytophthora cinnamomi*, necessitating the closing of the areas to vehicles and people as fungal spores are carried on vehicle tyres and feet. The reddish-brown timber is resistant to termites and is used for flooring, furniture making, railway sleepers, telegraph poles and even as woodblocks for road construction in the 1890s. Some 850,000

Jarrah blocks were supplied to the London City Council in 1897 to surface 13 kilometres of streets in the West End. In modern times it is considered so valuable that it is recovered from old buildings and resold. The Jarrah forests have been ruthlessly exploited since European colonisation and less than half the original forests now exist due to clearing for agriculture and logging for timber. The remaining forests are a rich resource, not only for timber but because of the diverse flora and fauna that inhabit them. Over 1200 species of plants are recorded from them and they are the home for the endangered Western Quoll and the Brush-tailed Bettong as well as 27 other mammal species, 45 reptiles and 150 birds. Jarrah has not been successful when grown overseas and is not commonly cultivated in Australia as it requires specific soil and climatic conditions.

Two other subspecies are recorded: subsp. *elegantella*, which has a restricted distribution just south of Perth, forming a small compact tree to 8 metres high with smaller, narrower leaves than the type species; and subsp. *thalassica*, which has blue-grey leaves and a spreading, often weeping, crown and is common in the northern part of the Darling Range.

Far left: A mature Jarrah tree in the forest near Tonebridge, Western Australia.

Left: The flowers are usually too high to be seen on forest trees.

English had concessions on 400,000 hectares in leases and owned 27 sawmills. The state government was loath to give support or to consider forest conservation proposals, even after several royal commissions, until the 1930s when it realised that forestry provided an opportunity to employ the many men put out of work in the Depression. Fire control also became essential and lookouts were constructed on tall trees in the 1940s to monitor fires. The famous Gloucester Tree at Pemberton was pegged for this purpose in 1946.

In the early 1920s, it was noticed that some groups of Jarrah trees were dying but little was done until 1964 when the culprit was identified as the root fungus *Phytophthora cinnamomi*. This soil-borne pathogen was spread by the movement of machinery and human activity, and in 1971 a hygiene program was initiated; access to forests was restricted, and equipment sterilised. By 1977 about one-third of the Jarrah forests had been quarantined, preventing public access, and these restrictions remain today. It is thought that early settlers may have brought the fungus to Australia in the soil of live plants, as it is now present in much of the country.

In 1967, Japanese interests were keen to obtain Karri, Jarrah and Marri (*Corymbia calophylla*) woodchips as raw material for paper manufacture. The government approved the construction of a woodchip plant at Manjimup to produce 700,000 tonnes of chip annually, using Bunbury as the export harbour. The company used mainly Karri and Marri thinnings, sawmill waste and timber that was unfit as sawlogs. The mill is still in operation.

Victoria

The discovery of gold in Victoria in 1851 coincided with the ferocious fires of 'Black Thursday' on 6 February of that year, when one-third of the state was ablaze. Timber was needed urgently for construction, mining timbers and firewood in the Ballarat–Bendigo area, as well as for the hundreds of settlers who had heard of the fine grazing land on the Murray River. After self-government was granted to Victoria in 1855, the realisation dawned that a stop had to be made to the reckless exploitation of timber

in the state. In 1869 a report was given to the President of the Board of Lands and Works on the 'advisability of establishing state forests'. Various unenacted Bills concerning forest management were presented to the government in ensuing years, but it was not until a royal commission was held in 1897 and the subsequent *Forests Act* of 1907 that a State Forests Department was created under a Minister for Forests. Today, Victoria consumes about half of the timber it produces. The main source of high-quality timber for furniture, flooring and joinery is sourced from the high-rainfall forests of the mountain country. It includes Mountain Ash (*E. regnans*), Alpine

This log tramway through the Mountain Ash (*Eucalyptus regnans*) forests in eastern Victoria allowed logs to be extracted in steep terrain (1888).

An unlogged forest (top) and a logged area (above) near Ben Lomond, Tasmania, 1988. Forestry practices in the state continue to generate controversy.

Ash (*E. delegatensis*), and Shining Gum (*E. nitens*). Heavy construction timber is logged from some River Red Gum forests along the Murray River.

Tasmania

In Tasmania, the logging of Mountain Ash, Alpine Ash, Messmate (*E. obliqua*) and Tasmanian Blue Gum (*E. globulus*) began about 1810. As Hobart Town began to expand, the forests were cleared for agriculture and in the 1850s steam was introduced, expanding the industry further. The number of mills increased from two in 1850 to 22 in 1855. The government was keen to export timber to England but the industry was hampered by the use of unseasoned timber. Eventually with the establishment of the *State Forests Act* in 1885, quality controls were introduced and by this time the number of mills had risen to 62. The prolonged depression of the 1890s forced the closure of all but 37 mills. As the economy improved by 1937–38, Tasmania led the states in the production of timber for paper and pulp and it was then that Associated Pulp and Paper Mills Ltd (APPM) commenced operations at Burnie in northern Tasmania. In the 1990s, huge areas of land were leased by Gunn's Plantation Ltd from farmers who were having difficulty in making an income from their farms. These areas, and others acquired by Gunn's, have allowed it to have some 110,000 hectares planted with Tasmanian Blue Gum and in both the east and central areas of the state, massive plantations can now be seen. Proposals for the construction of a further pulp mill in northern Tasmania have encountered strong opposition from environmentalists despite conditional approval from state and Commonwealth governments in 2009.

MOUNTAIN ASH (*Eucalyptus regnans*)

The tallest hardwood tree in the world, Mountain Ash is found in the ranges of eastern Victoria, the Otway Ranges and in moist forests of Tasmania. The tallest individual tree has been located near the Tahune Airwalk tourist attraction some 80 kilometres south-west of Hobart. It was reported in October 2008, measured at 99.6 metres high and named 'Centurion'. The timber is light brown and is used extensively in the building industry, as well as for paper and pulp. Mountain Ash has smooth cream, grey or brown bark except for a skirt of rough fibrous bark up to 15 metres at the base. Trees are straight and commonly 80–90 metres tall in pure stands in these high rainfall areas. With no lignotuber, Mountain Ash is destroyed by fire, often resulting in forests that consist of more or less equal-age trees as seed germination is promoted by the nutrients in the ash bed. These forests are of high conservation value as they are important habitat for such birds as the Powerful Owl and the Lyre Bird as well as Victoria's animal emblem, the rare Leadbeater's Possum. Nevertheless, Mountain Ash forests are still being clear-felled in Victoria and Tasmania for pulp and timber but plantations are also being established in Australia and overseas in New Zealand and South Africa.

Below left: Even-aged stands of Mountain Ash are common, resulting from forest fires in the past.

Below right: The base of a giant Mountain Ash near Mt Fatique in the Strzelecki Ranges, Victoria.
PHOTO: BRETT MIFSUD.

Many postcards used eucalypts to remind the troops of home. PHOTO: AWM (NEG. NO. RC09086).

14 Eucalypts in Wartime

LINKING EUCALYPTS WITH WAR MIGHT AT FIRST SEEM STRANGE, BUT THEY OFFER A STRONG symbolic link when Australians are away from home, and at no time is this more evident than during war. For many Australians in times past, war zones became their first and last overseas destination.

While wattle was seized upon as a national symbol within Australia, it appears that eucalypts, with their unmistakeable leaves and strong smell, were the symbolic link with home for overseas troops.

During the First World War families and loved ones sent postcards to the troops with eucalypt leaves attached. Initially these would have been handmade, with gumleaves glued or stitched to a backing card, but soon they were available commercially with printed text. Just like today's cards, they varied to suit the occasion:

> To My Dear Son on Active Service.
> May You Soon Return to Me.
> A Gum Leaf from Australia

> To My Old Pal at the Front.
> A Speedy and Safe Return.
> A Gum Leaf from Australia

OFF TO THE WAR
Goodby my little Gum Blossom
And don't you fret for me
We'll soon be back together
In the Old Gum Tree

Copyright

One of a series of postcards May Gibbs produced at the outbreak of war in 1914, which helped introduce her gumnut babies to the public.

But the traffic was not all in one direction. The South Australian artist Laurence Howie, who served with the 13th Field Engineers in Egypt and France, employed his artistic skills to design the regimental Christmas cards, probably printed in London. His card for 1917 sets military insignia within an Art Nouveau design of eucalypt flowers and gumleaves.

In North Africa and the Middle East the troops would have found planted eucalypts, most likely River Red Gum (*Eucalyptus camaldulensis*), and it is obvious these struck a real

Christmas card designed by Laurence Howie, probably based on the Scarlet Gum (*Eucalyptus phoenicea*). COURTESY OF MARY HOWIE.

chord. A photograph in the Australian War Memorial shows the Heliopolis Sporting Club in Egypt, converted to an Australian Auxiliary Hospital in 1915, with the caption: 'The patients have decorated the wooden building with eucalypt branches for Christmas.' Other photos depicting the limited festive occasions for the troops show indoor tables decorated with eucalypt foliage.

For the many youth from rural Australia, the smell of gumleaves must have stirred strong feelings of home. These feelings were reflected also in remembrance for the fallen. Graves for Australian war dead in these regions were often planted with eucalypts. Those who never returned home were buried among the eucalypts—a symbolic return, if not a real one. Following the First World War, the Imperial War Graves Commission made every effort to have eucalypts planted in each war cemetery dedicated to fallen Australians.

The Second World War saw Australian soldiers return to the Middle East and there are numerous photos of 'troops resting beneath gum trees planted during the last war'. Eucalypts still held their strong symbolic link with home, as illustrated by the wreath of gumleaves placed on the war graves in El Alamein, Egypt, on Remembrance Day 1943, from 'the Australian people in honour of the AIF who fell in the Battle of Alamein'.

The practice of sending eucalypt leaves to servicemen and women overseas continued in the Second World War. The War Memorial has a package of six such leaves, carefully pressed in its original cardboard, each leaf inscribed from a different member of the Hibbens family of Orange to Viv Hibbens, who joined the RAAF in 1940 at the age of eighteen. Written on the cardboard are the words, 'Give Jim Leahy one of the gum leaves if he is still with you. Lots of love Mum.'

This strong emotive link between serving troops and eucalypts has continued. At a 1949 Anzac Day ceremony at Kure in Japan, the Australian contingent of the British Commonwealth Occupation Force planted 500 eucalypts brought from Australia. Two decades later Australian troops were planting eucalypt trees in Vietnam. In this conflict the Australian Civil Affairs Unit had an agricultural attachment and records show that they planted 150 River Red Gums around Nui Dat in 1970.

In more modern times, many of our activities in overseas areas of conflict have been more humanitarian than military, and it is often civilian groups such as CARE and AusAID who find themselves in war or disaster zones. In recognition of their exceptional bravery, the Australian Government established the 'Humanitarian Overseas Service Medal' in 1999. Fittingly, the eucalypt tree is the central symbol of this medal, the branches spreading from the Australian land at the base of the medal to the world, which is represented by a circle. A ring of gumnuts surrounds the circle, symbolising hope and life after disaster. The back of the medal repeats the ring of gumnuts and details of the award and recipient.

Above left: Heliopolis Sporting Club in Egypt, converted to an Australian Auxiliary Hospital, decorated with eucalypt branches for Christmas, 1917. PHOTO: AWM (NEG. NO. C00354).

Above right: An Australian soldier shows local schoolchildren how to care for eucalypt trees planted at their school in Nui Dat, Vietnam, 1970. PHOTO: AWM (NEG. NO. FAI/70/0150/VN).

Left: Wreath of locally sourced eucalypt leaves in El Alamein Cemetery, Egypt, in honour of fallen Australians, 11 November 1943. PHOTO: AWM (NEG. NO. MEC2505).

Far left: War graves of Australians who fell during the taking of Beersheba, then Palestine, planted with eucalypts, 1917. PHOTO: AWM (NEG. NO. J01160).

Left: A stylised eucalypt tree is the central symbol of the Australian Humanitarian Overseas Service Medal, introduced in 1999. PHOTO: DPMC.

PART 4

UTILISING
EUCALYPTS TODAY

After drying, the seed and the chaff are released. Cup Gum (*Eucalyptus cosmophylla*) (left). The larger particles are the seeds; the smaller particles are chaff. Yellow Bloodwood (*Corymbia eximia*) (right), showing the typical urn-shaped fruits of *Corymbia*. Here, the larger seeds are more easily distinguished from the chaff.

15 Propagation and Cultivation

EUCALYPTS ARE GENERALLY PROPAGATED FROM SEED. THE SEED IS BORNE IN capsules, often called gumnuts, which may remain on the tree for some years after maturity. Ripening time varies considerably between species and some species will shed their seed within twelve months. Eventually the valves of the gumnut open and the seed is released. This may happen if the branch bearing the fruits is dislodged by wind, birds or simply by ageing. If collecting seed, make certain that you have an appropriate permit or, if on private land, that the owner has given permission to collect.

Ensure that the seed has not already been shed by firstly checking that the valves are still closed and that the seed is mature—the gumnut should be hard and brown. Place the nuts in a paper bag and leave them in a warm spot. In a few days the seed will be released but care should be taken as the seed will be mixed with chaff (the non-fertile particles). The shape and size of the seed varies greatly from species to species but generally the seed is more solid than the chaff and usually darker.

A limited range of eucalypt seeds suitable for the home garden can be bought in packets.

In most cases pre-treatment of the seed is unnecessary, but those species that occur in subalpine and alpine areas will give improved results if the seed is stratified, a process that simulates the winter extremes in the wild. To stratify seed, mix with damp sand and place in a plastic bag in the refrigerator for about eight to ten weeks prior to sowing.

An alternative for those who cannot collect their own seed, or who want seed of unusual species, is to purchase seed in packets. A limited range of species can be bought from nurseries or botanic gardens shops. These are often the more colourful flowering species and usually have photos on the packet. There are also online suppliers of seed.

Seed may be sown in seed trays or directly into tubes. Use a commercial seed-sowing medium in the trays, or a well-drained potting mix with a little slow-release fertiliser in tubes. A wetting agent is a useful addition if one is not already in the mix. If tubes are used it is suggested that at least two to four seeds are placed in each tube and covered with

This Alpine Ash (*Eucalyptus delegatensis*) seedling, bearing its first true leaves, is ready for transplanting into a larger pot or tube. The pair of seed leaves, or cotyledons, can be seen below.

about 3 millimetres of mix. Germination usually occurs in one to two weeks. After germination remove all but one seedling from the tube. If seed is sown in trays, pot on the seedlings into tubes or pots at the appearance of the first pair of true leaves, which develop above the cotyledons, or seed leaves. This minimises the chance of the plant developing a curled root system. Keep the seedlings in half shade until ready to plant.

Eucalypts are difficult to propagate from cuttings but cuttings taken from seedlings with juvenile foliage will form roots under good nursery conditions. The one exception is tropical *Eucalyptus deglupta*, which does not occur naturally in Australia. With this species, some success has been reported from branch cuttings taken from plants up to five years old. Young shoots taken from a lignotuber or epicormic shoots after a fire have also been struck as cuttings.

Grafting, a technique which allows a growing shoot of a plant to be joined to an established seedling, has been used successfully in the propagation of hybrids. Using an approach graft or a top wedge graft, some fine colourful hybrids have been released onto the market. This technique allows plants to retain their clonal properties, such as flower colour or form, which may be lost from seed propagation. By using a hardy root stock, they are readily adapted to cultivation.

Many papers have been written on the propagation of eucalypts by tissue culture and until recently this was not commercially feasible. Now a tissue culture laboratory has been developed in north Queensland, where production is being successfully achieved. Tissue culture is a technique which allows huge numbers of plants of the same genetic composition to be produced in sterile culture and transferred to normal potting soil.

Cultivation

When plants reach 20 centimetres high, they are ready to be planted in their final location in the ground. A hole should be dug larger than the container and the soil loosened for about 30 centimetres around the plant. As the plant is removed from its container, a check should be made on the root system to ensure that the roots have not begun to curl around the pot or tube. If this has happened, the roots must be pruned to remove the curl. A curled root system will result in an unstable plant, which is vulnerable to wind.

Place the plant in the prepared hole and firm the soil around the stem, leaving the plant at the same level as it was in the container, and water well. Apply some slow-release fertiliser around the plant. It is beneficial to spread a mulch around the new plant to help conserve moisture, but keep the stem of the seedling clear of mulch. See the diagram below as a general guide. Once established, eucalypts respond to a dressing of a general fertiliser every six months for the first year or so and then they may be left to their own devices.

There is a eucalypt for almost any site but, in general, most species prefer a full sun position. They are tolerant of most soil conditions, but many of the species that occur in arid environments will need good drainage and those from the south-west of Australia do not fare well on the humid east coast.

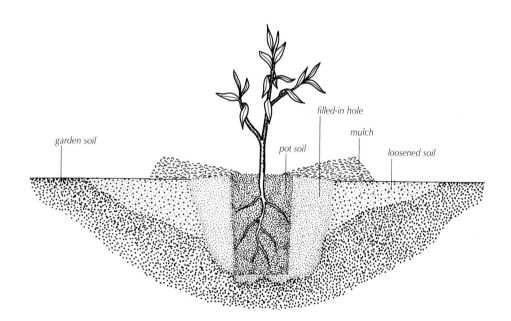

garden soil   pot soil   filled-in hole   mulch   loosened soil

Loosen the soil for at least 30 centimetres around the hole where the plant is to be positioned and ensure that the roots are not curled in the pot. Water well and apply a mulch, keeping the stem of the seedling free of mulch.

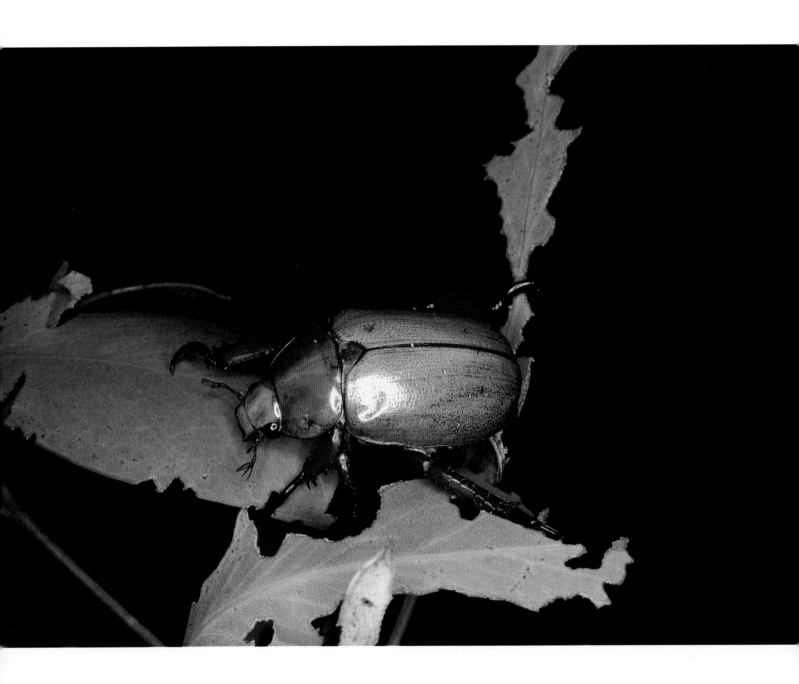

Christmas beetles, such as this one in the genus *Anoplognathus*, can defoliate the young growth of eucalypts at the height of summer.

16 Managing Pests and Diseases

EUCALYPTS ARE PRONE TO MANY PESTS AND DISEASES BUT WITH BALANCED NUTRITION AND normal climatic conditions, most are not considered major problems. We will examine a few of the more serious pests that are encountered, as well as possible means of control.

Probably one of the most serious problems is known as dieback. This begins with the loss of foliage from the crown of a tree and may proceed to the loss of branches and ultimately, in serious cases, the death of the tree. The basic cause can be traced back to human activity. Clearing of land has resulted in the isolation of trees, or small groups of trees. Roads and structures have been built, causing changes in drainage patterns. The reduction in understorey vegetation has limited the natural fauna that inhabited the area and when foliage feeders such as scarab beetles or psyllids attack a tree, there are insufficient predators to keep them under control. In a forest situation, scarab beetles are normally controlled by birds and sugar gliders and their larvae numbers are regulated by parasitic wasps. When these predators are absent, the beetles can cause severe defoliation, resulting in dieback.

A heavy infestation of lerp on this Mallee Red Gum (*Eucalyptus nandewarica*) gave the whole foliage a silvery-grey appearance. The stress of such an infestation was probably responsible for the tree's death during Canberra's drought in 2006–08.

Similarly, sap-sucking psyllids are normally controlled by a variety of birds, sugar gliders and other possums. In north-eastern New South Wales, serious dieback in populations of Flooded Gum (*Eucalyptus grandis*), Sydney Blue Gum, (*E. saligna*) and Grey Gum (*E. propinqua*) has been noted. These forests have a disturbed understorey, often with a dense shrub layer of the exotic weed *Lantana camara*, and are associated with large colonies of Bell Miners and Noisy Miners in the upper branches. These birds are very aggressive, excluding smaller birds from their territory. Furthermore, they are thought to 'farm' the psyllids by eating their sugary covering but leaving the insect. Similar problems have been experienced in forests of the Narrow-leaved Peppermint (*E. radiata*) in Victoria and southern New South Wales.

Another major cause of dieback is root damage by the fungus *Phytophthora cinnamomi*. This is a soil-borne pathogen that attacks the growing tips of roots and is transmitted

through the soil by spores in moving water. When the roots are infected, they are prevented from taking up water and nutrients, often resulting in a tree with a full foliage of dead leaves. This is followed by leaf drop and usually the death of the tree. It is a major problem in the Jarrah forests of the south-west of Western Australia and is associated with forestry work and the construction of roads, which tend to change the drainage and water movement throughout the soil. Some of these forestry areas have been quarantined in an attempt to restrict the spread of the disease. In eastern Australia, the stringybarks and the ashes are the most susceptible of the eucalypts to attack from *P. cinnamomi*. Some control of *Phytophthora* has been achieved for avocados by injecting the trees with phosphorous acid (Avoguard 500SL), but no information is available for eucalypts. Dieback may also occur in times of drought or increased salinity in the soil, and if coupled with any of the former situations then plant death will often occur.

Another serious fungal disease is *Armillaria*, which can attack many native and exotic plant species. Several *Armillaria* species have been recorded as causing death in eucalypts. Known commonly as Honey Fungus, *Armillaria mellea* and *A. luteobubalina* have caused considerable concern in both cultivated situations and native forests in southern Australia. Their presence is usually first noticed by clumps of brownish mushrooms

near the base of the tree trunk in autumn or by the death of limbs. The fungus attacks the roots of the tree, but fungal threads are also often seen under the bark. The fungus spreads through the soil by these threads, which may travel at up to one metre per year. There is no known cure for the disease and the best precautions are to remove any infected material and soil surrounding the dead plant. Several Australian botanic gardens have suffered serious damage from this pest.

Many insects may affect eucalypts by chewing the foliage or sucking the sap in young stems. In healthy trees they do not pose a threat to the tree. Many of these chewing insects, such as sawfly larvae, paropsis beetles and grasshoppers, tend to attack juvenile foliage or tender young growth and in garden situations may cause serious damage. They may be controlled by physically removing the pests or by using an appropriate insecticide.

Gum Tree Scale (*Eriococcus coriaceus*) was a serious threat to eucalypt plantations in New Zealand but has now been brought under control by the importation of some natural Australian predators. The ladybird beetle (*Rhysobius ventralis*) and the larva of a moth, *Stathmopoda melanochra*, both feed on the scale and with their introduction chemical control is no longer necessary.

Galls have been mentioned briefly in Chapter 5 and may be caused by a great variety of organisms. Their control is very difficult, as once the gall is noticed it is

Western Australian Jarrah dieback sign in 1979, proclaiming the forest a quarantine area due to *Phytophthora cinnamomi* infestation.

usually too late to do anything but cut off the affected branches and burn them. This control is largely cosmetic and is obviously impractical in plantations.

Powdery mildew is a fungus that often attacks eucalypt seedlings, causing greyish blotches on the leaves. It tends to occur when seedlings are watered overhead in the cooler weather and the foliage remains wet overnight. It is seldom fatal and is best controlled by keeping the foliage dry and using sub-irrigation.

The most worrying threat to eucalypts is a fungus known as Guava Rust (*Puccinia psidii*). This disease was first observed in Brazil in the 1960s when it caused serious defoliation in plantations of young hybrid eucalypts (*Eucalyptus grandis* x *E. urophylla*) grown for timber. The fungus is specific to plants of the family Myrtaceae and previously had caused damage to the fruit trees, guava and jaboticaba. At this stage the fungus has not appeared in Australia, although it has been noted in the Australian *Melaleuca quinquenervia* plants in the Florida Everglades. Quarantine authorities are concerned, as are foresters and scientists—if the fungus appears in Australia it could devastate our natural flora as well as our timber plantations. Our flora is well represented by the family Myrtaceae, with about 140 genera and thousands of species. Overseas travellers must be on the alert and ensure that they strictly obey quarantine regulations as they return to Australia.

Above far left: A Honey Fungus, *Armilaria luteobubalina*, growing around the base of Broad-leaved Stringybark (*Eucalyptus caliginosa*) shows the typical habit of these fungi.

Above left: A typical cluster of sawfly larvae of the genus *Perga*, which raise their heads and spit when disturbed.

Above centre: A heavy infestation of the sap-sucking scale insect *Eriococcus confusus* on the young stems of a eucalypt. Physical removal is the best remedy.

Above right: A plant infected by Guava Rust (*Puccinia psidii*) in South America. PHOTO: CSIRO.

Grafted cultivar, *Corymbia* 'Summer Beauty',
photographed at Coffs Harbour, New South Wales.

17 Hybrids and Cultivars

A HYBRID IS THE OFFSPRING OF TWO GENETICALLY DIFFERENT PARENTS USUALLY WHEN THE parents are different species. These may occur naturally in the field or may be made deliberately to achieve some special purpose. A cultivar (a cultivated variety) is a selected form of a plant that has been brought into cultivation because of special characteristics that may be useful to horticulture, forestry or agriculture. Many cultivars are hybrids.

The naming of cultivars must follow a prescribed format set down by the *International Code of Nomenclature for Cultivated Plants*. The cultivar name should consist of no more than three words (for example, *Corymbia* 'Summer Red'), they should be capitalised, and they should be included in single quotes. This name should follow the genus or the genus and species name. Once named, the cultivar may be presented with full description and photographs to the Australian Cultivar Registration Authority (ACRA) or to the Plant Breeder's Rights (PBR) office to determine the distinctness of the cultivar.

The natural hybridisation of eucalypts occurs frequently in many parts of eastern Australia, adding considerably to the difficulty in identifying eucalypts there. More than 134 hybrids have been given names over the years by botanists who, at the time, have considered them actual species. Later and closer examination of these has revealed their true origin. Species that are often prone to hybridisation include *Eucalyptus botryoides*, *E. camaldulensis*, *E. crebra*, *E. globulus*, *E. robusta*, *E. sideroxylon*, *E. tereticornis*, *E. radiata*, *Corymbia calophylla*, *C. maculata* and *C. tessellaris*, but there are also many others.

Foresters have attempted to hybridise some of the economic eucalypts to improve their growth rate, tolerance to salinity and the structure of their timber. Some clones of River Red Gum (*E. camaldulensis*) have shown good tolerance to salty soils and these have been crossed with Flooded Gum (*E. grandis*) and Tasmanian Blue Gum (*E. globulus*). While the cross has been successful, propagation of the resulting hybrid had proved difficult until recent advances in techniques enabled them to be produced by tissue culture. These hybrids are now available in Australia and are being distributed to combat soil salinity.

Grafted cultivar, *Corymbia* 'Summer Red'. The ample flow of nectar attracts birds.

By contrast, a number of man-made hybrids intended for the ornamental trade have been successfully marketed. These have been propagated by grafting. The most outstanding of these are hybrids between the Red Flowering Gum (*Corymbia ficifolia*) from Western Australia and the Swamp Bloodwood (*C. ptychocarpa*) from northern Australia. As both of these species occur in several colour forms, their progeny display a range of different colours. The best known of these are *C.* 'Summer Red' and *C.* 'Summer Beauty'. These have been grafted on to the hardy Red Bloodwood (*C. gummifera*) and the Spotted Gum (*C. maculata*). *Corymbia* 'Summer Red' has masses of deep-red flowers for many months of the year and *C.* 'Summer Beauty' has large bunches of pink flowers. It is very important for these grafts to be prepared by competent operators as poorly executed grafts will result in disappointment when the graft fractures and the tree collapses. Two other cultivars with similar parents are *C.* 'Summer Snow' with white

The cultivar *Eucalyptus cladocalyx* 'Vintage Red' displays colourful foliage. It has been developed by the company OzBreed. PHOTO: OZBREED.

flowers and *C.* 'Summer Glory' with flowers paler than 'Summer Red'. All have been granted Plant Breeders Rights.

A chance hybrid that occurred in cultivation in South Australia is *Eucalyptus* 'Urrbrae Gem'. This is a cross between the Red Flowered Mallee (*E. erythronema*) and Strickland's Gum (*E. stricklandii*), both Western Australian species. Some modest success has been had by propagating this hybrid from tissue culture and it has been grafted on to Strickland's Gum stock. *E.* 'Urrbrae Gem' has red flowers borne in small bunches along the stems and is best suited to growing in arid and semi-arid areas.

The following four cultivars have been registered with the Australian Cultivar Registration Authority based at the Australian National Botanic Gardens in Canberra.

- *E. camaldulensis* 'Dale Chapman' is the only cultivar to be registered because of its value as a timber plant. It was selected in Florida in 1978 because of its fast growth in dense plantations and it can be propagated from cuttings using mist propagation. It has been estimated to produce 127 tonnes dry weight per hectare per year in plantations of 6250 trees per hectare. This is in excess of normal clones.
- *E. scoparia* 'Golden Crown' is a selected seedling, the new foliage of which is a bronze colour, gradually turning gold. As the foliage matures, the gold changes to a lime-green colour. The foliage contrasts well with the red branchlets. This cultivar was received for registration by the Australian Cultivar Registration Authority in 1984, but as it has not appeared in nursery lists it is doubtful if it still persists.
- *C. citriodora* 'Marion' is said to be a dwarf form of the species with a dense crown, larger leaves, and branches produced low down from the trunk. It is said to come true from seed.
- *C. ficifolia* 'Vermillion Blaze' is a selected form of the species, with large orange flowers that remain on the tree for longer than normal. It has to be propagated by grafting.

SWAMP BLOODWOOD
(*Corymbia ptychocarpa*)

A rough-barked bloodwood from the Kimberley, Top End of the Northern Territory and far western Queensland, this tropical species is often seen in cultivation in subtropical and tropical areas where it forms a small tree to 15 metres. In nature it is found near lagoons, creeks and springs, where it may grow taller. The large, leathery leaves are paler on the underside and the large, showy terminal flower sprays may be creamy white, pink or red, and are full of nectar for visiting parrots and honeyeaters. The gumnuts are very large and ridged, reaching 5.5 centimetres long. When grown from seed, the flower colour of the progeny is uncertain. The species has been used to form hybrids with the Red Flowering Gum (*Corymbia ficifolia*) from Western Australia. There are two subspecies of *E. ptychocarpa*, with subsp. *aptycha* being restricted to the Top End of the Northern Territory. It is characterised by the lack of longitudinal ridges on the buds and gumnuts.

A Swamp Bloodwood flowering in a Brisbane garden.

Another hybrid that has been grown for many years in arid areas is known as *E.* 'Torwood'. This is a hybrid between *E. torquata* and *E. woodwardii*. As this hybrid has been propagated from seed, the progeny show great variability, but some clones are outstanding and they should be perpetuated by propagating them by grafting. It is commonly used as a street tree in Alice Springs and many rural towns in South Australia. The flower colour varies from red, through pink to yellow. It is widely grown in America. *Eucalyptus torquata* has also been used in another hybrid, this time with *E. erythronema*. The progeny are sold as *E.* 'Augusta Wonder'.

Two dwarf cultivars of *C. ficifolia*, known as *C.* 'Dwarf Crimson' and *C.* 'Dwarf Orange' are available and are said to reach 3 metres with a similar spread.

Eucalyptus cladocalyx 'Vintage Red' is a cultivar released at the 2009 Melbourne International Flower and Garden Show. It produces red foliage, which can appear to change colour from red to purple or grey depending on the direction of the sunlight and the age of the foliage. It is grafted onto normal Sugar Gum (*E. cladocalyx*) stock. It has been submitted for Plant Breeders Rights.

Isolated eucalypts on farms often have their bark damaged or even removed when they become a 'scratching post' for livestock.

18 Landscaping and Planting

DUE TO THE VARIETY OF HABIT, BARK TEXTURE, LEAF AND FLOWER AND THEIR hardiness in such a wide range of climates and soil types, eucalypts have a broad use in landscaping situations.

Eucalypts on farms

As trees on farms, the broad spreading crowns of many species create shade and shelter for stock. On the often harsh climate of the eastern tablelands, the Yellow Box (*Eucalyptus melliodora*) and the Apple Box (*E. bridgesiana*) are ideal for this purpose. As well as improving the ambience of the landscape, the planting of wood lots on larger farms also has the added advantage of attracting birds and providing a long-term income for the farmer for log or oil production. To get optimum benefit for bird habitat, lots greater than five hectares are required. In some instances where individual trees are grown on farms, it has been observed that cattle have caused damage and even death to eucalypts by continually rubbing themselves against the trunks. On the western slopes of New South Wales and in central Queensland the Poplar Box (*E. populnea*) is often used as an assurance against drought, when it is lopped or coppiced and the foliage used as fodder.

In the final years of the twentieth century, Australia saw a 'landcare' movement among the farming community which resulted in huge numbers of trees, mostly eucalypts, being planted on agricultural and grazing land. Greater awareness of salinity problems and a realisation that we were losing biodiversity, coupled with programs of government grants and paid coordinators, contributed to the landcare success.

Poplar Box (*Eucalyptus populnea*) was often left when grazing land was cleared because its foliage could be used as fodder in times of drought.

A massive 'landcare' program in many parts of Australia saw eucalypts planted in vast numbers at the end of the twentieth century. Here plastic guards protect young trees in northern Victoria.

Combating soil salinity

Soil salinity is one of the most serious environmental problems facing the Australian landscape. The clearing of land for farming and grazing has allowed the watertable to rise in many parts of the country, resulting in high salt levels near the surface. This degrades the soil to such an extent that grasses and other pasture species will not survive.

In parts of Western Australia, native eucalypts have been planted on farms in order to lower the watertable. There are a number of species that occur naturally on saline soils and these are being used with some success. Species such as Kondinin Blackbutt (*Eucalyptus kondininensis*), Swamp Yate (*E. occidentalis*), Salt Gum (*E. salicola*), *E. sargentii* subsp. *onesia*, *E. utilis*, and *E. spathulata* subsp. *salina* are all suitable to use for this purpose. In recent years, hybrid clones brought in from Brazil are also proving successful. These are *E. camaldulensis* x *E. grandis* and *E. camaldulensis* x *E. globulus*. These are being propagated by tissue culture by Yuruga Nursery at Walkamin in north Queensland and are being distributed to most states where salinity is a problem.

In addition to controlling soil salinity, other mallee species are being grown by Western Australian wheat farmers in association with the Oil Mallee Company in order to provide a secondary income by producing eucalyptus oil and other possible by-products (see Chapter 25). The alternate swathes of wheat crop about 80 metres wide and mallee shrubs about 10 metres wide give the landscape an unusual striped appearance.

Salt-tolerant hybrids *Eucalyptus camaldulensis* x *E. grandis*, produced in quantity at Yuruga Nursery, north Queensland.

Left: Swamp Mallet (*Eucalyptus spathulata*) has a subspecies *salina* which occurs naturally on saline soils.

Top: An extreme example of salinity where rising salt in the watertable has killed a eucalypt woodland community in northern Victoria. Salt crystals can be seen on the soil surface.

Eucalypts in urban landscaping

Urbanisation of the natural forests surrounding Australia's capital cities has created fire hazards, and despite the frequent advice of fire authorities to clear areas around houses and remove leaves from gutters, many properties are lost each summer to bushfires.

But in general trees in towns and cities provide a variety of utility and environmental benefits. They have been shown to reduce the amount of stormwater run–off, thus minimising flooding and allowing easier water penetration into the soil. They tend to reduce urban air temperatures by the evapo-transpiration of their leaves and lessen pollution by the direct absorption of gaseous contaminants. Their shade in car parks is appreciated by motorists and in suburban streets by the people who walk their dogs along shaded footpaths. As street trees and avenue plantings, they have been successful provided correct selection of species has been achieved.

Trees have to be allowed to reach their full potential, so in general they are unsatisfactory when planted under power lines. A fine example of avenue planting may be seen at the entrance to Kings Park in Perth, where

the road is lined with Lemon-scented Gums (*Corymbia citriodora*). Unfortunately in hindsight, as this species is native to eastern Australia, it was not an ideal choice for the location as seeds from these trees have spread into nearby bushland and the species is now considered a weed in Western Australia. This emphasises the need for careful selection.

In another example, a species with restricted natural distribution, the Cadaghi (*Corymbia torelliana*) has become a weed species in northern New South Wales and south-east Queensland. Cadaghi occurs in the fringes of rainforests west of Cairns and as it is a fast-growing, handsome tree, it was used extensively in subtropical areas, where it seeded prolifically and is now a declared environmental weed in Brisbane and surrounding areas. It is also a host tree for scale insects, which attract black smut fungus, making the tree unsightly.

Excellent choices for street planting have been made in many semi-arid rural towns and cities where small eucalypts with colourful flowers such as Coral Gum (*Eucalyptus torquata*), the hybrid *E.* 'Torwood', Fuchsia Gum (*E. dolichorhyncha*), Lemon Gum (*E. woodwardii*) and Red Flowering Gum (*Corymbia ficifolia*) have been used to great effect.

Not all choices have been as fortunate. Several species around Sydney's wealthy northern suburbs have been christened 'widow makers' by foresters because of their habit of dropping branches. The Sydney Red Gum (*Angophora costata*) and the Blackbutt (*Eucalyptus pilularis*) are particularly dangerous and homes are often built adjacent to these giants, endangering both the houses

Above left: Lemon-scented Gum (*Corymbia citriodora*) with an expected height of 30 metres, was not a good choice to plant under electricity wires at Gunnedah in New South Wales.

Above: This photograph, taken in the 1960s as Perth's Kings Park was being developed, shows the spectacular effect of an avenue of Lemon Scented Gums (*Corymbia citriodora*).

and the residents. Another eucalypt, whose common name reflects its propensity to drop branches, is the Brittle Gum (*E. mannifera*).

Eucalypts have featured in the landscaping of the streets of Australia's capital, Canberra, where the well-known eucalypt botanist, Lindsay Pryor, was Director of Parks and Gardens from 1944 to 1958. His use of eucalypts created a pleasant human ambience where the effects of winds, frosts and sun were modified by his plantings. He was also involved with establishing many of the first eucalypts to be planted in the Australian National Botanic Gardens and it is here that the Eucalypt Lawn features many species grown as specimen trees. The first tree planted in these botanic gardens was a eucalypt, a Brittle Gum (*E. mannifera*) planted in 1949 by Sir Edward Salisbury, Director of the Royal Botanic Gardens at Kew, London. The Australian National University campus houses no less than 49 species of eucalypts, allowed to grow to their full potential in the absence of power lines.

Parklands have featured eucalypts since the early European history of Australia. The site of the Royal Botanic Gardens, Sydney, was well vegetated when

Captain Arthur Phillip arrived in 1788, but the only surviving trees from this original forest are two Forest Red Gums (*E. tereticornis*) now seen in two of the lawn areas of the gardens. In 1816, a row of Swamp Mahogany (*E. robusta*) was planted to define the boundary of Mrs Macquarie's Road, adjacent to the present botanic gardens. This became the first row of street trees planted in Australia. These were replaced in 1991 with the same species and the original trees gradually removed as their health deteriorated. When Ferdinand von Mueller was made Director of the Melbourne Botanic Gardens in 1857, he planted avenues of trees including the Tasmanian Blue Gum (*E. globulus*). These rows were later replaced to form a more aesthetic landscape style by his successor, William Guilfoyle, in 1873.

Lindsay Pryor planted Canberra's streets with an interesting range of eucalypts, including these Red Box (*Eucalyptus polyanthemos*) with their attractive grey foliage.

Above left: Cadaghi (*Corymbia torelliana*) with its attractive green trunk, is becoming a weed in some parts of Queensland.

Above centre: Brittle Gum (*Eucalyptus mannifera*) is aptly named for its propensity to drop limbs. The branches of this street tree fell during a still night in Canberra.

Above right: The western Victorian town of Warracknabeal has planted a range of colour forms of *Corymbia ficifolia* in its main street. They make a stunning display in summer.

In the United Kingdom, where only the hardiest eucalypts survive the winter, the Royal Horticultural Society's National Collection for Eucalypts is held by Dr Doug Smith at his property in Hampshire, England. Some 35 species have survived in this collection, mostly from Tasmanian or southern tablelands collections. Temperatures to −7°C have been experienced and although some defoliation and trunk damage occurs, many of these cold-tolerant species have survived and grown well. Shining Gum (*E. nitens*) is one of the fastest-growing eucalypts in the UK, with a tree in Oxfordshire reaching 16 metres in four years and possessing a fine straight trunk. Cider Gum (*E. gunnii*) has also achieved rapid growth in the UK as, once established, it will grow at the rate of 3 metres per year. As a shelter belt, it should be densely planted at six plants per metre for best results. Tasmanian Blue Gum seedlings are used in some London parks as bedding plants. Their grey juvenile foliage contrasts well with other plants. This fine species, however, is not considered generally hardy when grown as a tree.

A list of cold-tolerant species that have survived and grown well in the UK and North America follows:

E. archeri	E. macarthuri
E. bridgesiana	E. morrisbyi
E. cinerea	E. neglecta
E. coccifera	E. nitens
E. crenulata	E. nova-anglica
E. dalympleana	E. pauciflora
E. delegatensis subsp. tasmaniensis	E. rodwayi
E. elliptica	E. rubida
E. gregsoniana	E. stellulata
E. gunnii	E. subcrenulata
E. kybeanensis	E. urnigera

Tasmanian Blue Gum (*Eucalyptus globulus*) grown as a hedge in New Zealand. Many trees are grown as tall hedges there, kept trimmed by huge machines.

Opposite:

Top: The first row of trees planted in Australia in 1816 were these Swamp Mahogany (*Eucalyptus robusta*) with the Macquarie Wall in the background, at the Royal Botanic Gardens, Sydney, 1996. PHOTO: JAIME PLAZA.

Far left: A Cider Gum (*Eucalyptus gunnii*) planted in the Royal Botanic Garden, Edinburgh, Scotland. It is one of a few eucalypts able to be grown outdoors in the UK.

Left: Tasmanian Blue Gum (*Eucalyptus globulus*) grown for its juvenile blue-grey foliage as a bedding plant at London's Regent's Park, UK.

Even with these species it is important to ensure that the seed used is collected from plants that occur naturally in the coldest areas.

In Australia, New Zealand, America and the United Kingdom, it is not uncommon to see eucalypts used as clipped hedges for windbreaks and shelter for stock. The Shining Gum (*E. nitens*), despite its tall stature in nature, has been successfully clipped to a hedge some 2 metres high when planted at about 1.5 metre centres in Tasmania. Tasmanian Blue Gum is frequently used as a noise barrier along roads in California, with the cultivar 'Compacta' preferred for farm sites. It is also used in New Zealand as a windbreak. Also common in New Zealand urban plantings is Red Flowering Gum, spectacular in autumn. Yellow Box (*E. melliodora*), Red Ironbark (*E. sideroxylon*) and Red Flowering Gum are seen as street trees in San Francisco. One specialised use for eucalypts is found in alpine tourist areas in New South Wales, where Snow Gum (*E. pauciflora*) has been planted under ski-lifts to define the ski-runs.

Eucalypts in private gardens

In older, larger gardens where it was usually not necessary to consider space and even height restrictions, the choice of eucalypts for the home garden was easy. Today, with ever-diminishing suburban garden sizes, it is much more critical to choose carefully. Height and spread are of the utmost importance, as is the selection of species suitable for the climate.

Many of the mallees that occur in areas of Western Australia have the size characteristics that make them suitable for home gardens, but as they grow naturally in areas with winter rainfall, they will not survive the humid, moist summers of the east coast and will succumb to root fungus diseases such as *Phytophthora cinnamomi*. They are, however, excellent subjects for gardens in areas with a Mediterranean climate, and cities such as Melbourne, Adelaide and Perth can readily accommodate these wonderful plants as well as the drier parts of the inland and western slopes of New South Wales. The Bell-fruited Mallee (*E. preissiana*) with

It might not have been anticipated that this Sydney Red Gum (*Angophora costata*) would get so large when it was planted in Auckland, New Zealand, in the late 1800s. It is 27.2 metres high with a girth of 7.94 metres.
PHOTO: WILLY COENRADI.

yellow flowers, Square-fruited Mallee (*E. tetraptera*) with red flowers, Round-leafed Mallee (*E. orbifolia*) with yellow flowers and wonderful peeling and colourful bark, and the Silver Princess (*E. caesia* subsp. *magna*) with red flowers and a weeping habit, are just a few from which to choose.

In Tasmania, the Western Australian Red Flowering Gum has been used effectively in many areas and in late summer and autumn the various coloured forms make spectacular garden displays. While Sydney Red Gum (*Angophora costata*) is frequently allowed to remain in gardens in the northern suburbs of Sydney, it has the potential to drop large branches on calm days, causing substantial damage to property. In New Zealand, where it tends to produce a more spreading habit, this may not be such a problem.

For the subtropics and tropical areas, there are a number of diminutive species that are excellent for small gardens. The Plunkett Mallee (*E. curtisii*), with large clusters of cream flowers, hails from near Brisbane and adapts well to garden conditions in these areas. The Yellow-top Mallee Ash (*E. luehmanniana*) from the Sydney sandstone is also a handsome, small mallee with yellowish stems and shiny green leaves. For a long-term colourful display, none are better than *Corymbia* 'Summer Red' and *C.* 'Summer Beauty'. From the tropics, the red-flowered Bristle-leaved Bloodwood

(*C. dunlopiana*) grows well as far south as Coffs Harbour, New South Wales, and two grey foliage species, the Twin-leaf Bloodwood (*C. cadophora*) and the Silver Box (*E. pruinosa*) make interesting foliage contrasts in tropical gardens.

In suburban gardens one has to be careful of the roots of large eucalypts, for as they spread in search of moisture they tend to clog up drains and pipes. This same quest for moisture is seen when smaller plants are grown beneath eucalypts as constant watering is required to keep them in good condition.

Eucalypts as bonsai

Although far from the traditional species used in bonsai, eucalypts have been successfully grown as bonsai subjects. Of the specimens seen, the most successful have been the River Red Gum (*E. camaldulensis*) and the Narrow-leaved Black Peppermint (*E. nicholii*). Attempts have also been made with Yellow Box (*E. melliodora*), Snow Gum (*E. pauciflora*), Cider Gum (*E. gunnii*) and Sydney Red Gum (*Angophora costata*) with some success. Some experimental work is underway with some of the mallee species and it is likely that examples of these will be seen in the future.

Bonsai from Narrow-leaved Black Peppermint (*Eucalyptus nicholii*). It has been trained as a bonsai for ten years, repotted three times, and its lower portion carved to give it a gum tree style.

RED FLOWERING GUM (*Corymbia ficifolia*)

Occurring in a very restricted area south-east of Perth and in the Stirling Ranges, the Red Flowering Gum is very common in cultivation in areas with a Mediterranean climate (dry summers/wet winters) and also in parts of New Zealand. Many fine specimens are seen in Tasmania. The tree has a spreading crown and is usually less than 15 metres high. The flowers are borne in large terminal sprays and vary in colour, from white to pink to red and orange. If grown from seed, the flower colour may be any of the above despite being collected from a particular coloured tree. Flowers have been recorded from summer through to autumn. They are highly ornamental and are frequently visited by lorikeets and honeyeaters for their nectar. Plants grafted on to *C. gummifera* are frequently used to increase the tree's hardiness in subtropical areas. The species has also been used to produce hybrids with the northern species *C. ptychocarpa*, in order to grow it in more humid climates.

The brilliant flowers make the Red Flowering Gum one of Australia's favourite ornamental trees.

A tree in full flower in Tasmania, a long way from its original home. PHOTO: MARCIA WRIGLEY.

CAESIA (*Eucalyptus caesia*)

During the Elder Scientific Exploring Expedition of 1891–92, Richard Helms gathered specimens of a *Eucalyptus* that the Aboriginals of the area called 'Gungurru'. This was almost certainly *E. woodwardii*, but in 1896 it was misidentified by Ferdinand von Mueller and Ralph Tate as *E. caesia*. This led to the incorrect application of the common name 'Gungurru' to *E. caesia*. The common name 'Caesia' is now used in most references. This species is probably the best known of the small ornamental eucalypts in cultivation. In nature it is rare, always associated with granite outcrops in the eastern wheatbelt of Western Australia. It has a mallee habit usually less than 10 metres high, with minnirichi bark, the reddish-brown old bark peeling to reveal a smooth green bark beneath. The silvery-grey branches are pendulous and often weighed down in late winter and spring by the large pink flowers and urn-shaped gumnuts. A subspecies (subsp. *magna*), often sold as 'Silver Princess', has larger flowers and fruits, with the pendulous branches often touching the ground. Both subspecies thrive in well-drained soil on sunny sites in areas of winter rainfall.

The pendulous buds, flowers and fruits are decorative.

PLUNKETT MALLEE
(*Eucalyptus curtisii*)

This mallee or slender, small tree may reach 7 metres high and is endemic to the forests of south-east Queensland. Fires are frequent in these forests and encourage the mallee habit as trees shoot from the lignotuber after fire. The bark sheds in thin strips to reveal the smooth, greyish-green trunks. In spring and early summer, masses of white flowers are borne terminally on the branches, giving a fine floral display. Flowers are laden with nectar, attracting both insects and nectar-seeking birds. The Plunkett Mallee's small size and showy flowers make it an ideal garden subject for subtropical and temperate areas, yet it will also withstand quite heavy frosts and has flowered well in Canberra. It will tolerate most soils and aspects and often produces flowers in its second year from seed.

Prolific flowering at a height that can be easily seen make the Plunkett Mallee a popular home garden eucalypt.

NARROW-LEAVED BLACK PEPPERMINT (*Eucalyptus nicholii*)

Although restricted to a small area between Armidale and Glen Innes on the northern tablelands of New South Wales, this species is widely seen in cultivation in south-eastern Australia as an ornamental in home gardens and parks. It is found in grassy woodland on poor soils and is frequently exposed to heavy frosts. It grows to 15 metres high with a spreading crown of handsome, blue-green, drooping leaves and rough bark extending to the upper branches. The leaves are pleasantly aromatic and are grazed by Koalas. As its habitat has been subject to extensive clearing and seed collectors have exploited the species, it is listed as vulnerable under the Australian Government *Environment Protection and Biodiversity Conservation Act 1999.*

A Narrow-leaved Black Peppermint growing in a front garden in Coffs Harbour, New South Wales.

SQUARE-FRUITED MALLEE (*Eucalyptus tetraptera*)

This straggly, spreading mallee is common along the south coast of Western Australia and inland to the Stirling Ranges. It rarely exceeds 4 metres high but may spread to 8 metres. Leaves are thickly textured and the unique square red buds, borne singly in the leaf axils, are about 5 centimetres in diameter. The flowers are also red or deep pink and seen in spring and summer. The square gumnuts age to brown and are frequently used in floral arrangements. As a garden novelty for semi-arid or non-humid areas, it is a great conversation piece. The Square-fruited Mallee requires good drainage and a sunny location and is hardy to most frosts and resistant to salt-laden winds. Its ungainly habit can be improved by pruning, with branches taken back to the lignotuber.

For those who like things in fours.

Part of Dean Nicolle's Currency Creek Arboretum in South Australia showing nine-year-old eucalypts planted in the 1990s. PHOTO: DEAN NICOLLE.

19 Eucalypt Arboreta

FOR MOST LARGE PLANT GROUPS THERE IS A SPECIALIST GARDEN OR ARBORETUM SOMEWHERE in the world that has concentrated on growing them. Some plant groups seem to attract more of these specialist gardens than others—orchids, cacti, palms and cycads spring to mind.

You would expect a plant group like the eucalypts to also have plantations displaying the diversity of species, but of course the very size of many of the trees makes this a daunting project. In Australia we have several arboreta or gardens where a broad range of eucalypts can be seen in one place. In discussing the size of the collections we will use the word 'taxa' to include species, subspecies and varieties as this is how computers generate their count.

Currency Creek Arboretum

The largest collection, in excess of 900 taxa, is in fact privately owned and located off the beaten track in South Australia. This labour of love has been assembled by Dean Nicolle, who has had a passion for eucalypts since his school days. Dean grew up in Adelaide and with the help of his father obtained land at Currency Creek, near Goolwa, where he started planting eucalypts as an arboretum. In most cases he collected the seed himself, often travelling to very remote areas, sometimes on Aboriginal land. Shortly after graduating from the University of Adelaide, Nicolle published his first book, *Eucalypts of South Australia* (1997), describing 95 taxa from that state, with his own photos taken in the field for each plant. He went on to do a PhD in Melbourne, on the classification of eucalypts of course, and continues to publish books and work as a consultant. His arboretum is 32 hectares in area and concentrates almost exclusively on eucalypts from all parts of Australia. Each seed collection is carefully documented and trees grown from it are replicated in several parts of the arboretum. It is open to the public from time to time through the Open Garden Scheme; it's best to check the details on his website: www.dn.com.au

Australian National Botanic Gardens

The Eucalypt Lawn of the Australian National Botanic Gardens in Canberra. Eucalypts are also scattered throughout the various sections of the gardens.

The next largest collection of eucalypts is in the Australian National Botanic Gardens in Canberra. Started in the late 1940s, these gardens do not focus on eucalypts in particular—in fact they grow about 6000 species of Australian native plants—but this includes just over 500 taxa of eucalypts, and eucalypts were the first plantings. They were officially opened in 1970 and are now administered by the Commonwealth's Director of National Parks. The gardens jointly manages the Australian National Herbarium with the CSIRO, and this herbarium has the largest number of eucalypt specimens in its collection, numbering about 67,000 in

2009. In most cases plantings in the gardens are linked to herbarium specimens and all seeds are sourced from the wild with full scientific data. Eucalypts in the gardens are not planted in rows like most arboreta, but are scattered throughout the garden beds, often as part of an ecological theme planting. One concentration of these plants is the Eucalypt Lawn in the centre of the gardens, a great place for picnics and even music concerts on warm summer weekend evenings. Entry is free, with a charge for parking, and the gardens are open seven days a week throughout the year.

Peter Francis
Points Arboretum

The plantations of the Peter Francis Points Arboretum are on the slope of a hill overlooking the town of Coleraine in western Victoria.

Coleraine is a small town about halfway between Melbourne and Adelaide, just south-east of the Grampians in Victoria. The arboretum is a community effort, but the driving force for its establishment was a local man, Peter Francis, who from 1966 until his death in 1989 saw the conversion of an abandoned quarry and rubbish dump, known as 'the Points', into a plantation which now contains about 500 eucalypts. The spectacular site is high on a hill overlooking the town. About 700 other native plant species are grown, but the focus of the collection is the eucalypts, planted in rows along the contours of the quite steep site. Seeds and plants were sourced throughout Australia, although the collection does not have the scientific rigour of the previous two plantations. The arboretum occupies 37 hectares and is now administered by the Victorian Department of Conservation Forests and Lands. The arboretum is associated with the Eucalyptus Discovery Centre, located in the heart of Coleraine. Entry is free and the arboretum is open seven days a week throughout the year.

Mount Annan Botanic Gardens

This annexe to Sydney's Royal Botanic Gardens is located near Campbelltown in what are now the outer south-western suburbs of Sydney. It was established in 1984 and unlike the city garden it grows only Australian native plants. It is on a very large site of 416 hectares with concentrated plantings scattered in various places over that area. Most of the plantings are laid out according to the botanical classification of the plants. The collection contains about 380 taxa of eucalypts spread over a fairly large area (it is designed for vehicular access). The collection is well documented scientifically, with vouchers held at the National Herbarium of New South Wales. Some of the labels on trees reflect the conceptual taxonomy of Johnson and Hill in the 1980s, with eucalypt genera such as *Symphyomyrtus*, which were not later accepted. Entry to this botanic gardens at the time of writing was $9 per car. The gardens are open seven days a week.

Waite Arboretum

Located at Glen Osmond at the foot of the Mt Lofty Ranges on the plains south of Adelaide, the Waite Arboretum forms part of the Waite Campus of the University of Adelaide. It occupies 30 hectares of land and was established in 1928. The arboretum contains trees from Australia and around the world, planted in rows with roughly mown grass beneath. While most of the older plantings are exotic, in recent years the emphasis has been on eucalypts, with about 360 taxa currently grown. The more recent plantings are well documented and vouchered and the Waite herbarium has now been incorporated into the State Herbarium of South Australia. This arboretum is not primarily intended as a public park and labels or tags are sometimes difficult to find. There is free public access seven days a week and it deserves to have more visitors than it currently receives.

One of the mallee eucalypt sections of the Mount Annan Botanic Gardens in Campbelltown, Sydney. There is an extensive drive-through area of eucalypt plantings, with trees planted in taxonomic groupings.

Older dryland eucalypt plantings at the Waite Arboretum, Adelaide. More recent eucalypt plantings are in straight rows for ease of maintenance. PHOTO: NEIL SHIRLEY.

Burrendong Arboretum near Wellington in New South Wales has widely spaced plantings of eucalypts in rolling grasslands.

Burrendong Botanic Garden and Arboretum

Located at Mumbil, near Wellington on the western slopes of the Great Dividing Range in New South Wales, the 167-hectare Burrendong Arboretum was established in 1964. As well as the typical arboretum layout of trees with rough mown grass beneath, there are more intensively planted garden beds of plants from all over Australia. About 150 taxa of eucalypts are recorded and the spacious layout enables the forms of mature trees to be clearly seen. The large area is best seen by car, with walks to the various garden beds. The arboretum maintains its own herbarium of vouchers. It is administered by the Burrendong Arboretum Trust. There is a charge for entry, which at the time of writing was $5 per car via an honour system at the entrance gate.

Eucalypt display centres

Not many plant groups have special museums or education centres devoted to them, but the eucalypts have at least two, and not necessarily where you would expect them.

The oldest of these is in South America, in Brazil, and is called Museu do Eucalipto. It arose from the efforts of Edmundo Navarro de Andrade (1881–1941). He was born in Brazil and educated at a school of agronomy in Portugal. After his studies he joined the research team of the Jundiai Forest Garden in Brazil and had planted 32,000 eucalypts by 1906. In 1913 he visited Joseph Maiden in Sydney and brought seeds of an additional 150 species back to Brazil. Shortly after this, in 1916, work commenced on the Museu do Eucalipto at Rio Claro in the São Paulo area. Its aim was to store and display artefacts and wood samples and become a centre of knowledge on eucalypts. The museum still exists.

The Museu do Eucalipto in Brazil. At the entrance to the museum displaying eucalypts and their products is a bust of Edmundo Navarro de Andrade, a pioneer eucalypt advocate in South America.
PHOTO: AUGUSTO JERONIMO MARTINI.

The Eucalyptus Discovery Centre in Coleraine, western Victoria, in 2008.

The second display centre is in Coleraine, Victoria, and is associated with the Peter Francis Points Arboretum mentioned above. With the amalgamation of local governments in Victoria in 1994, the Council Chambers in Coleraine became vacant and the town initiated the Eucalyptus Discovery Centre as an interactive learning environment to showcase the genus. Discovery rooms explain the natural history and uses of different species and the ecosystems to which they belong. Combined with visits to the Arboretum, this centre became the focus for school and tertiary excursions to the region. Visits to the centre have waned in recent years following reduced funding for school excursions. Its future is now uncertain, with a proposal that the site be used for a new Coleraine hospital.

The interior of the Eucalyptus Discovery Centre at Coleraine in 2008, with displays about eucalypts and the nearby Peter Francis Points Arboretum.

WEEPING MALLEE (*Eucalyptus sepulcralis*)

A slender mallee, often with only two or three stems, this species occurs in a small area of Fitzgerald River National Park, Western Australia. At 6–7 metres it stands well above the surrounding low heath in an area known as Sepulcralis Hill. The smooth greyish bark on the trunks contrasts with the reddish bark on the mature branchlets. The graceful weeping habit ensures that it cannot be mistaken for any other tree in the area. The juvenile leaves are grey, but the adult leaves are glossy green and the creamy yellow flowers and prominent, barrel-shaped gumnuts help to weigh down the already pendulous branches. This rare plant is in limited cultivation but should be suitable for semi-arid areas. A similar species, *E. pendens*, occurs near Badgingarra, north of Perth. It differs by having a more spreading habit, smaller buds and fruits, and rarely exceeds 4 metres in height.

The flowers are held on slender weeping branches.

The wispy weeping habit of this tree ensures it cannot be confused with any other eucalypt.

Sydney Blue Gum (*Eucalyptus saligna*) used for flooring. Its main appeal is the wood's distinctive colour range. Classic Grade has less variation in the colour, while this Australiana Grade shows wide colour variation. PHOTO: BORAL TIMBER FLOORING.

20 Timber Production

THE 150 MILLION HECTARES OF AUSTRALIAN NATIVE FORESTS SET ASIDE FOR COMMERCIAL logging are concentrated in Tasmania, Victoria and the south-west of Western Australia, with significant areas still in coastal New South Wales and Queensland. These are managed on what is claimed to be a 'sustainable yield' basis by their respective authorities. There are also more than 800,000 hectares of eucalypt plantations, of which almost half are in Western Australia.

The timber industry in Australia produces an annual turnover of about $19 billion and in 2006–07 employed about 83,400 people. Australia has become the world's largest exporter of woodchips, shipping a record of over 6 million oven-dry metric tonnes (odmt) in 2007. Eucalypt chips, most of which are still from native forests, are by far the most common exported, accounting for approximately 70 per cent of the total woodchip exports in 2007, the remainder being softwood from pine plantations. Australia is the major supplier of hardwood chips to Japan and currently supplies 34 per cent of the Japanese total import volume. Eucalypt chip export prices more than doubled in the six years to 2008 and in that year were US$167/odmt when delivered on board a vessel in Tasmania.

The industry has not been without controversy in recent decades, where examples of clear-felling for woodchips and logging of old-growth forests have been highlighted and caused anger from environment movements. To some extent these problems have been alleviated through the signing of ten 'Regional Forest Agreements' between 1997 and 2001. Under these agreements, significant areas of eucalypt forest in New South Wales, Victoria, Western Australia and Tasmania were declared new conservation reserves, and stronger commitments were given to the sustainable management of forest outside the reserve estate. However, there is still considerable opposition in many quarters to any continued logging of old-growth forest, a position supported by recent research which shows their value as carbon sinks to alleviate human-induced greenhouse gas emissions. Eucalypts have been exported to most temperate and subtropical countries of the world and significant plantations are being grown in Brazil, Chile, Hawaii, India, China, Africa, New Zealand and South-East Asia.

Top timber eucalypts

In Victoria and Tasmania, Mountain Ash (*E. regnans*) is considered the best timber for the pulp and paper industry and is also used for heavy construction, plywood, furniture and flooring, where its pale-blonde colouring is favoured by builders. Alpine Ash (*E. delegatensis*) from Victoria, Tasmania and southern New South Wales is used increasingly for sliced and peeled veneer because of its pale colour and uniform, straight grain, but it is also used both in Australia and overseas for flooring and cupboards.

Tallowwood (*E. microcorys*) is generally considered the best hardwood in New South Wales. It is used for heavy engineering construction, poles, flooring and decking. The timber is a pale yellowish-brown, slightly oily in nature and extremely durable, with an interlocking grain, but its greasy texture makes it difficult to glue. It occurs in north coastal New South Wales and is frequently associated with other good timber trees such as Flooded Gum (*E. grandis*), Sydney Blue Gum (*E. saligna*) and Blackbutt (*E. pilularis*). The Stringybark Messmate (*E. obliqua*), widespread in hilly and mountainous country in south-eastern Australia including Tasmania, produces a straight-grained, brown timber, which is easily worked and glued and is used extensively for furniture, house building and flooring, as well as for pulp.

In Western Australia, Jarrah (*E. marginata*) represents about two-thirds of the total timber production of the state. It occurs on red loams on the Darling Range escarpment and on poorer soils, where it may only reach mallee proportions. The timber is red to reddish-brown and is resistant to termites, making it suitable for house building, piles and wharf construction. It finishes well and is prized in high-quality furniture making.

The other important timber tree in Western Australia is Karri (*E. diversicolor*). Occurring in the wet forest of the south-west, it produces larger lengths of straight, knot-free timber than any other hardwood species. The wood is red, hard and tough and is used for roof construction, flooring and as support timbers in mines.

Marri (*Corymbia calophylla*) usually occurs in forests dominated by Jarrah and Karri. Although still used for tool handles, case manufacture and fence posts, it is now the principal species used for woodchip production in Western Australia. It is resistant to the fungus disease *Phytophthora cinnamomi*.

Of the other *Corymbia* species, the Spotted Gum (*C. maculata*) and the related Lemon-scented Gum (*C. citriodora*) and Large-leaved Spotted Gum (*C. henryi*) are probably the most significant timber trees. Occurring in and near coastal areas of New South Wales and Queensland, the timber has been used for tool handles, poles and plywood. In recent times these

Unfinished timber samples, *left to right:* Mountain Ash (*Eucalyptus regnans*), Jarrah (*E. marginata*), Tallowwood (*E. microcorys*) and River Red Gum (*E. camaldulensis*).

species have also been used in plantations in Queensland and South Africa for their pulp production potential.

The Tasmanian Blue Gum (*E. globulus*) and the River Red Gum (*E. camaldulensis*) are probably the two most widely grown eucalypts in the world but although their timber is used for construction work, its main use is for pulp, firewood and charcoal production. As River Red Gum is termite resistant, it is popular for landscaping, fencing and outdoor furniture, and better quality logs may be used for furniture and veneer.

Today, the timber resource presented by the above species and many other eucalypts is still enormous. Due to their abundance and variety, eucalypts provide timber for many different applications, from heavy construction work, flooring, firewood, cabinet making, fence posts, charcoal and farm use, and inevitably as wood pulp for the chipboard and paper industries. The timber varies in colour, hardness, durability and resistance to borers and termites.

FLOODED GUM (*Eucalyptus grandis*)

Occurring in wet forests from near Newcastle to north Queensland, this tall, fast-growing tree reaching up to 75 metres high is used extensively in forestry plantations in northern New South Wales. It has smooth bark with a permanent stocking of rough greyish bark reaching several metres up the trunk. It is closely related to the Sydney Blue Gum (*E. saligna*), differing mainly in the nature of the valves of the gumnuts and the fact that Flooded Gum does not have a lignotuber. The leaves are paler on the underside and the small white flowers are seen from late summer to winter. The pinkish timber is used for general construction, joinery, plywood, panelling, boat building and flooring. While it is an important timber tree in Australia, massive planting programs have been carried out in South Africa and Brazil, where hybrids with River Red Gum (*E. camaldulensis*) have been developed.

Right: Straight trunks showing the bark in a picnic area near Wauchope, New South Wales.

Far right: A beautiful example of a Flooded Gum in the Royal Botanic Gardens, Sydney.

Naming eucalypt timbers

Some mention should be made of the naming of timber as distinct from the naming of tree species. There are quite a few anomalies, but we will use one example. The common name 'Mountain Ash' is used for *E. regnans*, but timber from this tree is usually sold as 'Victorian Ash' if it comes from Victoria. The timber merchant is likely to tell you that it is the same timber as 'Tasmanian Oak' from Tasmania. But don't be too sure. The Tasmanian Government's tastimber website states that Tasmanian Oak

is the name used for three almost identical species of eucalypt hardwoods that are normally marketed collectively: *E. delegatensis* grows at higher altitudes, while *E. regnans* is found in wetter sites, and *E. obliqua*, which has a wide distribution, occurs in wet forests but also extends into drier areas.

This website also states that Tasmanian Oak has the alternative name of 'Australian Ash'.

BLACKBUTT (*Eucalyptus pilularis*)

This tall forest tree may reach 70 metres high and occurs in coastal areas from Eden in southern New South Wales to south-east Queensland. It is one of the most important timber trees in eastern Australia, where its timber is used for house construction, flooring, plywood and veneer. Blackbutt timber was considered the best for woodblocks used in the construction of roads in the early days of the colony. About 40 per cent of the plantation timber in New South Wales is Blackbutt and it is also planted in New Zealand. It is readily recognised by the persistent bark on the lower part of the trunk and the smooth white bark above, which sheds in long ribbons. The timber is brown to yellow-brown and is resistant to termites and lyctid borer. Trees grow quickly in moist forests on rich loamy soils.

The contrasting lower and upper bark of the Blackbutt can be clearly seen.
PHOTO: D. GREIG/APII.

TALLOWWOOD (*Eucalyptus microcorys*)

Tallowwood grows in wet forests from Newcastle in New South Wales to Fraser Island in south-east Queensland. This eucalypt forms a medium-sized to tall tree, occasionally reaching 60 metres high and often occurring in pure stands. Its bark is soft and fibrous and is retained into the small branches. Tallowwood gets its name from the brown, oily timber which makes excellent flooring that may be given a high polish. The white or cream flowers tend to be produced heavily every three to four years. Extensive forest plantations may be seen in northern New South Wales and also in many parts of Africa and Hawaii. As a tree for farms and rural properties, it forms a handsome shade specimen but is resistant only to light frosts. Tallowwood is a favourite food tree for Koalas and is frequently planted for this purpose.

The base of a Tallowwood tree, showing the fibrous bark.

The flowers of the Tallowwood are quite small.

A dining table and chairs made of Jarrah (*Eucalyptus marginata*), at the Wood Works Gallery, Canberra.

21 | Timber Crafts

THERE IS A BROAD RANGE OF USES FOR EUCALYPT TIMBER—FROM THE ROUGH-HEWN structures of the early colonists and subsequent major infrastructure projects, to the furniture and craft objects discussed here. In exploring the use of eucalypts by artisans and craftsmen, we will look firstly at eucalypts as cabinet timbers for the construction of furniture, and then at their use in craft and art objects, although there is often not a clear distinction between the two.

Eucalypts were certainly not a first choice for cabinet timber in Australia. There were other, more suitable, local timbers like Red Cedar (*Toona ciliata*) which could be worked much like the timbers more familiar to the early furniture makers, and there was ready access to imported timber such as Mahogany (*Swietenia* spp. from the Americas and *Khaya* spp. from Africa). The one exception was Jarrah (*Eucalyptus marginata*), which had use as a cabinet timber because of its working properties and its appearance. There was also a niche use of River Red Gum (*E. camaldulensis*). But most others—even Mountain Ash (*E. regnans*)—were seen as 'timbers of last resort'.

There was another major problem with the use of eucalypts as cabinet timbers—glue. The traditional glues developed for cabinet making did not work well on most eucalypt wood. But with little interest in the timber, there was not much incentive to innovate.

Then international events intervened. The 1992 Rio Earth Summit in Brazil came up with a set of principles to underlie the sustainable management of forests worldwide. In Australia the supply of many imported timbers started to dry up. The industry had to reinvent itself and take another look at those timbers of last resort. And a glue had to be developed that was suitable for eucalypt wood.

Spotted Gum (*Corymbia maculata*) was one of those difficult-to-glue timbers, but its grain was appealing to the Asian market. In the early 1990s, Australia attempted a marketing campaign in Asia for furniture made from Spotted Gum. Unfortunately, the furniture soon fell to pieces when the glued joints failed in the humid Asian environment—with a very negative impact on Australia's export reputation.

A table and chair made from Spotted Gum (*Corymbia maculata*), demonstrating its high strength and elasticity and its suitability for fine workmanship. These demonstration pieces were made by George Ingham and Ian Guthridge at the Canberra School of Art (1997–98) to explore the potential of plantation Spotted Gum despite its difficulties.
PHOTO: KATE SHAW.

161

The solution was to manufacture glues developed specifically with eucalypts in mind, and by the mid-1990s companies like AV Syntec were bringing such glues onto the market. As new glues became available, a range of timbers such as Blackbutt (*E. pilularis*) and Messmate (*E. obliqua*) could be used as cabinet timbers. Even the notoriously difficult Spotted Gum now had potential as a furniture timber.

At the same time there was a marketing campaign promoting the appeal of native timber species. 'Ash' was extensively promoted as 'Oak' for marketing purposes and Tasmanian Oak started to become a prestige timber. What had previously been considered blemishes in eucalypt timber grain began to be promoted under the banner of 'natural feature hardwoods'.

The rising awareness of the devastation of the world's tropical hardwood forests following the Rio Earth Summit enabled another marketing initiative: buying eucalypt timbers helped save the world's rainforests.

Eucalypts and artist craftsmen

Many decorative uses of timber involve wood-turning—using metal tools to change the shape of a fast-spinning piece of wood in a lathe. Wood-turning had been part of nineteenth-century cabinet making in Australia, with door knobs, stair balustrades and the like, but of course eucalypts were not a timber of choice. Spinning eucalypt wood would blunt the soft steel of the old turning tools much faster than tools, such as a plane, working fixed wood.

Even at the height of the Arts and Crafts Movement in Australia in the early twentieth century, when wood-carving was popular, wood-turning was not part of that scene, nor was the use of eucalypt timber. In fact it was *Acacia* timber that first brought our native hardwoods to prominence as suitable for wood-turning when King Edward VII was given a walking-stick made of turned Gidgee (*Acacia cambagei*). It was not long before items of turned Mulga (*Acacia aneura*) with its distinctive yellow and chocolate grain, were so common they became kitsch.

By the 1970s, wood-turning as a genuine artist craftsman activity in Australia had been in decline for many years. In North America it was in revival mode, and visits in the mid-1970s by people such as Canadian Stephen Hogbin (b. 1942) had a profound influence on the way Australian craftsmen started to view the possibilities of Australian timber. Instead of seeing the eucalypts' idiosyncratic grain, rough edges and insect damage as faults, people started to see them as features that could be highlighted.

While this was happening on the amateur front, there was also a revival in incorporating wood design courses in Australian art schools, notably those in Hobart, Canberra and Launceston. In 1979 the Crafts Council of Australia organised the first National Wood Conference, and various local guilds started to form.

Artists started to see the beauty of using recycled timber, especially eucalypt wood, not only in wood-turning but in a range of sculptural objects and furniture. As old buildings were demolished, the beams and joists were keenly sought. Even old timber fence posts have found a second life in the hands of craftsmen.

One feature of eucalypt timber which has contributed considerably to its popularity as a wood-turning and sculpture medium is the common presence of 'burls' on the trunks of trees. These are woody growths in which the grain has grown in a deformed manner, often filled with knots and dormant buds, usually as a result of some sort of stress. It is not unusual to find beautiful eucalypt trees with part of their 'character', in the form of a burl, removed by chainsaw. While this does not destroy the tree, it does leave an ugly visual legacy.

With the rise in popularity of wood crafts in the last 30 years, there has also arisen a range of wood galleries to show off and sell the objects created by these artists. These include the Bungendore Wood Works Gallery near Canberra and the South Coast Wood Works Gallery near Denmark in Western Australia. Others, like the Sturt School for Wood at Mittagong in the southern highlands of New South Wales, combine a gallery with workshops and courses.

Above: A living trunk of a forest eucalypt with its burl removed by chainsaw. There is now a keen demand for such burls by wood workers. This one has a fungus growing from the wounded wood; damaging the tree always raises the potential for infection.

Top left: A bowl turned from the fine wood of a River Red Gum (*Eucalyptus camaldulensis*) by wood craftsman Terry Baker. PHOTO: BUNGENDORE WOOD WORKS GALLERY.

Second from top: The burl from a River Red Gum (*Eucalyptus camaldulensis*) has been turned into a platter with very strong markings.

Left: Wood-turned vases of Jarrah (*Eucalyptus marginata*) show off the beautiful colour of the timber.

Bottom left: Volute, a sculpture by artist Matthew Harding using the timber of Jarrah (*Eucalyptus marginata*). The deep red grain of the timber provides a contrast with the 'ebonised' dark surface. The ebonising stain technique uses a ferric solution to react with the tannins in the wood. Many artists use eucalypt timber as a medium and an inspiration, in this case part of a seed/regeneration series inspired by the 2003 Canberra bushfires. Harding said 'Eucalypts remind me of the phoenix metaphor with their inner vitality rising from the ashes.'
PHOTO: MATTHEW HARDING.

Bee hives located in eucalypt forest. They are moved around
on pallets to locations where eucalypts are flowering.

22 Honey Production

THE HONEY BEE (*APIS MELLIFERA*) WAS INTRODUCED TO AUSTRALIA IN 1822 AS a food source and also to pollinate crops in the new colony. It soon became established, despite the presence of many native bees, and is now the source of an important Australian industry.

Honey production in Australia is worth about $60 million annually and approximately 77 per cent of this production comes from the flowers of eucalypts. Almost 10,000 apiarists manage about 500,000 hives and we export honey to 38 countries. Australia now ranks about ninth in the world for its honey production, behind China, America and Argentina.

Three types of honey from the supermarket that indicate from which eucalypt the honey was largely produced. *From left,* Ironbark (*Eucalyptus sideroxylon*), Pink Gum (*E. fasciculosa*) and Yellow Box (*E. melliodora*).

Honey bees require a supply of both nectar and pollen for their survival. Nectar is a sugary solution consisting mainly of sucrose, with some dextrose and levulose, and is produced by the nectar glands of the flower. Pollen or pollen grains are the male cells produced by the anthers of the flower. They vary in colour but are mostly cream or yellow.

After collecting the nectar in its proboscis, the bee stores it in its stomach and carries it back to the hive. On reaching the hive, the nectar is regurgitated and mixed with an enzyme known as invertase. It is stored in honeycomb cells in the hive and is thickened by the bees, who fan the cells with their wings to evaporate the water. When the nectar becomes sufficiently viscous, the bees seal each cell with beeswax produced by glands in the abdomen. The stored honey may be used by the bees as food in cold weather or may be mixed with pollen to feed their brood.

Pollen consists mainly of protein and fat, in addition to carbohydrates, vitamins and minerals, and provides the bees with half of their food requirements. Pollen is collected using small brushes on the front pairs of legs and transferred during flight to the sacs on the rear legs. Back at the hive, the pollen is transferred to empty honeycomb cells and made available to the brood as required. Pollen is mixed with nectar to make 'bee bread' and this is fed to the larvae as a food rich in protein. Bees are able to comfortably

Red Ironbark, or Mugga (*Eucalyptus sideroxylon*) is a favourite with beekeepers. Its flowers can be white, pink or red.

travel 1–3 kilometres and have been recorded moving up to 8 kilometres from their hive to collect their payload.

Apiarists who use eucalypts as their target species follow the flowering patterns of the eucalypts in their area and move their hives accordingly. The flowering habits of eucalypts are strongly influenced by the weather, particularly the rainfall. In extended drought conditions flowering is often sparse. Also, some eucalypts tend to flower heavily every two to three years, others even less frequently. Honey production comes mainly from southern Australia, where New South Wales yields about 42 per cent of Australia's output, followed by Victoria with 19 per cent, Queensland with 15 per cent and South Australia with 13 per cent.

Most species of eucalypt yield some nectar and pollen, but the amount varies considerably between species and certain species are favoured for their nectar production while others are targeted for their pollen. Some of the major species used by the industry and their properties are summarised below.

- River Red Gum (*Eucalyptus camaldulensis*)—widely favoured for both its nectar and pollen production as well as its long flowering period. The honey is a light amber colour and has a distinctive but mild flavour. For this reason it is preferred in many overseas countries.
- White Box (*E. albens*)—a major source of both nectar and pollen in New South Wales, Victoria and southern Queensland. The honey is deep gold with amber tones, is smooth in the mouth and has a clean, light texture. In cold, wet winters bees may suffer digestive disorders when harvesting this species.

- Yellow Box (*E. melliodora*)—once regarded as the best honey producer in Queensland, New South Wales and Victoria, this species is becoming less common with clearing of its habitat. It is still an excellent nectar producer in good seasons but is not rich in pollen. The honey is a light amber colour and its light fluid texture is quite buttery in the mouth.
- Apple Box (*E. bridgesiana*)—produces excellent nectar and pollen and its flowering follows Yellow Box. As the two species share similar habitats, these areas are frequently favoured by apiarists.
- Red Ironbark or Mugga (*E. sideroxylon*)—considered the most reliable nectar producer in Australia but is poor in pollen. The honey is amber in colour and said to have an aroma of almonds and coconut.
- Snow Gum (*E. pauciflora*)—this widespread species produces good quantities of pollen but its nectar supply is poor. It complements other species with excellent nectar production.
- White Mallee (*E. dumosa*)—in good seasons the White Mallee is a major contributor to honey production in the semi-arid areas of New South Wales and South Australia. It gives a high yield of both nectar and pollen.

Kangaroo Island has a unique place in Australia's honey industry as it is thought to be the only place in the world where pure strains of the Ligurian bee exist. Importations were made from Liguria in Italy between 1881 and 1885 with the intention of breeding the bees to provide a future source of purebred queen bees for the beekeeping industry. The island was declared a Bee Sanctuary in 1885 and as the island is beyond the bee flight range from the mainland, the strain has remained pure and the island free of bee diseases. The Ligurian bee is very docile and produces a fine range of honeys from the several native eucalypts on the island. Sugar Gum (*E. cladocalyx*), White Mallee (*E. cylindriflora*) and Cup Gum (*E. cosmophylla*) are the main species concerned.

Eucalypt honey is said to have a variety of therapeutic and germicidal properties. It may be massaged into the skin to relieve muscle and joint pains, rheumatism and sprained ligaments. It is effective in the relief of insect bites and stings. As it produces ozone on exposure to the air, it has an antiseptic effect when applied to wounds, ulcers, burns and abrasions.

Overseas, eucalypt honey is widely produced, with River Red Gum and Tasmanian Blue Gum (*E. globulus*) being the most popular. In Portugal, honey produced from Tasmanian Blue Gum is said to have a taste resembling muscatel grapes.

Australian native bees

Australia has about ten species of social native bees which are stingless. These form their hives in hollows in eucalypt trees and gather nectar and pollen from eucalypts and other native wildflowers, often providing a useful pollination means for some of our native flora. As with the exotic honey bee, they also produce a tasty, tangy honey known as 'sugarbag honey', but the volume of production is very limited. Whereas a hive of honey bees may produce about 75 kilograms of honey per year, native bees produce about 1 kilogram. The flavour of sugarbag honey is said to be reminiscent of lemon and eucalyptus. In recent years native beekeeping has become popular as a hobby and as a means of pollinating crops. Hives are available commercially, using specially modified boxes from which honey may be harvested without harming the bees.

One of the species of native bee—stingless and much smaller than introduced honey bees.
PHOTO: GERARD SATHERLEY.

YELLOW BOX (*Eucalyptus melliodora*)

Renowned for its tasty honey production, the Yellow Box is widespread from western Victoria through the eastern tablelands and western slopes of New South Wales to south-east Queensland. It occurs on a variety of soils and varies in height from 10 to 30 metres, with a shady crown of green to grey-green leaves, sometimes with pendulous branches. The sweetly scented flowers are white, although a rare pink form has been recorded.

Yellow Box trees have been recorded flowering in most months, probably depending on rainfall. The bark is very variable, making the species difficult to identify without examining the flowers and gumnuts. Sometimes the whole trunk is rough with fibrous, thin, yellow-brown to grey flakes; in other specimens the trunk is almost all smooth and pale grey to yellow. The flowers produce huge quantities of honey and in a controlled taste test with other single-flower honeys, Yellow Box honey was the most favoured. The timber is hard and durable and is used for heavy construction, sleepers and poles. It also makes excellent firewood.

Yellow Box is frost hardy and on the tablelands it is highly regarded as a shelter tree on farms, providing protection for sheep and cattle.

Flowering trees are sought after by apiarists.

Trees are often left in farm paddocks for shelter.

RED IRONBARK OR MUGGA (*Eucalyptus sideroxylon*)

Red Ironbark forms a handsome tree to 25 metres, its grey to blue-grey foliage contrasting well with its dark-grey to black deeply furrowed and hard bark. Occurring in open woodland on the western slopes of New South Wales and extending to northern Victoria and south-east Queensland, it is used frequently in street and rural plantings in inland towns, where it is resistant to frosts. In Canberra it is planted extensively in open areas between residential developments and recovered well after the disastrous fires of 2003. The bark is impregnated with kino and this red, resinous material is seen secreting from the bark. Flowers are borne in sevens in the leaf axils and may be white, pink or red. They are seen for many months, from autumn to early summer, and their nectar is enjoyed by parrots and honeyeaters.

Favoured by apiarists for its reliable nectar production, the honey is said to have a flavour of almonds and coconut. The foliage has been used for oil extraction and the timber is hard and used for heavy construction and sleepers. It is also good for firewood, as it burns slowly and generates good heat. Red Ironbark is easy to propagate from seed and accepts most soils in a sunny situation.

A closely related species, *E. tricarpa*, occurs in coastal south-eastern New South Wales and Victoria. It differs in having its flowers in threes instead of sevens and has slightly larger buds and gumnuts. Some intermediates have been found in Gippsland, Victoria and near Eden in New South Wales.

This section of an Ironbark trunk shows the pockets of dark kino gum in the bark. The kino is responsible for the tree's black colour.

Top: From a distance the bark of these trees looks black. This one is near Mudgee, New South Wales.

23 Cut Flowers, Foliage and Gumnuts

INTEREST IN NATIVE PLANTS FOR USE IN THE CUT-FLOWER MARKET HAS INCREASED dramatically in the last 30 years, with members of the Proteaceae family being particularly popular, but more recently eucalypts have come to the fore and they now form a large part of the market, both locally and on the export scene. The export market for Australian cut flowers and foliage was estimated at about $50 million in 2007, with eucalypt material rated about ninth in the popularity stakes. About 50 per cent of this export market goes to Japan, 30 per cent to North America and about 14 per cent to Europe. The expanding consumer market in China is also seen as a huge potential market. Locally, interest is high as well, but it is difficult to isolate the figures for eucalypts. Eucalypts are being grown for foliage in several places overseas; Israel, Ireland, South America, the Mediterranean countries, New Zealand and parts of Africa all have plantations for this purpose.

The market for cut eucalypts may be considered in several categories:

- foliage used as fillers for floral arrangements
- foliage with buds, which may be colourful and add a focus to an arrangement
- flowers, which may be used as a feature for an arrangement
- gumnuts, which may or may not be used with foliage
- dried foliage.

Foliage as fillers

The foliage used as fillers is usually grey, bluish or silvery and often has a unique shape. This is usually juvenile growth before the foliage changes to the adult form. There are many species involved. Those from eastern Australia include Argyle Apple, often marketed as Silver Dollar Gum (*Eucalyptus cinerea*), Silver-leaved Mountain Gum (*E. pulverulenta*), Spinning Gum (*E. perriniana*), Apple Box (*E. bridgesiana*), Victorian

Opposite: The large, bold flowers of the Red Bull Mallee (*Eucalyptus pachyphylla*) are being assessed for their vase life.

Silver Gum (*E. crenulata*), Tasmanian Blue Gum (*E. globulus*) and two endemic Tasmanian species—Cider Gum (*E. gunnii*) and Heart-leaved Silver Gum (*E. cordata*). These all develop into trees and need to be pruned to enable them to be harvested readily and to maintain growth of the juvenile foliage.

From South Australia and Western Australia, the preferred species for foliage production are mallees. These include Book-leaf Mallee (*E. kruseana*), Southern Cross Mallee (*E. crucis*), Curly Mallee (*E. gillii*), and the most popular of all, Tallerack (*E. pleurocarpa*—still marketed under the incorrect name *E. tetragona*). These species mostly carry their juvenile foliage through to the adult stage, so they are more readily managed for harvesting, but some hard pruning encourages more shoots from the lignotubers and thus increases production. The foliage of these species often includes buds and even gumnuts, which add to the charm and interest of the branches.

TALLERACK (*Eucalyptus pleurocarpa*)

Tallerack occurs on the sandplains of southern Western Australia, near Esperance, and also has a small population north of Perth in similar situations. This mallee has smooth, grey-brown stems rarely exceeding 4 metres high and spreading to 8 metres. The young stems are squarish and clothed with a silvery-grey bloom. Grey-green leaves are oval with a short stalk and the buds and four-sided gumnuts are also silvery grey. The flowers are cream and seen mainly in late spring and summer. This species was grown and sold incorrectly as *E. tetragona* for many years. The forced name change is unfortunate as 'tetragona', meaning four-sided, so aptly described the plant's characteristics. Although this plant tends to become straggly with age, it may be pruned hard to the lignotuber and new growths will rejuvenate its appearance. Tallerack is one of the most popular species for cut foliage, both dried and fresh, for the florist trade and the gumnuts are exported. Cultivation is easy in well-drained soil and a sunny situation with low humidity, provided heavy frosts are avoided. Unlike many grey foliage eucalypts, little insect damage has been experienced with the foliage.

The beautiful grey foliage makes Tallerack an attractive feature shrub for the garden.

As well as having square stems, the flowers have four divisions.

CORAL GUM
(*Eucalyptus torquata*)

Coral Gum forms a small, spreading tree to about 10 metres high, usually with a single trunk of hard, dark-grey, rough bark. It occurs naturally in the Goldfields area of Western Australia. The small branches are smooth and grey. The buds are swollen and ribbed at the base and have a long, curved cap that is also ribbed at the base. The flowers are usually pink but sometimes cream and are seen for much of the year. This ornamental tree is used extensively in roadside plantings and parks and gardens in semi-arid and winter rainfall areas, where it frequently hybridises with *E. woodwardii*. It will survive in areas that have become slightly saline. The flowers are useful for cutting and have a good vase life. Most soils are suitable and a well-drained sunny site is preferred. Coral Gum has been used in California and Israel and is suitable as a container plant as it flowers when very young. It is a good honey producer.

Coral Gum beautifully describes the most common flower colour for this tree.

Foliage with colourful buds or flowers

Most of the species used in this category are found naturally in Western Australia. The one exception is the pink-flowered form of the Red Ironbark, or Mugga (*E. sideroxylon*). This eastern species has attractive blue-grey foliage and delicate, drooping sprays of small pink flowers, which are recorded for many months of the year. Of the more popular western species we have Coral Gum (*E. torquata*), Fuchsia Gum (*E. dolichorhyncha* or *E. forrestiana*), Silver Princess (*E. caesia* subsp. *magna*), Illyarrie (*E. erythrocorys*), Yarldarlba (*E. youngiana*) and Lemon-flowered Gum (*E. woodwardii*). The flowers of these species are not large, but enhance the foliage with their colour.

Flowers which may be used as features

The eucalypts used as features in arrangements are Western Australian or tropical species with large, colourful flowers. It is only in the last few years that eucalypt species have been considered for the cut-flower market and some of them are still being assessed for their vase life and production requirements. Those that appear to have the most potential are Mottlecah (*E. macrocarpa*), Rose Mallee (*E. rhodantha*), Bell-fruited Mallee (*E. preissiana*), Dowerin Rose (*E. pyriformis*), Red Bull Mallee (*E. pachyphylla*), the tropical species Scarlet Gum (*E. phoenicea*), Darwin Woollybutt (*E. miniata*) and Swamp Bloodwood (*Corymbia ptychocarpa*) and its various hybrids with the Western Australian Red Flowering Gum (*C. ficifolia*).

SCARLET GUM (*Eucalyptus phoenicea*)

One of several colourful eucalypts in the tropics, Scarlet Gum occurs from the eastern Kimberley through the Northern Territory, with an isolated occurrence near Cooktown in Queensland. It has soft, flaky, orange-brown bark retained to the small branches and brilliant clusters of orange to scarlet flowers for much of the year. Its fruit are also interesting, being cylindrical with a flared mouth and about 3 centimetres long. Occurring on sandstone escarpments and stony ridges, the Scarlet Gum may reach 12 metres high and is occasionally multi-trunked. It is a wonderful plant for home gardens in the tropics, where its ample flow of nectar encourages honeyeaters and parrots. It is readily propagated from seed and is reputed to flower in its second year. Research is currently underway to consider its potential as a cut flower.

A closely related species, *E. ceracea*, known as the Seppelt Range Gum, occurs in a remote and inaccessible part of the northern Kimberleys. Its grey stalkless juvenile leaves are retained into the crown of the tree and its buds and gumnuts are also grey. It is listed as vulnerable under the Australian Government *Environment Protection and Biodiversity Conservation Act 1999*. When seed becomes available, it would be a handsome addition to the garden.

A Scarlet Gum from near Timber Creek in the Northern Territory.

This plant is growing in a private garden in Brisbane, Queensland.

SPINNING GUM (*Eucalyptus perriniana*)

Forming a mallee or small straggly tree to 7 metres, the Spinning Gum makes an intriguing specimen tree for gardens in cold areas. Its bark is smooth and sheds in long ribbons. The grey foliage is its unique feature. The juvenile leaves are round, about 8 centimetres in diameter and joined at the base to form a circle around the stem. When dry, they remain on the stem and are free to spin in the wind. The juvenile leaves are retained well into the tree, when in most cases some conventional adult, lance-shaped leaves are formed. The Spinning Gum occurs in subalpine areas in south-eastern New South Wales, Victoria and at lower altitudes in Tasmania, where it is listed as rare. It adapts well to cultivation, accepting heavy frosts and temperatures down to −10°C. The foliage is cut for the florist trade and used both fresh and dried. It is being cultivated in the United Kingdom and America.

Because the leaves of the Spinning Gum are joined around the stem, they cannot fall off when they die.

DOWERIN ROSE (*Eucalyptus pyriformis*)

This low mallee, found north and north-east of Perth. is readily distinguished by its large, pendulous flowers and gumnuts, which may reach 5.5 centimetres across. It is sometimes known as the Pear-fruited Mallee. The bark is smooth, shedding to a brownish grey and the foliage is bluish-green. The buds are prominently ribbed and the flowers, seen from winter to spring, may be yellow, cream or red. The gumnuts are also ribbed, with a raised disc, and are frequently used for floral arrangements. Plants grow well in arid and semi-arid areas, where they need a sunny site with excellent drainage. They are sensitive to heavy frosts.

These flowers will develop into attractive ribbed fruit.

LEMON-FLOWERED GUM (*Eucalyptus woodwardii*)

This small- to medium-sized mallet may reach 10 metres high with a smooth white bark, shedding in long ribbons to reveal pale-pink bark beneath. The branches are pendulous and grey and the thick leaves are also blue-grey. The handsome, bright-yellow flowers are borne in clusters of seven, about 5 centimetres in diameter, and tend to weigh down the branches, adding to its ornamental effect. Lemon-flowered Gum occurs in a restricted area near Kalgoorlie in Western Australia in slightly alkaline sandy loam. It is commonly used as a street tree in semi-arid areas of western Victoria and South Australia and is also useful in gardens and parks in America and Israel, as it is resistant to drought and frosts. The species has hybridised with *E. torquata* to form the well-known hybrid *E.* 'Torwood'. The flowers are valued by apiarists for honey production.

A roadside planting of the Lemon-flowered Gum in Kerang, northern Victoria.

Clusters of flowers make this tree spectacular in season.

The woody fruit of Kingsmill's Mallee (*Eucalyptus kingsmillii*) adds interest to dried floral arrangements.

Gumnuts used with or without foliage

The unique shape and often silvery appearance of many eucalypt gumnuts have made them popular for floral arrangements. The Tallerack leads the way with its waxy silver foliage and gumnuts of the same colour. Book-leaf Mallee, Mottlecah, Rose Mallee, Silver Princess and Curly Mallee have similar properties. Others with uniquely shaped gumnuts include Red Bull Mallee, Dowerin Rose, Kingsmill's Mallee (*E. kingsmillii*) and most of the *Corymbia* species. Marri (*C. calophylla*) is particularly popular and large bunches of the gumnuts are frequently exported.

Dried foliage

Eucalypt foliage has been dried for floral work for many years. There are two methods used for drying:

1. Bunches may be hung upside down on stretched wires in a dark, airy shed or room until most of the water in the product has been removed. By hanging the bunches upside down, the stems remain straight. It is important to remove the picked foliage from sunlight as quickly as possible to retain the natural colour. The presence of light and the water in the fresh foliage causes oxidation and the leaves may discolour. The length of time for the foliage to dry is dependent on the humidity and the temperature of the area.

2. The second method is to stand the freshly picked foliage in a plastic container in a mixture of glycerine and water and allow the stems to suck up the liquid. The optimum environment to use this method is at a temperature of about 22°C, 50 per cent humidity, and in good light but not direct sunlight.

A stock preserving solution may be made by adding 250 millilitres of glycerine to 600 millilitres of water and adding half a teaspoon of powdered citric acid. Use 100 millilitres of this solution to every 100 grams of foliage. The quantities are important as too little solution will make the foliage brittle and too much may cause bleeding of the foliage and lead to staining of furnishings. Cut 2 centimetres off the base of the stems just prior to immersing them in the liquid. Allow the foliage to remain in the container until it has absorbed the solution. For most eucalypts this may take five to seven days. The treated foliage will remain soft and more lifelike and will remain this way indefinitely.

Some floral decorators prefer to artificially colour their foliage by adding a systemic vegetable dye to the above solution. While this may not be to everyone's taste, some suppliers in America offer up to ten different-coloured eucalypt foliage lines. The industry is shrinking, with only about three to five businesses left that actually grow, preserve and process their own leaves.

Another innovation used by florists with species such as Spinning Gum (*E. perriniana*), where the leaves surround the stems, is to wait until the leaves have loosened from the stem and push them to the end of the stem to form a flower-like rosette.

In America 'preserved eucalyptus' is sold in a range of colours. This is listed as 'Paprika' in the catalogue of the International Decoratives Co., which started marketing preserved eucalypt leaves in the 1950s.
PHOTO: INTERNATIONAL DECORATIVES.

Cultivation of eucalypts for foliage production

Before embarking on a eucalypt foliage project, it is important to recognise both the natural habitat of the target species and climatic and soil conditions of the proposed site. As many of the species suitable for use as ornamental foliage occur naturally in semi-arid zones, it would be useless to try to cultivate them on the humid east coast. Similarly, tropical species must be grown in a frost-free zone.

Soil should generally be well drained, with a pH of between 6 and 7. If the pH is far outside this range, some attempt should be made to adjust it, as problems with trace elements may occur. Access to irrigation is also essential as even semi-arid species will require additional water in extreme conditions. When planting, consider the ultimate height and spread of the species and space plants to ensure that plenty of air movement occurs through the plantation. This will minimise leaf fungal infections, which can cause serious disfiguration of the leaf surface. Weed control is also vital to ensure a healthy plantation.

Some fertiliser will benefit the plant response, particularly in the first few years of growth. A dressing of processed fowl manure (such as Dynamic Lifter) should be applied in the late spring and again in autumn when the soil is moist. It should be followed by a further watering.

The degree of pruning required will depend on the species. Mallees will benefit by annual hard pruning to encourage new shoots from the lignotuber. Tree species whose cut foliage relies on the production of juvenile foliage should also be regularly pruned. Other tree species grown for flower or gumnut production must be pruned from time to time to allow easy harvesting.

Many of the desirable eucalypt species with silvery foliage are also subject to insect and fungal disease attack. While it is worthwhile to keep spraying to a minimum, chewing insects such as Christmas Beetles, Paropsis Beetles and looper caterpillars may reach serious proportions and must be controlled by the relevant insecticide. Similarly, scale insects and psyllids

ILLYARRIE
(*Eucalyptus erythrocorys*)

Remarkable for its colourful flowers, the Illyarrie is commonly used as a street tree in drier, frost-free areas of all states. It forms a small tree to 8 metres, or sometimes develops a mallee habit. The trunks are smooth and the emerging flowers have a bright-red, four-lobed bud cap. The large flowers are borne in threes and have four tufts of vivid yellow stamens. The sculptured gumnuts are large and grooved and often used in floral arrangements. Although it occurs naturally in undulating limestone soils in coastal areas north of Perth, Illyarrie has been cultivated in most soil types.

The red, sculptural buds of the Illyarrie contrast with the bright-yellow flowers.

ARGYLE APPLE (*Eucalyptus cinerea*)

A tree that grows to 15 metres high, Argyle Apple retains its rough, fibrous bark into the small branches. The bark is grey at the surface but reddish-brown underneath. The tree's main feature is its handsome, silvery-grey juvenile foliage, which is round and stem-clasping and retained into the canopy of the tree. Adult leaves are also grey, but lance-shaped with a short stalk. Argyle Apple occurs in the central and southern tablelands of New South Wales and into Victoria. The flowers are white and borne in threes in winter and spring. The juvenile foliage, marketed as Silver Dollar Gum, is harvested for floral arrangements and may be used fresh or dried. Coppiced plantations are grown in southern Europe for this purpose. In America it has been used as a pot plant and kept small by regular pruning. Its small size makes it suitable for small gardens, where it is hardy in most soils and resistant to frosts. Trees may be seen in the United Kingdom, where the tallest specimen is recorded in Devon at 18 metres high. A second subspecies, subsp. *triplex*, has been described. It has a high percentage of adult leaves and occurs in three isolated locations near Canberra.

An Argyle Apple flowering, with its silver-grey foliage.

Top: The silvery-grey foliage makes Argyle Apple popular for urban ornamental plantings.

may cause damage, and treatment with white oil applied in the early morning or evening is an effective control.

Leaf spotting is usually caused by a fungus and the most common causal organism is a pathogen known as *Mycosphaerella*, several species being involved. It causes lesions on the leaf which vary in size from a few millimetres to 80 per cent of the leaf surface. Fungal infection is worse in humid conditions and good aeration of the plantation is beneficial. Advice on treatment should be sought from the local Department of Agriculture.

Harvesting the crop is best done in the early morning when the foliage is turgid, ensuring that the tips are not too soft or they will droop. For standard bunches, cuts should be about 50 centimetres long and placed in a bucket of water as soon as possible after harvest. They are then stored in a coolroom kept at about 2°C until ready to pack in boxes for market.

The Plant Research Centre at the Waite Institute of the University of Adelaide has an ongoing and active involvement in examining potential species for use as cut foliage and flowers.

BOOKLEAF MALLEE
(*Eucalyptus kruseana*)

More common in cultivation than it is in the wild, this small mallee rarely exceeds 3 metres high. It is prized for its handsome foliage, which is silvery-grey with stem-clasping round leaves about 2 centimetres in diameter. The juvenile leaves are retained throughout the tree. The bark is smooth and coppery bronze, near the base shedding in ribbons. The greenish-yellow flowers are borne close together near the ends of branches in autumn and winter. Bookleaf Mallee is rare but not considered endangered as it occurs on three granite outcrops east and south-east of Kalgoorlie, Western Australia. While it grows well in climates with a winter rainfall, success has also been had on the east coast. It may be propagated readily from seed and enjoys a well-drained sunny site in the garden. Flowers may be expected in the second year from seed. Although often growing in an ungainly shape, being a mallee, it responds well to pruning and is hardy to all but the severest frosts. In America, potted specimens have been used indoors and it is generally available in American nurseries. The foliage is sought after for floral arrangements and it may be used fresh or dried. Ferdinand von Mueller named the species after a fellow German pharmacist, John Kruse.

A Bookleaf Mallee flowering beautifully at the Australian Arid Zone Botanic Gardens in Port Augusta, South Australia.

MOTTLECAH
(*Eucalyptus macrocarpa*)

Mottlecah is a sprawling mallee reaching 3 metres high and growing in dry sand plains north and east of Perth in Western Australia. It has the largest flowers and fruits of any eucalypt. The leaves are silvery-grey, more or less heart-shaped and clasp the stems, while the red, stalkless flowers are borne singly in the leaf axils and are about 10 centimetres in diameter with yellow tips to the anthers. The huge gumnuts are squat, up to 9 centimetres across and coated with a grey bloom. Flowers, gumnuts and foliage are used in floral arrangements. The plant grows best in semi-arid areas, or temperate regions with a winter rainfall. It is in cultivation in California. A second subspecies, subsp. *elachantha*, is recognised. It occurs in the northern part of the range and has smaller buds and gumnuts. The Rose Mallee (*Eucalyptus rhodantha*) is very similar to

the Mottlecah but differs in the flowers being borne on a short stalk. It occurs in a restricted area north of Perth and is listed as vulnerable.

Eucalyptus macrocarpa subsp. *elachantha*.

The plant is usually a straggly shrub.

DARWIN WOOLLYBUTT (*Eucalyptus miniata*)

A common, medium-sized tree to 25 metres in the Kimberley and across the Northern Territory just into Queensland, the Darwin Woollybutt is recognised most easily by its bark. The trunk is clothed with rough, fibrous, reddish-brown bark for several metres and the upper bark is smooth and white. It is very common in open grassy forests in deep sandy soils, and visitors to Kakadu National Park will pass many hectares of this attractive tree along the Arnhem Highway. The branches, buds and gumnuts have a silvery-grey bloom. Clusters of showy orange flowers are borne in the leaf axils from summer through to spring and are followed by the large, barrel-shaped ribbed gumnuts to 6 centimetres long. This is an ideal tree for gardens and parks in the drier tropics, as birds are attracted to the nectar and cockatoos enjoy the seed when the gumnuts are near mature.

Darwin Woollybutt may be propagated readily from seed and on germination the seed leaves are produced just above ground level, an unusual characteristic for eucalypts. Preferring a sunny well-drained position, it is small enough for the average garden. This species may be readily distinguished from the related *E. phoenicea* by its distinctive bark, much larger gumnuts and the flower clusters, which have fewer flowers. Hollowed trunks have been used by Aborigines for making didgeridoos.

The contrasting bark of the lower and upper parts of the tree can be seen in the photo at top right.

The orange flowers make the Darwin Woollybutt attractive for home gardens in the drier north.

A wool and cotton rug, woven and dyed by Eva Butchart using natural eucalypt dyes, in about 1928. The motif probably represents the Red Flowering Gum (*Corymbia ficifolia*). GIFT OF NAIRNE BUTCHART, 1981/NGA.

24 Dyes

Five thousand years ago the Chinese are known to have used vegetable matter to dye the fibres used in weaving. By about 4000 years ago we know that the Egyptians had refined this process by using a mordant to increase the range and depth of colours. This technique remained basically unchanged around the world until the mid-nineteenth century, when chemical dyes started to be developed, initially derived from coal tar.

In the late twentieth century, fabric dyeing using vegetable dyes had a revival in Western countries, with a return to the basics through various handweavers and spinners guilds. During this revival, people sought to add a local or national element by exploring the potential of their own native plants. In Australia, eucalypts proved a rich source of colouring.

In explaining the use of natural dyes, we must first look at the fibres used in weaving. These are basically protein fibres such as wool and silk, derived from animals, and cellulose fibres such as cotton, linen and hemp, derived from plants.

In very simple terms, the dyes derived from plants such as eucalypts tend to be slightly acidic and bond readily to the slightly alkaline protein fibres. The cellulose fibres tend to be neutral and require pre-treatment by soaking in a protein-rich or alkaline solution before being introduced to the dye.

Mordants are basically substances that are added to the process in order to assist, fix or change the reaction between the fibre and the dye. They act as a bridge or catalyst in the process. Usually fibres are introduced to the mordant before being introduced to the dye, but the mordant can in fact be the container, such as a copper, aluminium or iron pot, in which the process takes place. Different metal containers can influence the dye reaction in different ways.

In the early history of European settlement in Australia, the dyeing industry did not develop. The First Fleet, on their way to Australia via South America, picked up prickly pear plants (*Opuntia* sp.) and the cochineal scale insects that feed on them, with the obvious intention that these insects would provide the red dye for the soldiers' coats, but

A selection of colours achieved using eucalypt dyes by Jean Carman in the mid 1970s.

nothing seems to have come of this. The colony seems to have relied on the looms and industry of England for all its fabrics.

Joseph Maiden in 1887 commented on a yellow colouring from the Red Stringybark (*Eucalyptus macrorhyncha*), but a couple of years later, in his book *Useful Native Plants of Australia* (1889), he says:

> Australia certainly does not appear to be a land which can boast of its native vegetable dyes. But it is only fair to observe that practically nothing has been done in the way of experiments with our raw dyestuffs.

Henry Smith (1852–1924), an industrial chemist in Sydney working with the Technological Museum, followed Maiden's lead. In 1898 he published a paper 'On Myrticolorin, the Yellow Dye Material of Eucalyptus Leaves'. Later that year he followed with another paper in which he analysed the commercial potential of the dye and compared it with the less easily produced equivalent, quercitron, derived from the bark of the American Black Oak (*Quercus velutina*), which at the time sold for £6 10s. per ton. Smith had successfully tested the myrticolorin dye on striped calico, and explained how simple it would be to set up a native industry to extract it, but it seemed no one took up his proposal. Perhaps business people could see that natural dyes were on the way out.

In the 1930s there was minor interest in eucalypts as dye sources, with a few people dabbling in the craft as part of the Arts and Crafts movement. Eva Butchart (c. 1875–1955) produced a small booklet entitled *Table Looms and Some Australian Dyes as Home Crafts* in which she devotes a few paragraphs to the extraction technique and colours obtained from eucalypts. Illustrated in the booklet is a rug in which she has woven a design of Red Flowering Gum (*Corymbia ficifolia*) using dyed wool, now in the National Gallery of Australia (see p. 182).

The real interest in Australian native dyes came in the 1970s with the rise of groups such as the Handweavers and Spinners Guild of Victoria. One person experimenting with eucalypts, first in Victoria and later in Queensland, was Jean Carman (1909–2005),

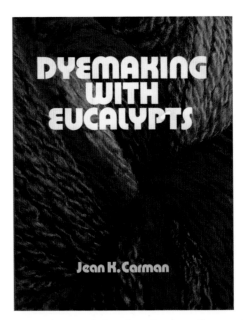

Dyemaking with Eucalypts by Jean Carman (1978).

who published *Dyemaking with Eucalypts* in 1978. She tested 240 species, sent to her from around Australia, and documented the colours produced in wool with different mordants and treatments.

In recent years another enthusiast has taken up the cause of eucalypt dyes—artist and designer India Flint (b. 1958). She has broadened the scope of her investigations to include fibres other than wool and tested a further 203 eucalypt species using a far more rigorous experimental approach. Flint pioneered another method of assessing the outcome of a eucalypt-mordant combination, which she calls 'eco-prints'. It involves steaming the leaf wrapped tightly in the fibre sample. The resulting take-up of the dye by the fabric not only gives a quickly assessable result, but to Flint offers the potential of various pattern designs on fabrics, which she has developed commercially.

For plain-coloured dyeing with protein fabrics such as wool, she suggests simmering the leaves of the chosen eucalypt in rainwater for about 45 minutes, then straining off all the leaf material. Next, immerse the textile or fibre to be dyed in the warm dye water, and heat slowly for 45 minutes but do not boil. Then allow the fibre to cool in the dye-bath. Remove excess

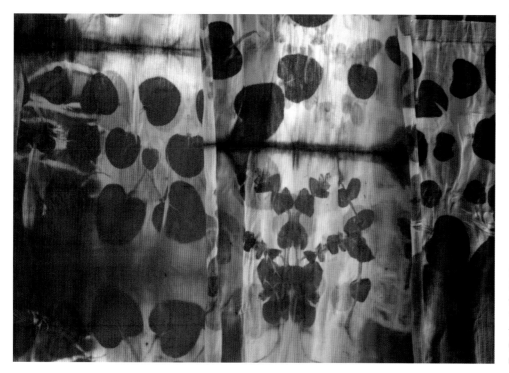

Merino wool fabric dyed by India Flint using her 'eco-print' method. The deep rich reds are from the leaves of Argyle Apple (*Eucalyptus cinerea*). PHOTO: INDIA FLINT.

Recycled Japanese kimono silk displaying the detail of India Flint's 'eco-print' method using the Tasmanian Blue Gum (*Eucalyptus globulus*). PHOTO: INDIA FLINT.

dye-water with the spin cycle of a washing machine and allow the fibre to dry in the shade.

Flint has concluded that mordant additives are rarely required for eucalypt dyeing, using the 'vessel as mordant' approach instead. She gives an example of *Eucalyptus globulus*, which in a stainless steel vessel gives a khaki green colour to silk, but using an iron vessel in acidic water (from a splash of vinegar) gives almost purple results; a copper vessel enhances the golden tones of the dye.

Cellulose fibres such as cotton require pre-treatment in order for the dyes to be fixed. Among other possible treatments, Flint advocates using the Japanese traditional method of soaking them in water in which soybeans have been ground up. Fabric so treated can be stored for up to a year before the dyeing takes place.

The leaves are not the only part of the eucalypt from which dyes can be derived; flowers, fruit and bark provide rich potential. It is interesting that 100 years after Smith advocated an Australian industry around dyes derived from eucalypts, there is a small but thriving eucalypt dyeing industry catering for a boutique market in designer fabric and clothing.

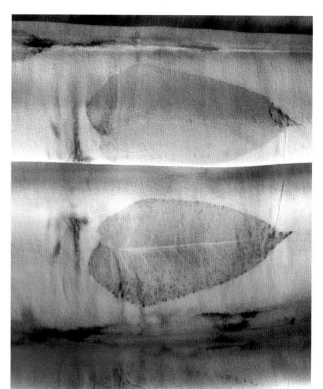

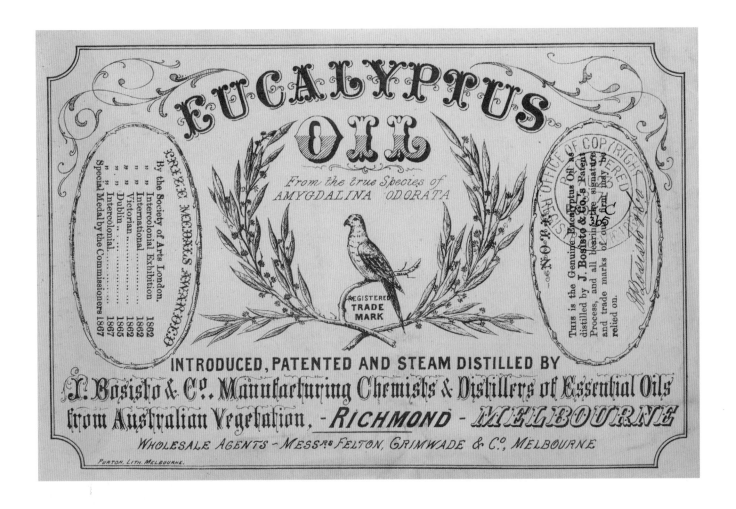

This Bosisto label from 1871 lists the medals already won for his eucalyptus oil. It is hard to be clear about the species responsible for the oil as the name *Eucalyptus amygdalina* was used very broadly at the time. The parrot logo was to persist on these labels into the 21st century. PHOTO: SLV.

25 Eucalyptus Oil

ABORIGINALS RECOGNISED THE THERAPEUTIC PROPERTIES OF EUCALYPTS WELL BEFORE Europeans arrived in Australia. They used infusions of the leaves of a number of species to relieve sinus congestion, body pains, colds and fever. When the First Fleet arrived in Sydney in 1788, it was surgeon Dennis Considen who distilled oil from the leaves of the Sydney Peppermint (*Eucalyptus piperita*) to successfully treat the wounds of convicts and sailors. On realising the effectiveness of the treatment, he distilled a litre of the oil to send to Sir Joseph Banks in England for his assessment. Testing showed that it was more effective in the treatment of head colds than the conventional European peppermint herb, *Mentha piperita*. J.H. Maiden, New South Wales Government Botanist, later honoured Considen by naming *E. consideniana* after him and stating that he was 'the father of the eucalyptus oil industry'.

An advertisement for Bosisto's eucalyptus oil from 1898.

Crude stills were set up by colonists in the late eighteenth century to extract the oil for their own use, but no commercial operation was established for many years. It took the work of Victorian botanist Ferdinand von Mueller, who experimented with different species, to convince Melbourne pharmacist Joseph Bosisto to develop a distillery at Dandenong Creek in 1854 to extract oil from the Narrow-leaved Peppermint (*E. radiata*). Bosisto was an entrepreneur and he exhibited samples of the oil at seventeen international expositions throughout the world from 1854 to 1891. He was awarded many gold, silver and bronze medals for his product. When Bosisto died in 1898, the Felton Grimwade Company became the owners of Bosisto's Parrot Brand Eucalyptus Oil. Although the founders have all passed away, the oil is still marketed under that name by Felton, Grimwade and Bosisto's Pty Ltd.

In the 1870s, the chemical analysis of eucalyptus oil began to be examined, particularly by the French chemist F.S. Cloez, who was researching essential oils to ascertain their suitability for medicinal, industrial and perfumery purposes. He looked at Tasmanian Blue Gum (*Eucalyptus globulus*) which had already been widely planted in Europe and identified the major component of its oil as 'eucalyptol', now usually known as cineole. Mueller was impressed by Cloez's work and honoured him by naming the Gympie Messmate (*E. cloeziana*) after him. Australian chemists R.T. Baker and H.G. Smith of the Museum of Applied Arts and Science in Sydney followed in the early 1900s, and then A.R. Penfold in the 1930s. They analysed many species, finding not only that the oil composition varied from species to species but also that the composition varied within a species. Following Cloez's work, the Australian chemists also categorised the various oils into those that can best be used for medicinal, industrial and perfumery applications.

Analysis of the oil

The above analyses showed that cineole was the most important component for use in medicinal and germicidal applications. It has an odour that in low concentrations is considered pleasant and clean by most people, and has mild bactericidal and antimicrobial properties. It has been reported that eucalypts with high cineole content in their oil have shown less damage from Christmas Beetle attack, indicating that these oils have potential as a carrier solvent in pesticides. Some eucalypts have as much as 90 per cent cineole in the composition of their oils. Cineole's action is that of a mild irritant of the nasal and bronchial passages which stimulates mucous secretion, unblocking the nose and bronchial tubes.

Other important components of eucalyptus oil include phellandrene and piperitone. Those species with significant quantities of these chemicals in their oil were favoured for the production of solvents and industrial oils used in the mining industry to separate metallic sulphides by flotation. Eucalyptus oil for use in the perfumery and flavouring industries required the presence of citronellal, citral, geranyl acetate and/or geranial in its components.

Many eucalypt species from eastern and southern Australia were analysed but only about twenty were considered worthy of more detailed examination.

Extraction of the oil

Following his early work at Dandenong Creek, Bosisto could see the potential for the industry and in 1880, backed by Melbourne businessmen Alfred Felton and Frederick Grimwade, he established the first large-scale still in Australia, near Dimboola in north-west Victoria. It was known as the Eucalyptus Mallee Company. By the turn of the century, many stills were in operation, the largest being Ockenden's at Spring Bay in Tasmania and Fauldings at Punyelroo in South Australia. Other small

The 1920 caption for this Lemon-scented Gum (*Corymbia citriodora*) photo read: 'Climbing a tree, in order to procure leaves for distillation'. It was a fairly labour-intensive industry. PHOTO: BAKER AND SMITH'S *EUCALYPTS AND THEIR ESSENTIAL OILS.*

bush stills were also constructed in New South Wales, Victoria and Kangaroo Island in South Australia.

The laborious work of gathering material to feed these early stills was often carried out by Aboriginals, or unemployed miners from the goldfields. The branches were cut by hand with slashers or sickles and loaded into horse-drawn wagons to be taken to the stills, where the load was dumped into vertical steel vats set in the ground. Steam was passed over the foliage and the volatile oil collected from cooling condensers. The water was drawn off and the oil, which floated to the

top of the container, was finally bottled. These bush stills were anything but fine engineering constructions and ad hoc repairs were frequently necessary to keep the operation going.

Production quantities

Up until the 1950s, Australia was the leading producer of eucalyptus oil, with some 1000 tonnes exported annually and supplying about 70 per cent of the world's market. Currently, the estimated world production of eucalyptus oil of the cineole type is in the order of 3000 tonnes annually and of oil for perfumery use about 1500 tonnes. Demand for industrial-type oils is very limited in today's market. Australia's dominance in oil production declined dramatically after the Second World War, with cheaper overseas production, variable world prices and, at times, inconsistent quality of the local product.

China is now the major supplier of eucalyptus oil, with more than 70 per cent of the world market. Australia's annual production is about 120 tonnes. The farmgate value of Australian oil is about $1.5 million and the retail value when sold in small bottles is in the order of $5 million. Australian production of oil is expected to rise, with large plantations of eucalypts being used in Western Australia to control salinity. Some of these are oil-producing species and with more sophisticated distilling techniques and equipment, a high-quality product is anticipated.

Cineole-rich oils used strictly for medicinal purposes must satisfy national or international pharmacopoeia specifications and this may introduce further requirements for compliance, sometimes requiring a second distillation process. A product that has been available in Australia for many years is Double 'D' Eucalyptus Oil, indicating that it has been through a double distillation process.

Broad-leaved Peppermint (*Eucalyptus dives*). The 1920 caption indicated the tree showed this growth six months after its foliage had been 'lopped' for oil distillation.
PHOTO: BAKER AND SMITH'S *EUCALYPTS AND THEIR ESSENTIAL OILS.*

McKean's Eucalyptus Works, 1923, showing the 'lump' of foliage being removed from the container after distillation.
PHOTO: NLA.

World Eucalyptus Oil Production, 2004.

Double 'D' eucalyptus
oil is twice distilled.

India
6%

Swaziland
3%

Chile
3%

Australia
3%

Brazil
4%

Spain
2%

Portugal
5%

South Africa
5%

China
69%

Sources of eucalyptus oil

Medicinal and germicidal use

Tasmanian Blue Gum (*E. globulus*) has been so widely planted throughout the world it is now the main source of cineole-rich eucalyptus oil and is grown for this purpose in China, Portugal, Spain, India, Brazil and Chile. The cineole content of the oil from Tasmanian Blue Gum varies, but averages about 62 per cent, so in order to meet the British Pharmacopoeia requirements of 70 per cent minimum cineole content, production has to be refined if the oil is to be used for medicinal purposes. Australia imports some of this lower-priced oil and refines it further for re-export, or for blending with locally produced oil.

Blue mallee (*E. polybractea*), which occurs in the West Wyalong area of New South Wales and in north-west Victoria, has up to 90 per cent cineole in its oil, the highest of any species. Due to its semi-arid habitat it is not as adaptable to general cultivation as many other species and is not being grown overseas to any extent. Being a mallee, harvesting of the leaves can be done mechanically and regular coppicing (removal of the leafy tops) of the plants increases the production of new growth. It is being grown in plantations and viable stills are in operation in both New South Wales and Victoria. Experiments with selected clones offering an improved yield of oil should enhance the production in these states. It is also one of the species being tested in Western Australia by the Oil Mallee Association.

The Gully Gum (*E. smithii*), from southern New South Wales and eastern Victoria, is grown extensively in South Africa and Swaziland where it produces masses of leafy growth and has a relatively high cineole content in the oil. In Swaziland, the species is coppiced, with the first cut being made 20–24 months after planting. Subsequent cuts of the coppice regrowth are made at approximately sixteen-month intervals, at which time the plants are 5–6 metres tall. Harvesting may continue for many years and in Swaziland some areas of Gully Gum are still being harvested after twenty years or more.

The Narrow-leaved Peppermint (*E. radiata*), also from southern New South Wales and eastern Victoria, was used in Australia but it is now considered unviable due to the difficulty and cost of harvesting the high branches. The oil has a high cineole content of 70–80 per cent and has a pleasant aroma. It is still being used in South Africa, where production quantities are expected to increase.

Broad-leaved Peppermint (*E. dives*), from the northern and southern tablelands of New South Wales and Victoria, varies considerably in the nature of its oil, with some clones being rich in cineole (60–75 per cent), others favouring phellandrene (60–80 per cent) and still other clones with piperitone (40–56 per cent). Clones with high phellandrene content were preferred for industrial oils, but their present use is minimal and production has now ceased in Australia. Piperitone has been used for the synthesis of menthol but more recently it has been produced from the mint *Mentha arvensis*.

River Red Gum (*E. camaldulensis*) is being harvested for oil in Nepal, but this species varies greatly in the composition of its oil and only clones from north Queensland have proved satisfactory for medicinal oil production. Other species used in the past have included the Apple Jack (*E. elaeophora*), Red Ironbark (*E. sideroxylon*), Yellow Gum (*E. leucoxylon*), Green Mallee (*E. viridis*), White Mallee (*E. dumosa*), Red Morrell (*E. oleosa*) and Kangaroo Island Narrow-leaved Mallee (*E. cneorifolia*), which is still being distilled and sold as a cottage industry on the island.

Plantation of Blue Mallee (*Eucalyptus polybractea*), grown for oil production near West Wyalong, New South Wales. Planting density is 3300 plants per hectare, in rows 3 metres apart.

Mechanical harvesting every eighteen months removes everything above 20 centimetres from the ground. Here the mallee stump is starting to shoot again with red new growth.

The mechanical harvester spits all the leaves and stems into the huge trailer of this truck. The trailer acts as the distillation container when a sealed lid is dropped over it.

The trailer filled with foliage is backed into the distillation shed. The edge is being cleared of debris to allow the lid in the background to be lowered into place for a sealed fit.

The furnace which heats the water to produce steam is fuelled from leaves that have had their oil removed during earlier distillation.

Steam produced from the heat of the furnace is forced into the trailer and the resulting mixture of steam and eucalyptus oil is condensed and separated in this small still. The bucket collects the oil.

Perfumery and flavouring use

Several species of eucalypts produce oil that is satisfactory for use in the perfumery industry. These oils usually contain citronellal as their major component, but are used in their whole form for their lemony aroma. Lemon-scented Gum (*Corymbia citriodora*) is the main species used and again the major supplier is China (1000 tonnes), with Brazil (500 tonnes) and India (50 tonnes) providing significant quantities. The oil is not distilled in Australia. Lemon-scented Ironbark (*E. staigeriana*), a rare tree from Cape York Peninsula, is being grown in Brazil which produces about 60 tonnes of oil annually. No single chemical predominates in this oil but it has a pleasant lemon aroma.

Another species that was used in the perfumery industry was Camden Woollybutt (*E. macarthurii*), a presently endangered species from the central and southern tablelands of New South Wales. It has 60–70 per cent geranyl acetate in the oil of its bark, which was extracted by distillation at the beginning of the twentieth century. Finally, the Strawberry Gum (*E. olida*) contains an unusual component in its oil known as methyl cinnamate, which imparts a fruity aroma and flavour and is present at up to 98 per cent in the oil. Not only the oil is used, but the leaves may be used fresh or dry and as a ground spice to enhance the flavour of cooked fruit dishes, desserts, spiced jams and confectionery. It has been harvested since the 1980s but its use tends to be limited to the Australian Bush Food industry.

Strawberry Gum (*Eucalyptus olida*) looks like many other eucalypts, but the oil extracted from its leaves is unique, containing unusual components that give it a fruity odour.
PHOTO: BROOKER & KLEINIG/APII.

Opposite: The basic distillation process for eucalyptus oil involves putting the leaves in a sealed container into which steam is forced. The heat of the steam vaporises the oil in the leaves and the resulting mixture of steam and oil is taken by pipe to a still, where it is cooled in a container surrounded by cold water. The steam and the oil vapour condense to form water and oil which floats above the water. The oil is then separated from the water.

Products and uses

After 156 years, Bosisto's Parrot Brand Eucalyptus Oil is still available from pharmacists and supermarkets in various-sized bottles, from 55 to 250 millilitres. It is said to help relieve the symptoms of colds and flu and muscular and arthritic pain. It removes stubborn stains and grease marks from clothes and carpet and is a natural air freshener which can also be used in the laundry wash. It may be used as a toilet cleaner and deodoriser and is effective as an insect repellent. It is made from the leaves of the Blue Mallee and is thus high in the active ingredient, cineole. Eucalyptus oil is also sold as a convenient aerosol spray. Other brands made from Blue Mallee are distributed from other Australian distilleries, and overseas the product made from the leaves of Tasmanian Blue Gum is sold.

As a chest rub to relieve congestion, eucalyptus oil is mixed with methyl salicylate, menthol and a carrier oil and is available in tubes and tubs. An inhalant is also sold. This is mixed with other fragrant oils and used in a steam vaporiser, or in hot water, to relieve nasal congestion. It is also available as a nasal spray. Sugar-free sweets sold as Eucalyptus Drops are said to clear the nose and soothe the throat. These are often flavoured with honey and lemon and may be sucked to freshen the breath and reduce the urge to cough. A eucalyptus wool wash is also being marketed. The oil in the wool wash serves three purposes: it acts as a solvent for removing grease, it imparts a fresh, clean odour to the garment, and it softens the texture of the wool.

As well as products produced from pharmaceutical-grade oil, which meet the standards prescribed in the European and British Pharmacopoeias and the US National Formulary, industrial-grade oils are also sold for other purposes. These have a lower cineole content and may be used as a fragrance for wax candles, perfumed soaps, in garden sprays, insect repellents and to remove spots and stains from carpets and clothes.

An interesting by-product of the distilling industry is the residue of leaves after the distillation process is completed. This is sold as a mulch for gardens and parks and is used by many Victorian local councils and other institutions.

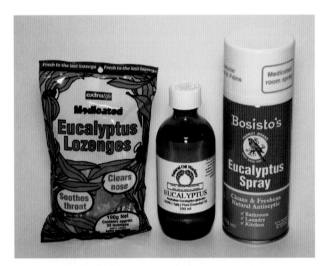

Eucalyptus oil products: lozenges that claim to clear the nose and soothe the throat, oil from the Tasmanian Blue Gum (*Eucalyptus globulus*) and a pressure-pack antiseptic spray.

Other potential markets
As a degreaser

There is a significant opportunity for eucalyptus oil to be used in industrial degreasing and solvent applications as a partial replacement for the conventional use of trichloroethane. This product has been criticised internationally as a significant contributor to ozone depletion and its use is being phased out. Experiments at Murdoch University in Western Australia have shown that high-cineole eucalyptus oil is effective as a workshop degreaser. Following the trials, it is now used routinely in the Kwinana workshops of Alcoa Australia.

As a fuel additive

Eucalyptus oil has value as an additive to ethanol/petrol blends as the cineole prevents phase separation in the presence of water. It acts as a co-solvent and assists in maintaining a homogenous blend.

By-products from the oil mallee plantations of Western Australia

In the early 1990s Professor Alan Barton of Murdoch University approached the Western Australia Department of Conservation and Land Management to examine the potential of planting oil mallees across the Western Australian wheatbelt to assist in overcoming the serious soil degradation occurring in the area because of the presence of high salinity. With the cooperation of local farmers, the Oil Mallee Association was formed and in 1998 it received a $2.2 million grant from the Australian Government's Natural Heritage Trust to propagate and maintain mallees for planting in the Western Australian wheatbelt. The Association now has over 900 growers throughout the region. Today, the Oil Mallee Project has target plantings of 500 million mallees, to be planted over 1 million hectares, by the year 2025. While high-quality eucalyptus oil production is one of the expected outcomes from the project, other by-products are likely to be of equal or even greater benefit.

Once mallees are established, the foliage may be harvested every two years with subsequent regrowth emerging from the lignotuber. It is estimated that this enormous quantity of foliage produced by the harvesting will result in about 3.5 million tonnes of biomass annually when the plantings are completed. The construction of an integrated wood-processing plant is currently being investigated by the association, the Western Australian Government and power companies to yield a range of products in addition to eucalyptus oil. These include:

* Activated carbon—a high-value product used in water treatment, gold recovery and in the food and beverage industry.
* Charcoal—there is a large Australian and international market for charcoal as a cooking fuel and for use in metallurgical processes.
* Renewable energy—Western Power has identified biomass combustion as one of the cheapest sources of renewable energy.

As well as these products, the value of the mallees as carbon sinks (the 'locking up' of carbon resulting in less CO_2 in the atmosphere) cannot be underestimated. As part of the global initiatives to reduce greenhouse gases, carbon credits to plant trees may be sold to polluting companies to offset their CO_2 emissions.

Research is also underway to examine other possible products emanating from these huge mallee plantations, such as:

* Wood pellets—wood is ground to a small particle size and then dried to make wood pellets. Compared with the original wood, these pellets are light, easily stored and transported as a source of heat and power. The market for wood pellets in Europe and Japan is forecast to expand as pellets are used increasingly as a source of renewable energy.
* Fast pyrolysis—a process where woody material is converted into a liquid called bio-oil. This process heats small, particle-sized wood to 500°C in approximately one second and converts about two-thirds of the biomass into liquid bio-oil. The remaining biomass is converted into charcoal and non-condensable gases reused in the process to heat the pyrolysis reactor. This bio-oil can compete with fossil fuels in a number of situations and can be used to generate heat and power.
* Ethanol production—several processes are available to produce ethanol from the sugars that exist in the wood. These involve breaking down the wood into components and then reforming them into ethanol by either fermentation or catalytic synthesis.

While eucalyptus oil will continue to be a marketable product in its own right, these potential by-products may offer an encouraging solution to some of the world's environmental problems.

PART 5

SPECIAL EUCALYPTS

Coolabah (*Eucalyptus coolabah*), forming an open woodland on the
banks above the Darling River, south-west of Bourke, New South Wales.

26 Iconic Groups of Eucalypts

SOME EUCALYPT SPECIES ARE GROUPED TOGETHER IN THE PUBLIC IMAGINATION BY THEIR common names. Five of these groups are discussed in this chapter.

Coolabahs (*Eucalyptus coolabah* and *E. microtheca*)

There is still much confusion as to the correct name of the iconic Coolabah. We have followed *EUCLID* in applying the above names. These two species differ in their bark characteristics and also in their distribution. *E. microtheca* has a more northerly distribution, from the Kimberleys in Western Australia through the Northern Territory to north Queensland, and holds its rough, fissured bark into the small branches. *E. coolabah* occurs further south in Queensland, central Australia, northern South Australia and northern New South Wales and has powdery, smooth white bark on the small branches. Both species occupy similar environments in that they prefer seasonally inundated heavy soil plains, although *E. coolabah* often prefers a drier location. The common name, which may be spelled Coolabah or Coolibah, is derived from the Aboriginal name for the tree, '*gulabaa*'.

There is concern that these trees, made famous by Banjo Paterson's song 'Waltzing Matilda', may be at risk because of dams, irrigation and overuse of ground water from bores, and also from excessive land clearing. This is quaintly portrayed by The Wilderness Society's modified lines of the song:

> Now a jolly swagman can't find a billabong
> 'cos they have bulldozed the Coolabah trees.

The name Coolabah has found a place in the Australian language, used in many commercial enterprises such as motels, cafés and estate agents, and even as the name of

Coolabah (*Eucalyptus microtheca*), north of Elliot in the Northern Territory. PHOTO: BROOKER & KLEINIG/APII.

a small town situated between Nyngan and Bourke in western New South Wales.

Seed germinates readily but when sown should not be covered, as light is required for germination. Both species adapt well to cultivation, accepting very dry conditions and some exposure to frosts. Their greyish-green leaves are a feature.

Ghost Gums (*Corymbia papuana, C. bella, C. arafurica, C. aspera* and *C. aparrerinja*)

Confusion reigns over the correct botanic name for the iconic Ghost Gum and it is apparent that botanists still argue about it. The beautiful white-barked eucalypt made famous by the artist Albert Namatjira is a feature of many parts of tropical and arid savannah lands of Australia. Before 1995, the name *E. papuana* was applied loosely to almost any narrow-leaved, white-barked eucalypt in northern and central Australia. However, in 1995, when the botanists Hill and Johnson decided that this whole group of plants (subgenus *Blakella*) should be placed in the genus *Corymbia*, the individual plants were examined more thoroughly. This revealed that the true

C. papuana occurs widely in Papua New Guinea and Irian Jaya but only in a small area of Australia, at the tip of Cape York. The remaining Ghost Gums were split into a number of new species. They occur from warm temperate latitudes to the monsoonal tropics and there are now 24 species and subspecies.

In general these trees have a mid-green crown with smooth white bark, sometimes with flaky or tessellated bark on the trunk. They are frequently partly deciduous in the dry season and at the beginning of the wet season the new growth on some species develops a rich claret colour. Some may begin to form buds before the new leaves are seen and, in a hurry to catch the moisture of the sometimes limited wet season, they may shed their seed six to eight weeks after flowering. Their differences are often difficult for the casual observer to distinguish. Key features used to identify them may be the length of flower stalk, the width of juvenile or adult leaves and whether the leaves are rough or smooth.

Only the more common species are mentioned here. *C. bella* occurs in the Kimberley, the Top End and north Queensland, preferring seasonally wet sites. It has an expanded spray of flowers and usually dull green leaves. *C. arafurica* occurs only in the monsoonal top end of the Northern Territory and is distinguished from the

A central Australian Ghost Gum (*Corymbia aparrerinja*) west of Alice Springs, the species captured in many Albert Namatjira paintings.

A northern Ghost Gum (*Corymbia bella*) near the Bungle Bungle Ranges, east of the Kimberley, Western Australia.

closely related *C. bella* by having much larger juvenile leaves. The Rough-leaved Ghost Gum (*C. aspera*) is a handsome small tree to 15 metres occurring on rocky ridges in the monsoonal north, from the eastern Kimberleys to north-west Queensland.

The Ghost Gum from central Australia is now *C. aparrerinja* and is found from the Gibson Desert in Western Australia, north to Tennant Creek and east to Mt Isa and Barcaldine . The species name is derived from the Aboriginal name for the tree. It is also the species of the 'Tree of Knowledge' (now dead) in Barcaldine, under which the Australian Labor Party was said to be formed. It occurs mainly on red sand and rocky slopes and is distinguished by its completely white, powdery bark and somewhat shiny, bright-green, narrow leaves.

Gimlets (*E. salubris* and related species)

The Gimlets, named for the resemblance of their trunks to a small carpenter's tool with a twisted shank used for boring holes, are characterised by their spirally, fluted smooth trunks, which vary in colour from a rich orange-brown to grey, depending on the season. The

A Gimlet (*Eucalyptus salubris*) tree near Hyden in the Goldfields region of Western Australia, here with orange-brown bark.

The stems of the Gimlet (*Eucalyptus salubris*) showing the fluted shape with the characteristic twist. Here the bark is silver-grey.

bark sheds in long ribbons. *E. salubris*, the most common species is widespread in the semi-arid wheatbelt and Goldfields areas of Western Australia, where the soil is often verging on alkaline. It is a mallet and is frequently multi-trunked.

Several other species are closely related to *E. salubris*. These are the Silver Gimlet (*E. campaspe*), the Large-fruited Gimlet (*E. creta*), the Two-winged Gimlet (*E. diptera*), and the Rough-barked Gimlet (*E. effusa*). All are mallets except the last, which develops a mallee habit, and despite its common name only the base of the trunk is rough. Other related species are *E. terebra*, *E. ravida* and *E. tortilis*. All of these have restricted distributions in the Goldfields and drier areas of Western Australia and differ in the silvery-grey branchlets of *E. campaspe* and *E. ravida* and the larger, crowded buds of *E. terebra*. *E. tortilis* differs only in its slightly larger buds and fruits.

The beautiful, twisted, shiny trunks of the Gimlets are their main feature and travellers along the Eyre Highway will marvel at their beauty in the Norseman area. The flowers, which are seen in spring and summer, are a good source of nectar and pollen and the timber has been used for poles in the mining industry. As an ornamental for parks and gardens in semi-arid areas, Gimlets will survive in most well-drained soils and tolerate moderately heavy frosts. They are used extensively in drier parts of America and are also grown in several parts of Africa, India and Israel.

Scribbly Gums
(*E. haemastoma*, *E. racemosa* and *E. rossii*)

These three species are known as Scribbly Gums as their smooth bark is covered with the scribbles made by the larvae of a moth of the genus *Ogmograptis*. This very small moth lays its eggs under the new bark of the tree and as the emerging grub grows it leaves a scar on the bark which increases in size and forms a scribble, which is revealed as the bark falls. It is not certain if the grub pupates under the bark or whether it falls to the ground.

The trunk of a Scribbly Gum (*Eucalyptus rossii*) showing last year's shedding bark with its scribbles, while underneath can be seen another set of scribbles on the new bark.

A cluster of Scribbly Gums (*Eucalyptus racemosa*) near Forster on the New South Wales north coast.

While the three species described here bear the common name, several other eucalypts are found with scribbles, possibly made by other species of *Ogmograptis*.

E. *haemastoma* is a small, often twisted tree to 10 metres high and is a common component of the Sydney sandstone flora around Sydney. Its informal shape and colourful trunk make it an ideal plant for native gardens. E. *racemosa* occurs on the east coast, from Nowra in New South Wales to Bundaberg in Queensland, and forms a taller, straighter tree reaching up to 20 metres. The gumnuts are smaller than E. *haemastoma*. E. *rossii* occurs on the New South Wales tablelands and western slopes, where it is a straight tree to 15 metres. These last two species are very similar and apart from their different distribution the only other difference is that the juvenile leaves of E. *rossii* are narrower than E. *racemosa*. The trunks of all these species become a rich yellow in spring prior to shedding their bark.

Snow Gums (*E. pauciflora, E. lacrimans, E. coccifera* and *E. gregsoniana*)

Snow Gums in general inhabit high country but many individuals may never experience snow. Five subspecies are recognised for E. *pauciflora* with subspecies *pauciflora* occurring over the entire range of the species, from south Queensland through New South Wales and Victoria to South Australia and Tasmania. Over this range it varies from a tree to 30 metres to a vigorous mallee. The bark is smooth and white with scribbles and some occasional yellowish patches; the juvenile leaves are blue-green and the adult leaves are glossy green with parallel veins. The white flowers are borne profusely in summer and autumn and the gumnuts often have a greyish bloom. Subspecies *debeuzevillei*, known as the Jounama Snow Gum differs in having angular mature buds and occurs in the southern Australian Capital Territory and nearby ranges. Subspecies *acerina* occurs in eastern Victoria and lacks any greyish bloom. Subspecies *hedraia* is found only in the Falls Creek area of Victoria and may be distinguished by its large, greyish, stemless

A Snow Gum (*Eucalyptus pauciflora* subsp. *pauciflora*), the most widespread subspecies, here becoming a medium-sized tree in the Brindabella Ranges of New South Wales.

buds and hemispherical gumnuts to 1.5 centimetres across. Subspecies *niphophila* is restricted to the highest alpine areas of the mainland. It forms a stocky mallee to 7 metres with colourful twisted trunks and is frequently the subject of alpine vegetation photographs. In all cases the above plants are readily cultivated and will tolerate extremes of cold. They have been introduced to England and even Norway where they are said to have survived temperatures down to −23°C. The timber has been used for fence posts and firewood, and apiarists have welcomed the flowers for their honey.

E. *lacrimans* is known as the Weeping Snow Gum and forms a slender tree to 12 metres, with smooth white bark marked with cream and grey patches. It occurs in subalpine areas around Kiandra, New South Wales, and its pendulous branches and gumnuts have a greyish bloom. Its handsome habit has made it popular for cultivation in southern areas. The Wolgan Snow Gum (E. *gregsoniana*), from the Blue Mountains and southern tablelands, is a mallee to 4 metres and has narrow juvenile leaves and small buds and fruits.

E. *coccifera* is the Tasmanian Snow Gum, which only occurs at the high altitudes of Mt Wellington and the central plateau of Tasmania. It may form a small tree to 15 metres but is more often seen as a mallee with smooth, beautifully figured bark with colours of cream, pink, fawn and grey. Like E. *pauciflora* ssp. *niphophila*, it is frequently represented in alpine photographs.

A Snow Gum (*Eucalyptus pauciflora* subsp. *niphophila*) growing under windswept conditions right on the tree line near Blue Cow in the Kosciuszko National Park, New South Wales.

A cluster of Weeping Snow Gums (*Eucalyptus lacrimans*) with their wispy, weeping foliage, near Kiandra in the Kosciuszko National Park, New South Wales.

Shrub of the Mongarlowe Mallee (*Eucalyptus recurva*), one of our rarest eucalypts, from near Braidwood in New South Wales. PHOTOS: M. CRISP/APII.

27 Endangered Eucalypts

In 1981, the Australian National Parks and Wildlife Service published a book by Professor Lindsay Pryor entitled *Endangered Species: Eucalypts*. It included some 73 species that he considered endangered or potentially endangered. Since that time, more field work has been carried out and many more species have been described. Also, more accurate definitions of the conservation status of a species have been made, enabling more accurate assessment of its plight.

The *Environment Protection and Biodiversity Conservation Act 1999* (the EPBC Act) was passed by the Australian Government and came into effect in 2000. It lists the threatened Australian flora in several categories: extinct, extinct in the wild, critically endangered, endangered, vulnerable and conservation dependent. Eucalypts are found in two of these categories, endangered and vulnerable. An endangered species is one that is likely to become extinct unless various threats and pressures affecting them cease.

In 2009 some twenty *Eucalyptus* species and one subspecies were listed as endangered and two *Angophora* spp., four *Corymbia* spp. and 49 *Eucalyptus* spp. were designated as vulnerable. The reasons why these species find themselves in this predicament are many and varied. While some species range over many kilometres, others are restricted to very small areas. This may be due to excessive land clearing for agriculture, grazing, road construction, mining or other human endeavours. On the other hand, where small populations of a species occur in remote areas, one can suppose that environmental conditions may have changed and the species cannot compete with others in the new conditions. Perhaps altered soil conditions or weather patterns may have reduced the capacity of a species to thrive.

Flowers of the Mongarlowe Mallee (*Eucalyptus recurva*). Note the turned down tip of the leaves.

Let us consider some of the species that are most threatened and examine the efforts that are being made to lessen these threats.

The Mongarlowe Mallee (*Eucalyptus recurva*) is known from only five plants in the wild. It is a shrubby, smooth-barked mallee usually less than 3 metres high with distinctive juvenile leaves that are retained into the mature foliage. They are shiny green, borne in opposite pairs and have a turned-down tip. The small cream flowers are borne in threes in January. These plants occur east of Braidwood on the southern tablelands of New South Wales on four separate sites separated by some 30 kilometres. It is thought that they are relict occurrences of a previously much more prevalent species. All of the individuals have huge lignotubers, suggesting that they could be several hundred years old. Attempts were made to cross-pollinate the species and grow the progeny in botanic gardens before re-establishing them in the wild, but this has so far been unsuccessful.

Even more precarious is *E. copulans*, which was presumed extinct until two individual trees were rediscovered in 2006 near Wentworth Falls in the Blue Mountains of New South Wales. Its original population has been reduced by clearing and filling of swampy land for housing development. This species forms a smooth-barked tree to 6 metres, with grey bark shedding in ribbons. The white flowers are borne in clusters of eleven in the leaf axils. It is believed to be a stabilised hybrid between Black Sally (*E. stellulata*) and Narrow-leaved Sally (*E. moorei*). One would assume that the authorities should reschedule this species to be critically endangered. Some seedlings have been produced by the Mt Annan Botanic Gardens and three individuals have been reintroduced into the Wentworth Falls area.

The Imlay Mallee (*E. imlayensis*) is another New South Wales eucalypt that is living on the edge. Although about 80 plants are known, they are clustered together on the upper slopes of Mt Imlay, near Eden in southern New South Wales. Although Mt Imlay is now included in a national park, there are significant threats to this species. No seedlings have been observed, flowering produces very few seeds and the seeds are difficult to germinate. The existing plants have very large lignotubers, which it is hoped renders them reasonably safe from fire, but it is thought that they are likely to be susceptible to the fungus disease *Phytophthora cinnamomi* and to attack by gall-forming psyllids. The Imlay Mallee forms a multi-trunked plant to 7 metres high with smooth, greyish bark shedding in ribbons to reveal a green trunk ageing to orange brown.

The Imlay Mallee (*Eucalyptus imlayensis*), known from about 80 plants near Eden, New South Wales.
PHOTO: BROOKER & KLEINIG/APII.

The white flowers are borne in threes. At the time of writing, several plants were growing in the Australian National Botanic Gardens in Canberra.

The situation with the Victorian Silver Gum or Buxton Gum (*E. crenulata*) is somewhat different to the above species as it is much more common in cultivation than it is in the wild. It is known naturally from two sites in south-central Victoria separated by about 60 kilometres. In total there are less than 700 trees and many are not in good health suffering from insect attack, weed invasion and disturbance of the locations. Victorian Silver Gum is grown extensively for its handsome grey foliage, which is used in the florist industry. Many plantations exist both in Victoria and southern New South Wales and as a result it has become naturalised

While rare in the wild, the Victorian Silver Gum (*Eucalyptus crenulata*) is common in cultivation.

some of the old specimens have huge lignotubers with a number of stems arising from them. We will look at a few species that are in the most perilous positions.

The Mt Misery or Dandaragan Mallee (*E. dolorosa*) is confined to a single population west of Dandaragan on the upper lateritic slopes of Mt Misery. Some eight clumps are known in this area of remnant mallee heath which has been fenced to reduce the risk of damage by grazing. Some believe that the Mt Misery Mallee is a relict species, barely surviving extinction as a consequence of a drying climate in the late Pleistocene period. The Western Australian Government has declared this species critically endangered. The Mt Misery Mallee forms a low shrub 1.5–2 metres high with rough, grey to brown bark and with white flowers borne in sevens and clustered at the leafless ends of the branchlets. The species currently exists only on private land and has at least once suffered fire damage from which it has recovered and flowered, albeit sparsely. The present owners are sympathetic to supporting its survival. Several other rare plants are also found in this community. Seed collections have shown poor germination but a few have been produced from tissue culture at botanic gardens. Efforts are continuing to produce more plants for eventual reintroduction to the site and to a nearby site with similar environmental conditions.

The Eneabba Mallee (*E. impensa*) is closely related to the beautiful Mottlecah (*E. macrocarpa*) and the Rose Mallee (*E. rhodantha*). It differs in that its foliage is green rather than grey and its leaves and buds are on short stalks. The flowers are pink and the gumnuts are about 5.5 centimetres in diameter. The Eneabba Mallee occurs in six populations spread over about 3 kilometres and includes about 36 individual plants. Five populations occur in a nature reserve and the sixth on private land. The reserve is a C-class reserve, which does not offer sound protection and, as mineral sands and other mineral commodities exist in the area, some concern for these populations exists. All populations have been burnt in recent years and although plants have reshot from the lignotuber, the new foliage has been seriously damaged by insects and no seedlings have appeared after the fires. The Western Australian Government has designated this

in both states. There is a need, however, to preserve the integrity of the natural populations and a recovery plan is being implemented by the Victorian Department of Sustainability and Environment. At one site the species is hybridising with Swamp Gum (*E. ovata*) and most of this population appears to be lacking pure *E. crenulata* specimens. However, the larger population near Buxton appears to be maintaining its genetic integrity.

The situation in Western Australia is different again as the state is so large and with extensive clearing for grazing and agriculture, thirteen of the 23 species listed under the EPBC Act as endangered occur in this state. All are mallees and most populations are thought to exist with fewer than 100 individuals. With mallees it is often difficult to be sure of the number of plants as species critically endangered. While some germination from seed has been achieved by botanic gardens, seedling survival was poor. Several plants were produced from tissue culture, but insect damage to the foliage from the larva of a moth was a major problem.

The Meelup Mallee (*E. phylacis*) is known only from a single population near Meelup, west of Bussleton. Its stems may reach 5 metres high with unique brown and grey, rough, corky bark forming multi-layered plates and strips and extending to the small branches. The creamy-white flowers are borne in the leaf axils, in clusters of eleven in winter and early spring. The gumnuts have markedly exserted valves. The population, overlooking Eagle Bay, is adjacent to a car park, the construction of which divided it in two and most likely destroyed some plants prior to their discovery in 1981. Initially the species was thought to be a hybrid as it had not produced any viable seed, but searches failed to find a second parent. DNA testing subsequently found that all the plants were

Perhaps the oldest eucalypt known, this rare Meelup Mallee (*Eucalyptus phylacis*) has had its only known population disturbed by the building of a car park near Bussleton, Western Australia. PHOTO: BROOKER & KLEINIG/APII.

Very few of the 50 known plants of the Badgingarra Box (*Eucalyptus absita*) occur in a nature reserve.
PHOTO: BROOKER & KLEINIG/APII.

a single clone and that previous natural events had caused the original lignotubers to separate. This gave rise to the theory that the plant was more than 6000 years old and was probably the oldest eucalypt in existence.

Twenty-seven plants were recorded in 2003, all with the same genetic make-up and all showing some stem splitting and signs of aerial canker caused by fungal attack. Some control burning of plants was carried out and all resprouted with healthy new growth, suggesting that the old stems were more susceptible to disease than young, healthy stems. In 2003, six seeds were collected and three plants have resulted. They will be tested genetically and their form examined as they develop. To date, no further information is available as the seed-testing laboratory still considers it to be a hybrid and has given it low priority. Several plants have also been produced by tissue culture but, of course, these are clonally identical to their parent. The Western Australian Government has designated the Meelup Mallee as critically endangered.

The Badgingarra Box (*E. absita*) is found in several locations over a 15-kilometre range between Badgingarra and Dandaragan, north of Perth. It forms a mallee 4–10 metres high, with smooth bark or sometimes with rough, yellow-brown bark at the base. Leaves are glossy green and the white flowers are borne in sevens between April and July. It is estimated that about 50 plants exist over this range, but being a mallee with a number of stems the precise number of plants is difficult to estimate. Most plants are found on private property that has been cleared for grazing and any seedlings that may have appeared could have been eaten by stock. A few plants are in a nature reserve but seed collected from this population appears to be sterile. Seed from the other areas has been collected for storage in the Department of Environment and Conservation's Threatened Flora Seed Centre. Proposals exist to fence the areas on private property and to carefully monitor these populations and those that exist alongside roads. This species has been designated as critically endangered by the Western Australian Government.

In addition to the above species, the following table lists the remaining eucalypts designated as endangered under the EPBC Act.

Two other subspecies are listed in the EPBC Act. These are *E. gunnii* subsp. *divaricata* and *E. pachycalyx* subsp. *banyabba*, but neither of these is recognised as distinct in the Australian Plant Census.

SPECIES	COMMON NAME	OCCURRENCE	APPROXIMATE NUMBER OF PLANTS
Eucalyptus balanites	Cadda Road Mallee	WA	50–100
E. beardiana	Beard's Mallee	WA	1300
E. brevipes	Mukinbudin Mallee	WA	320+
E. burdettiana	Burdett's Mallee	WA	140
E. conglomerata	Swamp Stringybark	Qld	1100
E. crucis subsp. *praecipua*	——	WA	56
E. cuprea	Mallee Box	WA	200+
E. insularis	North Twin Peak Mallee	WA	70–120 on mainland+ island population
E. leprophloia	Scaly-butt Mallee	WA	50–90
E. morrisbyi	Morrisby's Gum	Tas.	2000+
E. paludicola	Fleurieu Swamp Gum	SA	15 known populations
E. pruiniramus	Jingymia Gum	WA	58
E. sp. Howe's Swamp Creek	——	NSW	Uncertain

Morrisby's Gum (*Eucalyptus morrisbyi*) is restricted to four populations, two of which are very small and being reduced by urbanisation. The two remaining populations are remnants of larger populations and are now in reserves.

RED-FLOWERED MALLEE BOX
(*Eucalyptus lansdowneana*)

This small mallee reaches 6 metres and is restricted to rocky ridges of the Gawler Range in South Australia, where its status is designated as 'rare' by the South Australian Government. Its often twisted trunks have generally smooth bark but some individuals may have grey flaky bark at the base. The red or mauve-pink flowers are borne in groups of seven, both terminally and in the upper leaf axils, and have been recorded in autumn and spring. It is suitable for planting in most temperate areas, provided good drainage is available. It is frost-hardy to –7°C and a good bird attractor.

Despite its rare status in the wild, it is quite common in cultivation.

The Red-flowered Mallee Box is shown here with red flowers, but it can also bear mauve-pink flowers.

Beard's Mallee (*Eucalyptus beardiana*) has a very scattered and restricted distribution south of Shark Bay, Western Australia. Its name commemorates John Beard (b. 1916), a noted ecologist in that state. PHOTO: BROOKER & KLEINIG/APII.

North Twin Peak Mallee (*Eucalyptus insularis*) is known from four populations, three on the mainland east of Esperance in Western Australia, and one on North Twin Peak Island, where it occurs at the base of a steep slope adjacent to a granite cliff. PHOTO: BROOKER & KLEINIG/APII.

28 Significant Individual Eucalypts

We have, for most of this book, looked at eucalypts as genera and species, but humankind has the propensity to single out and name those individuals that have a special significance. This chapter examines some of the individual eucalypts that have become important because of their own special attributes, or their association in some way with human history.

The first usually involves our fascination with magnitude—the *Guinness Book of Records* view of the world—and in the case of trees this has usually focused on height. But there are other claims to fame—the girth of the tree trunk, usually measured 'at breast height', the diameter of the tree trunk, the age of the tree, and even the height from ground to first branch.

This all seemed of little consequence for the Australian colonists in the first half of the nineteenth century, but as soon as the Americans started staking claims to have the tallest and oldest trees anywhere, there arose some international rivalry. However, it is usually considered that Australia left its run too late; by the time measurements were made, most of our magnificent individuals had been cut down. One of the major problems was the inability to accurately measure the height of standing trees and many of the early records must be viewed with scepticism. In this chapter, only metric units are used, although early measurements were in feet.

It is also apparent that those involved—even scientists like Ferdinand von Mueller—were quite sloppy in their record keeping and in verifying the information they were producing. In the 1866–67 Intercolonial Exhibition in Melbourne, Mueller claimed that on the Black's Spur there was a Mountain Ash (*Eucalyptus regnans*) with a height of 146 metres, another at 128 metres, and rumours of some reaching 'half a thousand feet' (152 metres). By comparison, today's known tallest tree, Hyperion, a Coast Redwood (*Sequoia sempervirens*) in California, is officially recorded at 115.5 metres. This would have given Australia the claim to the world's tallest trees.

Following similar claims leading up to the Centennial International Exhibition in

Opposite: Big Ash One. The devastating 2009 Black Saturday bushfires not only killed 173 people and destroyed thousands of houses, they also killed mainland Australia's tallest trees. The tallest of these, Big Ash One, a Mountain Ash (*Eucalyptus regnans*), stood 92.4 metres tall before the fires, with its first branch 55 metres above the ground. Although now dead, it was still standing late in 2009, along with the skeletons of thousands of other 300-year-old trees in the Kinglake National Park, Victoria. PHOTO: BRETT MIFSUD.

Melbourne in 1888, a prize of £100 was offered to anyone who could authenticate any tree over 122 metres. The prize was never claimed, though the fine print did include some exacting conditions. At the same time there was a photographic exercise to record Victoria's tallest trees, with Mr Duncan Peirce eventually being commissioned to photograph them. The tallest found only measured 99 metres, but it did result in the publication of the large folio, *The Giant Trees of Victoria*.

For many years claims of Australia having the world's tallest trees were put down to exaggeration, but in 1982 a document was found in the records of the Victorian Forestry Department, written by the Inspector of State Forests on 21 February 1872:

> In one instance I measured with the tape line one huge specimen that lay prostrate across a tributary of the Watts and found it to be 435 feet [132.6 metres] from the roots to the top of its trunk. At 5 feet from the ground it measures 18 feet [5.5 metres] in diameter. At the extreme end where it has broken in its fall, it is 3 feet [0.9 metres] in diameter. This tree has been much burnt by fire, and I fully believe that before it fell it must have been more than 500 feet [152 metres] high.

This reported tree has been given the popular name 'Ferguson Tree' in honour of that Inspector of Forests. This is generally regarded as the record for the 'tallest tree in the world', although there is considerable scepticism among some of those engaged in tree measurement today. At the present time we can only regard living eucalypts as 'the tallest flowering plant', with North American conifers holding the 'tree' record.

Today, we have no records of trees even approaching this height after a century of logging and the periodic extreme bushfires like those of 1939 and 2009. At the time of these earlier debates, much of the old-growth forests of Tasmania would have been unexplored. Today, the focus of the hunt for the tallest trees has moved to that state.

These very tall or very big trees, are often given individual names, especially in Tasmania. They are given these nicknames by the public, foresters, tree climbers and conservationists. At one time the names were listed, with the trees' details, on Forestry Tasmania's website. But, in a move to cut out sentimentality from the forestry debate, such names were removed from the site in December 2003. They still persisted in the popular mind without an official government listing, and tree enthusiasts kept the names alive on websites. In 2009 Forestry Tasmania supported a group called the Giant Tree Consultative Committee to provide independent advice on the protection, management and promotion of giant trees and this group set up a new website listing trees, including their nicknames, at www.gianttrees.com.au. It appears that other states have not embraced nicknames for individual trees to the same extent as Tasmania.

Some states, via government or National Trust registers, give significant trees a code number. The lack of an official Australia-wide system for registering such trees is surprising given the public interest.

During the writing of this book several trees listed for Victoria had to be removed due to their death in the devastating Black Saturday 2009 bushfires.

This etching, *The Giant Gum-tree*, from *Australian Pictures: Drawn with Pen and Pencil* published in 1886, reflects the fascination with huge trees at the time. The accompanying text compares the size of Australian trees with those of California, with considerable exaggeration.

Some well-known tall trees are listed below by their nicknames and code numbers.

INDIVIDUAL NAME	SPECIES	LOCATION	HEIGHT	GIRTH/DIAMETER
Hyperion	*Sequoia sempervirens*	Redwood National Park, California, USA	115.5 m	4.84 m diam
Centurion (TT443)	*Eucalyptus regnans*	Tahune Forest, Tasmania	99.6 m	4.05 m diam
Icarus Dream (TT326)	*E. regnans*	Andromeda Reserve, Tasmania	97 m	2.9 m diam
Mount Tree (TT094)	*E. regnans*	Andromeda Reserve, Tasmania	96 m	12 m girth 3.8 m diam
Damocles (TT099)	*E. regnans*	Diogenes Creek, Tasmania	92.9 m	9 m girth 3.39 m diam
The Grandis	*E. grandis*	Bulahdelah State Forest, NSW	?86 m	8.5 m girth
Bunjil's Spear	*E. regnans*	Kirth Kiln State Park, Beenak, Victoria	86.4 m	1.2 m diam
Noble Tree	*E. nobilis*	Cunnawarra Flora Reserve, NSW	79 m	NA
Bird Tree	*E. pilularis*	Middle Brother National Park, Kendall, NSW	69 m	3.6 m diam
Big Fella Gum	*E. grandis*	Middle Brother National Park, Kendall, NSW	67 m	2.5 m diam

When assessed by their girth (circumference), diameter, or the estimated volume of the timber they contain, trees are usually called 'big trees'. A selection of well-known big trees is listed below.

INDIVIDUAL NAME	SPECIES	LOCATION	HEIGHT	GIRTH/DIAMETER	VOLUME
General Sherman	*Sequoiadendron giganteum*	Sequoia National Park, California, USA	84.2 m	24 m girth	1487 m³
Arve Big Tree (TT048)	*E. regnans*	Arve, Tasmania	87 m	17.2 m girth 5.4 m diam	360 m³
Two Towers (TT038)	*E. regnans*	Styx Tall Trees Forest Reserve, Tasmania	75.3 m	20.55 m girth 45 m² footprint	358 m³
Rullah Longatyle (TT372)	*E. globulus*	Geeveston, Tasmania	82 m	17 m girth 5.5 m diam	368 m³
Still Sorrow (TT191)	*E. regnans*	Glow Worm Creek, Tasmania	82 m	5.80 m diam	358 m³
Bigfoot (TT328)	*E. regnans*	Arve Valley, Tasmania	82 m	20.45 m girth	344 m³
Ada Tree T11202	*E. regnans*	Ada River Valley, Powelltown, Victoria	76 m	15.5 m girth	250 m³
Vincent Tree	*E. grandis*	Bruxner Park, Coffs Harbour, NSW	65 m	7.01 m girth 2.26 m diam	NA
Darejo	*E. denticulata*	Results Creek, Errinundra, Victoria	62 m	14 m girth	200 m³
Monkira Monster	*E. coolabah*	Neuragully Waterhole, western Queensland	60 m	14 m girth	NA
Eagle Tree (T11490)	*E. camaldulensis*	Gunbower Island, Victoria	52 m	9 m girth	NA

Left: Icarus Dream, at 97 metres tall was the tallest known *Eucalyptus regnans* in Australia until the discovery of Centurion in October 2008. It is located in the Andromeda Reserve in the Styx Valley, Tasmania. The stand is small and the trees are around 300 years old and are beginning to decline. However, it still contains twelve trees that exceed 90 metres in height and retains the title of the tallest known patch of forest in the southern hemisphere. PHOTO: BRETT MIFSUD.

It is interesting to note that around the world individual eucalypts are also given nicknames. In Spain there is a Tasmanian Blue Gum (*E. globulus*) known as 'O Avó de Chavín' (The Grandfather), which is 67 metres tall. In Portugal a Karri (*E. diversicolor*) with the name 'Karri Knight' is known as the tallest eucalypt in Europe, at 78 metres.

Historic eucalypts

The next group of individually named eucalypts have some historical significance or are associated with some event that the local community finds significant. Many of these trees relate to the colonial exploration of Australia. Unlike most other continents, we have an ancient history of our indigenous inhabitants and a very recent and comparatively well-documented history, since 1770, of European colonisation. Part of this recent history is the so-called exploration by Europeans of a land already well known to the Aboriginal people.

These explorers left a legacy of marked trees which have become part of our heritage. These markings were not random acts of graffiti but in most cases a vital part of the exploration procedure, allowing routes to be retraced and assisting rescue missions. The handbook

Opposite:

Top left: Papa Zig, a *Eucalyptus regnans*, thrives in the combination of abundant rainfall, fertile deep soil and long intervals between large bushfires in the southern forests of Tasmania. These trees can reach an enormous size but can also hide themselves extremely well. Although not listed among the top few in our table, Papa Zig is over 17 metres in girth and 84 metres tall and yet it was missed in various surveys and explorations for giant trees in the area despite the fact it is just 30 metres from a busy forestry road. PHOTO: BRETT MIFSUD.

Left: Two Towers, a *Eucalyptus regnans*, has dominated this patch of land for over 450 years. During this time it has accrued a wood volume of over 358 square metres and its footprint on the earth covers over 45 square metres, larger than some inner-city units! To accurately measure the volume of these giant eucalypts, a tape is wrapped around the trunk at various heights up the trunk. Two Towers bifurcates at about 15 metres up; in the photo, climber Tom Greenwood is seen about 20 metres up, where each fork of the tree is still over 2 metres in diameter. PHOTO: BRETT MIFSUD.

of instructions to the Elder Scientific Exploration Expedition (1891–92) includes:

> The Leader will cause all important camping places to be marked on the ground as permanently as possible. Where there are trees, they should be marked, after removing a sheet of bark, by cutting with a chisel the initial letters of his name with the date and number …

It is interesting to note that the explorer Thomas Mitchell, in 1836, found such blazes so meaningful that he sketched and later painted one made by an earlier explorer, John Oxley, who had camped by the Lachlan River nineteen years earlier.

Around the world there is a movement for countries to record their significant trees in some sort of national register, but this does not appear to have happened in

Watercolour painting by explorer Thomas Mitchell in 1836 of a tree marked by a previous explorer, John Oxley, on 17 May 1817. PHOTO: MITCHELL LIBRARY, SLNSW.

Australia. A few tree sites were placed on the Register of the National Estate by the Australian Heritage Commission, some states have a database maintained by the local chapter of the National Trust, and some local government authorities maintain a list for their district. Recently, some private individuals have attempted to set up a website register, but such sites have no permanence or status. There is also debate as to whether only living trees should be on such registers, or whether they should include dead relic trees.

In a book of this nature it will only be possible to mention a few examples that illustrate various ways in which individual eucalypts have achieved iconic status. Bob Beale eloquently describes his sense of wonder of some of these in far more detail in his book *If Trees Could Speak* (2007).

The Explorers Tree
(Katoomba, New South Wales)

This Blackbutt (*E. pilularis*) which is today commemorated by a dead stump under a shelter near Katoomba is supposed to be a tree blazed by Blaxland, Lawson and Wentworth during their historic crossing of the Blue Mountains in 1813. William Woolls, in a letter to *The Sydney Morning Herald* on 26 August 1867, said:

> To show how little some of the trees alter in the course of half a century, I may mention that the blackbut on which the late Mr W Lawson cut his initials with a tomahawk in 1813 still presents the letters as legible as ever.

In 1884 a wall and fence were erected around the tree on the authority of the Minister for Lands. However, reports around the turn of the last century suggest the initials could no longer be seen, but a few years later in a tourist promotional guide they are mysteriously reported to be clearly visible. Tourism in the Blue Mountains was a significant industry in the early twentieth century and it was important to have objects for people to visit. Whether this involved enhancing history is a matter of debate.

MARKED TREE.

The Explorer's Tree, Katoomba, as depicted in the *Picturesque Atlas of Australia* in 1888.

The Proclamation Tree (Glenelg, South Australia)

The colony of South Australia was proclaimed under the shade of a gum tree in the area now known as Glenelg on 28 December 1836. However, by the time of the celebrations of the colony's 21st anniversary, there was already controversy as to which tree it was. Notwithstanding regular commemorative ceremonies under an arched River Red Gum (*E. camaldulensis*) over the next 100 years, the South Australian branch of the Royal Geographical Society of Australasia declared it the wrong tree at the time of the state's centenary. In recent years, the finding of a sketch made at the time seems to support the celebrated tree as being the correct one, but the controversy certainly has not been settled. Currently, the remains of this tree are protected by an arched metal roof in a small garden in the suburb of Glenelg.

The Proclamation Tree at Glenelg as it looked in the 1950s, with one of the authors standing at its base.

The Separation Tree (Royal Botanic Gardens, Melbourne, Victoria)

The citizens of Melbourne gathered on 15 November 1850 under this River Red Gum to celebrate the news of the separation of Victoria from the colony of New South Wales. The planned celebrations included 'refreshements being at the same time furnished to the children on the hill about the Botanic Gardens' near

The Separation Tree as it looked in 1946 when Crosbie Morrison used it in a book on the Royal Botanic Gardens, Melbourne. The plaque on the tree is enlarged.

the lagoon that then superintendent John Dallachy was developing into a lake. A plaque was attached to the tree one year later. On 15 November 1951 a replacement tree was planted from seeds taken from the original to ensure continuity. It is interesting to note that a metal spike some way up the trunk marks the level of the 1891 flood of the Yarra River.

Herbig's Tree (Springton, 60 kilometres north-east of Adelaide, South Australia)

Not all fame springs from major political events. This mighty River Red Gum with its hollowed-out base was home to a humble Polish migrant and his family. Johann Friedrich Herbig emigrated from Silesia in 1855 and worked on a property at Black Springs, now Springton. He soon managed to lease his own farm, marry, and

The Herbig Tree is still alive, 150 years after it was large enough and hollow enough to house a family.
PHOTO: ROSEMARY PURDIE.

The Dig Tree photographed in 1997 with a boardwalk protecting its root system.

The Dig Tree photographed in 1911, as published in the *Sydney Mail*. Part of the original 1861 stockade can still be seen in the background, as can part of the word 'DIG' and the arrow.

father the first two of his sixteen children while living in the hollow of the tree from 1855 to 1860. After his departure to better accommodation, the tree grew on, sheltering a range of activities. In 1968 the descendants of the Herbig family formed a memorial trust and bought the land containing the tree. About 900 of those descendants gathered there to celebrate the 150th anniversary of Herbig's occupation of the tree.

The Dig Tree (south-west Queensland, near Innaminka in South Australia)

Perhaps Australia's most famous tree, this Coolabah (*E. coolabah*) commemorated a sad episode in our history. The ill-fated Burke and Wills expedition (1860–61) had become part of a de facto race to cross the continent of Australia, from south to north. On 16 December 1860 Robert O'Hara Burke, the leader, split his party in two, leaving the larger group on the banks of Coopers Creek in south-west Queensland while he and three others, including surveyor William John Wills, made a dash to the Gulf of Carpentaria. The party left at Coopers

Creek was told to wait three months, uncertain as to whether Burke's party would return that way or head for the settled areas of Queensland. On 21 April 1861, suffering from heat and boredom and with food running low, this party headed south for Melbourne after leaving a message buried beneath a campfire site and marking a tree with the word 'DIG'. By a quirk of fate, later that day Burke, Wills and the third surviving member, King, staggered exhausted to the camp site and discovered the buried message. They had crossed the continent and missed their support team by nine hours. Too exhausted to catch up, all but King perished in the weeks ahead.

The marked tree lived on, taking the name 'Dig Tree'. In 1898 a fellow called John Dick carved the face of Burke into the trunk of another tree about 30 metres away, which became known as the 'Face Tree'. The Dig Tree survives into the 21st century as a local landmark and tourist attraction. It has a boardwalk surrounding it to reduce soil compaction and some excellent interpretation explaining its historic background.

The Kelly Tree (near Mansfield, north-eastern Victoria)

The Kelly Tree is associated with Australia's most famous bushranger, Ned Kelly. On 26 October 1878, a gunfight occurred between the Mansfield police and what became the Kelly gang. Three policemen (Lonigan, Kennedy and Scanlon) were shot. So began the chain of events leading to the capture of Ned Kelly twenty months later, and his eventual hanging. The Kelly Tree marks the spot where the gunfight occurred. The tree is a Mountain Gum (*E. dalrympleana* subsp. *dalrympleana*), and is still a healthy specimen with a forked trunk, located alongside the Stringybark Creek. At some stage someone has attached a large metal plate to the tree in the vague shape of Ned Kelly's armour, which has almost been enveloped by the growing bark.

Top right: The Kelly Tree, a Mountain Gum (*Eucalyptus dalrympleana*) next to Stringybark Creek, Toombullup State Forest, near Mansfield, Victoria.

Right: The Kelly Tree plaque, slowly being overgrown by bark.

The Tree of Knowledge (Barcaldine, Queensland)

In the heady days of industrial disputes during the depression of the 1890s, the town of Barcaldine in central Queensland became the focus of a widespread shearers' strike. On 1 May 1890 at least 1300 took part in one of the world's first May Day marches, most of the participants being striking shearers. Soon, mounted infantrymen with bayonets drawn were sent in to break the strike. Out of this conflict was born the political movement which eventually became the Australian Labor Party, soon winning seats in elections in all the colonial legislative assemblies. With time, and the need to establish historical 'roots', one huge Ghost Gum (*Corymbia aparrerinja*) was credited with being the tree under which the striking shearers met, and was named the 'Tree of Knowledge', as the place of origin of the Australian Labor Party.

Situated in the main street of Barcaldine, the tree was often the focus of Labor Party celebrations and a major tourist attraction for the town. After surviving more than a hundred years of Australian political rivalry, the tree was noticed to be in poor shape leading up to the May Day celebrations of 2006, and it was soon revealed to have been poisoned. An estimated 30 litres of weedkiller had been poured beneath the tree to kill it via the roots. In 2009, a controversial 18-metre tall timber and steel monument was opened to mark the spot where the tree had once lived.

The Fairies' Tree (Fitzroy Gardens, Melbourne, Victoria)

This River Red Gum achieved fame after the tree died. It was a Centenary gift to the children of Melbourne from sculptor Ola Cohn (1892–1964). She carved the base of a dead tree, which had been part of the original vegetation of the area, with imps, fairies and a strange

The Tree of Knowledge, photographed in 1992 in the main street of Barcaldine. It was killed by poison fourteen years later.

The Fairies' Tree in 2005, after conservation and repainting. PHOTO: TAKVER.

The Fairies' Tree, being carved by Ola Cohn, in Fitzroy Gardens, Melbourne (1934).

The Cazneaux Tree (Flinders Ranges, South Australia)

It is remarkable that the act of photographing a tree would confer on it the status of a tourist attraction, but that is what happened to this River Red Gum. Harold Cazneaux (1878–1953) photographed the tree on a visit to the Flinders Ranges in 1937 and within three months of his trip a version was exhibited in the London Salon of Photography under the title *A Giant of the Arid North*. It was not until 1941, while Australia was at war, that Cazneaux exhibited a version under the title it is now known by—*The Spirit of Endurance*. Photos were taken

mixture of Australian native birds and mammals. She undertook the carving from 1931 to 1934. In 1944 Cohn started to paint the carvings in colour 'as a Christmas gift to the children whose soldier fathers are fighting overseas'. In 1977, the trunk was extracted from the ground for chemical treatment and the removal of rotted wood. The tree was then remounted on a concrete base to prolong its life. It was repainted as recently as 1998. To this day, children often insert notes in the tree 'to communicate with the fairies', a practice that is causing problems for its conservation.

Top right: The Cazneaux Tree in 2007. PHOTO: MARCIA WRIGLEY

Right: One of the photographic versions of the same tree photographed by Harold Cazneaux in 1937. PHOTO: THE CAZNEAUX NEGATIVE COLLECTION/NLA.

from various angles and there are several versions of the prints, cropped and retouched in different ways, in various galleries around Australia. The tree, however, lives on and has become a popular spot for tourists in the Wilpena region of the Flinders Ranges (see also p. 253).

The Gloucester Tree (Pemberton, Western Australia)

This giant Karri (*E. diversicolor*) is famed for its fire-watch cabin perched 58 metres above the ground. The cabin was built in 1947 and happened to coincide with a bush picnic visit to the site by the governor general of the day, the Duke of Gloucester, hence its name. The tree had been 15 metres taller when the epic six-hour climb was undertaken by Jack Watson, using climbing irons and a belt, to ascertain its suitability. At that time the first limbs were encountered from 39 metres above the ground and it had a girth of 7.3 metres. Early photos show that most limbs were removed during the cabin construction and today's branches are secondary growth. It is still very much alive and is a popular tourist attraction. The original wooden cabin was replaced with a metal viewing platform in 1973. Today, about 400,000 people visit the tree each year, about a quarter of those climbing to the top.

The first of these Karri tree-top fire-watch cabins had been built in 1938, and by 1958 eight had been constructed. Today two others are available for the public to climb: the Diamond Tree near Manjimup at 51 metres, and the Dave Evans Bicentennial Tree, also near Pemberton, at 70 metres.

The Gloucester Tree has a 'staircase' of pegs that allows visitors to climb to the fire-watch cabin, which can just be seen through the foliage at the top. PHOTO: DEC.

The Monkira Monster photographed in 1952 by Arthur Groom, with the then manager of Monkira Station, Bob Gunther, sitting on one of the lower branches. This tree is a Coolabah (*E. coolabah*). PHOTO: NLA.

The Monkira Monster (Neuragully Waterhole, western Queensland)

This tree would fit into the topic of 'big trees' discussed earlier in this chapter, but its story is unusual. It is a Coolabah, seldom seen by tourists due to its remoteness on private land on Monkira Station, 130 kilometres east of Bedourie. It was mentioned by Jim Willis in the 1963 *Australian Encyclopaedia* and by Albert Brooks in *Tree Wonders of Australia* in 1964. Brooks gave its dimensions, when converted to metric, as 60 metres tall with a girth of 14 metres, and the circumference of its outer foliage was 228 metres. This means that the longest branches reached out about 37 metres from the main trunk. The tree is still alive and in recent years has been fenced to protect it from stock under a federal government conservation program. Access to the tree is allowed only with the permission of the station managers.

In Espirito Santo, Brazil, stacked eucalypt logs await pick-up. Plantations of eucalypts have replaced 3.4 million hectares of forest, becoming the world's biggest source of eucalypt pulp for paper. PHOTO: MARK MOFFETT/NATIONAL GEOGRAPHIC.

29 Eucalypts Overseas

THERE ARE MORE EUCALYPT TREES IN CULTIVATION OVERSEAS THAN THERE ARE BEING cultivated in Australia. Massive plantations are being grown in most temperate and subtropical countries of the world, with one estimate suggesting they could cover 20 million hectares. Such plantations are only absent from the extremely cold areas and the lowland tropics.

Since Ferdinand von Mueller sent Tasmanian Blue Gums to Italy in the 1860s, their value as timber, charcoal and oil, as well as amenity planting has been widely recognised, but their introduction to many countries has not been without controversy. Eucalypt plantations have often had an adverse effect on local farmers, sucking moisture and nutrients from previously arable soil. It has been said by environmentalists that eucalypts create an almost sterile environment with an absence of birds and other wildlife. However, observations by unbiased researchers in Africa and South America have shown that nectar-seeking birds and those large birds that nest and roost in tall trees have benefited from eucalypt plantations. Small animals, especially reptiles, also use the thick litter under the trees for cover.

Let us first examine some of the countries where eucalypt plantations occupy large tracts of land and have replaced forested areas where the natural forests have been ruthlessly cleared for firewood and agriculture.

India

India was perhaps the first country to grow eucalypts for ornamentation when the ruler of Mysore State, Tippu Sultan, a keen gardener, received seeds of several species. He planted the seeds in the Nandi Hills, some 60 kilometres from the city of Bangalore in southern India, in the late eighteenth century. A specimen of Forest Red Gum (*Eucalyptus tereticornis*) from these plantings was measured in 1984 as 60 metres high, with a 4.6-metre girth and aged at 194 years. Although some further sporadic plantings were undertaken, it was not until the 1950s that roadside and garden plantings were promoted using

FOREST RED GUM (*Eucalyptus tereticornis*)

Forest Red Gum is one of the most common eucalypts on the east coast. It occurs, mostly in open forests, from Bega on the south coast of New South Wales to Cape York in north Queensland and possibly Papua New Guinea. A subspecies, subsp. *mediana*, occurs in Gippsland, Victoria, and may have resulted from hybridisation with River Red Gum. Forest Red Gum may reach 50 metres high but is usually around 30 metres. It has smooth, mottled bark with patches of grey, pink, cream and white shedding in large sheets, sometimes leaving a small skirt of rough bark at the base. The long, conical bud cap is distinctive and the flowers are normally white, but pink forms have been recorded. Flowers produce ample nectar and pollen and are sought after by apiarists. Heavy flowering has been noticed every four years and flowers have been recorded in most months. The wood is resistant to termite attack and is used for heavy construction, poles and firewood. Forest Red Gum provides excellent wildlife habitat for farm and rural properties as birds and flying foxes are attracted to the flowers and the foliage is one of the most important food sources for Koalas. This species has been known to hybridise with many other species and these plants have frequently been given species names. One of the most common of these is a hybrid with Swamp Mahogany (*E. robusta*) which has been called '*E. patentinervis*'; the two parents share common habitats along the New South Wales and Queensland coasts.

This tree occurs naturally in Mt Annan Botanic Gardens, Campbelltown, New South Wales.

The bark is one of the Forest Red Gum's attractive features.

progeny from the Nandi Hills Forest Red Gums. The characteristics of these trees were unique and the name Mysore Gum was applied to them. Although confirmed as a form of Forest Red Gum, they were more drought-tolerant than other Australian provenances and were very adaptable to a range of climates and soil types. In the 1960s huge plantations were established in many parts of India.

Subsequently, many other species have been introduced, but the Mysore Gum is still favoured in most areas for its excellent coppicing powers, which make it ideal for the paper and pulp industries. Tasmanian Blue Gum, River Red Gum, Flooded Gum and Lemon-scented Gum are also widely planted and in all there are about 7.5 million hectares of eucalypt plantations in the country. The fast-growing Tasmanian Blue Gum is preferred in many areas where the local hills have been denuded due to the collection of timber for firewood.

Another interesting industry that has emerged in India is the production of rutin. This glycoside has several therapeutic properties and is extracted from the leaves of Red Stringybark (*E. macrorhyncha*) and Youman's Stringybark (*E. youmanii*). Although production is limited at present, it is expected to expand in future years.

We have mentioned earlier that the introduction of eucalypts has not been without controversy. The early plantations in India caused many problems for the local rural people eking out a living from their crops. They claimed that the eucalypts dried out their soil, starved their crops of nutrients and killed the grass grazed by their cattle. While the rich landowners were making money selling their timber to the pulp and paper mills, the poor were becoming poorer. Eventually, these problems were resolved by more sensitive positioning of the plantations and ensuring that there was sufficient distance between the water-seeking roots of the eucalypts and the farmers' crops.

Recent advances in selection of species and hybrids of eucalypts have allowed farmers to develop a technique of agroforestry known as polyculture, where eucalypts are interplanted with annual crops of wheat, fodder, green manure and other grains.

Brazil

Second only to India, the eucalypt plantations of Brazil cover an estimated 3.6 million hectares. Plantations began in the early 1900s under the guidance of Edmundo Navarro de Andrade (see p. 151) but received a boost in 1948 to supply charcoal for the iron and steel industries. These later plantations consisted mainly of Tasmanian Blue Gum. In the 1970s there was an increase in plantation development, with a demand for short fibre pulp for the paper industry. Improved cultural techniques and the production of cloned planting stock using hybrids *E. camaldulensis* x *E. globulus* and *E. camaldulensis* x *E. grandis* led to a huge expansion of the industry and exportation of these fast-growing and hardy hybrid clones to places like Australia.

In addition to pulp production, Brazil began using Lemon-scented Gums, firstly for charcoal and timber but later harvesting the leaf material for the production of essential oils high in citronellal, which is used in perfumes and insecticides. It is now the second-largest producer of this oil in the world, behind China. The Lemon-scented Ironbark (*E. staigeriana*) which yields a complex range of essential oils is also being used for this purpose.

As in India, the wide use of eucalypt plantations is causing some problems for the local population. Farmers who had been fully occupied in caring for their small areas of crops find themselves unemployed after their land has been taken over by the large timber companies, as the labour required to manage a eucalypt plantation is much less than that needed for cultivating crops. In addition to this, much of the diverse natural rainforest is being cleared and replaced by the fast-growing eucalypts. One of the many consequences is the threat to the huge variety of epiphytes that inhabit these forests, as plants such as orchids and bromeliads are unable to re-establish on the deciduous eucalypt bark.

Environmentalists, disturbed at the devastation that has been wrought on the native rainforest, are encouraging local native species to be used in reafforestation projects. Nevertheless, companies continue to expand their eucalypt plantations; the growth rate of eucalypts is greater than that of the native Brazilian trees. In March 2006, hundreds of women from a rural worker's movement occupied the research centre of one of the companies, Aracruz Celulose, in Rio Grande do Sul. They destroyed thousands of eucalyptus seedlings and damaged the research facilities. This confrontation is continuing.

China

Although eucalypts were first introduced to China in 1890, it was not until the 1950s that plantations were established. The main species planted were Lemon-scented Gum and Queensland Peppermint (*E. exserta*). Today, more than 300 species of eucalypts are being grown in China; as well as the above species, the dominant ones are Tasmanian Blue Gum and River Red Gum, with Flooded Gum and the non-Australian Timor Gum (*E. urophylla*) in the warmer areas. It is estimated that there are now more than 2.6 million hectares of plantations.

China has mainly used timber for firewood, woodchips, charcoal and plywood, but now it is the major producer of eucalyptus oil for medicinal purposes and perfumes. The medicinal oil is extracted chiefly from Tasmanian Blue Gum, most of which is relatively low grade and is exported for further refining. The perfumery oil is sourced from Lemon-scented Gum. Some traditional Chinese medicines use eucalyptus oil in their formulation to treat headaches, nasal congestion, muscular and abdominal pain, and also as an antiseptic. An extract of the leaves of Swamp Mahogany (*E. robusta*) is sometimes preferred to ethyl alcohol as a disinfecting agent after operations.

Swamp Mahogany (*Eucalyptus robusta*) is providing a disinfectant in China.

LEMON-SCENTED GUM
(*Corymbia citriodora*)

Lemon-scented Gum is a tall, slender, smooth-barked tree which may reach 50 metres and occurs from northern New South Wales to Cooktown in north Queensland and west to the Carnarvon Range. The bark is white to pink or coppery and sheds in small, curling flakes and the leaves are strongly lemon-scented, containing the essential oil, citronellal. While the aromatic leaves are appreciated in the garden, the foliage is also harvested commercially for the distillation of oil, which is used in insecticides, perfumes and menthol. Lemon-scented Gum is grown widely around the world, but the commercial product comes mainly from China and Brazil. While large for the average garden, it is frequently planted in parks in tropical and temperate climates where frosts are not experienced. It is best used in the eastern states as established plantings in Western Australia have allowed the species to escape and it has become naturalised in that state.

Often grown in urban parks, this Lemon-scented Gum is growing in Adelaide, South Australia.

SUGAR GUM (*Eucalyptus cladocalyx*)

Sugar Gum occurs naturally in three distinct regions in South Australia. In the Flinders Ranges it forms a medium-sized tree to 35 metres high. On the Eyre Peninsula and Kangaroo Island, it forms a small, often crooked tree to 10 metres high. Progeny of these small trees are sometimes marketed as *E. cladocalyx* var. *nana* or Dwarf or Bushy Sugar Gum. The greyish, mottled bark is smooth, shedding in patches to reveal a yellow-brown bark beneath. The juvenile foliage and coppice growth are round and grey-green and very distinctive, while the adult leaves are glossy green and much paler on the underside. The white flowers, seen in summer, are borne in clusters of seven to eleven flowers on leafless sections of the branches—another unique feature. The barrel-shaped gumnuts are longitudinally ridged and up to 1.5 cm long.

Sugar Gum has been planted extensively as shelter belts on farms in South Australia and western Victoria. As it has a tendency to grow upright, constant coppicing (trimming of the leafy tops) has been necessary to encourage a bushy habit. The pruned branches have been used as posts and fencing as the timber is hard and resistant to termites. It has also been milled for construction work. The flowers are also valued for honey production. Sugar Gum is resistant to drought and all but the severest frosts. In Israel it is grown without irrigation. As a result of its use in woodlots for firewood in Victoria and Western Australia, it has become an environmental weed, invading grasslands and forests. The cultivar *E. cladocalyx* 'Vintage Red' develops red foliage.

Sugar Gum flowers spasmodically—in some places there can be a 5–15 year gap between flowerings.

A typical scene in many country towns in the drier parts of southern Australia is trees forming a coppice after being lopped above head-height.

Not in Australia! This river course lined with River Red Gums (*Eucalyptus camaldulensis*) is the Olifants River in South Africa, where they are a declared weed. PHOTO: LESLIE HENDERSON.

Africa

With so many countries on the African continent, it is difficult to obtain accurate figures for the area under eucalypt plantations, but it is believed to be in excess of 2 million hectares. Initially, Tasmanian Blue Gum was the main species grown, but due to drought-related dieback and insect attack it is now confined to cooler tropical climates such as higher parts of Ethiopia. The main commercial species are Flooded Gum on the most fertile soils, River Red Gum in more arid areas, Tuart (*E. gomphocephala*) on the sandy soils of northern Africa

A plantation of Gimlet (*Eucalyptus salubris*) in Morocco, northern Africa. Many Australian species are being trialled for their adaptability to African conditions.
PHOTO: PIERRE-ARNAUD CHOUVY.

Constructing traditional houses using locally grown eucalypt poles in Zimbabwe, Africa. PHOTO: CSIRO.

and Swamp Mahogany in more tropical areas such as Madagascar. A range of other species is being trialled in different environments.

Timber was used initially for pit props in the mines, but now is used for pulp and paper production as well as being valued by the native populations as a source of firewood, charcoal and building materials to replace the native vegetation that had been ravaged by overuse. However, in South Africa the eucalypt is causing some problems; it has become a weed in sensitive environments such as the fynbos in the Western Cape, where this unique wildflower ecosystem is threatened.

South Africa's *National Environmental Management Biodiversity Act 2004* has listed ten eucalypts as invasive; the Bald Island Marlock (*Eucalyptus conferuminata*) and Sugar Gum (*E. cladocalyx*) are seen as threats to the fynbos and must not be grown less than 50 metres from these sensitive areas. Eight other eucalypts are listed as invasive and may only be grown in demarcated areas. These species are River Red Gum, which invades watercourses, Karri, Flooded Gum, Grey Gum, Tuart, Coolabah, Tasmanian Blue Gum and Forest Red Gum.

In the last twenty years the Gully Gum (*E. smithii*) has been cultivated in southern and central Africa for its oil as well as its timber. The oil is high in cineole, making it suitable for medicinal use.

An Ethiopian story

After the thirteenth century, the royal establishment of Ethiopia had to be moved every few years as the local areas were stripped of firewood. In 1895, with the Empress Taitu complaining of existing in such uncomfortable circumstances, the Emperor Menelik II established a permanent capital at Addis Ababa. He planted the city with groves of the fast-growing Australian trees that had been established in Kenya, and Addis Ababa became a leafy oasis for the Royal Court. These trees were Tasmanian Blue Gums and the surrounding bare hills were densely planted to provide firewood for the native population. While these trees were eventually stripped, plantings have continued in more recent times, with funding from the United Nations and the Ethiopian Government.

North America

There is some debate as to who first introduced eucalypts to the United States. It is said that W.C. Walker, owner of the Golden Gate Nursery in San Francisco, planted the first seeds in 1853. Another report suggests that a retired clipper captain, Captain Robert H. Waterman, planted seeds on his property in the Suisun Valley, California, in 1853. However, it seems that it was Frank Havens, a local entrepreneur, who in 1856 set about clearing the grass-covered hills around San Francisco Bay and planting hundreds of Tasmanian Blue Gums in the hope of making a quick fortune. He promoted these trees in his company's prospectus as 'the most valuable tree on the face of the globe', noting that the timber was perfect for a wide range of uses 'from telegraph poles to railway sleepers or from violins to ecclesiastical furniture and insulator pins'. Havens went on to build nine plant nurseries and employed 200 workers at planting time, covering the Californian hills with Blue Gums.

In 1908, the State Board of Forestry issued a publication entitled *A Handbook for Eucalyptus Planters*. Shortly after this, there were indications that the trees were not performing as well as expected—the timber had a tendency to chip when planed and crack when dried. After failing to find reasons for this, Havens decided to call it a day in 1914. The reason for the failure of the industry is still uncertain, but it is possibly due to the rapid growth of the trees in the Mediterranean climate and the harvesting of the timber at a very young age.

Although the nurseries have all disappeared, the trees remain and are part of the permanent landscape of California. The grass-covered hills, with their springtime display of colourful wildflowers, no longer exist and this is thought to have contributed to the extinction of the Xerces Blue Butterfly (*Glaucopsyche xerces*), the larva of which fed on native *Lotus* and *Lupinus*. Birds, too, have suffered by the reduction of their habitat as many are unable to find food in the eucalypt forests, and the gum that exudes from some eucalypt species seals their beaks and prevents them eating.

These days many local people consider eucalypts to be native to California and actively lobby against their removal. In fact in Santa Cruz, eucalypts are protected under a Heritage Tree Ordinance and anyone who cuts down a tree more than sixteen years old incurs a criminal offence and a fine of not less than US$500. Others call them 'America's biggest weed' and the 'gasoline tree'. The latter is due to the highly flammable oil content of their leaves and the tragic loss of lives and property after frequent bushfires. One of the worst of these was in 1991 when almost 3000 homes were lost, and again in 2003 when a further 850 homes were lost and more than fifteen people were killed. In 2009, fires fanned by strong winds raged again through the hills.

The answer to this 'weed' problem may be in the production of bio-oil by a technique called fast pyrolysis. One hundred tonnes of eucalypt timber would generate 75,000 litres of bio-oil for use as crude oil for generation of electricity and production of fuel for vehicles. Research is still progressing along these lines and may at least partly solve the problems, both in California and other countries where the eucalypt has caused controversy.

Genetically modified eucalypts are being produced by a company in the United States to increase the frost tolerance of tropical eucalypts and to improve their productivity and make them less invasive. This would allow eucalypts to be grown in south-eastern states where pines are now being grown as timber plantations. The selected trees are mainly hybrids between the Timor Mountain Gum (*E. urophylla*) and Flooded Gum (*E. grandis*). It is claimed they have a higher productivity than pines and a shorter crop rotation. Trials have indicated that trees may be harvested each 5–7 years by coppicing.

The genetic composition has been changed by the introduction of a cold inducible promoter and a pollen control gene in order to reduce the likelihood of seed production. In trials they have shown minimal invasive characteristics, producing few seeds; those seeds that do set result in poor germination. Because of their infertility, these trees can only be propagated by tissue culture.

TASMANIAN BLUE GUM (*Eucalyptus globulus*)

Tasmania's floral emblem, the Blue Gum, occurs also in the mainland forests of eastern Victoria and southern New South Wales, with one isolated occurrence near Burra in South Australia. A tall tree reaching 70 metres high, it is easily recognised by its juvenile foliage, which consists of large, silvery-grey, stem-clasping leaves borne on square-winged stems. The adult, lance-shaped leaves are glossy green and up to 30 centimetres long. The flowers are creamy-white and quite large, while the buds, fruits and young stems are clothed with a grey bloom.

Four subspecies are named, three of which occur only on the mainland, and although these tend to intergrade, some authorities still regard them as distinct species. Subspecies *bicostata*, often known as Eurabbie, has slightly smaller buds with flowers in threes and occurs in southern New South Wales and Victoria, with the singular occurrence near Burra, South Australia. Subspecies *pseudoglobulus*, known as Victorian Eurabbie, occurs in east Gippsland and is similar to subsp. *bicostata* but has its buds on a stout stem. Subspecies *maidenii* occurs in southern New South Wales and eastern Victoria and has its buds in sevens, with less greyish bloom on the buds and fruits. The foliage and the gumnuts are sometimes used for floral arrangements.

Tasmanian Blue Gum is probably the most widely grown eucalypt in the world. Its timber is used for construction, railway sleepers, firewood and paper. It is also commonly planted as an ornamental and shade tree and has become naturalised in many overseas countries, where it is sometimes considered a weed. In China, Spain and Portugal, oil is distilled from the foliage for use in perfumes and soap making.

Eucalyptus globulus subsp. *bicostata*, with its buds in threes, covered in a grey bloom.

A giant forest tree beside a track in Tasmania; the figure gives an idea of its size.

The company claims that these trees provide land holders and rural areas with more economic options and address the unmet needs of the pulp and paper industry and the developing bio-energy industry.

Some 60 trials were underway in 2008 and were being examined by a Government Regulatory Authority of the US Department of Agriculture. Not everyone is happy with these developments, as the memory of the Californian experience is still fresh, but the use of timber for the production of bio-oil by fast pyrolysis may change some minds and be the answer to the 'weed' problem in California as well.

Other countries

Other countries that have given over huge tracts of land to eucalypt plantations are Spain, Portugal, Chile, Pakistan, New Zealand and more recently South-East Asian countries such as Cambodia, Thailand and Vietnam. In South-East Asia landholders have planted fast-growing species such as Lemon-scented Gum, expecting them to be coppiced at five years old and selling the cuttings for about US$5 per tree for paper and pulp use. These figures would be repeated in another five years as the coppice growth matures.

Although it might seem an odd combination, these pineapples are growing under a canopy of River Red Gums (*Eucalyptus camaldulensis*) in Thailand. PHOTO: CSIRO.

First cultivation records for eucalypts in Europe appear in Portugal by 1829, Italy around 1830 and Spain by 1847. These Tasmanian Blue Gums (*Eucalyptus globulus*) are growing at Galicia in north-west Spain. There are about 600 trees in this forest, ranging from 95 to 115 years old. PHOTO: GUSTAVO IGLESIAS.

PART 6

EUCALYPTS IN ART AND CULTURE

Augustus Earle, *June Park, Van Dieman's Land, the general appearance of the country in its natural state, perfect park scenery,* watercolour, c. 1825. The distant trees have a eucalypt 'look', but the subject tree, assuming it is a eucalypt, is not a very successful representation. PHOTO: NLA.

30 Painting Gum Trees

IN A BOOK OF THIS NATURE WE ARE NOT GOING TO DELVE INTO THE WORLD OF ART CRITICISM. There is, however, an interesting story in the evolution of the European immigrant's abilities to draw or paint the unique form of eucalypts. For those who travel overseas, it is not unusual to spot a tree in the distance and immediately proclaim it to be a eucalypt from Australia. These trees have a special 'look', no matter whether they have been planted in Africa or China.

For Europeans coming to Australia in the years after 1788, the eucalypts must have looked quite different to trees they were familiar with, but capturing that difference on paper or canvas proved a challenge. This is perhaps more intriguing when we consider that most of the artists were trying to capture the 'exotic' nature of Australia, often for an audience in England that would never see the real thing.

Most of these artists, by influence or training, were saddled with the artistic trends of Europe at the time. The neoclassical view of the eighteenth century was that nature was to be rendered with its imperfections tidied up, to represent things as they should be rather than as they are. The early nineteenth century saw the rise of the Picturesque movement, introducing a variation and irregularity of elements that went together to produce 'the kind of beauty that would look well in a picture'.

In seeking out these picturesque landscapes, the artists had as their benchmark the European painters Claude Lorrain, Salvator Rosa and Nicolas Poussin. Rather than capturing a 'snapshot' of what they saw, the artists were influenced by what a picturesque landscape in the hands of these masters would look like.

Artists 'learned' how to draw trees, just as they learned how to draw the human figure. It has been suggested that figure-drawing lessons based on classical marble statues in art class studios resulted in difficulties in giving accurate renditions of Oceanic peoples when these artists came to the Pacific. Similarly, no art instruction in Europe had provided these artists with models of the open foliage, vertical arrangement of leaves and general asymmetry of the eucalypts.

Added to this was the fact that, by and large, newcomers to Australian shores did not like the appearance of eucalypts. They were seen as 'monotonous'; as William Bligh commented in 1807, the country was covered 'with trees of a dark, sombre hue, without any variety of tinge to relieve the eye'—certainly a failing for those seeking the picturesque, for whom variety was crucial.

Barron Field, judge of the Supreme Court of New South Wales from 1816 to 1823, lamented the restricted palette: 'What can a painter do with one cold olive green?' He goes on to say that there is no scene in New South Wales 'of which a painter could make a landscape, without greatly disguising the character of the trees'.

So how long did it take for these early artists to 'get their eye in' when painting eucalypts in the landscape? A few examples might suffice to show this evolution.

Thomas Watling (b. 1762?) was transported to Australia for forgery in 1792. There is some evidence to suggest that he had taught drawing in Scotland. During his eight years in Australia he painted detailed and reasonably accurate illustrations of flowers, birds and other animals. However, his attempts to represent drawing of eucalypts in his landscape *South View of Sydney-Cove taken from the General Spring nigh the Eastern entrance to Pitt's Row* have not captured the distinctive look of the trees. It is notable that he has illustrated quite accurately a dead tree and possibly stumps showing regrowth.

Joseph Lycett (c. 1775–1828) was another artist transported to Australia for forgery, in 1814. Like Watling, his artistic talents were put to use by the colonial authorities. Lycett was joined in Australia by members of his family, who came as free migrants. The family returned to England after Lycett received an absolute pardon in 1822. There he proceeded to publish *Views in Australia*, which was issued in thirteen monthly parts from 1824. As part of this process he produced a series of watercolours in apparent preparation for the engravings to be published, and they show an interesting insight into the representation of eucalypts. In his watercolour *View of Salt Pan Plains, Van Diemen's Land*, painted in 1824, we have what could be interpreted as a fair representation of a eucalypt and eucalypt vegetation. But in the subsequent engraving based on the painting—*Salt Pan Plain, Van Diemen's Land*—we find this transformed into a very un-eucalypt tree and less-Australian vegetation. It has been suggested that these changes were to appeal to the picturesque ideals of the time, to make the commercial publications more appealing.

Perhaps these artists could draw eucalypts, but the English audiences to which they were catering would have seen such representations as 'wrong' and this would have depreciated their artistic skills. Perhaps, as Baron Field suggested, they were deliberately 'disguising the character of the trees'.

Augustus Earle (1793–1838) was the first artist to come to Australia with a Royal Academy background,

Thomas Watling's, *South View of Sydney-Cove taken from the General Spring nigh the Eastern entrance to Pitt's Row*. Pencil, ink and wash, 1792–96. PHOTO: NHM.

Joseph Lycett's *View of the Salt Pan Plains, Van Diemen's Land*, watercolour, 1824.
PHOTO: DIXSON GALLERIES, SLNSW.

Left: Joseph Lycett's *Salt Pan Plain, Van Diemen's Land*, hand-coloured engraving, from *Views in Australia*, Plate 19, 1824.
PHOTO: NLA.

John Glover, *The Last Muster of the Aborigines at Risdon*, oil on canvas, 1836. PHOTO: QVMAG.

Right: Typical eucalypts, possibly *Eucalyptus pulchella*, photographed at Risdon today at the place where Glover set his painting of the Last Muster. They show nothing of the sinuous form portrayed in Glover's painting.

for his paintings as predominantly the new rich of the colony. These people knew what eucalypts looked like.

Martens did not usually make trees the central focus of his paintings, but one, simply titled *Blue Gum*, painted in 1843, shows that he has captured the look of these trees. It is interesting that he is the first artist to prominently show the ribbons of bark hanging down from the trunk and branches of the tree, despite numerous literary references to this phenomenon over the previous 50 years. Perhaps earlier artists 'tidied up' their paintings to remove such bark, which would have seemed incongruous to English viewers.

Thus by the 1850s we find that artists in general have 'got their eye in', and we see a range of skills, artistic

Conrad Martens, *Blue Gum*, watercolour, 1843. This is probably the Southern Blue Gum (*Eucalyptus globulus* subsp. *bicostata*), with its ribbons of hanging bark. PHOTO: DIXSON GALLERIES, SLNSW.

Albert Namatjira's *MacDonnell Range*, watercolour on paper, c. 1965. The tree is the central Australian Ghost Gum (*Corymbia aparrerinja*). PHOTO: NAA: A1500, K13420 © LEGEND PRESS.

interpretations and art styles in the works that follow.

Mention should be made of the artist Henry James Johnstone (1835–1910) who came to Australia in 1853. He had worked in his father's photographic firm, a trade he reverted to in Melbourne after a successful stint on the Victorian goldfields. But painting was his passion, and he took lessons in Melbourne and started exhibiting. One of his oil paintings, *Evening Shadows, Backwater of the Murray, South Australia*, became the first acquisition of the Art Gallery of South Australia in 1880 and is an almost 'photographic' representation of eucalypts. Ironically, it was painted in England after he left Australia permanently in 1878. Apart from being a landmark for Australian galleries acquiring Australian landscapes, it is also reputed to be 'Australia's most copied painting'.

Johnstone's painting would also have considerable influence on the young Hans Heysen (1877–1968). Heysen grew up in South Australia after arriving from Germany at the age of six. He has been called 'the most prolific and influential Australian landscape painter in the first half of the twentieth century', and certainly made the vision of the gnarled River Red Gums in a dry landscape one of our icons. In the watercolour *The Clearing, Early Morning* painted in 1919, we typically see his detailed portrayal of the bark and dead twigs as well as the form of the young and old trees.

No mention of painting eucalypts would be complete without reference to the art of Albert Namatjira (1902–59). He did for the central Australian Ghost Gums what Heysen had done for the River Red Gums. As an Aboriginal man growing up on Hermannsburg Mission in central Australia, he was strongly influenced by the commercially trained artist Rex Battarbee, who exhibited his watercolour paintings at the mission in 1934. Battarbee and others mentored Namatjira and arranged for his paintings to be exhibited. Within ten years he had become famous and his delicate watercolours, many featuring the iconic eucalypts of the so-called 'red centre', were sold throughout Australia. While eucalypts and their white trunks were the focus of only a few of his paintings, it is his use of them to frame the dramatic colours of central Australia that most typifies his works.

Henry James Johnstone, *Evening Shadows, Backwater of the Murray, South Australia* (1880). The trees are River Red Gums (*Eucalyptus camaldulensis*). GIFT OF MR HENRY YORKE SPARKS 1881/AGSA.

Left: Hans Heysen's watercolour, *The Clearing, Early Morning* (1919). The trees are River Red Gums (*Eucalyptus camaldulensis*). BEQUEST OF SIR JAMES MCGREGOR, 1974/NGA. © HANS HEYSEN/ LICENSED BY VISCOPY, 2010.

One of the lantern slides (cracked in the top corner) Archibald James Campbell used for public lectures. This one is of a Jarrah (*Eucalyptus marginata*) forest. PHOTO: NLA.

31 Photographing Gum Trees

TODAY WE TAKE PHOTOGRAPHY VERY MUCH FOR GRANTED, BUT THE DIFFICULTIES encountered when the early photographers wanted to move from their studio laboratories to the bush were considerable. Before the availability of dry-plate photographic plates in the 1880s, the photographer had to have a mobile darkroom in which to make up his wet plates, which had to be used within two to three minutes. Nicholas J. Caire (1837–1918) commented on a photograph at the Erskine River Waterfall, Victoria, in 1876:

> An idea of the difficulty with which the present very beautiful illustration was obtained may be gained from the fact that it took our assistants several days to convey the apparatus a distance of six miles and back.

Duncan J. Peirce, Plate 2 from *The Giant Trees of Victoria* (1888–89), labelled *Eucalyptus Amygdalina Regnans*. This is the Mountain Ash (*E. regnans*). Photographers of this period had difficulty getting the tree in their camera frame and had no qualms about destroying the surrounding vegetation to get their view.

The earliest photographs of eucalypts were mainly 'record shots'; the photo was a technical means of communicating information and wonder. The 1880s saw a rising interest in travel and tourism, as well as national identity, and the railways enabled people to get away from the cities. Photography helped to fuel this interest and the giant eucalypts became objects of fascination for the public.

The 1880s also saw the rise of competitive interest in 'giant trees', not just in Australia but also in America as photos of the Californian Redwoods began to circulate. Several photos of large eucalypt trees were exhibited in the 1888 Centennial Exhibition in Melbourne. This resulted in prize money being offered for the finders of trees over 400 feet (120 metres) tall, and a total of £600 was raised for the purpose of more systematically obtaining pictures of Victoria's highest trees.

John Duncan Peirce (credited as Duncan J. Peirce) photographed significant trees for the resulting book *The Giant Trees of Victoria*, which came out in 1888–89 as a large folio volume with botanical names beneath each photo. In these photos human figures are an important element for scale.

Nicholas Caire continued to promote these giants of the forest with his photos accompanying numerous newspaper articles and with sales to the public. He commented to the Victorian Field Naturalists in 1904 that he was a photographer not a botanist, and if his eucalypt photos be 'the means of awakening official and public interest in them, and lead to the collecting and recording of information for the benefit of future generations, then I will consider myself well repaid in the interest that has been aroused'.

While Caire and Peirce were professional photographers, others like Archibald James Campbell (1835–1929) and Walter Gill (1851–1929) used photography as a medium for education and to raise public awareness. Campbell was a government officer who took up photography through a course at the Working Men's College in Melbourne and often used that same venue to give public lectures illustrated with lantern slides (see p. 250). Recalling one of these talks given in 1893, he later commented, 'It was intended as a pictorial protest to the Government of the Day who were about to despoil a magnificent State Forest Resource on the crown of the Dandenongs …'

Walter Gill was appointed Conservator of Forests for South Australia in 1890 and was described as 'a skilful and enthusiastic photographer, having made it a special private hobby for many years'. Of a free public lecture given by Gill in 1899, the *Observer* newspaper reported:

> the Conservator brought the forests to his audience by means of numerous magnificent lantern slides, made from photographs taken by himself on the reserves … The limelight views gave an excellent idea of the growth and character of the towering sugar and red gums, stringybark, and other trees grown in the natural forests.

AUSTRALIA BEAUTIFUL
THE HOME PICTORIAL ANNUAL 1929
PRICE TWO SHILLINGS AND SIX PENCE

Above right: John Bertram Eaton (1881–1966): cover of *Australia Beautiful: The Home Pictorial Annual 1929*. Eaton was a keen tree photographer—this one is most likely Yellow Box (*Eucalyptus melliodora*).

Right: John Kauffmann, *Golden Gleams*, a carbon photograph (c. 1908). PHOTO: NGA.

Opposite: Harold Cazneaux's *The Spirit of Endurance*, one of many versions printed from several negatives in the years after it was photographed in 1937. Compare with p. 225 for differences. PHOTO: NGA.

These photographers were taking photos before the advent in Australia of the worldwide movement that aimed to promote photography as an art form, and they aimed for photos that were technically correct in terms of sharpness and exposure. Once photography became a little easier, the more artistic looked for 'atmosphere' in their photos. These photographers were interested in entering the works in salons, and in manipulating the image after it left the camera. Photos were given titles, just like other works of art.

The Adelaide-born photographer John Kauffmann (1864–1942), on returning from Europe in 1897, was full of pictorial ideas from the salons and exhibitions he had seen there. He promoted the soft-focus impressionist imagery, where trees seen through the early morning mist were the order of the day, imposing European 'atmosphere' on the Australian scene.

It was not until about 1917 that Australia found its own artistic photographic vision to 'interpret something in the bright light and spaciousness of Australia'. These photographers were sometimes dubbed 'the Sunshine School' and were influenced by artists such as Tom Roberts and Hans Heysen. Australian photographers started to present themselves on the international scene and eucalypts provided a characteristic icon for their work. The English photographer, Mrs Alfred Milson, noted in 1923: 'In this year's London Salon … there was a distinct evidence of Australian artists working together, and the gum trees were overdone.'

In Australia, the upper middle class looked to the lavish periodical *Australia Beautiful: The Home Pictorial Annual* to compare the Australian art scene with the rest of the world. Here was a venue for our leading photographers and nothing could be more Australian than eucalypts.

Harold Cazneaux (1878–1953) was born in Adelaide and had seen an exhibition by Kauffman in 1898; then and there he decided to spend his life taking similar pictures. But Cazneaux was of the new school, with

Opposite: Charles P. Mountford 'The Ghost Gum' from *Australian Tree Portraits*. He named it *Eucalyptus papuana*, but this central Australian species is now *Corymbia aparrerinja*. PHOTO: SLSA.

a new relationship to light. Early mornings and late evenings fell out of favour, as did mist to achieve a soft focus.

Cazneaux's iconic photo *The Spirit of Endurance*, taken in the harsh midday sun in 1937, is one of the best-known tree portraits in Australia. But which photo is 'the' photo? There are many different versions, vertical and horizontal formats, with dead branches added, moved or removed in the darkroom. This River Red Gum (*E. camaldulensis*) was still alive in 2007 and has become a tourist feature in the Flinders Ranges.

While other photographers took the occasional eucalypt photo, one often overlooked in reviews of Australian photography is the ethnographer Charles Pearcy Mountford (1890–1976). His 1956 book *Australian Tree Portraits* was definitely aimed at the art pictorial market, an early 'coffee table' book of well-composed black and white photographs. But Mountford combines his art photography with botanical pen portraits and scientific names. Mountford wrote one of the earliest books on the Aboriginal artist Albert Namatjira, and there is an unsettling similarity to the composition of some of his central Australian photographs with the work of that artist.

Once we reach the 1950s we are in the era of accessible colour photography via the 35-millimetre slide and we again see, as in the 1880s, photos used mainly for documentation and the transmission of information. The slideshow presentation to field naturalist clubs mirrored the lantern slide presentations to similar clubs in an earlier time.

No mention of tree portraits in Australia would be complete without reference to two Tasmanian photographers who raised the standard of colour photography to a true art form: Lithuanian-born Olegas Truchanas (1923–72) and the man he influenced, Peter Dombrovskis (1945–96), born of Latvian parents. Like Campbell 75 years earlier, these men used the medium of photography to raise public awareness about the threat to our wilderness from government and government-sanctioned projects, although eucalypts were rarely the main focus of images.

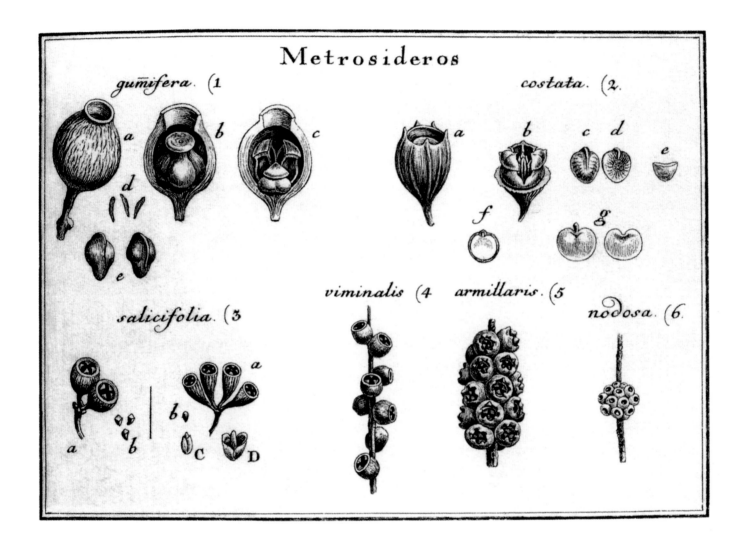

The first published illustrations of eucalypts, as fruit, in Gaertner's *De Fructibus et Seminibus Plantarum* (1788). He included them under the genus name *Metrosideros*. They include what we now know as *Corymbia gummifera*, *Angophora costata* and *Eucalyptus amygdalina* (as *salicifolia*), plus some *Melaleuca* species.

32 Flower Painters and Illustrators

THERE IS A RICH TRADITION OF SCIENTIFIC ILLUSTRATION AND POPULAR FLOWER PAINTING IN Australia. Those with a special interest in the technical aspects of botanical illustration should read Helen Hewson's *Australia: 300 Years of Botanical Illustration*, published in 1999, for a detailed history of the craft.

The artist on board the *Endeavour*, assisting Joseph Banks on Cook's voyage to Australia in 1770, was Sydney Parkinson. He was probably the first to make detailed drawings of eucalypts, but died before the voyage returned to England. Unfortunately, the copper plates engraved from his drawings were not printed in colour for another 200 years; they finally appeared in *The Florilegium* in 1988.

It is interesting to note that the first published illustrations of eucalypts were printed before the name *Eucalyptus* was even in use. The German botanist Joseph Gaertner (1732–91) was given some fruit and seed samples when he visited Joseph Banks in 1787, and a year later illustrated some of these under the name *Metrosideros* in his huge book on seeds and fruit, *De Fructibus et Seminibus Plantarum*.

It was not until 1792 that L'Heritier de Brutelle published the first illustration using the name *Eucalyptus*, establishing that name for the genus with *Eucalyptus obliqua*. The first illustration of an *Angophora* resulted from the visit to Sydney of a Spanish expedition in 1793. Material collected there was passed on to the Spanish botanist Antonio Cavanilles, who did his own drawings from which the metal plates for *Angophora cordifolia* (now *A. hispida*) were engraved and published in 1797.

Around this time we start to see the Australian flora being illustrated in periodicals such as *Curtis's Botanical Magazine* and J.E. Smith's *Exotic Botany*, fulfilling an English appetite for knowledge about plants from foreign lands. Many of these illustrations were fairly crude and executed purely for printing and hand-colouring in the journals, but a couple of artists stood out for their artistic skills.

Pierre Joseph Redouté (1759–1840) was born in Belgium but spent most of his life in France. He became an associate of L'Heritier and they spent time together in London

The genus *Angophora* was first described in Cavanilles' *Icones et Descriptiones Plantarum* (1797). This plate shows the Dwarf Apple (*Angophora hispida*) under the name *A. cordifolia*.

where they were able to see a eucalypt flowering at Kew and the specimens in Banks' herbarium. It was Redouté who did the painting on which the engraved plate of *Eucalyptus obliqua* is based (see p. 54). However, it was under the patronage of Napoléon's wife, the Empress Joséphine, that his botanical output flourished. Not only did he do beautiful paintings to impress the empress, but she had the financial means to have them published. Many were growing in Josephine's garden at Malmaison where Australian plants seemed to be a special favourite.

Ferdinand Bauer (1760–1826) was born in Austria, one of seven children, three of whom would become involved in botanical art. His association with Australian plants began when he came to the attention of Joseph Banks, who recommended him as botanical artist on Flinders' expedition to navigate the coast of Australia in 1801–03 with botanist Robert Brown. At the end of the trip he advised Banks that he had 'sketches of plants above one Thousand and Animals two Hunderd (sic)'. Despite the gruelling conditions he was working under in the cramped quarters of the ship, he is regarded as one of the best botanical artists of all times. It is unfortunate that only a small proportion of his paintings have been published.

While eucalypts continued to be painted from time to time for various scientific publications in Europe, it is the flower painters who called Australia home that we will now concentrate on.

Louisa Anne Meredith (1812–95) had already published books of poetry with her own illustrations before she arrived in Australia, leaving England shortly after her marriage in 1839. Her relationship with eucalypts changed over the course of her life; she referred to them in very negative terms on arrival but later featured eucalypt flowers on the cover of one of her many popular books, *Our Island Home: A Tasmanian Sketch Book*. She painted 'studies' of individual flowers before preparing plates for publication, which usually combined several species in an assemblage.

These paintings of assemblages of several unrelated species of native flowers became the hallmark of Victorian lady artists of the period. It was a respectable pastime

and could earn women an income. Harriet and Helena Scott, for example, produced scientific illustrations of insects and their host plants, but also produced attractive assemblages for postcards and Christmas cards.

None of these Victorian women could match the output of Australia's most famous flower painter, Ellis Rowan (1848–1922). She continued in the tradition of artistically arranged assemblages, but it is the sheer number of her paintings and her intrepid adventurism that most marks her life. Despite the lack of scientific rigour in her paintings, between 1872 and 1893 she won ten gold and fifteen silver medals in International Exhibitions held throughout the world. It is estimated

Ferdinand Bauer's detailed painting of the Bald Island Marlock (*Eucalyptus conferruminata*). Although painted about 1811, this species was not formally described until 1980. PHOTO: NHM.

Original watercolour painting of Soap Mallee (*Eucalyptus diversifolia*), signed by Pierre-Joseph Redouté in 1811. This was later published as a mirror-image print to accompany Aimé Bonpland's description of the species in 1813. PHOTO: FMC.

Louisa Anne Meredith's watercolour study of Tasmanian Blue Gum (*Eucalyptus globulus*) for a painting she later published as *Gum Flowers and Love* in 1860. PRESENTED THROUGH THE ART FOUNDATION OF VICTORIA BY MRS JAMES EVANS, GOVERNOR, 1989/NGV.

One of the few paintings by Ellis Rowan where she has concentrated on a single species—Coral Gum (*Eucalyptus torquata*)—as subject, rather than a mixed 'bunch'. PHOTO: NLA.

that she produced about 3000 works. While Rowan did not specialise in eucalypts, the volume of her work dictates that eucalypts are included in many paintings and are the sole subject of a few.

Rowan travelled widely, not only to conventional places but also the rainforests of north Queensland and Papua New Guinea, where she suffered considerable hardships while maintaining her demeanour in long dresses and whalebone corsets. She was equally at home in the jungle, or society openings of her exhibitions in London or New York. She also painted extensively in the United States, where she illustrated three textbooks on American wildflowers.

On one of her travels to Western Australia in 1880, Rowan met up with the English flower painter Marianne North (1830–90), and the two women shared a cottage at Albany for a few days of painting together as their travelling paths crossed. North, too, was an intrepid traveller and Rowan was able to introduce her to the

wonders of Australia's western flora. It was here that North produced the painting of *Eucalyptus macrocarpa* that now hangs in the gallery named after her in the Royal Botanic Gardens in Kew, London.

Rosa Fiveash (1854–1938) was a contemporary of Rowan, but worked in a far less glamorous world, only leaving Adelaide for a single two-year period overseas. Fiveash is credited with introducing the art of china painting to Australia, but it is for her accurate botanical illustrations that she is most remembered. She was engaged by the forester John Ednie Brown to illustrate his *Forest Flora of South Australia*, on which she worked with lithographer H. Barrett to produce some incredibly detailed, coloured lithographic plates of eucalypts between 1882 and 1890. Fiveash would produce a watercolour painting from live material and Barrett would etch the lithographic stones, one stone for each coloured ink, with up to eleven stones needed to print one plate.

At about the same time that Fiveash was working in colour in South Australia, Ferdinand von Mueller was producing his *Eucalyptographia: A Descriptive Atlas of Eucalypts of Australia and Adjoining Islands*, published in Victoria between 1879 and 1884. The plates for this were printed from single lithographic stones in black ink, with often a single artist producing the image and etching the stone. In most cases these artists got little credit for their work: 'R. Austen delt et Lith' in fine print at the foot of the page was all that they could expect.

A few years later, in New South Wales, Joseph Maiden was publishing his *Critical Revision of the Genus Eucalyptus* between 1903 and 1930, with the artist Margaret Flockton (1861–1953) as his major illustrator. She started work at the National Herbarium

Marianne North's painting of Mottlecah (*Eucalyptus macrocarpa*), produced when she visited Western Australia in 1880. She put more detail in her backgrounds than Ellis Rowan. PHOTO: RBGK.

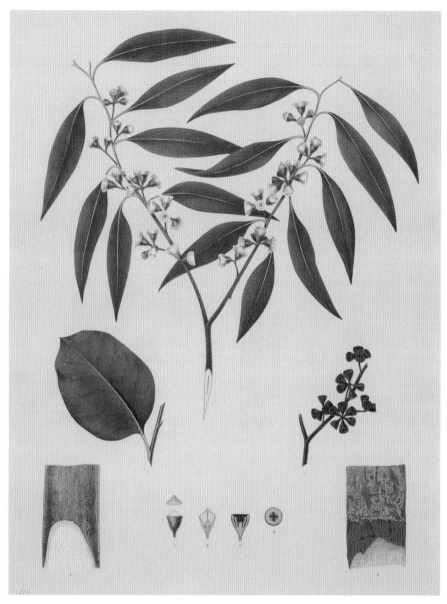

Artist R. Austen's plate of Ilyarrie (*Eucalyptus erythrocorys*) in Ferdinand von Mueller's *Eucalyptographia* in the 1880s. His name appears in fine print in the bottom left corner of the page.

Rosa Fiveash's plate of Cider Gum (*Eucalyptus gunnii*) for the *Forest Flora of South Australia*, published by John Ednie Brown in 1882. PHOTO: NGA.

of New South Wales in 1901 'at the rate of 2 shillings per hour'. Flockton stayed with the project until her retirement in 1927, two years after Maiden's death. Unusual for the time, Maiden had prepared two pages of acknowledgements to be inserted in the final volume published several years after his death, and there he described her contribution as 'immense' and Margaret as 'practically a joint author'.

In the twentieth century one artist stands out from all others when it comes to painting eucalypts. Stan Kelly (1911–2001) spent most of his working life as an engine driver with the Victorian Railways, but his favourite pastime was watercolour painting and searching for rare eucalypts. In 1949 he published *40 Australian Eucalypts in Colour*, a lavish coffee-table book in those post-war years when times were still tough and quality paper hard to get. Kelly accompanied his colour plates with descriptions of each species in plain English. Twenty years later Kelly published 250 paintings in the book *Eucalypts*, with text by George Chippendale and Robert Johnstone, and nine years later in 1978 *Eucalypts Volume II* with a further 258 paintings. In 2009 Kelly's paintings of eucalypts were incorporated into the pages of Australian passports as part of their anti-fraud security.

In the latter part of the twentieth century there have been many botanical illustrators and flower painters of high standard who from time to time have tackled eucalypts, but none stand out as specifically a eucalypt painter. The modern trend is for detailed photographs instead of illustrations in both technical books and popular field guides.

Stan Kelly, photographed in 1973.

Margaret Flockton's detailed illustrations of the fruit of Dowerin Rose (*Eucalyptus pyriformis*) in Joseph Maiden's *Critical Revision of the Genus Eucalyptus* could have inspired the designer of the 1966 Australian $5 note (see p. 281). PHOTO: NGA.

Stan Kelly's published plate of Sand Mallee (*Eucalyptus eremophila*) from *40 Australian Eucalypts in Colour* (1949).

A hall settle made by Gertrude Rushton working for Hamlyn Bros of Adelaide in 1913. It shows beautifully rendered eucalypt flowers with kookaburras carved in Blackwood timber (*Acacia melanoxylon*).
PHOTO: PENELOPE CLAY/PHM.

33 Eucalypts in Applied Art

IN THE LATTER PART OF THE NINETEENTH CENTURY, ENGLAND SAW THE RISE OF THE ARTS and Crafts movement, with strong advocates such as the artist, socialist and writer William Morris. This reflected a reaction against the mass production of the industrial revolution and a return to craftsmanship, where the value of an object should derive from the effort and delight which had been put into creating it. There was also an emphasis on drawing on motifs from the natural world, especially those appropriate to the place of manufacture.

This movement affected technical and art education, not only in Britain, but also in North America and Australia. Movements such as this spread rapidly with various International Expositions held around the world, including the Sydney International Exhibition held in the Garden Palace adjacent to the botanic gardens in 1879.

One of the earliest advocates of the Arts and Crafts movement in Australia was ironically a Frenchman, Lucien Henry (1850–96), fresh out of prison in New Caledonia for his involvement in the Paris Commune of 1871. From his position as a lecturer at the Sydney Technical College, he had great influence in raising the profile of Australian botanical motifs in applied art and architecture in Australia. While his use of the Waratah has been well documented, and he used a range of other native floral motifs, his complete lack of interest in eucalypts is puzzling.

When Henry left Australia in 1891 it was Richard Thomas Baker (1854–1941) who took up the cause for Australian flora in art and craft. Baker arrived from England in 1879 with teaching, art and science qualifications, and within ten years became Joseph Maiden's assistant at the Sydney Technological Museum (now the Powerhouse Museum). One of his keen interests at the Museum was to build up the collection known as 'Australian Flora in Applied Art', which was a popular exhibit at the time. While Baker was also passionate about the Waratah, he was more inclusive of all botanical motifs, including the eucalypts.

At this time there was a strong feeling of nationalism as Australia headed towards

Detail of a section of Gertrude Rushton's hall settle showing the eucalypt flowers.

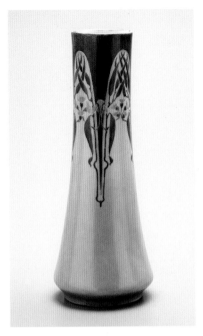

Federation and these two influences came together with the formation of Arts and Crafts societies around Australia in the first years of the twentieth century. Tasmania had a strong Arts and Craft movement, with the first group established in Hobart in 1903 and a second in Launceston in 1906. They quickly followed in other eastern states—New South Wales in 1906, Victoria in 1908, Queensland in 1912. The private Linton School of Art in Perth and the state School of Design in Adelaide promoted similar ideals. The membership of these was drawn from three main groups: professional artisan craftsmen, educators at the various technical institutions and the numerous amateur individuals proficient in traditional craft techniques. The latter were sometimes referred to as 'women's crafts' and helped relieve the isolation and sometimes boredom of women in the Australian outback. These societies held exhibitions on a local, and sometimes a national level, and many offered classes and arranged guest speakers.

Baker showed a keen interest in the New South Wales Society for Arts and Crafts and often addressed their meetings. When he was approached to send his lantern slides to Adelaide so that the South Australian Society could see his Australian flora in art, he immediately suggested he come and speak himself. Baker delivered

two lectures in Adelaide titled 'Australian Flora in Applied Art' and 'Our Natural Heritage, the Gum Tree' in July 1910. Hans Heysen was in the audience.

While Baker was in Adelaide to deliver his talk, he was busy building up his collection and brought back several items for the museum. These included a copper repoussé vase featuring eucalypt blossom and an Art Nouveau porcelain vase with eucalypt flowers and intertwined leaves.

Woodcarving was one of the crafts promoted by the Arts and Crafts societies. Perhaps less well known is that this craft was seen as quite suitable for women at that time, with artists like Ellen Nora Payne (1865–1962) in Tasmania and Gertrude Rushton (1884–1957) in South Australia making sturdy pieces of furniture with intricate carvings, often depicting eucalypts and Australian animals (see p. 266).

The Melbourne industrial chemist and poet, John Kendrick Blogg (1851–1936) was another woodcarver who was especially fond of eucalypt subjects. He emigrated to Australia from Canada when in his twenties, but it was not until the death of his wife when he was in his fifties that he took up carving in a major way, some say to relieve his grief.

The influence of the movement extended to

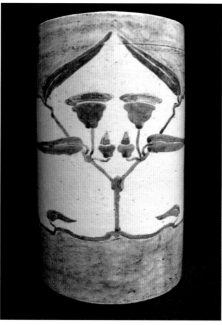

architecture, especially to decorative projects such as public buildings. A fine example can be seen in St John's Church in Launceston, where the architect Alexander North engaged local craftspeople to produce interior decoration incorporating native plants and animals. As well as woodcarving, we have columns with eucalypt flowers, gumnuts and leaves modelled in wet cement by craftsman artist Gordon Cumming (1894–1972).

The world of pottery and ceramics is so full of eucalypt designs that a whole book could be produced on the topic. These range from the products of individual craftspeople to those produced by small-scale industries. Most states had a 'school of Arts and Crafts' in some form, and these offered a range of courses including pottery and china painting. There was rivalry between the 'hand-built' pottery and those that used a potter's wheel, the latter being shunned by some as being a mechanical device suitable only for the making of mass-produced pottery and too far from the tenets of the Arts and Crafts movement.

China painting was popular, using imported ceramic blanks on which the artist painted with fusible enamels mixed with oil, later to be fired in a kiln. Adelaide in the early 1900s became a centre for promoting Australian flora in china painting under the influence of Rosa

A column capital in St John's Church, Launceston, with flowering gums carved in wet cement by Gordon Cumming to a design by Tasmanian architect Alexander North. PHOTO: GARY HAYES.

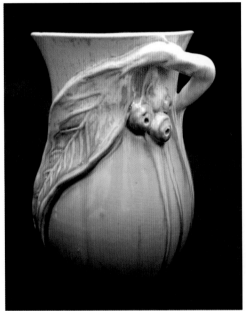

This hand-painted vase was produced by Bakewell Brothers Ltd, who started making bricks and pipes in Erskineville, Sydney, in 1884. They later developed tiles, pots and other domestic wares. This vase was produced in the 1930s and the eucalypt design was painted by D.V. Merton. PHOTO: KRISTEN CLARKE/PHM.

This typical piece of Remued ware from Premier Pottery shows their hallmark use of eucalypt motifs of leaves and gumnuts. PHOTO: NORIS IOANNOU.

Fiveash (1854–1938), who illustrated the *Forest Flora of South Australia*, and Laurence Howie (1876–1963), who became First Assistant Master at the School of Design. Howie seemed particularly interested in eucalypts and they were the subject of many of his works.

Occasionally, individual potters set up businesses to produce very 'Australian' ceramics on a commercial basis. This was the case with artists David Dee (1877–1934) and Reg Hawkins (1894–1971) and their families, who set up a pottery at Darebin, Victoria, during the Depression. Their ceramics were known as Remued ware, and were marketed from Premier Pottery in Preston from 1929 to 1956. Gumnuts and gumleaves became the hallmark of this very distinctive ware.

Embroidery, leatherwork, copper repoussé and marquetry were all crafts where eucalypts were used as strong motifs promoting a nationalist theme.

Perhaps more surprising is the use of eucalypt motifs overseas at this time. It was most noticeable after agents for some of the English ceramic companies set up offices in Australian cities at the end of the nineteenth century, despatching local orders back to their home factories. There was a long tradition of using floral decoration on ceramics in Europe and many of these companies had excellent artists who could turn their hands to the Australian flora.

Both Doulton & Co. and the Royal Worcester Porcelain Company produced ranges of tableware incorporating Australian plant designs. Doulton prided itself on the realistic manner in which it reproduced the Australian flora and even went so far as to have specimens frozen solid in blocks of ice and transported to England by ship so their artists could see the flowers 'fresh'.

When Ellis Rowan held a major exhibition of her works at Angus & Robertson's bookshop in 1910, the Sydney jewellers Flavelle Brothers commissioned Rowan to produce gum blossom designs, which they forwarded to Royal Worcester in England. There, one of their artists would hand-paint the design onto cups and saucers. The tea sets were later sold in the Flavelle shop. Worcester still have several dozen original Rowan designs in their archive.

A frame for a mirror, showing raised eucalypt foliage, buds and fruit, using copper repoussé on cedar wood by Eirene Mort (1879–1977) (c. 1906). PHOTO: NGA.

This porcelain saucer was painted by Ernest John Phillips from a drawing by Ellis Rowan for the Royal Worcester Porcelain Company, England. PHOTO: MARINCO KOJDANOVSKI/PHM.

Tasmanian Blue Gum (*Eucalyptus globulus*) lampshade made in c. 1900 by the internationally famous Daum crystal studio founded by Jean Daum (1825–85) and based in Nancy, France. JAMES AND DIANA RAMSAY FUND 1997/AGSA.

Tiara in silver gilt and topaz, made in France around 1900 by Charles Lefebvre of Lefebvre and Sons, Paris. Gumleaves were a favourite design element for Art Nouveau artists probably representing Tasmanian Blue Gum (*Eucalyptus globulus*). PHOTO: ANDREW FROLOWS/PHM.

Red Flowering Gum (*Corymbia ficifolia*) was the motif used by artist Olive Nock in her prize-winning design, eventually used by the Liberty Silk Company of London in 1928. PHOTO: ANDREW FROLOWS/PHM.

But it was not just tableware that caught the eye of overseas designers. The gentle curve of the eucalypt leaf lent itself to the Art Nouveau style of the time and French designers such as Lalique, Daum and Charles Lefebvre saw possibilities that the expatriate Frenchman Lucien Henry had missed.

The Arts and Crafts movement also used eucalypts in fabric design. Designer Olive Nock (1893–1977) consistently employed Australian floral and faunal motifs in her wide-ranging craft interests, and submitted a design to a competition held by Henderson's Silk Company in Sydney. Her winning entry of Red Flowering Eucalypts was printed by the famous Liberty Silk Company of London in 1928.

It is not surprising, with all this interest in eucalypt motifs, that the 'temporary' Parliament House in Canberra, opened in 1927, chose specially designed carpets featuring gumnuts. The carpet in the Senate Chamber was red, while that in the House of Representatives was green, with a repeat gumnut pattern and an edging of eucalypt leaves.

This is but a small taste of the breadth of eucalypt motifs in Australian applied art. Eucalypts' distinctive appearance, recognisable in the shape of the leaves alone, make them perfect for pottery and woodcarving where colour is not an issue, while those seeking the colourful also have ample scope, especially among the Western Australian species.

'The Lights of Adelaide, from the Mount Lofty Ranges', a 1930s poster from the Publicity and Tourist Bureau, South Australia, with the artist signed as McLean. The eucalypt looks like a representation of a River Red Gum (*Eucalyptus camaldulensis*) but this might be artistic licence for this lookout does not seem a typical habitat for this species. PHOTO: NLA.

34 Eucalypts in Advertising

WITH EUCALYPTS BEING THE MOST DOMINANT TREE IN MOST PARTS OF AUSTRALIA, AND second only to *Acacia* in the number of different species, it is perhaps surprising that they have not featured more prominently in our advertising. Certainly, the other Australian icons—the kangaroo, emu and koala—monopolised our early trademarks.

In the earliest years of the colonies, most products were transported in bulk, taken out of a barrel, box or tin and wrapped for the customer. Choice was minimal. By the end of the nineteenth century, more and more goods were being sold to the customer in bottles, tins and jars, choice had increased and manufacturers needed to differentiate their products. It was only after the 1860s that the various colonial governments enacted laws to register trademarks. From 1906 this role was taken over by the Commonwealth.

Immediately after Federation in 1901, there was a flood of nationalism in our brands and logos featuring maps of Australia, iconic animals and iconic plants, especially eucalypts, wattles and waratahs.

The marketing of eucalyptus oil often featured visual references to eucalypts, but it is their use on other products that is interesting: the 'Mallee Brand' for preserved fruit, 'Ironbark' for a Sydney paper manufacturer, 'Golden Gum' for imported foods, and even a pair of trees linked by a eucalypt leaf for the 'Prima' hosiery company, presumably because socks and stockings come in pairs.

In modern times one of the most distinctive logos is that of the National Trust of Australia—three very simple eucalypt leaves with the characteristic insect nibble on one. Far less obvious is the national logo for Scouts Australia—the three-element north-point of the logo designed in England for the boy scout movement in 1908 has been transformed by artist John Coburn into stylised eucalypt leaves incorporating the Southern Cross.

Another use of eucalypts in advertising was to promote Australia itself, and this was done in travel posters, especially in the 1930s. The most famous of these was 'Australia, the tallest trees in the British Empire' by the artist Percy Trompf, produced by the

NATIONAL TRUST

The logo of the National Trust of Australia—easily recognised and very Australian.

The Scouts Australia logo, with its subtle use of eucalypt leaves.

Australian National Travel Association. It features only the trunks of giant Mountain Ash (*Eucalyptus regnans*) dwarfing two horse riders. Eucalypts feature prominently in other posters of the time such as those promoting Adelaide and the Blue Mountains.

An interesting example of incorporating eucalypts into advertising art could once be found in the glass paintings in New South Wales hotels controlled by Tooth's brewery. During the 1930s, Tooth's was under pressure from the temperance movement and declining beer sales in their 600 pubs. They decided to counter this by changing their corporate image and between 1930 and 1969 commissioned almost 6000 unique glass paintings to decorate the exteriors of their hotels. While many of these were traditional sporting subjects, quite a few were rural scenes, with eucalypts prominently featured to give the paintings a definite Australian identity. They also tried to counter the traditional 'blokey' beer image by including women in some of the paintings.

We must not forget Australia's fascination with 'big' landmarks scattered throughout the country. Eucalypts did not miss out on this treatment, with the creation of the Big Gumnut as part of the marketing at Austraflora Nursery in Melbourne in the 1980s. The glass-fronted giant gumnut was built as a teahouse and gallery. From its shape we would have to conclude it is modelled on a *Corymbia* fruit.

The Gumnut Teahouse, photographed at Austraflora Nursery in Melbourne in 1989.

'Australia, the tallest trees in the British Empire'—Marysville, Victoria. A c. 1939 colour lithograph by acclaimed poster artist Percy Trompf. The trees are Mountain Ash (*Eucalyptus regnans*). PHOTO: COURTESY PERCY TROMPF ARTISTIC TRUST AND JOSEF LEBOVIC GALLERY.

This Tooth's KB Lager painted-glass pub panel by artist Tom Woodman was part of a campaign to change the beer's image to reflect a more outdoorsy and healthy lifestyle. Eucalypts helped give a typically Australian feel to the images.
PHOTO: PHM.

The Mallee Brand was the trademark of the Mildura Fruit Preserving Company in 1893.

Golden Gum was the trademark of the Australian Manufacturing and Importing Company of Sydney. It was being used to label food in 1920.

Prima Hosiery was a Melbourne-based company using this trademark, which dates from 1928.

Australian postage stamps featuring eucalypts, showing
the year of their issue. See p. 280 for details

35 Australiana and Collectables

'AUSTRALIANA' IS A LOOSE TERM TO DESCRIBE OBJECTS, BOOKS AND EPHEMERA CONSIDERED to be typical of Australia. The desire of both children and adults to collect 'things' is commonly recognised but seldom studied. Indeed, whole industries have grown up around this need and websites like eBay thrive on it. While some collect for investment, many collect for pure enjoyment.

Eucalypts, being so iconic in Australian culture, have featured prominently in a wide range of collectables.

Collecting cards

Before Australia produced its first postage stamp in 1913, the cigarette companies were capitalising on the collecting urge and strengthening customer loyalty by producing series of cards on a wide range of topics. W.D. & H.O. Wills produced a series of 50 cards on Australian wildflowers between 1901 and 1917, including two eucalypts, *Angophora cordifolia* (now *A. hispida*) and *Eucalyptus corymbosa* (now *Corymbia gummifera*). A second series of these cards was produced a few years later, this time printed on silk, featuring different illustrations of the same species. It has been suggested that silk became cheaper than card as a result of paper shortages during the First World War. The artist Henry Baron (1863–1948) is assumed to have painted the illustrations for these cards. He is known to have worked for Wills on cigarette cards and he also did illustrations for J.H. Maiden's botanical publications.

After the Second World War and with advanced colour printing processes, the inclusion of card sets to encourage customer loyalty to a range of products became common. Cards were included in many breakfast cereals, packets of tea and to accompany filling the petrol tank with the 'Discover Australia with Shell' promotion, which included cards, albums and posters. Eucalypts featured in many natural history sets. Even the Redhead match company produced a series of labels for their matchboxes that included a couple of eucalypts among a series on Australian native plants.

A pre-First World War W.D. & H.O. Wills cigarette card. Captioned 'Bloodwood, *Eucalyptus corymbosa*', this eucalypt is now known as *Corymbia gummifera*.

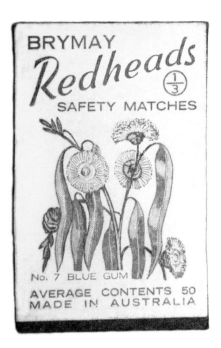

A Shell Petrol collecting card from the early 1960s featuring Tasmanian Blue Gum (*Eucalyptus globulus*).

Redhead matchbox cover, 1960s. Tasmanian Blue Gum, (*Eucalyptus globulus*). PHOTO: LYNN COLLINS.

Postage stamps

It is on the pre-eminent collectable, the postage stamp, that eucalypts have most often caught the imagination of Australian designers. Wattles, our national flower, with about 1000 species have only appeared on seven stamps, while eucalypts, with about 870 species have appeared on seventeen stamp designs.

The first appearance of a eucalypt on an Australian stamp was the result of a historic event. In 1936 the Post Office issued a series of stamps designed by F.D. Manley commemorating the centenary of the founding of the colony of South Australia. Each stamp featured the 'Proclamation Tree' at Glenelg, an arching River Red Gum (*E. camaldulensis*), no longer with any foliage, under whose shade the colony had been proclaimed 100 years earlier.

It was 1968 before the first eucalypt was featured on a stamp for its own sake. The Tasmanian Blue Gum (*E. globulus*), showing flowers, buds and fruit, designed by D. Thornhill, was part of a series featuring six native plants. The next eucalypt stamp, in 1974, was again an indirect

inclusion—the reproduction of a painting by South Australian artist Hans Heysen that beautifully captures the character of River Red Gums in an arid setting. A series featuring Australian trees with designs by D. Rose was issued in 1978 and featured a Ghost Gum (*Corymbia aparrerinja*) in a stark central Australian setting.

Eucalypts got their own stamp series in 1982, issued in booklets and designed by artist Betty Conabere. These stamps featured flower portraits of five species and included their botanical names: *E. calophylla* 'Rosea' (now *C. calophylla*, which can have red or cream flowers), *E. caesia*, *E. ficifolia* (now *C. ficifolia*), *E. globulus* and *E. forrestiana*. The last of these was an incorrect identification, as the species was the closely related *E. dolichorhyncha*.

The next stamp featuring eucalypts was rather more whimsical. The May Gibbs' characters Snugglepot and Cuddlepie sticking their heads out of a gumnut, with red and cream gum flowers in the background, was issued as one of a series of five stamps commemorating children's literature in 1985. The issue of which eucalypt these gumnut babies derived from is a matter of hot debate, eastern Australians claiming *Corymbia gummifera* or *C. eximia*, while Western Australians insist on their *C. calophylla* or *C. ficifolia* since May Gibbs lived in both parts of Australia at different times of her life.

In 1988 a 'panorama' series was issued, with one stamp called 'The Bush'. It was a photographic representation of a eucalypt forest.

Art was the basis for the next eucalypt stamp, this time the work of artist Albert Namatjira featuring a Ghost Gum (*Corymbia aparrerinja*) for Australia Day 1993. In 1996 a large vertical $5 stamp featured a photographic collage of the Mountain Ash (*E. regnans*), together with the fronds of a tree fern. Another Albert Namatjira painting of a Ghost Gum was featured on a stamp in 2002.

A close-up photographic image of the flowers of a Coarse-leaved Mallee (*E. grossa*) was included in a series of native flower stamps designed by Janet Boschen in July 2005.

In August 2005 eucalypts featured on two of the five-stamp series of Australian trees designed by Lisa Christensen: Snowgum (*E. pauciflora*) and Karri (*E. diversicolor*).

Money

Currency is considered a 'collectable' in more ways than one and these days some coins are minted mainly for their collection value. The earliest banknote to feature a eucalypt was the £20 note in circulation from 1914 to 1938. This was not a celebration of the beauty of eucalypts but a depiction of several men felling a giant Tasmanian Blue Gum (*E. globulus*). The engraving on the banknote is based on a photograph taken on Bruny Island, Tasmania, in 1895.

Australia introduced decimal currency in 1966, and the following year a paper $5 note featuring Joseph Banks depicted a range of botanical elements in the background. Among these were several eucalypts including prominent fruits and a bud of Dowerin Rose (*E. pyriformis*), buds of Comet Vale Mallee

(*E. comitae-vallis*), and fruit of White Ash (*E. fraxinoides*), Black Sally (*E. stellulata*) and Yellow-top Mallee Ash (*E. luehmanniana*).

With the introduction of polymer banknotes, a new $5 note was issued in 1992 with a portrait of Queen Elizabeth II on the front accompanied by a spray of the Scribbly Gum (*E. haemastoma*), showing flowers, buds and fruit. The polymer banknotes provided the opportunity to include a transparent security feature and on this note a stylised eucalypt flower is used.

Legal tender coins specifically featuring eucalypts were part of a coin series on Australia's floral emblems produced by the Royal Australian Mint in 1996. This series included gold $150 and $100 coins featuring Tasmanian Blue Gum (*E. globulus*).

Top: The reverse of the 1914 Australian £20 note featuring axemen felling a Tasmanian Blue Gum (*Eucalyptus globulus*) in Tasmania. PHOTO: MICK VORT-RONALD.

Above: Part of the Australian $5 note, issued from 1966 to 1992, featuring a range of eucalypts. A key to their names has been added on the left.

The Perth Mint specialises in 'bullion' legal tender coins in precious metals and has issued a series of platinum 'Discover Australia' coins, with a Flora Series. The third coin in this series, issued in May 2007, featured 'Tasmanian Bluegum' with a coloured representation of flowers and buds. They are available in half an ounce or one-tenth of an ounce of 99.95 per cent pure platinum in proof quality.

Part of the current Australian $5 note, showing the Scribbly Gum (*Eucalyptus haemastoma*) to the left of the Queen's portrait. On the right is the security feature in the lower corner of the note in the form of a stylised eucalypt flower.

Legal tender gold coin featuring Tasmanian Blue Gum (*Eucalyptus globulus*), 1996 (left). Bullion coin featuring Tasmanian Blue Gum (*E. globulus*), Perth Mint, 2007 (right). PHOTOS: ROYAL AUSTRALIAN MINT, PERTH MINT.

Souvenirs and memorabilia

Eucalypts have featured prominently in Australia's souvenirs, memorabilia and ephemera. One person's short-lived souvenir is another person's lifelong treasure. An interesting evolution of memorabilia can be seen with painted gumleaves.

Hand-painted gumleaves were part of the Australian scene in the latter half of the nineteenth century. This may have started out as a personal hobby—we certainly know that the artist Alfred Eustice (1820–1907) started painting on eucalypt leaves when he was a shepherd in the Ovens district of Victoria. These leaves measured about 15 centimetres wide by 10 centimetres long. Some years later his leaf miniatures were featured in an 'Art and Art Treasures' exhibition in Melbourne, and it soon became a trend. The large immature leaves of Messmate (*E. obliqua*) were favoured for this purpose, but others have used Narrow-leaved Peppermint (*E. radiata*), White Box (*E. albens*) and Ribbon Gum (*E. viminalis*). This personal endeavour was soon commercialised, with the hand-painted leaves being glued or sewn onto preprinted blank postcards with words such as 'A Gum-leaf from the Mountain-side to wish you a Merry Christmas' added. Soon afterwards fully printed postcards were designed to look as if they had a eucalypt leaf attached (often embossed for realism), with the postcard scene confined to the surface of the printed leaf. By the time of the First World War we find our troops overseas were being sent all three iterations of this: the personalised hand-painted gumleaves, often with iconic images such as the kookaburra; commercial cards using real leaves; and printed cards designed to look like a painted leaf.

We are fortunate that painted leaves and postcards are flat and relatively easily preserved. Other ephemeral memorabilia with a more three-dimensional form, such as the more recent painted gumnuts as fridge magnets are much less likely to survive long enough to get into one of our museums.

There is no shortage of eucalypt memorabilia and souvenirs available today. These range from fridge magnets to the wares of expensive gift shops; from gold-plated eucalypt leaf jewellery to leadlight glass mobiles and silk scarfs. For the thematic collector, there are endless opportunities.

A leaf painted by an amateur, signed S. Wadsworth, of a scene in the Blue Mountains, undated. The leaf is 17 centimetres long. PHOTO: VANE LINDESAY.

This postcard is rather crudely printed, with an even cruder seascape of a departing ship mid-leaf. The words 'Greetings for the New Year' and some lines of verse are printed in gold, with a flowering gum blossom in the corner. It probably dates from the early 1900s.

Using a special alloy with a silver appearance, the Don Sheil Collection has used the eucalypt theme to create a wide range of products. COURTESY: AUSTRALIAN CHOICE, CANBERRA.

Eucalypt leaves as 2009 giftware: a silk scarf by Helen Joyce with gold printed leaves; a silk eucalypt leaf bookmark with real gumnuts from Creative Silk; a leather gumleaf bookmark with veins and a nibbled bit. COURTESY: AUSTRALIAN CHOICE, CANBERRA.

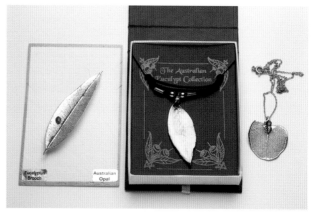

Right: Once the technology for metal-plating plant parts became available in the 1990s, eucalypt leaves were a prime subject. This selection of 2009 jewellery includes a eucalypt brooch with opal in 22-carat gold from Desert Gems; a pendant from the Australian Eucalypt Collection of leaves coated in nickel or copper; and a gold-plated, skeletonised immature eucalypt leaf pendant from Tanplaters of Pt Neill, South Australia.
COURTESY: AUSTRALIAN CHOICE, CANBERRA.

The May Gibbs product line has provided much scope for
collectors. This 1994 plate has an individual number on
the back and was produced by the Bradford Exchange.

FUCHSIA GUMS (*Eucalyptus dolichorhyncha* and *E. forrestiana*)

These two species are known as Fuchsia Gum, differing only in their bud cap. The former has a long beaked cap and in the latter it is flat. *E. dolichorhyncha* has been sold as *E. forrestiana* and this has been the cause of much confusion. Both trees are mallets (i.e. small trees without a lignotuber), forming dense, shrubby trees 4–8 metres high with smooth bark. The beautiful red, slightly squarish, winged buds are pendulous and the flowers are yellow and seen in spring and summer. Both species are commonly used as ornamentals in inland areas with dry summers. They both occur on or near the south coast of Western Australia, north of Esperance on sandy clay soils.

The long, beaked cap of *Eucalyptus dolichorhyncha* can clearly be seen.

A tree of the true *Eucalyptus forrestiana* near Ravensthorpe, Western Australia. PHOTO: *EUCLID*.

Although originally an instrument of northern tribes only, the didgeridoo has
become a powerful symbol for all Aboriginal Australians. In this photograph
the didgeridoo is playing a part in the 30th anniversary of the Aboriginal
Tent Embassy in Canberra, 2002. PHOTO: NLA.

36 Music, Stage and Screen

EUCALYPTS RELATE TO MUSIC IN TWO COMPLETELY DIFFERENT WAYS—AS A MATERIAL FROM which music can be made, and as a theme that has influenced music generated in Australia.

Aboriginal traditional music consists mainly of rhythmic singing supported by a limited number of musical instruments. The simplest of these Aboriginal instruments are known as 'clapsticks' in English. They are usually two wooden sticks, often eucalypts, one held in each hand, which are brought sharply together to make a percussive rhythm. In some areas, wooden boomerangs are used in the same manner as clapsticks. In northern Australia the wood used to make clapsticks is often the ubiquitous Darwin Stringybark (*Eucalyptus tetrodonta*).

The 'bullroarer' is the English name given to another group of Aboriginal instruments that are also often made of eucalypt timber. A bullroarer is a piece of flattened wood that is attached to a fibre string and swung around above the head, causing it to oscillate at a frequency that produces a roaring sound.

Perhaps the best-known Aboriginal instrument is the didgeridoo. Ironically, this name is thought not to be Aboriginal but to have been coined by the anthropologist Herbert Basedow in 1926 on the basis of sounds made by the instrument. Traditionally, the didgeridoo was only used by the most northern tribes, south to about the current settlement of Wave Hill. Most didgeridoos were made from a slender branch or log of Darwin Stringybark (*E. tetrodonta*) that had been hollowed out by termites, the hollow sometimes being enhanced by fire. Didgeridoos are usually about 100–160 centimetres long and flared slightly at one end. The diameter of the inside hollow is 3–5 centimetres. The smaller end is smoothed to form a mouthpiece. The didgeridoo is played by blowing through vibrating lips directly into the mouthpiece. There are many different playing styles and in recent years it has crossed into the realm of Western music with the support of composers such as Peter Sculthorpe.

Another musical instrument that bridged the divide between traditional Aboriginal

Didgeridoos made from Darwin Stringybark (*Eucalyptus tetrodonta*) are now popular tourist souvenirs in the Northern Territory.

Aboriginal gumleaf bands were popular at rural activities in the early 1900s. Here, a group entertains a crowd at Deniliquin in New South Wales, in 1934. PHOTO: NLA.

Herbert Patten (b. 1943) is one of Australia's pre-eminent gumleaf players. He gave his first public performance when he was eight years old and went on to win many awards. Here, he plays on a Yellow Box (*Eucalyptus melliodora*) leaf. PHOTO: SHANNON MATTINSON/MU.

culture and the popular culture of the European settlers is the humble gumleaf. To what extent the gumleaf as a sound-producing instrument was part of pre-European Aboriginal culture seems uncertain. By the end of the nineteenth century, gumleaf players or bands were part of the vaudeville circuit. These bands were often Aboriginal, or white performers claiming to have learned the art from Aboriginals.

In its simplest form, the gumleaf was held against the lower lip with the air forced over the top edge, causing it to vibrate. Mostly the leaves were fresh, but some players had 'cured' leaves that they used over many years. In modern times the art of gumleaf playing had a revival, with the town of Maryborough in Victoria introducing a national competition in 1977 as part of its 'Golden Wattle Festival'. By the final competition in 1997 the prize had climbed to $1000 with a $500 travel voucher, with many interstate competitors and wide coverage by the popular press. The competition usually involved one fixed tune,

often Waltzing Matilda, plus a tune of choice.

It is interesting to note that two Australian movies have incorporated Aboriginal gumleaf bands: Ken Hall's *The Squatter's Daughter* in 1933, and *Rangle River* in 1936, an Australian 'western' based on a story by Zane Grey.

While botanical themes for music for the early European settlers usually reflected a pining for 'the old country', by the end of the nineteenth century the eucalypt as an element of romance was starting to make its appearance. A series of 'Eucalyptus Waltzes' for the pianoforte by Walter Cope was released in 1879 in a folio titled *The Eucalypti Waltzes*, published in Sydney.

The 1910 ballad 'In the Valley Where the Gum Trees Grow' by Percy Foster, printed as sheet music in Sydney, includes the words:

In the valley where the gum trees grow,
It is there my heart is longing to go,
For there dwells the sweetest girl
Who has set my heart a-whirl.

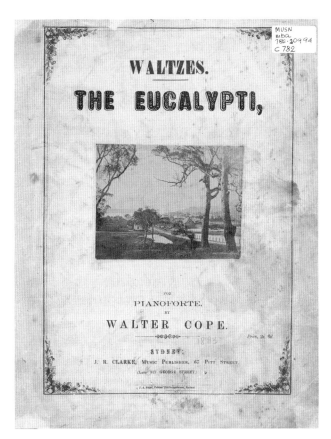

Sheet music for *The Eucalypti Waltzes* by Walter Cope, 1893. PHOTO: NLA.

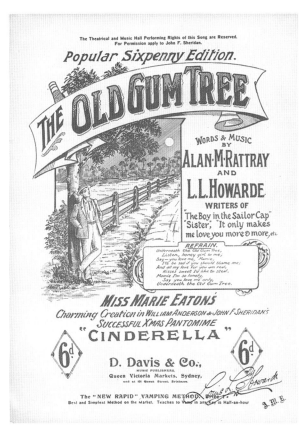

Sheet music for 'The Old Gum Tree' by Rattray and Howarde, published by D. Davis & Co. sometime after 1910. PHOTO: NLA.

Soon after, the popular sixpenny edition of 'The Old Gum Tree' by Rattray and Howarde, also published in Sydney, opens with the words:

> By the little gum lagoon,
> 'Neath the gum tree shade there dwells my lady love.

There is a progression of eucalypt-themed music right to the present day, including 'The Mallee Root Song' by Edith Harrhy, released by Palings in 1932, and John Williamson's 'Mallee Boy' and 'Give Me a Home among the Gum Trees' in recent years. In 2009 composer Peter Sculthorpe was working on music about gum trees based on Patrick White's novel *A Fringe of Leaves*.

Live theatre may seem to have less potential for eucalypt themes, but it pops up when there is a need for national identity. One early example is the J.C. Williamson pantomime of 1895 called *Djin Djin*. As was usual for this Australian Christmas tradition, the pantomime had a principal boy played by a female actor and a dame played by a man, and many allusions to popular topics. It was written and produced in Australia by Williamson and Bert Royle, but the story was set in Japan. While the production is full of colourful Japanese characters and sets, the two Australian heroes visiting this exotic land need to be clearly identified with the names 'Prince Eucalyptus' and his faithful servant 'Tom Wallaby'. The production's popularity and success was thought to have saved J.C. Williamson from bankruptcy in the depression of the 1890s.

In more modern times, eucalypts have had their place on the Australian stage. Barry Humphries, in the guise of Dame Edna Everage, produced a sequinned eucalypt dress for his stage production 'Getting Back to My Roots, and Other Suckers' in 2003.

The ultimate star of Australia, Barry Humphries as Dame Edna Everage, wearing the ultimate Australian eveningwear—a eucalypt-enhanced sequinned frock—in Melbourne in 2007. PHOTO: SHANNON MORRIS/*THE AGE*. COURTESY OF BARRY HUMPHRIES.

Above right: Scene from a performance of the ballet *Snugglepot and Cuddlepie.* PHOTO: DON MCMURDO/NLA.

When discussing costumes, we should not forget the Snow Gum costume of hand-painted nylon lycra and silk featured in the 'Nature' segment of the opening ceremony of the Sydney 2000 Olympic Games. It was designed by Eamon D'Arcy and 50 were manufactured at the Ceremonies Costume Workshop at Redfern. The costume was designed and constructed to 'transform', with the performers beginning the segment rolled up in the leaf structure on the ground and gradually uncurling into the open gumleaf structure.

Both ballet and stage productions for children have been dominated by May Gibbs' legacy of Snugglepot and Cuddlepie and her other gumnut characters. Richard Mills wrote the score for the ballet *Snugglepot and Cuddlepie* while artist-in-residence with the Australian Ballet in 1987. This piece was subsequently recorded and released by the ABC and won a PPRA Award for Contemporary Classical Composition in 1991. There have also been several stage productions based on Snugglepot

and Cuddlepie over the years. One musical by Peter and Carolyn Combe premiered at the Adelaide Festival of Arts in 1992 and has been performed by casts of children. In 2006, the satirist John Clarke wrote the words for a new production entitled *The Adventures of Snugglepot & Cuddlepie and Little Ragged Blossom*, with music by Alan John. Although written for children, it has plenty of appeal to adults and includes the song 'Eucalyptus Blues'.

When it comes to the silver screen, eucalypts have been bit players wherever there has been a need to identify the Australian setting. Ironically, many movie-goers play 'spot the eucalypt' when watching Hollywood productions or telemovies set not only in America but almost anywhere else in the world. Watching Cortés riding beneath gum trees on his way to conquer the Aztecs brings a smile to many naturalists.

Only a few movies have actually dealt with the topic of eucalypts and these have concentrated on the timber industry. One of the sixteen films produced in 1913, when Australia had a thriving silent movie industry, was called *Blue Gum Romance*, and was set near Gosford in New South Wales. The story, like others to follow, was set in a timber logging camp, perhaps Australia's equivalent of the Wild West of American movies. White boys from Gosford played the parts of Aboriginals in a corroboree scene.

Hand-produced lobby cards were a standard part of early cinema. This one promotes the silent film *Tall Timber*, set in a eucalypt logging camp. PHOTO: NFSA.

Above right: A model set for the Ken Hall film *Tall Timbers*, set in a logging camp. The model eucalypt trees had to fall in a domino effect—a vital part of the storyline. PHOTO: NFSA.

The next two films to deal with the Australian timber industry have almost identical names. *Tall Timber*, a 1926 silent film by Dunstan Webb, is set mostly in a timber camp. It involves a story of blackmail and love and includes a violent fight on the swaying trucks of a runaway logging train. The timber scenes were filmed at Langley Vale on the north coast of New South Wales and the movie cost about £3000 to produce.

Tall Timbers, a 1937 talking film by Ken Hall, involves a young forestry graduate and a race between two timber companies to fill a major contract. The climax of the film involves an innovative logging technique where a whole hillside of trees are partially cut through, then the tree at the top is dynamited to produce a domino chain reaction that fells all the lower trees. The film is noted for its special effects because, after two failed attempts with six cameras to film the mass felling, Alan Kenyon resorted to making a model of the timber slope and filming the drive in miniature. Close-up shots of the aborted attempts were intercut with those from the

model. It was filmed near Gloucester in New South Wales and cost about £18,000 to produce.

The Winds of Jarrah, a 1985 film produced by Mark Egerton, had limited commercial success. Set in 1946, it involves a love story between an English governess and the boss of a sawmilling operation, ironically based on a Mills & Boon novel. In another ironic twist, it was backed by the Film Corporation of Western Australia, and as the title might suggest was intended to be shot near Pemberton in Western Australia. But it was finally filmed near Dorrigo in northern New South Wales in what was considered 'similar vegetation'. It had a $2.5 million budget.

Mention should be made of Ray Lawrence's *Bliss*, a 1985 film based on the novel of the same name by Peter Carey. The end of the film has the lead character, Harry Joy, planting honey-producing eucalypts to impress the love of his life, Honey Barbara, in what is described as 'writing a love letter that takes eight years to be sent'.

This chapter should have concluded with the movie of Murray Bail's novel *Eucalyptus*, but production stopped in early 2005. The film was given a lot of publicity, actors Russell Crowe and Nicole Kidman were to be the stars, and sets were built at Bellingen, near Coffs Harbour in northern New South Wales. Perhaps it is yet destined to be the best movie about eucalypts.

WHITE GUM.

"And you, oh gaunt gum tree,
   Why white? Why white?"
"The ghosts of all the bush passed, creepingly
   One night ; one night."

A poem for children entitled 'White Gum' by Ethel Turner,
illustrated by David Souter, from *Gum Leaves* (1900).

37 Eucalypts and Children

IN NINETEENTH-CENTURY AUSTRALIA MOST OF THE INFLUENCES ON CHILDREN IN THE FORM of books and stories were of European, mostly English origin. Fairytales by the Brothers Grimm contain a story about a juniper tree, or Hans Christian Andersen's fir trees and elder trees, while almost every magic forest is populated by oak trees.

This was quickly recognised by the young James Bonwick (1817–1906), who arrived in Tasmania in 1841 and was a teacher there for the next eight years. He later established a boarding school in Victoria and went on to become the Government Inspector of Denominational Schools. In 1857 he published *How Does a Tree Grow? Or Botany for Young Australians*, a 42-page booklet in the form of a dialogue between father and son. The text is fairly heavy in content, but very Australian, with gum trees being the main focus of the conversation:

> But how is it that a gum-tree forest is kept up, for there must be a tremendous lot of lime, soda, flint, and the rest, removed from the soil?
> Yes, but when the trees fall, they rot, and the solid parts return to the ground.
> Oh, father, the remains are very small, compared to the living tree.
> True, because the principal part of a plant consists of the gases, which fly off, and of carbon, which unites with the oxygen of the air.
> How does God bring fresh carbon to the forest? . . .

Twenty years later Ferdinand von Mueller also saw the need to redress the lack of Australian content in the books available for teaching, publishing his *Introduction to Botanic Teachings at the Schools of Victoria* in 1877. This is no chatty dialogue, but a heavy botanical textbook, with the first chapter devoted to 'Eucalyptus Trees'.

It was a long time before home-grown literature was produced for children. One of the first was *Seven Little Australians* by Ethel Turner (1872–1958), which she published in 1894 when she was only 22 years old. Eucalypts don't get a very high or positive profile,

but they do provide young readers with settings they can relate to: 'miles and miles of monotonous gum saplings' or 'nothing but an endless vista of gum trees'. Turner published a stream of children's books over the next 30 years, including *Gum Leaves* in 1900, which, apart from some gum tree poems illustrated by David Henry Souter (1862–1935), had little to do with eucalypts.

The first significant fantasy story for Australian children was *Dot and the Kangaroo* written by Ethel Pedley (1860–98) and published a few months after her death. The story centres around a child being lost in the bush, a constant theme of literature and art in the nineteenth century. Eucalypts are introduced in the third paragraph: 'She gave up all hope of finding her home, and sat down at the foot of the biggest blackbutt tree, with her face buried in her hands.' (Would children have known the name 'blackbutt' in 1899?) Dot is 'saved' by a friendly kangaroo and climbs into her pouch. She has conversations with many animals in the forest and the narrative has a strong environmental message. The story spawned a series of Australian animated films following the original one in 1977.

A blending of traditional English 'fairies' within the context of an Australian bush setting was published in 1907 by Tarella Quin (1877–1934), with illustrations by Ida Rentoul Outhwaite (1888–1960) in a book titled *Gum Tree Brownie and Other Faërie Folk of the Never-Never*. The story concerned the relationship between a special gum tree fairy (called a 'brownie') and a woodcutter. The book was a great success. Quin seems to have faded from the literary scene, but Outhwaite went on to develop her fairy themes in recognisably Australian settings, with a host of Australian animals, for the rest of her life.

The germ of the most significant introduction of eucalypts to Australian children's reading occurred in 1913 when trained illustrator May Gibbs (1877–1969) was commissioned to draw a heading for one of Ethel

Top left: The cover of Ethel Turner's *Gum Leaves*, designed by David Souter, published in 1900.

Left: A plate by Ida Rentoul Outhwaite from *Gum Tree Brownie and Other Faërie Folk of the Never-Never*, showing one of her 'brownies' (1907).

The cover of *The Lone Hand* literary magazine in January
1914 saw the birth of May Gibbs' gumnut babies.

Turner's stories appearing in the *Sydney Mail* newspaper. Among the elements in the illustrated title 'The Magic Button' are some inconspicuous gumnuts with children's faces poking out. Gibbs was working on commission to illustrate a range of work, but wanted to venture into independent commercial areas for herself. In her own words:

> I thought of the Australian gumleaf, which was an ideal shape for a bookmark and a pretty thing. If only I could make it interesting on both sides. In the middle of the night I awoke, and, in fancy, saw peeping over a long gumleaf, a little bush sprite with a gumnut on its head. I hand painted them and Lucy Peacock of the Roycroft Library sold them for me at 5 shillings each. They became so popular, later we printed them and sold thousands for 6d each.

Gibbs developed her gumnut babies further in a commissioned cover for the literary magazine *The Lone Hand* in 1914. Although she created babies based on other Australian native flowers, the gumnut babies were always the favourite. With the onset of the First World War, and the wave of patriotism it generated, Gibbs created gumnut baby postcards to send to the diggers overseas.

By 1916 Angus & Robertson had agreed to publish two books written and illustrated by May Gibbs: the first sold for a shilling; the second, longer one, for two shillings and sixpence:

> The first Australian books I ever did were the flower books, *Gum-Nut Babies* and *Gum-Blossom Babies*. I thought to myself I'll make the pictures first and write the stories around them because the pictures will sell the book. The stories just rolled out of me, I had no trouble at all.

The most famous of her books, *Cuddlepot and Snugglepie*, appeared in 1918 and has never been out of print. She also produced a similar gumnut-baby cartoon strip for newspapers over many years titled 'Bib and Bub'. Gibbs continued to publish books drawing on these characters

until 1954. She generously left the royalties from her work to various children's charities following her death in 1969, and her artwork has been much commercialised in the years since.

Gibbs' works have had such an impact on Australian life that few would not recognise the illustrations even though they might not know the stories. They have spawned books and academic papers on her contribution to Australian identity and even anthropological studies on the sexual identity and orientation of the gumnut characters she portrayed.

May Gibbs never revealed which species of eucalypt inspired the gumnut babies. It is obvious that they are bloodwood fruits in the genus now known as *Corymbia*. But since she was influenced by her upbringing in Western Australia, then spent her creative years in Sydney, there is debate about eastern or western species. Possibilities are the western Marri (*C. calophylla*) or the eastern Red Bloodwood (*C. gummifera*) or Yellow Bloodwood (*C. eximia*), which would have grown close to her home of Nutcote in North Sydney.

While prominent children's authors and book illustrators who followed May Gibbs introduced eucalypts into their settings, they were hardly central to the story. These include Norman Lindsay (1879–1969) with his koala character 'Bunyip Bluegum' in the 1918 book *The Magic Pudding*—it is hard to have a koala without references to eucalypts! New Zealand-born Australian Dorothy Wall (1894–1942) introduced another 'anthropomorphic koala' to children with her book *Blinky Bill* in 1933. This was the first of several books and comic strips based on his adventures, all with a mild conservation message. The character was developed into a television puppet show, animated movie and even a computer game in later years.

Another writer of children's books from the 1930s to the 1960s was Nuri Mass (1918–1993), who published *Australian Wild-flower Fairies* in 1937. Mass's so-called 'fairies' were the flowers themselves, beautifully drawn in reasonable botanical detail, and these flowers spoke about themselves in botanical terms to children. However, she appears to have avoided *Eucalyptus*, perhaps thinking that May Gibbs had a monopoly on

A plate from May Gibbs' most famous book, *Snugglepot and Cuddlepie,* titled 'The Editor Writing His Leading Article'. Like many of her drawings it is based on a feature she would have been familiar with in her local Sydney bushland, the Scribbly Gum (*Eucalyptus haemastoma*), with the writing-like marks on its trunk. ILLUSTRATION © THE NORTHCOTT SOCIETY AND THE SPASTIC CENTRE OF NEW SOUTH WALES.

them, but she does feature *Angophora* as the 'Dwarf Apple Fairy'. Her 1967 book *Australian Wildflower Magic* was more straightforward in its botanical approach, and included *Eucalyptus*.

In the latter half of the twentieth century, books aimed specifically at Australian children proliferated, whether stories about children or about creatures of the bush, and eucalypts become part of the fabric of the story. It would be hard to single out individual books from this period as so many are of very high standard, especially with their illustrations capturing the spirit of the eucalypt-dominated bush.

Perhaps no mention of eucalypts and children should be left without a passing mention of one of the songs most beloved of small children, both in Australia and overseas:

> Kookaburra sits in the old gum tree,
> Merry merry king of the bush is he.
> Laugh, Kookaburra, laugh, Kookaburra,
> Gay your life must be!

The song was written in 1934 for a competition run by the Girl Guides Association of Victoria. It was the winning entry by Marion Sinclair, who died in 1988. It was first performed at a Victorian Jamboree in 1934 in the presence of the Scouting founder, Robert Baden-Powell.

38 Eucalypts in Australian Literature

EUCALYPTS ARE SO EMBEDDED IN THE AUSTRALIAN PSYCHE that it is hard to imagine literature without them and a chapter of this length will barely scratch the surface of such a complex topic.

The earliest writings in the colony were mostly narratives, descriptions of life and exploration, and it was to be many decades before the first home-grown novels appeared. Poetry, on the other hand, found early expression in the new land with the publication by Barron Field (1786–1846) of *First Fruits of Australian Poetry* in 1819. Field had arrived in 1816 to take up the role of judge of the Supreme Court and expressed in his long poem *Botany-bay Flowers* that the botanists had been busy but poetry neglected:

> Tho' thousands of thy vegetable works
> Have, by the hand of Science (as 'tis call'd)
> Been gather'd and dissected, press'd and dried, . . .
> Still fewer (perhaps none) of all these Flowers
> Have been by Poet sung. Poets are few.
> And Botanists are many, and good cheap.

Field waxes eloquent about our shrubby flowering plants, even incorporating Latin botanical names into his verse, but is acerbic about the eucalypts: 'no tree, to my taste, can be beautiful that is not deciduous'. He goes on to say 'all the dearest allegories of human life'

are bound to the seasonal generation and loss of leaves, and these 'are as essential to the poet as emblems, as they are to the painter as picturesque objects'.

Most of the poetry of the time concentrates on pining for the 'old country' and portraying the nature of Australia as grotesque. In 1840 a poem 'The Land of Contradictions' was published in newspapers, which, along with swans being black instead of white, eucalypt leaves are noted for their oddity:

On other trees—another wonder—
Leaves without upper side or under.

One of Australia's celebrated colonial poets, Adam Lindsay Gordon (1833–70) still harks back to European or classical allegories and comparisons when mentioning Australian trees, probably Scribbly Gums, in 1870:

When the gnarl'd, knotted trunks Eucalyptian
Seem carved, like weird columns Egyptian,
With curious device, quaint inscription,
And hieroglyph strange.

Almost half a century later, in 1913, the Jewish-Australian poet, Nathan Spielvogel (1874–1956), often writing under the name 'Gumsucker', reflected upon the attitude of his predecessors in this segment from the poem 'Our Gum Trees':

They thought of oak and of ash and elm;
They looked at the gum and sneered.
They thought his leaves were of sombre hue,
Too mean to provide them shade;
They sniffed his scent, when the breezes blew,
And sighed for a primrose glade.
They said his limbs were of uncouth shapes
Like threatening demon's arms,
His strings of bark were like widow's crapes;
They longed for their woodlands' charms.

It is usually considered that John Lang (1816–64) is the first Australian-born novelist with the publication of his book *Botany Bay* in 1859. Although he studied in England and worked for a while in India, he would not have seen the eucalypts as 'alien'. The novel is about murder, deception and people getting lost in the bush, but the role of eucalypts, and indeed Aboriginals, is just part of the fabric of life: 'Mr. Cox ordered the blacks to strip from a bluegum tree, with their tomahawks, a large sheet of bark. Upon this the remains were placed, carried straight away to Mr. Fisher's house.' He later describes a scene: 'we came upon a plain, an extensive valley skirted by gigantic gum-trees in full flower—a

whitish, sweet-smelling flower, filled with honey, upon which the parrots and other birds feed'. Here, we have a writer relaxed and accepting of eucalypts and their environment.

Marcus Clark (1846–81), best known for his novel *For the Term of His Natural Life,* also wrote another book, *Old Tales of a Young Country,* in 1871. In describing Hobart Town as it would have been in 1822, he is already reflecting on the eucalypt forests we had lost, noting the settlement:

consisted for the most part of thinly scattered cottages standing in the midst of unfenced allotments, while the roots and stumps of primeval gum-trees tripped up the unwary foot-passenger.

One of the best-known Australian novels of the nineteenth century, penned under the name of Rolf Boldrewood (1826–1915), is *Robbery Under Arms,* published in 1882. Here, eucalypts enter the text in a most unselfconscious manner:

There wasn't the smallest breeze. The air was that still and quiet you could have heard anything stir in the grass, or almost a 'possum digging his claws into the smooth bark of the white gum trees.

In this novel we start to see eucalypts incorporated into the idiom of the day: 'His hair was like a hay-coloured mop, half-hanging over his eyes, which looked sharp enough to see through a gum tree and out at the other side.' Boldrewood's character Starlight, when trying to impersonate a 'new chum' is described as acting: 'as green about all Australian ways as if he'd never seen a gum tree before'.

By the end of the century we find the writer/poets Banjo Paterson (1864–1941) and Henry Lawson (1867–1922) trying to outdo themselves in their 'Australianness'. By this time, Paterson assumes his audience will be familiar with different gum trees, and introduces into his poetry ironbarks, stringybarks, bloodwoods and the immortal Coolabah of 'Waltzing Matilda' fame.

Lawson, in his famous short story 'The Drover's Wife' (1892) commences with:

> The two-roomed house is built of round timber, slabs, and stringy bark, and floored with split slabs. A big bark kitchen standing at one end is larger than the house itself, verandah included.
>
> Bush all around—bush with no horizon, for the country is flat. No ranges in the distance. The bush consists of stunted, rotten native apple trees. No undergrowth. Nothing to relieve the eye . . .

In opening his bleak short story about the encounter of a lonely woman and her children with a venomous snake, Lawson underlines the role of eucalypts in country life at the time—every aspect of the dwelling is derived from these trees and their bark. He, too, assumes his readers will have some idea what 'native apple trees' are—most likely a dull blue-grey leaved eucalypt such as Argyle Apple (*Eucalyptus cinerea*), which would add to the sombre desolation of the scene.

Argyle Apple (*Eucalyptus cinerea*) may have been Lawson's 'rotten native apple trees'.

Around the turn of the century there was a spate of very 'Australian' stories about growing up in the outback, perhaps riding on a wave of nationalism as Australia moved towards Federation. These books weave eucalypts into their scenes and assume readers are aware of different sorts of gum trees. Joseph Furphy (1843–1912) drew on his background as a bullock-driver to write *Such is Life* in 1903 using the pen-name Tom Collins. In describing a scene on the Lachlan River he writes:

> The river itself fringed, and the adjacent low ground dotted, with swamp box, river coolibah, and red-gum—the latter small and stunted in comparison with the giants of its species on the Murray and Lower Goulburn.

A similar book, *On Our Selection,* was written under the pen-name Steele Rudd (1868–1935) and started life as a series of stories in the *Bulletin* in 1899, later giving rise to the characters of 'Dad and Dave'. Here, too, we have ironbarks and box trees distinguished from gum trees. He also introduces the concept of making a living in the bush by hunting Koalas for their skins, ten or twenty a day, by having the children climb the eucalypts and cut off the branch that supports them.

Perhaps the most significant author of this period is Miles Franklin (1879–1954), who published her novel *My Brilliant Career* in 1901. Franklin obviously loved gum trees and it shows in her writing. She opens this book, addressing the reader:

> My Dear Fellow Australians . . . This is not a romance . . . neither is it a novel, but simply a yarn—a real yarn. Oh! As real, as really real— . . . in its weariness and bitter heartache as the tall gum-trees, among which I first saw the light, are real in their stateliness and substantiality.

Henry Lawson, in a short story in 1896 titled 'His Country After All', touched on the topic of eucalypts growing overseas when a disgruntled expatriate Australian encounters eucalypts planted in New Zealand and the smell of their foliage has a transforming effect on his attitude to his homeland.

But how were non-Australian writers viewing the steady march of eucalypts around the world? One such author was the Englishman Norman Douglas (1868–1952) who was prominent in British literary circles in the early part of the twentieth century. It is unclear how widespread his views were, but they certainly come across strongly in his book *Old Calabria* about southern Italy, published in 1915:

> You walk to this building along an avenue of eucalypti planted some forty years ago. Detesting as I do the whole tribe of gum trees, I never lose an opportunity of saying exactly what I think about this particularly odious representative of the brood, this eyesore, this grey-haired scarecrow, this reptile of a growth with which a pack of misguided enthusiasts has disfigured the whole Mediterranean basin.

The author D.H. Lawrence (1885–1930) visited Australia in 1922 in the aftermath of the First World War and published his novel *Kangaroo* in 1923. He was obviously not at ease with eucalypts, preoccupied by dead trees in the landscape, as he introduces Australia to his readers in the opening chapter:

> But the bush, the grey, charred bush. It scared him . . . he let himself feel all sorts of things about the bush. It was so phantom-like, so ghostly, with its tall pale trees and many dead trees, like corpses, partly charred by bush fires: and then the foliage so dark, like grey-green iron. . . .
>
> He walked on, had just walked a mile or so into the bush, and had just come to a clump of tall, nude, dead trees, shining almost phosphorescent with the moon, when the terror of the bush overcame him. . . .
>
> It was strange that . . . the tree-covered land should be so gloomy and lightless. It is the sun-refusing leaves of the gum-trees that are like dark, hardened flakes of rubber.

Thirty years after the success of *My Brilliant Career*, Miles Franklin was living in London and giving advice to 'Australian writers' in a paper titled 'The Future of Australian Literature' in 1932:

> So with our eucalypts and other native features. The alphabet of their character and significance has not yet been realised. Note the oak and its acorns in English handicraft, the acanthus in Greek and Roman architecture, and return, oh, shallow Australian detractors, to the potential gumtree.

Up to the 1930s Australian poetry 'was infested with satyrs, fauns, nymphs, pans, elves, pixies and fairies'. Like Franklin, the poet and writer Rex Ingamells (1913–55) in 1938 urged poets to forsake the 'incongruous use of metaphors, similes, and adjectives' that used the 'same terminology as English writers apply to a countryside of oaks and elms and yews', giving an example:

> We find that dewdrops are spoken of as jewels sparkling on the foliage of gum trees. Jewels? Not amid the stark, contorted, shaggy informality of the Australian bushland. Nothing could be more incongruous. Jewels?

Ingamells was the leading light in a movement to connect Australian poetry far more to the environment and to the Aboriginal people. One of the poets influenced by this 'Jindyworobak' movement was Colin Thiele (1920–2006), who wrote 'The Gum' in 1940:

> He stands
> At evening, on a hillock,
> Over-looking fallow lands.
> Bark-scarred and riven he has stood
> Three centuries,
> While the black went and the white came.
> Great straggling limbs
> Untidy, outflung, long:
> Colossal trunk
> Massive, strong,
> Gnarled-rooted, with a crushing, eagle-taloned grip,
> To the rocky hillock.
> Here and there
> A dead branch, dry
> Barkless and bare,
> Points with tapering, skeletonic fingers to the sky.

The author that did most to put Australia on the world literary map was Patrick White (1912–90), who won the Nobel Prize for Literature in 1973. His fourth novel, published in America in 1955 while White was living in Sydney, was *The Tree of Man*. Like the novels written at the turn of the century, it is a domestic drama spanning many decades and describing life in the remote Australian bush. Like others, White uses eucalypts to establish a sense of place, not just in the first chapter but in the very opening lines:

A cart drove between the two big stringybarks and stopped. These were the dominant trees in that part of the bush, rising above the involved scrub with the simplicity of true grandeur. So the cart stopped, grazing the hairy side of a tree, and the horse, shaggy and stolid as the tree, sighed and took root.

Red Stringbarks (*Eucalyptus macrorhyncha*) might have inspired the opening lines of Patrick White's *The Tree of Man*.

Another writer of that time, George Johnston (1912–70), penned his most significant Australian novel while living on a Greek island. *My Brother Jack,* published in 1963, is written in the first person and uses smell and eucalypts as a memory link between the present and the story's setting in Australia:

It was a day of intense heat—that burning Mediterranean summer heat that should be measured in degrees of cicadas. The sort of heat and the sort of burnt-out light that always reminds one of Australia, the smell of bushfire smoke and dust blowing and the dry tangle of bark litter beneath the gum-trees.

Towards the end of the twentieth century novelists are much more specific about eucalypts and their names. Just as we saw unspecified 'gum-trees' becoming stringybarks, ironbarks and apples at the end of the nineteenth century, now authors have a sense of the importance of individual species.

In the 1981 novel *Bliss* by Peter Carey (b. 1943), the final part of the story hinges on the protagonist, Harry Joy, planting not just eucalypts but those species known for their honey production in an effort to woo his beloved 'Honey Barbara'. He has to distinguish between the Tallowwoods, Bloodwoods and Flooded Gums for timber, and the Silver-leaved Ironbark, Yellow Box and Red Flowering Gums that would produce honey. His five-year wait for flowering is rewarded with a happily-ever-after ending—almost. Ironically, in the last few pages he is killed by a falling branch, a 'branch of a tree he has planted himself, one of his precious yellow boxes, a variety prized by bee-keepers but known to forest workers as widow-makers (wider-makers) because of their habit, on quiet, windless days like this one, of dropping heavy limbs'.

The author Murray Bail (b. 1941) has written the ultimate taxonomic novel with his 1998 book *Eucalyptus*. Described as a fairy story, the title of each chapter is the specific epithet of a eucalypt species. The protagonist is a man named Holland (possibly a metaphor for New Holland) with a daughter, Ellen. Holland plants his property in country New South Wales with all the species of eucalypts and promises the hand of his daughter in marriage to any man who can name every species. There are numerous stories within the story, each relating to a particular eucalypt or some play on words relevant to its botanical name. Common names mingle with botanical names as science mingles with fairytale.

Poetry, too, has changed in the last 50 years. Certainly satyrs, fauns, nymphs and fairies are seldom to be found. While the Jindyworobak movement of the 1940s was short-lived, its influence on Australian poetry was long-lasting. Poets now reflect on the environment and man's place in it. In many cases they are an active voice in the environmental movement. Another significant change is the participation of Aboriginal poets in the national discourse.

Judith Wright (1915–2000) is perhaps our best-known poet of the latter half of the twentieth century. Of her large body of work, only one poem has been selected here for its particular relevance. In 1974, Sir Otto Frankel made a comment in a speech to a UNESCO conference linking the 'casual informality of form' of eucalypts to Australia's national character. A year later Judith Wright responded with a poem, 'The Eucalypt and the National Character,' including the lines:

Ready for any catastrophe, every extreme,
she leaves herself plenty of margin. Nothing is stiff,
symmetrical, indispensable. Everything bends
whip-supple, pivoting, loose, with a minimal mass.
She can wait grimly for months to break into flower
or willingly bloom in a day when the weather is right.
Meagre, careless, indifferent? With the toughest care,
The most economical tenderness, she provides for
seed and egg.

Kath Walker, later taking the name Oodgeroo Noonuccal (1920–93), is probably the best known Aboriginal poet. Her poem 'Municipal Gum' (1960) reflects not only her environmental concerns, but, in the last lines, the tree becomes a metaphor for her sense of Aboriginal alienation:

Gumtree in the city street,
Hard bitumen around your feet,
Rather you should be
In the cool world of leafy forest halls
And wild bird calls.
Here you seem to me
Like that poor cart-horse
Castrated, broken, a thing wronged,
Strapped and buckled, its hell prolonged,
Whose hung head and listless mien express
Its hopelessness.
Municipal gum, it is dolorous
To see you thus
Set in your black grass of bitumen—
O fellow citizen,
What have they done to us?

This very brief journey through Australian literature, and indeed all aspects of the arts and popular culture, gives an insight into Australians' changing attitudes to our most ubiquitous tree. Like most relationships it has had its high points and low points, but in the end our relationship with eucalypts is truly 'a celebration'.

Acknowledgements

Many people have generously assisted us during our long preparation of the manuscript for this book and we sincerely thank all of them. The topics took us into some areas with which neither of us were particularly familiar and we are grateful to all those who assisted us through this unfamiliar territory. Unlike other books that we have written, many people have generously contributed photographs to this work, as its breadth is beyond the photographic scope of the authors. We have also used images from a range of Commonwealth and state government institutions and appreciate the assistance offered by their staff.

We would particularly like to thank the management and staff of the Australian National Botanic Gardens and the associated Centre for Plant Biodiversity Research in Canberra for their support for the project and access to databases—in particular Cheryl Backhouse, the curator of the Australian Plant Photographic Index, and the librarians Catherine Jordan and Kirsten Cowley. Access to some images from the Australian Plant Image Index and the *EUCLID* interactive CD key is much appreciated.

Others who have provided assistance in a variety of ways, include: Natalie Barnett, CSIRO Entomology; Chris and Margaret Betteridge for their knowledge of Sydney woodblocking; Ian Brooker for his support and response to a wide range of questions; Tom and Lyndal Butt for access to items from their Australian Choice shop; Pierre-Arnaud Chouvy for his north African photo; Willy Coenradi for his New Zealand photo; Lynn Collins for his matchbox photo; Carol Cooper for access to the Australian National Gallery Library; Richard and Geoff Davis for access to their West Wyalong oil distillation plantations and plant; Rolf de Heer for his assistance with images from *Ten Canoes*; Nathan Dutschke of Ozbreed for *Corymbia* 'Vintage Red' photos; Louise Egerton for support and ideas that initiated the project; India Flint for photos of eucalypt dyeing; Alex Floyd for advice on jetty construction; Kevin and Bron Goss for chasing up Western Australian issues; the volunteer staff of the Grenfell Historical Society Museum for access to records; Barry Hadlow for his photos from Timor; Rodney Hayward of the ANU School of Art for his assistance on cabinet making; Leslie Henderson for South African photos; Matt Holmes of the Perth Mint; Mary Howie for permission to use her father's card design; Gustavo Iglesias for photos from Spain; Noris Ioannou for pottery photos; Jenny Kane for providing access to the Eucalyptus Discovery Centre in Coleraine; David Kaus of the National Museum of Australia for advice on historic Aboriginal photos; Ron Kawalilak of the WA Dept of Environment and Conservation for access to *Landscope* images; Anne Kelly for providing access to the collections of the National Museum of Australia; Nevil Lazarus for his Mistletoe Bird photo; Sarah Lethbridge of ANU pictorial archives; Daniel Letocart for New Caledonian *Arillastrum* photos; Amelia Leubscher for the *Eucalyptus deglupta* photo; Vane Lindesay for the painted gumleaf image; David MacLaren for images from the Bungendore Wood Works Gallery; Augusto Jeronimo Martini for photos and advice on the Musu do Eucalipto in Brazil; John McPhee for advice and support on artistic topics; Brett Mifsud for his photos and invaluable knowledge of giant eucalypts; the National Trust of Australia for permission to use their logo; Mark Neighbour from CSIRO's ScienceImage for access to their photos; Dean Nicolle for general assistance with questions; Tony Orchard as Australian Botanical Liaison Officer, Kew, UK; Jaime Plaza from the Royal Botanic Gardens, Sydney, for photos; Gerard Satherley for wildlife photos and assistance; Scouts Australia for permission to use their logo; Des Shiels for his eucalypt oil history book; Neil Shirley, for Waite Arboretum photos; John Smith for his help with the photo of the cement column in St John's Church, Launceston; Takver for his photo of the Fairy Tree; Mick Vort-Ronald for photos and advice on currency; David Welch for helping to track down NT Aboriginal photos; Mary White for her advice and fossil photos; and Cliff Winfield for his assistance with Western Australian photos.

Finally, a special thankyou to our wives for their patience and encouragement for the project over a couple of years: Marcia Wrigley who was a sounding board and whose belief in the book was a constant support through some difficult times and Rosemary Purdie who assisted with much of the fieldwork, eucalypt photography and proofreading the manuscript.

JOHN WRIGLEY
MURRAY FAGG

Abbreviations for Photo Credits

AGSA	Art Gallery of South Australia, Adelaide
ANBG	Australian National Botanic Gardens, Canberra
APII	Australian Plant Image Index, Canberra
AWM	Australian War Memorial, Canberra
CSIRO	CSIRO's Science Image Photo Library
DEC	Department of Environment and Conservation, Western Australia
DPMC	Department of Prime Minister and Cabinet
FMC	Fitzwilliam Museum, Cambridge, UK
ML	Mitchell Library, Sydney
MU	Monash University, Melbourne
MV	Museum Victoria, Melbourne
NGA	National Gallery of Australia, Canberra
NGV	National Gallery of Victoria, Melbourne
NHM	Natural History Museum, London, UK
NLA	National Library of Australia, Canberra
NMA	National Museum of Australia, Canberra
NTL	Northern Territory Library, Darwin
PHM	Powerhouse Museum, Sydney
QVMAG	Queen Victoria Museum and Art Gallery, Launceston
RBGK	Royal Botanic Gardens, Kew, UK
SLNSW	State Library of New South Wales, Sydney
SLQ	State Library of Queensland, Brisbane
SLV	State Library of Victoria, Melbourne
SLWA	State Library of Western Australia, Perth

References

'The Adventures of Snugglepot and Cuddlepie and Little Ragged Blossom', Program, UWA Perth International Arts Festival

Atkinson, Russell O. (1975), *Ellen Nora Payne: Woodcarver of Tasmania*, self-published, Launceston

Baker, Richard T. and Smith, Henry G. (1920), *A Research on The Eucalypts Especially in Regard to their Essential Oils*, 2nd ed, Technological Museum, NSW, Sydney

Barber, P.A., Smith, I.W. and Keane, P.J. (2003), 'Foliar diseases of *Eucalyptus* spp. grown for ornamental foliage', *Australian Plant Pathology*, vol. 32, pp. 109–11

Barton, A. (?1998), Industrial Uses of Eucalyptus Oil, Report, Division of Science and Engineering, Murdoch University, WA

Bate, Weston (1989), *Having a Go: Bill Boyd's Mallee*, Museum of Victoria, Melbourne

Beale, Bob (2007), *If Trees Could Speak: Stories of Australia's Greatest Trees*, Allen & Unwin, Sydney

Bennett, A. and Wilson, J. (2004), 'A Patchy Resource … Wildlife and Nectar', Information Sheet, Department of Primary Industries, Vic.

Betteridge, Margaret (1979), *Australian Flora in Art*, Sun Books, South Melbourne

Blake, S.T. (1977), '*Allosyncarpia ternata*, a new genus and species of Myrtaceae subfamily Leptospermoideae from northern Australia', *Austrobaileya*, vol. 1, no. 1, p. 43

Bohte, A. and Drinnan, A. (2005), 'Floral development and systematic position of *Arillastrum*, *Allosyncarpia*, *Stockwellia* and *Eucalyptopsis* (Myrtaceae)', *Plant Systematics and Evolution*, vol. 251, no. 1 March, pp. 53–70

Bonwick, James (1857), *How Does a Tree Grow? or Botany for Young Australians*, James Blundell & Co., Melbourne

Bonyhady, Tim (1985), *Images in Opposition: Australian Landscape Painting 1801–1890*, Oxford University Press, Melbourne

Bonyhady, Tim (2000), *The Colonial Earth*, Melbourne University Press, Melbourne

Boosey & Hawkes (1995), 'Richard Mills', Repertoire Guide, Boosey & Hawkes (Aust.) Pty Ltd, Artarmon

Briggs, B.G. and Johnson, L.A.S. (1979), 'Evolution of the Myrtaceae—evidence from inflorescence structure', *Proc. Lin. Soc NSW*, vol. 102, pt 4, pp. 157–256

Brooker, M.I.H. (2000), 'A new classification of the genus *Eucalyptus* L'Her. (Myrtaceae)', *Australian Systematic Botany*, vol. 13, no. 1, pp. 79–148

Brooks, A.E. (1964), *Tree Wonders of Australia*, Heinemann Educational Books, Melbourne

Brown, J.E. (1882), *Forest Flora of South Australia*, Government Printer, Adelaide

Butchart, Eva and Veitch, E.C. (1930s), *Table Looms and Some Australian Dyes as Home Crafts*, self-published, Melbourne

Butler, Roger (2007), *Printed Images in Colonial Australia*, National Gallery of Australia, Canberra

Cannon, Michael (1973), *Life in the Country: Australia in the Victorian Age*, Nelson, Melbourne

Carman, Jean K. (1978), *Dyemaking with Eucalypts*, Craft Council of Australia, Rigby, Adelaide

Carr, D.J. and Carr, S.G.M. (1987), *Eucalyptus II*, Phytoglyph Press, Canberra

Carritt, R. (1999), 'Natural Tree Hollows', Fact Sheet, Note 5, NSW National Parks and Wildlife Service

Carron, L.T. (1985), *A History of Forestry in Australia*, Australian National University Press, Canberra

Chippendale, G.M. (ed.) (1968), *Eucalyptus Buds and Fruits*, Forestry and Timber Bureau, Canberra

Chippendale, G.M. and Wolf, L. (1981), *The Natural Distribution of* Eucalyptus *in Australia*, Special Publication 6, Australian National Parks and Wildlife Service, Canberra

Clark, Garry (2007), 'Environmental themes in Australian literature', in *A Companion to Australian Literature Since 1900*, Burns and McNeer eds., Camden House, New York

Clarke, Marcus and Hislop, Andrew (2002), *Old Tales of a Young Country*, University of Sydney Library, PDF online

Clarke, Philip A. (2007), *Aboriginal People and their Plants*, Rosenberg Publishing, Dural, NSW

Clemson, Alan (1985), *Honey and Pollen Flora*, Inkata Press, Melbourne

Cliff, Paul (ed.) (2000), *The Endless Playground: Celebrating Australian Childhood*, National Library of Australia, Canberra

Coppen J.J.W. (ed.) (2002), *Eucalyptus—The Genus* Eucalyptus, Taylor & Francis, London and New York

Cozzolino, Mimmo (1987), *Symbols of Australia*, Penguin Books, Ringwood, Victoria

Cuffley, Peter (1984), *Chandeliers and Billy Tea*, Five Mile Press, Hawthorn, Victoria

Davis, Tony (2005), 'Crowe Scuttles Eucalyptus Film', *The Sydney Morning Herald*, 12 February 2005

Division of Entomology, CSIRO (1970), *The Insects of Australia*, Melbourne University Press

Doughty, Robin W. (2000), *The Eucalyptus: A Natural and Commercial History of the Gum Tree*, John Hopkins University Press, Baltimore, USA

Ducker, Sophie (2001), *Story of Gum Leaf Painting*, School of Botany, University of Melbourne

Ebes, Hank (compiler) (1988), *The Florilegium of Captain Cook's First Voyage to Australia 1768–1771*, Ebes Douwma Antique Prints and Maps and Sotheby's Australia, Melbourne

Ebury, Francis (2001), 'Trees as Subjects' in 'Making Pictures: Australian Pictorial Photography as Art 1897–1957', PhD Thesis, University of Melbourne

Ebury, Francis (2004), 'Archibald James Campbell: photographing the Australian environment', *History of Photography*, vol. 28, no. 1, pp. 57–70

Edwards, Robert (1973), *Aboriginal Bark Canoes of the Murray Valley*, Rigby, Adelaide

Eipper, Chris (2003), 'Snuggles, Cuddles and sexuality: An(other) anthropological interpretation of May Gibbs's *Snugglepot and Cuddlepie*', *Australian Journal of Anthropology*, vol. 14, no. 3, pp. 336–54

Ellis, Elizabeth (1994), *Conrad Martens: Life and Art*, State Library of NSW, Sydney

Enercon Pty Ltd (2007), 'Bioenergy in the Avon Study Report for Avongro', SEDO Project no. P588, Western Australian Government, Perth

Ennis, Helen (1999), 'Postwar Australian Landscape Photography: Olive Cotton and Max Dupain', *History of Photography*, vol. 23, no. 2, pp. 136–9

Fairley, A. (2004), *Seldom Seen: Rare Plants of Greater Sydney*, Reed New Holland, Sydney

Field, Barron (1823), *First Fruits of Australian Poetry*, R. Howe, Sydney

Field, Barron (1825), *Geographical Memoirs on New South Wales*, Murray, London

Fletcher, Marion (1989), *Needlework in Australia: A History of the Development of Embroidery*, Oxford University Press, Melbourne

Fletcher, Neville (2003), 'The Didjeridu, the Bullroarer and the Gumleaf', *Acoustics Australia*, vol. 31, no. 2

Flint, India (2008), *Eco Colour: Botanical Dyes for Beautiful Textiles*, Murdoch Books, Sydney

Forests NSW (2005–2008), 'Bush Telegraph', Occasional Publication, NSW Department of Primary Industries

Franklin, Miles (1932), 'The Future of Australian Literature', *Essays and Articles*, State Library of NSW, Sydney

French, Alison (2002), *Seeing the Centre: The Art of Albert Namatjira, 1902–1959*, National Gallery of Australia, Canberra

Gibbons, P. and Lindmeyer, D. (2002), *Tree Hollows and Wildlife Conservation in Australia*, CSIRO Publishing, Canberra

Gilbert, Kevin (ed.) (1988), *Inside Black Australia: An Anthology of Aboriginal Poetry*, Penguin, Victoria

Glasson, Mikki and Ian (1980), *Eucalypt Dyer's Handbook*, self-published, Carcoar, NSW

Glocke, P., Delaporte, K., Collins, G. and Sedgley, M. (2006), 'Micropropagation of Selected Ornamental Hybrids', *Australian Plants*, vol. 23, no. 188, pp. 301–5

Gooding, Janda (1991), *Wildflowers in Art: Artists' Impressions of Western Australian Wildflowers 1699–1991*, Art Gallery of Western Australia, Perth

Grimshaw, J.M. and Bayton, R.P. (2009), *New Trees, Recent Introductions to Cultivation*, Kew Publishing, London

Hackforth-Jones, Jocelyn (1980), *Augustus Earle, Travel Artist: Paintings and Drawings from the Rex Nan Kivell Collection, National Library of Australia*, National Library of Australia, Canberra

Hamilton, Annette (2003), 'Snugglepot and Cuddlepie revisited: a response to Chris Eipper', *Australian Journal of Anthropology*, vol. 14, no. 3, pp. 355–60

Hamilton, Jill, Duchess of (1989), *Napoleon, the Empress and the Artist: The Story of Napoleon, Josephine's Garden at Malmaison, Redouté and the Australian Plants*, Kangaroo Press, Sydney

Hamilton, Jill, Duchess of (1998), *The Flower Chain: The Early Discovery of Australian Plants*, Kangaroo Press, Sydney

Handrick, K. (1998), 'Potting Mixes and Soil Needs of Eucalypts', Proceedings, F.C. Rogers Memorial Eucalyptus Weekend, Society for Growing Australian Plants, Coleraine, Vic.

Handweavers and Spinners Guild of Victoria (1974), *Dyemaking with Australian Flora*, Rigby, Adelaide

Hansen, David (2003), *John Glover and the Colonial Picturesque*, Art Exhibitions Australia Ltd and Tasmania Museum and Art Gallery, Australia

Harden, G. (n.d.), 'Eucalypts—Evolution and Distribution', Australian Museum Fact Sheet

Harrison, Margaret J. (1997), 'Australian Gumleaf Playing Championship History 1977–1997', self-published, Victoria

Healey, Margaret (2002), 'Place and Space in the Rhetoric of Australian Colonial Poetry', PhD thesis, School of Behavioural and Social Sciences and Humanities, University of Ballarat, Victoria

Hewson, Helen (1999), *Australia: 300 Years of Botanical Illustration*, CSIRO, Melbourne

Hill, K.D. and Johnson, L.A.S. (2000), 'Systematic Studies in Eucalypts', *Telopea*, vol. 8, no. 4, pp. 503–39

Hill, R.S., Truswell, E.M. *et al.* (1999), *Evolution of the Australian Flora: Fossil Evidence*, Flora of Australia vol. 1 (2nd edition), pp. 251–321, ABRS/CSIRO, Australia

Horsman, C. and Delaporte, K. (eds) (2002), *Eucalypts for Floriculture–A Growers' Guide*, RIRDC publication no. 02/132, University of Adelaide

Hylton, Jane, (1999), *Reflections: H.J. Johnstone's Evening Shadows: Australia's Most Copied Painting*, Art Gallery of South Australia, Adelaide

Ingamells, Rex (1938), 'Conditional Culture', Pamphlet, F.W. Preece, Adelaide

Ioannou, Noris (1986), *Ceramics in South Australia 1836–1986, from Folk to Studio Pottery*, Wakefield Press, Adelaide

Isaacs, Jennifer (1987), *BushFood: Aboriginal Food and Herbal Medicine*, Weldons, Sydney

Johnson, L.A.S. and Briggs, B.G. (1981), 'Three Old Southern Families—Myrtaceae, Proteaceae and Restionaceae', *Ecological Biogeography of Australia*, vol. 1 (ed. A. Keast), W. Junk, Utrecht

Kelly, Stan (1949), *40 Australian Eucalypts in Colour*, Dymock's Book Arcade, Sydney

Kelly, Stan (1969), *Eucalypts*, Thomas Nelson, Australia

Kelly, Stan (1978), *Eucalypts*, vol. II, Thomas Nelson, Australia

Kerr, Joan (1992), *The Dictionary of Australian Artists: Painters, Sketchers, Photographers and Engravers to 1870*, Oxford University Press, Melbourne

Kerr, Joan (1995), *Heritage: The National Women's Art Book*, Craftsman House, Sydney

Kinsella, John (ed.) (2009), *The Penguin Anthology of Australian Poetry*, Penguin Books

Kraehenbuehl, Darrell (1966), *Pre-European Vegetation of Adelaide: A Survey from the Gawler River to Hallett Cove*, Nature Conservation Society, SA, Adelaide

Ladiges, P. (2007), 'Eucalypt taxonomy—from L'Héritier to DNA', Conference Paper, National Academies Forum, Tasmania

Ladiges, P., Udovicic, F. and Nelson, G. (2003), 'Australian biographical connections and the phylogeny of large genera in the plant family Myrtaceae', *Journal of Biogeography*, vol. 30, no. 7, pp. 989–98

'Land of Contradictions', *The Perth Gazette and Western Australian Journal*, 14 November 1840, p. 3.

Lang, John (2004), *Botany Bay, or, True Tales of Early Australia*, University of Sydney Press

Lindesay, Vane (1988), *Aussie-Osities*, Greenhouse Publications, Richmond, Victoria

Lockwood, L., Wilson, J. and Fagg, M. (2001), *Botanic Gardens of Australia*, New Holland Publishers, Sydney

Malouf, David (1998), 'A Complex Fate', Lecture 2, ABC Boyer Lectures, ABC transcript

Martin, Susan K. (2004), 'The Wood from the Trees: Taxonomy and the Eucalypt as the New National Hero in Recent Australian Writing', *J. Assoc. Study Aust. Lit.*, no. 3, pp. 81–94

Mass, Nuri (1937), *Australian Wildflower Fairies*, Shakespeare Head, Sydney

Mass, Nuri (1967), *Australian Wildflower Magic*, Writers' Press, Sydney

McDonald, John (2008), *Art of Australia, Vol.1: Exploration to Federation*, Pan Macmillan, Sydney

McKay, Judith (1990), *Ellis Rowan: A Flower-Hunter in Queensland*, Queensland Museum, Brisbane

McKeown, K.C. (1944), *Australian Insects*, Royal Zoological Society of NSW, Sydney

McPhee, John (1982), *Australian Decorative Arts in the Australian National Gallery*, Australian National Gallery, Canberra

Menz, Christopher (1996), *Australian Decorative Arts 1820s–1990s: Art Gallery of South Australia*, Art Gallery Board of South Australia

Miley, Caroline (1987), *Beautiful and Useful: The Arts and Crafts Movement in Tasmania*, Queen Victoria Museum and Art Gallery, Hobart

Minchin, Liz (2003), 'Still Playing the Dame', *The Age*, 1 May 2003

Mitchell, Elyne (1950), *Australian Treescapes: A Photographic Study*, Ure Smith, Sydney

Mountford, Charles P. (1956), *Australian Tree Portraits*, Melbourne University Press

Mueller, Ferdinand von (1877), *Introduction to Botanic Teachings at the Schools of Victoria*, Government Printer, Melbourne

Mueller, Ferdinand von (1879–84), *Eucalyptographia: A Descriptive Atlas of the Eucalypts of Australia and the Adjoining Islands*, Government Printer, Melbourne

Muir, Marcie (1985), *The Fairy World of Ida Rentoul Outhwaite*, Craftsman House, Sydney

Murray, Scott (1993), *Australian Film: 1978–1992, A Survey of Theatrical Features*, Oxford University Press, Melbourne

Nadolny, C. (2002), *Dieback and What to do About It*, NSW Dept of Land and Water Conservation, Sydney

National Association of Forest Industries (1996), 'Forest Evolution', NAFI Briefings, NAFI Occasional Publication, Canberra

Newton, Gael (1996), *John Kauffmann, Art Photographer*, National Gallery of Australia, Canberra

North, Ian, Carroll, Alison and Tregenza, John (1977), *Hans Heyson Centenary Retrospective 1877–1977*, Art Gallery of South Australia, Adelaide

North, Marianne (1980), *A Vision of Eden*, Web & Bower, Exeter, England

Noye, R.J. (2007), *Dictionary of South Australian Photography 1845–1915*, PDF on CD, Art Gallery of South Australia, Adelaide

Organ, Michael (2007), 'Ida Rentoul Outhwaite (1888–1960): A Chronological Bibliography' website www.uow.edu.au/~morgan/outhwaite.htm

Pearson, M. (1993), 'The good oil: Eucalyptus distilleries in Australia', *Australasian Historical Archaeology*, vol. 11, pp. 99–107

Penfold, A.R. (1920), *Eucalyptus: The Essence of Australia*, Government Printer, Sydney

Penfold, A.R. and Morrison, F.R. (1951), 'Commercial Eucalyptus Oils', Bulletin no. 2, Museum of Applied Arts and Science, Sydney

Penfold, A.R. and Willis, J.L. (1961), *The Eucalypts: Botany, Cultivation, Chemistry and Utilisation*, Leonard Hill Books Ltd, London

Pike, Andrew, and Cooper, Ross (1980), *Australian Film—1900–1977: A Guide to Feature Film Production*, Oxford University Press, Melbourne

Pitkethly, Anne and Don (1988), *N.J. Caire, Landscape Photographer*, self-published, Victoria

Platt, S. (1999), 'Wildlife need natural tree hollows', Information Sheet, Dept of Primary Industries, Vic.

Powerhouse Museum online catalogue <www.powerhousemuseum.com/collection/database/> 2008–2009

Primary Industries and Resources of SA (1994), 'Galls', Information Sheet no. 23

Pryor, L.D. (1981), *Australian Endangered Species: Eucalypts*, Special Publication 5, Australian National Parks and Wildlife Service, Canberra

Pryor, L.D. and Banks, J.C.G. (2001), *Trees and Shrubs in Canberra*, Little Hills Press, NSW

Pryor, L.D. and Johnson, L.A.S. (1981), 'Eucalyptus, the Universal Australian', *Ecological Biogeography of Australia*, vol. 1 (ed. A. Keast), W. Junk, Utrecht

Pyne, S.J. (1991), *Burning Bush: A Fire History of Australia*, Henry Holt & Co. New York

Queensland Parks and Wildlife Service (2002), 'Trees for Koalas', Occasional Publication, Queensland Government, Brisbane

Radford, Ron (1980), *An Exhibition of Art Nouveau in Australia*, Art Gallery Director's Council

Reeder, Warwick (2006), *Sunlight and Shadow: Pictorial Photography by John B. Eaton FRPS (1881–1966)*, Reeder Fine Art, Melbourne

Reserve Bank of Australia (1988), 'A Garden of Note', in *Note Printing in Australia*, Nucolorvue Productions, Victoria

Richie, Rod (1989), *Seeing the Rainforests in 19th-century Australia*, National Library of Australia, Canberra

Robinson, Julie (2007), *A Century in Focus: South Australian Photography 1840s–1940s*, Art Gallery of South Australia, Adelaide

Rowan, Ellis (1991), *The Flower Hunter: The Adventures in Northern Australia and New Zealand, of Flower painter Ellis Rowan*, Collins/Angus & Robertson, Sydney

Royappa, R.C. Sheila (2006), 'Natural and cultural landscape of Australia in Murray Bail's *Eucalyptus*' in *Explorations in Australian Literature*, Sarangi and Mishra (eds), Sarup & Sons, New Delhi, India

Ryan, Robin (2003), 'Jamming on the Gumleaves in the Bush "Down Under"; Black Tradition, White Novelty?', *Popular Music and Society*, vol. 26, no. 3

Sauer, Arline (1934), *The Magic Gum Tree: An Australian Play for Children*, Palings Music, Sydney

Sharp, Nonie (2007), 'A poet's feeling for the Earth', *Local-Global: Identity, Security, Community*, vol. 3, pp. 24–32

Shiel, D. (1985), *Eucalyptus, Essence of Australia*, Queensbury Hill Press, Victoria

Skinner, Graeme (2009), 'In Tune with a Nation', *The Sydney Morning Herald*, 27 April 2009

Smith, Bernard, (2001), *Australian Painting, 1788–2000*, Oxford University Press, Melbourne

Smith, Bernard, and Wheeler, Alwyne (1988), *The Art of the First Fleet and Other Early Australian Drawings*, Oxford University Press, Melbourne

Smith, Greg (2006), 'We Are Turned into a Great Tree: Judith Wright's strange word about trees', *Australian Journal of Theology*, issue 7

Smith, Henry G. (1898), 'Notes on Myrticolorin', *J. Proc. Roy. Soc. NSW,* vol. XXXI, pp. 377–80

Smith, Henry G. (1898), 'On Myrticolorin, the Yellow Dye Material of Eucalyptus Leaves', reprint from *Trans. Chem. Soc. NSW*

Spielvogel, Nathan F. (1913), *Our Gum Trees and Other Verse,* D.W. Paterson, Melbourne

Stearn, William T. (1983), *Botanical Latin,* 3rd edition (rev.), David & Charles, London

Stephen, Ann (ed.) (2001), *Visions of a Republic: The Work of Lucien Henry,* Powerhouse Publishing, Sydney

Tanre, Con (1977), 'The Mechanical Eye', Macleay Museum, University of Sydney

Thomas, Sarah (2002), *The Encounter, 1802: Art of the Flinders and Baudin Voyages,* Art Gallery Board of South Australia, Adelaide

Tregenza, John (1980), *George French Angus: Artist, Traveller and Naturalist 1822–1886,* Art Gallery Board of South Australia, Adelaide

Tudge, Colin (2006), *The Secret Life of Trees,* Penguin Books, London

Turner, Bev (1993), *Recipes: Eucalyptus Oil—Emu Ridge Kangaroo Island, SA,* Eureka Press, South Australia

Vellacott, Helen (ed.) (1986), *Some Recollections of a Happy Life: Marianne North in Australia and New Zealand,* Edward Arnold, Melbourne

Vort-Ronald, Michael P. (1983), *Australian Banknotes: Distinctive Australian Government Issues 1913–1966,* 2nd edition, self published, South Australia

Walsh, Maureen (1985), *May Gibbs, Mother of the Gumnuts,* Angus & Robertson, Sydney

Watts, Peter, Pomfrett, Jo Anne and Mabberley, David (1997), *An Exquisite Eye: The Australian Flora and Fauna Drawings 1801–1820 of Ferdinand Bauer,* Historic Houses Trust of NSW, Sydney

Web, Catherine, Hill, Gregory and Ioannou, Noris (2005), *Gumnuts and Glazes: The Story of Premier Pottery, Preston 1929–1956,* Bundoora Homestead Art Centre, Victoria.

White, M.E. (1994), *The Greening of Gondwana,* 2nd edition, Reed, Sydney

White, M.E. (1994), *After the Greening: The Browning of Australia,* Kangaroo Press, Sydney

Williams, T. (2002), *America's Largest Weed,* Audubon, New York

Wilson, Edwin (1992), *The Wishing Tree,* Kangaroo Press, Sydney

Zacharin, Robert Fyfe (1978), *Emigrant Eucalypts,* Melbourne University Press, Melbourne

Useful websites

Arborglen Biofuels— www.arborglen.us/index.php/bioenergy

Australian Aboriginal Musical Instruments— www.didjshop.com/austrAboriginalMusicInstruments. htm

Australian Honey bee Industry Council— www.honeybee.org.au/

Australian Koala Foundation— www.savethekoala.com/koalatrees.html

Australian National Botanic Gardens— www.anbg.gov.au

Cut Flowers Capability Overview, Australian Trade Commission—www.austrade.com/Cut-flowers-capability

EPBC Act List of Threatened Flora— www.environment.gov.au/cgi-bin/sprat/public/ publicthreatenedlist.pl?wanted=flora

EUCLID: Eucalypts of Australia— www.anbg.gov.au/cpbr/cd-keys/euclid3

GIT Forestry— www.git_forestry.com

Honey Production with Stingless Native Bees— www.zeta.org.au/~anbrc/honeyproduction

Oil Mallee Association—www.oilmallee.com.au

Preserving Flowers and Decorative Foliages with Glycerin and Dye— www.oznet.ksu.edu/library/hort2/mf2446.pdf

Grafted cultivar *Corymbia* 'Summer Red' flowering at the
Australian National Botanic Gardens in Canberra.

Checklist of Species

The tables that follow give the up-to-date names of all eucalypts as accepted by the Australian Plant Census (APC) at the time of writing. They include species and subspecies in the three genera, *Angophora*, *Corymbia* and *Eucalyptus*. Heights given should be used as a guide only, and may vary considerably depending on the growing conditions of the species. Common names are generally those used by *EUCLID* but these will also vary from district to district.

TABLE 1: ANGOPHORA

Name and Author	Date Desc.	Common Name	Where it Occurs	Tree Form and Size	Flower Colour	Name Meaning
Angophora Cav.	1797					Greek *angos* = a goblet, *phoros* = bearing; referring to the vase-like gumnuts
Angophora bakeri E.C.Hall subsp. *bakeri*	1913	Narrow-leaved Apple	NSW	Tree to 20m	Cream/white	Honours Richard Thomas Baker (1854–1941), Australian botanist
Angophora bakeri subsp. *crassifolia* G.J.Leach	1986		NSW	Tree/Mallee to 10m	Cream/white	Latin *crassus* = thick, *folium* = leaf
Angophora costata (Gaertn.) Britten subsp. *costata*	1916	Sydney Red Gum	NSW/Qld	Tree to 30m	Cream/white	Latin *costata* = ribbed; referring to the gumnut
Angophora costata subsp. *euryphylla* L.A.S.Johnson ex G.J.Leach	1986		NSW	Tree to 25m	Cream/white	Greek *eurys* = broad, *phyllon* = leaf
Angophora floribunda (Sm.) Sweet	1830	Rough-barked Apple	Vic/NSW/Qld	Tree to 30m	Cream/white	Latin *floribundus* = profuse flowering
Angophora hispida (Sm.) Blaxell	1976	Dwarf Apple	NSW	Shrub to 8m	Cream/white	Latin *hispidus* = rough; referring to leaves
Angophora inopina K.D.Hill	1997	Charmhaven Apple	NSW	Tree to 8m	Cream/white	Latin *inopinus* = unexpected; referring to its occurrence in a well-known area
Angophora leiocarpa (L.A.S.Johnson ex G.J.Leach) K.R.Thiele & Ladiges	1988	Smooth-barked Apple	NSW/Qld	Tree to 25m	Cream/white	Greek *leio* = smooth, *carpos* = fruit; referring to the gumnut
Angophora melanoxylon R.T.Baker	1900	Coolabah Apple	NSW/Qld	Tree to 15m	Cream/white	Greek *melanos* = black, *xylon* = wood; referring to the timber
Angophora robur L.A.S.Johnson & K.D.Hill	1990	Sandstone Rough-barked Apple	NSW	Tree to 10m	Cream/white	Latin *robur* = oak; referring to the spreading appearance of the tree
Angophora subvelutina F.Muell.	1858	Broad-leaved Apple	NSW/Qld	Tree to 20m	Cream/white	Latin *sub-* = somewhat, *velutinus* = velvety; referring to the leaves
Angophora woodsiana F.M.Bailey	1882	Smudgee	NSW/Qld	Tree to 20m	Cream/white	Honours Father J. Tenison Woods (1832–89), Catholic priest and biologist

10 species plus 2 subspecies

TABLE 2: CORYMBIA

Name and Author	Date Desc.*	Common Name	Where it Occurs	Tree Form and Size	Flower Colour	Name Meaning
Corymbia K.D.Hill & L.A.S.Johnson	1995	Bloodwoods and Ghost Gums				Latin *corymbium* = a corymb (botanical term describing the flower clusters)
Corymbia abbreviata (Blakely & Jacobs) K.D.Hill & L.A.S.Johnson	1995 (1934)	Scraggy Bloodwood	WA/NT	Tree to 20m	Cream/white	Latin *abbreviatus* = shortened; referring to the congested flower cluster
Corymbia abergiana (F.Muell.) K.D.Hill & L.A.S.Johnson	1995 (1878)	Range Bloodwood	Qld	Tree 3–12m	Cream/white	Honours Ernest Georg Aberg (1823–1907), a medical doctor who planted eucalypts in Argentina
Corymbia aparrerinja K.D.Hill & L.A.S.Johnson	1995	Ghost Gum	WA/NT/Qld	Tree to 20m	White	From the central Australian Aboriginal name for this species
Corymbia arafurica K.D.Hill & L.A.S.Johnson	1995		NT	Tree to 15m	Cream/white	From the Arafura Sea, near to where this species occurs
Corymbia arenaria (Blakely) K.D.Hill & L.A.S.Johnson	1995 (1934)	Bundah Bundah	WA	Tree to 7m	White	Latin *arenarius* = growing on sand; referring to its habitat
Corymbia arnhemensis (D.J.Carr & S.G.M.Carr) K.D.Hill & L.A.S.Johnson	1995 (1985)	Katherine Gorge Bloodwood	NT	Tree to 15m	White	Latin *–ensis* = place of origin; from Arnhem Land
Corymbia aspera (F.Muell.) K.D.Hill & L.A.S.Johnson	1995 (1859)	Rough-leaved Ghost Gum	WA/NT/Qld	Tree to 15m	Cream/white	Latin *asper* = rough; referring to the leaf texture
Corymbia aureola (Brooker & A.R.Bean) K.D.Hill & L.A.S.Johnson	1995 (1991)	Yellowjacket	Qld	Tree to 15m	?	Latin *aureolus* = golden; referring to the colour of the rough bark
Corymbia bella K.D.Hill & L.A.S.Johnson	1995	Ghost Gum	WA/NT/Qld	Tree to 20m	Cream/white	Latin *bellus* = beautiful; describing the tree
Corymbia blakei K.D.Hill & L.A.S.Johnson	1995	Ghost Gum	Qld	Tree to 10m	Cream/white	Honours Stanley T. Blake (1911–73), Qld botanist
Corymbia bleeseri (Blakely) K.D.Hill & L.A.S.Johnson	1995 (1927)	Glossy-leaved Bloodwood	WA/NT	Tree to 20m	Cream/white	Honours F.A.K. Bleeser (1871–1942), a Darwin postman who collected the type specimen
Corymbia bloxsomei (Maiden) K.D.Hill & L.A.S.Johnson	1995 (1926)	Yellowjack	Qld	Tree to 20m	Cream	Honours Hans Schreiber Bloxsome (1876–1952), Qld farmer who sent specimens to J.H. Maiden
Corymbia brachycarpa (D.J.Carr & S.G.M.Carr) K.D.Hill & L.A.S.Johnson	1995 (1987)		Qld	Tree to 15m	Cream/white	Greek *brachy-* = short, *carpos* = fruit; referring to the relatively short gumnuts

* Bracketed date indicates when species was first described as *Eucalyptus*.

TABLE 2: CORYMBIA

Name and Author	Date Desc.*	Common Name	Where it Occurs	Tree Form and Size	Flower Colour	Name Meaning
Corymbia bunites (Brooker & A.R.Bean) K.D.Hill & L.A.S.Johnson	1995 (1991)	Blackdown Yellowjacket	Qld	Tree to 25m	White	Greek *bounites* = hill dweller; referring to the habitat
Corymbia cadophora K.D.Hill & L.A.S.Johnson subsp. *cadophora*	1995	Twinleaf Bloodwood	WA	Tree to 6m	Cream/white	Greek *kados* = jar, *phoreus* = carrier; referring to the barrel-shaped gumnuts
Corymbia cadophora subsp. *pliantha* K.D.Hill & L.A.S.Johnson	1995	Twinleaf Bloodwood	WA	Tree to 6m	Red	Greek *pleios* = more, *anthos* = flowers; referring to the more branched flower clusters
Corymbia cadophora subsp. *polychroma* R.L.Barrett	2007		WA	Tree to 4m	White/pink	Greek *poly-* = many, *-chromus* = coloured; referring to the marked variation in flower colour
Corymbia calophylla (Lindl.) K.D.Hill & L.A.S.Johnson	1995 (1841)	Marri	WA	Tree to 40m	White or pink	Greek *calo-* = beautiful, *phyllon* = leaf; referring to the large leaves
Corymbia candida K.D.Hill & L.A.S.Johnson subsp. *candida*	1995	Ghost Gum	WA/NT	Tree to 10m	White	Latin *candidus* = glossy white; referring to the starkly white trunk
Corymbia candida subsp. X *lautifolia* K.D.Hill & L.A.S.Johnson	1995	Ghost Gum	WA	Tree to 15m	White	Latin *lautus* = brilliant, *folium* = leaf; referring to the somewhat glossy adult leaves
Corymbia chartacea K.D.Hill & L.A.S.Johnson	1995		NT	Tree to 8m	White or pink	Latin *chartaceus* = resembling paper; referring to the leaf texture
Corymbia chippendalei (D.J.Carr & S.G.M.Carr) K.D.Hill & L.A.S.Johnson	1995 (1985)	Sand-dune Bloodwood	WA/NT	Tree to 10m	White	Honours George McCartney Chippendale (1921–2010), Australian botanist and author
Corymbia citriodora (Hook.) K.D.Hill & L.A.S.Johnson	1995 (1848)	Lemon-scented Gum	Qld/NSW	Tree to 50m	White	Latin *citriodorus* = lemon-scented; referring to the aromatic foliage
Corymbia clandestina (A.R.Bean) K.D.Hill & L.A.S.Johnson	1995 (1994)		Qld	Tree to 8m	?	Latin *clandestinus* = hidden; referring to the small population hidden among the ironbarks
Corymbia clarksoniana (D.J.Carr & S.G.M.Carr) K.D.Hill & L.A.S.Johnson	1995 (1987)	Clarkson's Bloodwood	Qld/NSW	Tree to 15m	White	Honours John Richard Clarkson (b. 1950), Qld botanist
Corymbia clavigera (A.Cunn.ex Schauer) K.D.Hill & L.A.S.Johnson	1995 (1843)		WA	Tree to 15m	White	Latin *clavus* = a club; referring to the club-shaped stalk of the gumnut
Corymbia cliftoniana (W.Fitzg.) K.D.Hill & L.A.S.Johnson	1995 (1919)		WA/NT	Tree to 8m	Cream/white	Honours R.C. Clifton (1854–1931), Under-secretary of Lands, WA
Corymbia collina (W.Fitzg.) K.D.Hill & L.A.S.Johnson	1995 (1919)	Silver-leaved Bloodwood	WA	Tree to 10m	Cream/white	Latin *collinus* = located on a hill; referring to the habitat
Corymbia confertiflora (F.Muell.) K.D.Hill & L.A.S.Johnson	1995 (1859)	Cabbage Gum	WA/NT/Qld	Tree to 18m	Cream/white	Latin *confertus* = crowded, *florus* = flower; referring to the large flower clusters
Corymbia dallachiana (Benth.) K.D.Hill & L.A.S.Johnson	1995 (1867)	Dallachy's Ghost Gum	Qld	Tree to 15m	White	Honours John Dallachy (c. 1808–71), Superintendent, Melbourne Botanic Gardens, and collector
Corymbia dendromerinx K.D.Hill & L.A.S.Johnson	1995	Ghost Gum	WA	Tree to 10m	Cream/white	Greek *dendron* = tree, *merinx* = a bristle; referring to the bristles on leaves and stems
Corymbia deserticola (D.J.Carr & S.G.M.Carr) K.D.Hill & L.A.S.Johnson subsp. *deserticola*	1995 (1988)		WA	Tree/mallee to 6m	?	Latin *desertum* = desert, *cola* = dweller; referring to its arid habitat
Corymbia deserticola subsp. *mesogeotica* K.D.Hill & L.A.S.Johnson	1995		WA/NT	Tree/mallee to 5m	?	Greek *mesogeoticos* = inland; as it occurs further inland than the type species
Corymbia dichromophloia (F.Muell.) K.D.Hill & L.A.S.Johnson	1995 (1859)	Small-fruited Bloodwood	WA/NT/Qld	Tree to 15m	Cream/white	Greek *di-* = 2, *chromo* = colour, *phloia* = bark; referring to the white bark with red flakes
Corymbia disjuncta K.D.Hill & L.A.S.Johnson	1995		WA/NT/Qld	Tree to 15m	Cream/white	Latin *disjuncta* = separate; referring to its regional distribution pattern
Corymbia dunlopiana K.D.Hill & L.A.S.Johnson	1995	Bristled-leaved Bloodwood	NT	Tree to 7m	Pink/red	Honours Clyde Dunlop (b. 1946), senior botanist NT Herbarium (1972–2001)
Corymbia ellipsoidea (D.J.Carr & S.G.M.Carr) K.D.Hill & L.A.S.Johnson	1995 (1987)		Qld	Tree to 15m	Cream/white	Latin *ellipsoideus* = ellipsoid; referring to the shape of the gumnut
Corymbia eremaea (D.J.Carr & S.G.M.Carr) K.D.Hill & L.A.S.Johnson subsp. *eremaea*	1995 (1985)	Hills Bloodwood	NT	Tree/mallee to 10m	White	Greek *eremaeus* = of the desert; referring to its habitat
Corymbia eremaea subsp. *oligocarpa* (Blakely & Jacobs) K.D.Hill & L.A.S.Johnson	1995 (1934)	Hills Bloodwood	WA/NT/SA	Tree/mallee to 10m	White	Greek *oligo-* = few, *carpos* = fruit; referring to the smaller gumnuts of this subspecies
Corymbia erythrophloia (Blakely) K.D.Hill & L.A.S.Johnson	1995 (1934)	Red Bloodwood	Qld	Tree to 8m	Cream/white	Greek *erythro-* = red, *phloia* = bark; referring to the frequently red flaky bark
Corymbia eximia (Schauer) K.D.Hill & L.A.S.Johnson	1995 (1843)	Yellow Bloodwood	NSW	Tree to 20m	White	Latin *eximius* = uncommon, outstanding; reference obscure
Corymbia ferriticola (Brooker & Edgecombe) K.D.Hill & L.A.S.Johnson	1995 (1986)	Pilbara Ghost Gum	WA	Tree/mallee to 15m	White	Latin *ferreus* = relating to iron, *cola* = dweller; referring to the ironstone hills habitat
Corymbia ferruginea (Schauer) K.D.Hill & L.A.S.Johnson subsp. *ferruginea*	1995 (1843)	Rusty Bloodwood	WA/NT/Qld	Tree to 12m	Cream/yellow	Latin *ferrugineus* = rusty red; referring to rusty red hairs on branchlets, buds and young leaves
Corymbia ferruginea subsp. *stypophylla* K.D.Hill & L.A.S.Johnson	1995		WA/NT	Tree to 12m	Cream/white	Greek *stypos* = a stalk, *phyllon* = a leaf; referring to the stalked leaves in canopy of subspecies
Corymbia ficifolia (F.Muell.) K.D.Hill & L.A.S.Johnson	1995 (1860)	Red Flowering Gum	WA	Tree to 10m	Red/Orange	Latin *fici-* = of figs, *folium* = leaf; referring to the fig-like leaves
Corymbia flavescens K.D.Hill & L.A.S.Johnson	1995	Cabbage Ghost Gum	WA/NT	Tree to 15m	White	Latin *flavescens* = yellow; referring to the foliage and branchlets which are yellow-green
Corymbia foelscheana (F.Muell.) K.D.Hill & L.A.S.Johnson	1995 (1882)	Broad-leaved Bloodwood	NT	Tree to 10m	Cream/white	Honours Paul Foelsche (1831–1914), policeman/magistrate and photographer in NT
Corymbia gilbertensis (Maiden & Blakely) K.D.Hill & L.A.S.Johnson	1995 (1953)	Gilbert River Ghost Gum	Qld	Tree to 12m	Cream/white	Latin *-ensis* = place of origin; from Gilbert River in north Qld
Corymbia grandifolia (R.Br.ex Benth.) K.D.Hill & L.A.S.Johnson subsp. *grandifolia*	1995 (1867)	Cabbage Gum	NT/Qld	Tree to 20m	Cream/white	Latin *grandis* = of great stature, *folium* = leaf; referring to the very large leaves
Corymbia grandifolia subsp. *lamprocardia* L.A.S.Johnson	1995	Pungna	WA/NT	Tree to 10m	Cream/white	Greek *lampros* = shining, *cardia* = heart; referring to the glossy heart-shaped adult leaves
Corymbia grandifolia subsp. *longa* L.A.S.Johnson	1995	Cabbage Gum	WA/NT	Tree to 20m	Cream/white	Latin *longus* = long; referring to the longer leaves and flower stalks than the other subspecies
Corymbia greeniana (D.J.Carr & S.G.M.Carr) K.D.Hill & L.A.S.Johnson	1995 (1987)		WA/NT/Qld	Tree to 10m	Cream/white	Honours Marjorie Free (née Green), formerly Curator Forest Research Herbarium, ACT

TABLE 2: CORYMBIA

Name and Author	Date Desc.*	Common Name	Where it Occurs	Tree Form and Size	Flower Colour	Name Meaning
Corymbia gummifera (Gaertn.) K.D.Hill & L.A.S.Johnson	1995 (1788)	Red Bloodwood	Qld/NSW/ Vic	Tree to 35m	Cream/ white	Latin *gummi* = gum, *fera* = bearing; referring to the gum (kino) that oozes from the trunk
Corymbia haematoxylon (Maiden) K.D.Hill & L.A.S.Johnson	1995 (1913)	Mountain Marri	WA	Tree to 15m	White	Greek *haemato* = blood, *xylon* = wood; referring to the common exudate from the trunk
Corymbia hamersleyana (D.J.Carr & S.G.M.Carr) K.D.Hill & L.A.S.Johnson	1995 (1987)		WA	Tree/mallee to 8m	Cream/ white	After its location in the Hamersley Ranges
Corymbia hendersonii K.D.Hill & L.A.S.Johnson	1995	Henderson's Bloodwood	Qld	Tree to 25m	Cream/ white	Honours Rodney J. Henderson (b. 1938), Qld botanist
Corymbia henryi (S.T.Blake) K.D.Hill & L.A.S.Johnson	1995 (1977)	Large-leaved Spotted Gum	Qld/NSW	Tree to 25m	White or lemon	Honours Neil Buchanan Henry (b. 1927), forester
Corymbia hylandii (D.J.Carr & S.G.M.Carr) K.D.Hill & L.A.S.Johnson	1995 (1987)	Hyland's Bloodwood	Qld	Tree 5–15m	Cream/ white	Honours Dr Bernie Hyland (b. 1937), Qld botanist
Corymbia jacobsiana (Blakely) K.D.Hill & L.A.S.Johnson	1995 (1934)	Stringy-barked Bloodwood	NT	Tree to 15m	Cream/ white	Honours Dr Maxwell Ralph Jacobs (1905–79), forester
Corymbia kombolgiensis (Brooker & Dunlop) K.D.Hill & L.A.S.Johnson	1995 (1978)	Scarp Gum	NT	Tree to 12m	White	After the Kombolgie series of sandstone beds in Arnhem Land where this species is found
Corymbia lamprophylla (Brooker & A.R.Bean) K.D.Hill & L.A.S.Johnson	1995 (1987)	Shiny-leaved Bloodwood	Qld	Tree to 15m	Cream/ white	Greek *lampros* = shining, *phyllon* = leaf; referring to the glossy adult leaves
Corymbia latifolia (F.Muell.) K.D.Hill & L.A.S.Johnson	1995 (1859)	Round-leaved Bloodwood	WA/NT/ Qld	Tree to 12m	Cream/ white	Latin *latus* = broad, *folium* = leaf; referring to the leaf shape
Corymbia leichhardtii (F.M.Bailey) K.D.Hill & L.A.S.Johnson	1995 (1906)	Rustyjacket	Qld	Tree to 15m	White	Honours Friedrich Wilhelm Ludwig Leichhardt (1813–48), Prussian explorer
Corymbia lenziana (D.J.Carr & S.G.M.Carr) K.D.Hill & L.A.S.Johnson	1995 (1985)	Narrow-leaved Bloodwood	WA	Tree to 10m	White	Honours Janette Rosemary Lenz (b. 1948), Research Assistant
Corymbia leptoloma (Brooker & A.R.Bean) K.D.Hill & L.A.S.Johnson	1995 (1991)	Yellowjacket	Qld	Tree to 15m	White	Greek *lepto-* = narrow, *loma* = border; referring to slightly downturned edge of the adult leaves
Corymbia ligans K.D.Hill & L.A.S.Johnson	1995		Qld	Tree to 20m	?	Latin *ligo* = to bind or tie; reference obscure
Corymbia maculata (Hook.) K.D.Hill & L.A.S.Johnson	1995 (1844)	Spotted Gum	NSW/Vic	Tree to 45m	White	Latin *maculatus* = spotted; referring to the bark
Corymbia nesophila (Blakely) K.D.Hill & L.A.S.Johnson	1995 (1927)		WA/NT/ Qld	Tree to 30m	Cream/ white	Greek *nesos* = island, *philos* = loving; referring to its occurrence on offshore islands
Corymbia novoguinensis (D.J.Carr & S.G.M.Carr) K.D.Hill & L.A.S.Johnson	1995 (1987)		Qld/PNG	Tree to 25m	Cream/ white	Latin *novo* = new, Latinised *guinea*; the type species was collected in Papua New Guinea
Corymbia oocarpa (D.J.Carr & S.G.M.Carr) K.D.Hill & L.A.S.Johnson	1995 (1988)		NT	Tree to 15m	White	Greek *oo* = egg, *carpos* = fruit; referring to the egg-shaped gumnuts
Corymbia opacula L.A.S.Johnson	1995		WA	Tree to 10m	?	Latin *opacus* = obscure, *-ulus* diminutive suffix; generally smaller than *C. opaca* (now *C. terminalis*)
Corymbia pachycarpa K.D.Hill & L.A.S.Johnson	1995		WA/NT	Tree/mallee to 6m	White	Greek *pachy-* = thick, *carpos* = fruit; referring to the thick-walled gumnuts
Corymbia papillosa K.D.Hill & L.A.S.Johnson	1995		WA/NT	Tree to 8m	White	Latin *papillae* = a nipple, *-osus* = many; referring to the tiny hairs that cover the bristle glands
Corymbia papuana (F.Muell.) K.D.Hill & L.A.S.Johnson	1995 (1875)	Ghost Gum	Qld/PNG	Tree to 40m	Cream/ white	Referring to its occurrence in Papua New Guinea
Corymbia paractia K.D.Hill & L.A.S.Johnson	1995		WA	Tree to 8m	Cream/ white	Greek *paractios* = seaside; referring to its habitat
Corymbia pauciseta K.D.Hill & L.A.S.Johnson	1995		NT	Tree to 6m	Cream/ white	Latin *paucus* = few, *seta* = bristle; referring to the smooth adult leaves
Corymbia peltata (Benth.) K.D.Hill & L.A.S.Johnson	1995 (1867)	Yellowjacket	Qld	Tree to 10m	White	Latin *peltatus* = a small shield; referring to the leaves with leaf stalk joined to the underside of the leaf
Corymbia petalophylla (Brooker & A.R.Bean) K.D.Hill & L.A.S.Johnson	1995 (1991)		Qld	Tree to 15m	White	Greek *petalos* = broad, *phyllon* = leaf; referring to the broad juvenile leaves
Corymbia plena K.D.Hill & L.A.S.Johnson	1995		Qld	Tree to 15m	White	Latin *plena* = full or stout; referring to the large, thick-walled gumnuts
Corymbia polycarpa (F.Muell.) K.D.Hill & L.A.S.Johnson	1995 (1859)	Long-fruited Bloodwood	WA/NT/ Qld	Tree to 20m	Cream/ white	Greek *poly* = many, *carpos* = fruit; referring to the large bunches of gumnuts
Corymbia polysciada (F.Muell.) K.D.Hill & L.A.S.Johnson	1995 (1859)		NT	Tree to 15m	Cream/ white	Greek *poly* = many, *sciado* = canopy; referring to the spreading crown
Corymbia porrecta (S.T.Blake) K.D.Hill & L.A.S.Johnson	1995 (1953)	Grey Bloodwood	NT	Tree to 20m	Cream/ white	Latin *porrectus* = stretched outwards and forward; possibly referring to the long broad adult leaves
Corymbia ptychocarpa (F.Muell.) K.D.Hill & L.A.S.Johnson subsp. *ptychocarpa*	1995 (1859)	Swamp Bloodwood	WA/NT/ Qld	Tree to 20m	Cream/ pink/red	Greek *ptychos* = a fold, *carpos* = fruit; referring to the ribbed buds and gumnuts
Corymbia ptychocarpa subsp. *aptycha* K.D.Hill & L.A.S.Johnson	1995	Swamp Bloodwood	NT	Tree to 15m	Cream/ pink/red	Greek *a* = not, *ptychos* = a fold; referring to the lack of ribbing on the subspecies
Corymbia rhodops (D.J.Carr & S.G.M.Carr) K.D.Hill & L.A.S.Johnson	1995 (1987)		Qld	Tree to 15m	White and red	Greek *rhodo-* = rose, *ops* = eye; referring to the red centre of open flowers
Corymbia scabrida (Brooker & A.R.Bean) K.D.Hill & L.A.S.Johnson	1995 (1991)	Rough-leaved Yellowjacket	Qld	Tree to 18m	White	Latin *scabridus* = like sandpaper; referring to the leaves
Corymbia serendipita (Brooker & Kleinig) Bean	2003 (1994)		Qld	Tree to 12m	?	English *serendipity* = making happy; the species was an unexpected discovery
Corymbia setosa (Schauer) K.D.Hill & L.A.S.Johnson	1995 (1843)	Rough-leaved Bloodwood	NT/Qld	Tree/mallee to 4m	White	Latin *seta* = bristle; referring to the bristles on the young stems and flowers
Corymbia sp. Pentland Hills (P.I.Forster + PIF16644) Qld Herbarium			Qld			An undescribed species
Corymbia sp. Springsure (M.I.Brooker 9786) Qld Herbarium			Qld			An undescribed species
Corymbia sphaerica K.D.Hill & L.A.S.Johnson	1995		NT	Tree/shrub to 10m	?	Greek *sphaera* = sphere; referring to the shape of the buds and gumnuts
Corymbia stockeri (D.J.Carr & S.G.M.Carr) K.D.Hill & L.A.S.Johnson subsp. *stockeri*	1995 (1987)	Blotchy Bloodwood	Qld	Tree to 12m	Cream/ white	Honours Dr Geoff Stocker (b. 1941), Qld botanist

TABLE 2: CORYMBIA

Name and Author	Date Desc.*	Common Name	Where it Occurs	Tree Form and Size	Flower Colour	Name Meaning
Corymbia stockeri subsp. *peninsularis* (K.D.Hill & L.A.S.Johnson) Bean	2002 (1995)		Qld	Tree to 20m	Cream/white	Latin *peninsular*; referring to the occurrence of this subspecies on Cape York Peninsula
Corymbia terminalis (F.Muell.) K.D.Hill & L.A.S.Johnson	1995 (1859)	Tjuta	WA/NT/ Qld/ NSW/ SA	Tree to 18m	White	Latin *terminalis* = terminal; referring to the flower clusters on the branch ends
Corymbia tessellaris (F.Muell.) K.D.Hill & L.A.S.Johnson	1995 (1859)	Carbeen, Moreton Bay Ash	Qld/NSW	Tree to 35m	White	Latin *tessellaris* = tessellated; referring to the bark at the base of the trunk
Corymbia torelliana (F.Muell.) K.D.Hill & L.A.S.Johnson	1995 (1877)	Cadaghi	Qld	Tree to 30m	White	Honours Count Luigi Torelli (1810–77), Italian politician who planted eucalypts to drain swamps
Corymbia torta K.D.Hill & L.A.S.Johnson subsp. *torta*	1995		WA	Tree to 15m	White	Latin *tortus* = twisted; referring to the undulating leaf margins
Corymbia torta subsp. *allanii* K.D.Hill & L.A.S.Johnson	1995		WA	Tree to 15m	White	Honours Allan Cunningham, who was the first to collect this subspecies, in 1819
Corymbia torta subsp. *mixtifolia* K.D.Hill & L.A.S.Johnson	1995		WA	Tree to 15m	White	Latin *mixtus* = mixed, *folium* = leaf; referring to the mixture of juvenile and adult leaves in canopy
Corymbia trachyphloia (F.Muell.) K.D.Hill & L.A.S.Johnson	1995 (1859)	Brown Bloodwood	Qld/NSW	Tree to 15m	White	Greek *trachy-* = rough, *phloia* = bark; referring to the rough tessellated bark
Corymbia umbonata (D.J.Carr & S.G.M.Carr) K.D.Hill & L.A.S.Johnson	1995 (1985)	Rusty Bloodwood	NT	Tree to 17m	Cream/white	Latin *umbonatus* = having a rounded projection; possibly referring to the small knob on the bud cap
Corymbia watsoniana (F.Muell.) K.D.Hill & L.A.S.Johnson subsp. *watsoniana*	1995 (1876)	Large-fruited Yellowjacket	Qld	Tree to 15m	Cream/white	Honours Thomas Wentworth Watson, who collected the type specimen in 1876
Corymbia watsoniana subsp. *capillata* (Brooker & A.R.Bean) K.D.Hill & L.A.S.Johnson	1995 (1991)	Yellowjacket	Qld	Tree to 15m	Cream/white	Latin *capillatus* = hairy; referring to the hairy juvenile leaf stalks and stems
Corymbia xanthope (A.R.Bean & Brooker) K.D.Hill & L.A.S.Johnson	1995 (1989)	Glen Geddes Bloodwood	Qld	Tree to 12m	Cream/white	Greek *xanthos* = yellow, *ope* = hole; referring to yellow underbark seen through gaps in grey outer bark
Corymbia zygophylla (Blakely) K.D.Hill & L.A.S.Johnson	1995 (1934)	Broome Bloodwood	WA	Tree/mallee to 6m	White	Greek *zygo-* = joined, *phyllon* = leaf; referring to the opposite leaves present in the canopy

93 species plus 10 subspecies

TABLE 3: EUCALYPTUS

Name and Author	Date Desc.	Common Name	Where it Occurs	Tree Form and Size	Flower Colour	Name Meaning
Eucalyptus L'Her	1792					Greek *eu-* = well, *kalyptos* = covered; referring to the cap that protects the flower before it opens
Eucalyptus abdita Brooker & Hopper	1991		WA	Mallee to 3m	White	Latin *abditus* = hidden; referring to the author's failure to find the species
Eucalyptus absita Grayling & Brooker	1992	Badgingarra Box	WA	Mallee to 10m	White	Latin *absitus* = distant; referring to the remoteness of the species from other related box species
Eucalyptus acaciiformis H.Deane & Maiden	1899	Wattle-leaved Peppermint	NSW	Tree to 20m	White	Latin *acaciiformis* = *Acacia*-like; referring to the leaves
Eucalyptus accedens W.Fitzg.	1904	Powder-bark Wandoo	WA	Tree to 25m	Cream	Latin *accedens* = resembling; referring to its similarity to *E. wandoo*
Eucalyptus acies Brooker	1972	Woolbernup Mallee	WA	Mallee to 3m	Cream	Latin *acies* = sharp edge; referring to the strongly angled branchlets
Eucalyptus acmenoides Schauer	1843	White Mahogany	Qld/NSW	Tree to 45m	White	Latin *acmenoides* = resembling the genus *Acmena*; referring to the pale underside of the leaves
Eucalyptus acroleuca L.A.S.Johnson & K.D.Hill	1994	Lakefield Coolibah	Qld/NSW	Tree to 15m	White	Greek *acros* = highest, *leucos* = white; referring to the white, smooth-barked upper branches
Eucalyptus aequioperta Brooker & Hopper	1993		WA	Tree/mallee to 10m	White	Latin *aequi-* = equal, *opertus* = covered; referring to the similarity of the bud cap and the base
Eucalyptus agglomerata Maiden	1922	Blue-leaved Stringybark	NSW/Vic	Tree to 40m	Creamy white	Latin *agglomeratus* = collected in a head; referring to the densely clustered gumnuts
Eucalyptus aggregata H.Deane & Maiden	1900	Black Gum	NSW/Vic	Tree to 20m	Creamy white	Latin *aggregatus* = clustered together; referring to the gumnuts
Eucalyptus alaticaulis R.J.Watson & Ladiges	1987		Vic	Tree/mallee to 30m	White	Latin *alatus* = winged, *caulis* = stem; referring to the winged stems of the seedlings
Eucalyptus alba Reinw. ex Blume var. *alba*	1826	White Gum	Timor/ PNG	Tree to 20m	White	Latin *albus* = white; referring to its white bark
Eucalyptus alba var. *australasica* Blakely & Jacobs	1934	White Gum	WA/NT/ Qld	Tree to 20m	White	Latin *australasicus*; referring to its mainland occurrence
Eucalyptus albens Benth.	1904	White Box	Qld/NSW/ Vic/SA	Tree to 25m	White	Latin *albens* = whitened; referring to the general appearance and white wax on buds and gumnuts
Eucalyptus albida Maiden & Blakely	1925	White-leaved Mallee	WA	Mallee to 3m	Creamy white	Latin *albidus* = whitish; referring to the juvenile leaves
Eucalyptus albopurpurea (Boomsma) D.Nicolle	2000	Coffin Bay Mallee	SA	Mallee to 5m	White/ pink/ mauve	Latin *albus* = white, *purpureus* = purple; referring to the variation in flower colour
Eucalyptus alipes (L.A.S.Johnson & K.D.Hill) D.Nicolle & Brooker	2005		WA	Mallet to 8m	Creamy white	Latin *ala* = wing, *pes* = a foot; referring to the 2-winged bud stalks
Eucalyptus alligatrix L.A.S.Johnson & K.D.Hill subsp. *alligatrix*	1995		Vic	Tree to 15m	White	Latin *alligatrix* = she who binds together; this species is the link between *E. cinerea* and *E. cephalocarpa*
Eucalyptus alligatrix subsp. *limaensis* Brooker, Slee & J.D.Briggs	1995		Vic	Tree to 30m	White	Latin *limaensis* = from the farming district Lima in north-east Vic where the subspecies occurs
Eucalyptus alligatrix subsp. *miscella* Brooker, Slee & J.D.Briggs	1995		NSW	Tree to 15m	White	Latin *miscella* = mixed; referring to the 3 and 7 flowered flower clusters on the same tree
Eucalyptus ambigua DC.	1828	Smithton Peppermint	Tas	Tree to 40m	White	Latin *ambiguus* = uncertain; presumably due to its similarity to *E. amygdalina*

TABLE 3: EUCALYPTUS

Name and Author	Date Desc.	Common Name	Where it Occurs	Tree Form and Size	Flower Colour	Name Meaning
Eucalyptus ammophila Brooker & Slee	1994	Sandplain Red Gum	Qld	Mallee to 6m	White	Greek *ammos* = sand, *-phila* = loving; referring to the species preference for sandplains
Eucalyptus amplifolia Naudin subsp. *amplifolia*	1891	Cabbage Gum	NSW	Tree to 30m	White	Latin *amplus* = large, *folius* = leaf; referring to the large leaves
Eucalyptus amplifolia subsp. *sessiliflora* (Blakely) L.A.S.Johnson & K.D.Hill	1990	Cabbage Gum	Qld/NSW	Tree to 30m	White	Latin *sessili-* = stalkless, *florum* = of the flower; referring to the stalkless flowers of this subspecies
Eucalyptus amygdalina Labill.	1806	Black Peppermint	Tas	Tree to 30m	White	Latin *amygdala* = almond; reference unclear
Eucalyptus ancophila L.A.S.Johnson & K.D.Hill	1990		NSW	Tree to 35m	White	Greek *ancos* = valley, *-phila* = loving; referring to its habitat
Eucalyptus andrewsii Maiden	1904	New England Blackbutt	Qld/NSW	Tree to 45m	White	Honours Ernest Clayton Andrews (1870–1948), Government Geologist
Eucalyptus angophoroides R.T.Baker	1901	Apple-topped Box	NSW/Vic	Tree to 40m	White	Latin *angophoroides* = resembling the genus *Angophora*
Eucalyptus angularis Brooker & Hopper	1903	Leseuer Phantom Mallee	WA	Mallee to 3m	?	Latin *angularis* = angled; referring to the angled branchlets
Eucalyptus angulosa Schauer	1843	Ridge-fruited Mallee	SA/WA	Mallee to 5m	Cream/pink	Latin *angulosa* = strongly angled; referring to the branchlets and buds
Eucalyptus angustissima F.Muell.	1863	Narrow-leaved Mallee	WA	Mallee to 5m	Creamy white	Latin *angustissima* = very narrow; referring to the leaves
Eucalyptus annulata Benth.	1867	Open-fruited Mallee	WA	Mallee to 7m	Cream/yellow	Latin *annulatus* = marked with a ring; referring to the disc around the edge of the gumnut
Eucalyptus annuliformis Grayling & Brooker	1992	Badgerabbie Mallee	WA	Mallee to 3m	White	Latin *annuliformis* = ring-like; referring to the disc around the edge of the gumnut
Eucalyptus apiculata R.T.Baker & H.G.Sm.	1902	Narrow-leaved Mallee Ash	NSW	Mallee to 6m	White	Latin *apiculatus* = ending abruptly in a point; referring to the leaves
Eucalyptus apodophylla Blakely & Jacobs	1934	Whitebark	WA/NT	Tree to 20m	White	Greek *a-* = without, *podos* = a foot, *phyllon* = leaf; referring to the stalkless leaves
Eucalyptus apothalassica L.A.S.Johnson & K.D.Hill	1990	Inland White Mahogany	Qld/NSW	Tree to 20m	White	Greek *apo-* = away, *thalassicos* = the sea; referring to its inland distribution
Eucalyptus approximans Maiden	1919	Barren Mountain Mallee	NSW	Mallee to 6m	White	Latin *approximans* = approaching; referring to its similarity to *E. stricta*
Eucalyptus aquatica (Blakely) L.A.S.Johnson & K.D.Hill	1990	Water Gum	NSW	Mallee/sml tree to 4m	White	Latin *aquaticus* = growing in water; referring to the habitat of this rare species
Eucalyptus aquilina Brooker	1974	Cape Le Grand Mallee	WA	Mallee to 7m	White	Latin *aquilinus* = of an eagle; referring to the hooked lobes on the gumnut
Eucalyptus arachnaea Brooker & Hopper subsp. *arachnaea*	1991	Black-stemmed Mallee	WA	Mallee to 5m	Creamy white	Latin *arachnaeus* = spidery; referring to the bud clusters
Eucalyptus arachnaea subsp. *arrecta* Brooker & Hopper	1991	Black-stemmed Mallet	WA	Tree to 10m	Creamy white	Latin *arrectus* = upright; referring to the mallet form compared with the type
Eucalyptus arborella Brooker & Hopper	2002	Twertup Mallet	WA	Mallet to 7m	Greenish	Latin *arbor* = tree, *-ella* = small; referring to the stature of the species
Eucalyptus arcana (D.Nicolle & Brooker) Rule	2009		SA	Tree to 5m	White	Latin *arcana* = secret; referring to the unexpected discovery of this species
Eucalyptus archeri Maiden & Blakely	1929	Alpine Cider Gum	Tas	Mallee/tree to 12m	White	Honours William H. Archer (1829–74), keen collector of botanical specimens
Eucalyptus arenacea Marginson & Ladiges	1988	Desert Stringybark	Vic/SA	Mallee/tree to 10m	White	Latin *arenaceus* = sandy; referring to its habitat
Eucalyptus arenicola K.Rule	2008		Vic	Mallee/tree to 12m	White	Latin *arena* = sandy, *-cola* = dweller; referring to its sandy habitat
Eucalyptus argillacea W.Fitzg.	1919	Mt House Box	WA	Tree to 5m	Creamy white	Latin *argilla* = clay; referring to the soil where this species was first found
Eucalyptus argophloia Blakely	1934	Burncluith Gum	Qld	Tree to 30m	White	Greek *argos* = bright white, *phloios* = bark; referring to the white bark
Eucalyptus argutifolia Grayling & Brooker	1992	Wabling Hill Mallee	WA	Mallee to 4m	White	Latin *argutus* = sharp, clear, *folius* = leaf; referring to the way its foliage contrasted with other mallees
Eucalyptus argyphea L.A.S.Johnson & K.D.Hill	1992	Silver Mallet	WA	Mallet to 15m	Creamy white	Greek *argypheos* = silvery white; referring to the bark
Eucalyptus aromaphloia L.D.Pryor & J.H.Willis subsp. *aromaphloia*	1954	Creswick Apple-box	Vic	Tree to 18m	White	Greek *aroma* = smell, *phloios* = bark; referring to the young bark, which is aromatic when crushed
Eucalyptus aromaphloia subsp. Major Mitchell Plateau (K.Rule 04127) Vic Herbarium						An undescribed subspecies
Eucalyptus articulata Brooker & Hopper	1993		WA	Mallee to 3m	White	Latin *articulatus* = articulated or jointed; referring to the base of the style
Eucalyptus aspersa Brooker & Hopper	1993		WA	Mallee to 4m	White	Latin *aspersus* = scattered; referring to its occurrence in Jarrah forests
Eucalyptus aspratilis L.A.S.Johnson & K.D.Hill	1992	Soak Yate	WA	Mallee to 5m	Cream/yellow	Latin *aspratilis* = rough, scaly; referring to the bark
Eucalyptus assimilans L.A.S.Johnson & K.D.Hill	2001		WA	Tree to 15m	?	Latin *assimilans* = making like, resembling; referring to the similarity to the related *E. sheathiana*
Eucalyptus astringens (Maiden) Maiden subsp. *astringens*	1924	Brown Mallet	WA	Mallet to 15m	Cream/lemon	Latin *astringens* = astringent; referring to extracts from the bark
Eucalyptus astringens subsp. *redacta* Brooker & Hopper	2002		WA	Mallet to 5m	Cream/pink	Latin *redactus* = reduced; referring to the smaller habit, buds and fruits of this subspecies
Eucalyptus atrata L.A.S.Johnson & K.D.Hill	1991	Herberton Ironbark	Qld	Tree to 10m	White	Latin *atratus* = clothed in black; referring to the dark bark
Eucalyptus badjensis Beuzev. & M.B.Welch	1924	Big Badja Gum	NSW	Tree to 45m	White	Latin *-ensis* = origin of the species; referring to the occurrence of the species on Big Badja Mt
Eucalyptus baeuerlenii F.Muell.	1890	Baeuerlen's Gum	NSW	Mallee/tree to 20m	White	Honours William Bäuerlen (1840–1917), plant collector for Technological Museum, Sydney
Eucalyptus baileyana F.Muell.	1878	Bailey's Stringybark	Qld/NSW	Tree to 40m	White	Honours Frederick Manson Bailey (1827–1915), Qld Colonial Botanist, author of 7-volume *Flora of Queensland*
Eucalyptus baiophylla D.Nicolle & Brooker	2008		WA	Mallee to 4m	White	Greek *baios* = little, *phyllon* = leaf; referring to the small juvenile and adult leaves
Eucalyptus bakeri Maiden	1913	Baker's Mallee	Qld/NSW	Tree/mallee to 12m	White	Honours Richard Thomas Baker (1854–1941), Australian botanist

TABLE 3: EUCALYPTUS

Name and Author	Date Desc.	Common Name	Where it Occurs	Tree Form and Size	Flower Colour	Name Meaning
Eucalyptus balanites Grayling & Brooker	1992	Cadda Road Mallee	WA	Tree/mallee to 5m	Creamy white	Greek *balanites* = like an acorn; referring to the buds
Eucalyptus balanopelex L.A.S.Johnson & K.D.Hill	1992		WA	Mallee to 4m	Creamy white	Greek *balanos* = acorn, *pelex* = a helmet; referring to the bud cap
Eucalyptus balladoniensis Brooker subsp. *balladoniensis*	1976	Balladonia Mallee	WA	Mallee to 5m	Pale yellow	Latin *-ensis* = origin of the species; referring to its location near Balladonia
Eucalyptus balladoniensis subsp. *sedens* L.A.S.Johnson & K.D.Hill	1992	Balladonia Mallee	WA	Mallee to 5m	Pale yellow	Latin *sedens* = sitting; referring to the stalkless buds of this subspecies
Eucalyptus bancroftii (Maiden) Maiden	1917	Bancroft's Red Gum	Qld/NSW	Tree to 15m	White	Honours Thomas Lane Bancroft (1860–1933), medical doctor based in Qld, interested in biology
Eucalyptus banksii Maiden	1905	Tenterfield Woollybutt	Qld/NSW	Tree to 20m	White	Honours Sir Joseph Banks (1743–1820), botanist with Captain Cook's voyage to Australia (1770)
Eucalyptus barberi L.A.S.Johnson & Blaxell	1972	Barber's Gum	Tas	Tree/mallee to 8m	White	Honours Horace Newton Barber (1914–71), Professor of Botany, Uni of Tas (1947–63)
Eucalyptus baudiniana D.J.Carr & S.G.M.Carr	1976		WA	Tree/mallee to 10m	White	Honours Nicolas Thomas Baudin (1754–1803), French navigator and plant collector
Eucalyptus baueriana Schauer	1843	Blue Box	NSW/Vic	Tree to 20m	White	Honours Ferdinand Lukas Bauer (1760–1826), Austrian-born natural history painter with Matthew Flinders
Eucalyptus baxteri (Benth.) Maiden & Blakely ex J.M.Black	1926	Brown Stringybark	NSW/Vic/ SA	Tree to 40m	White	Honours William Baxter (1787–after 1830), English gardener and plant collector
Eucalyptus beaniana L.A.S.Johnson & K.D.Hill	1991	Bean's Ironbark	Qld	Tree to 10m	White	Honours Anthony Bean (b. 1957), Qld botanist with special interest in Ironbarks
Eucalyptus beardiana Brooker & Blaxell	1978	Beard's Mallee	WA	Mallee to 4m	Pale yellow	Honours John Stanley Beard (b. 1916), WA botanist and Director Kings Park (1961–70)
Eucalyptus behriana F.Muell.	1855	Bull Mallee	NSW/Vic/ SA	Tree/mallee to 12m	White	Honours Hermann Hans Behr (1818–1904), German doctor and plant collector
Eucalyptus bensonii L.A.S.Johnson & K.D.Hill	1990	Benson's Stringybark	NSW	Tree/mallee to 8m	White	Honours Douglas Howard Benson (b. 1949), plant ecologist with Royal Botanical Gardens, Sydney
Eucalyptus benthamii Maiden & Cambage	1915	Camden White Gum	NSW	Tree to 40m	White	Honours George Bentham (1800–84), author of the first Flora of Australia (1863–78)
Eucalyptus beyeriana L.A.S.Johnson & K.D.Hill	1990	Beyer's Ironbark	NSW	Tree to 25m	White	Honours George Beyer (1865–c. 1921), botanical assistant with Sydney Technological Museum
Eucalyptus bigalerita F.Muell.	1859	Northern Salmon Gum	WA/NT	Tree to 17m	White	Latin *bi-* = two, *galerum* = a cap; referring to the double bud cap of the buds
Eucalyptus blakelyi Maiden	1917	Blakely's Red Gum	Qld/NSW/ Vic	Tree to 25m	White	Honours William Faris Blakely (1875–1941), author of the first *A Key to the Eucalypts* (1934)
Eucalyptus blaxellii L.A.S.Johnson & K.D.Hill	1992		WA	Mallee to 3m	White	Honours Donald Frederick Blaxell (b. 1934), botanist with National Herbarium, NSW
Eucalyptus blaxlandii Maiden & Cambage	1919	Blaxland's Stringybark	NSW	Tree to 35m	White	Honours Gregory Blaxland (1778–1858), led the first successful crossing of the Blue Mountains
Eucalyptus boliviana J.B.Williams & K.D.Hill	2001	Bolivia Hill Stringybark	NSW	Mallee to 5m	?Yellow	From the Bolivia Hill Nature Reserve in northern NSW
Eucalyptus bosistoana F.Muell.	1895	Coast Grey Box	NSW/Vic	Tree to 60m	White	Honours Joseph Bosisto (1824–98), politician and pharmacist who extracted oil from eucalypts
Eucalyptus botryoides Sm.	1797	Southern Mahogany	NSW/Vic	Tree to 40m	White	Greek *botry-* = a bunch, *-oides* = resembling; referring to the bunches of gumnuts
Eucalyptus brachyandra F.Muell.	1859	Tropical Red Box	WA/NT	Tree to 8m	Creamy white	Greek *brachy-* = short, *andra* = male; probably referring to the short stamens
Eucalyptus brachycalyx Blakely	1934	Gilja	SA/WA	Tree/mallee to 10m	White	Greek *brachy-* = short, *kalyx* = calyx; referring to the small buds
Eucalyptus brachycorys Blakely	1934	Cowcowing Mallee	WA	Mallee to 5m	White	Greek *brachy-* = short, *korys* = helmet; referring to the short bud cap
Eucalyptus brachyphylla C.A.Gardner	1942	Binyarinrinna Mallee	WA	Tree/mallee to 4m	White	Greek *brachy-* = short, *phyllon* = leaf; referring to the short leaves
Eucalyptus brandiana Hopper & McQuoid	2009		WA	Mallet to 5m	Red/pink	Honours Grady Brand (b. 1961), Curator of WA Botanic Garden and associated nursery
Eucalyptus brassiana S.T.Blake	1977	Cape York Red Gum	Qld	Tree to 20m	White	Honours Leonard John Brass (1900–71), botanist and plant collector
Eucalyptus brevifolia F.Muell.	1859	Northern White Gum	WA/NT	Tree to 10m	White	Latin *brevis* = short, *folium* = leaf; referring to the small leaves
Eucalyptus brevipes Brooker	1986	Mukinbudin Mallee	WA	Mallee to 5m	White	Latin *brevis* = short, *pes* = foot; referring to the short flower stalk
Eucalyptus brevistylis Brooker	1974	Rate's Tingle	WA	Tree to 25m	White	Latin *brevis* = short, *stylis* = style; referring to the small style
Eucalyptus bridgesiana R.T.Baker	1898	Apple Box	Qld/NSW/ Vic	Tree to 25m	White	Honours Frederick Bridges (1840–1904), an education officer in NSW
Eucalyptus brockwayi C.A.Gardner	1942	Dundas Mahogany	WA	Tree to 15m	White	Honours George Ernest Emerson Brockway (1900–73), WA forester
Eucalyptus brookeriana A.M.Gray	1979	Brooker's Gum	Tas/Vic	Tree to 40m	White	Honours Murray Ian Hill Brooker (b. 1934), botanist, author and leading eucalypt researcher
Eucalyptus broviniensis A.R.Bean	2001		Qld	Tree to 10m	White	Named after the Brovinia State Forest in south-east Qld, where the species is found
Eucalyptus brownii Maiden & Cambage	1913	Brown's Box	Qld	Tree to 18m	White	Honours Robert Brown (1773–1858), eminent Scottish botanist who sailed with Matthew Flinders
Eucalyptus buprestium F.Muell.	1862	Ball-fruited Mallee	WA	Mallee to 4m	White	Latin *Buprestris* = a species of beetle; referring to the attraction of some mallees to beetles
Eucalyptus burdettiana Blakely & H.Steedman	1939	Burdett's Mallee	WA	Mallee to 4m	Yellow/ green	Honours William Burdett (1871–1940), orchardist and native plant gardener in SA
Eucalyptus burgessiana L.A.S.Johnson & Blaxell	1972	Faulconbridge Mallee Ash	NSW	Tree/mallee to 7m	White	Honours Rev. Colin Ernest Bryce Burgess (1907–87), Church of England curate and amateur botanist
Eucalyptus burracoppinensis Maiden & Blakely	1925	Burracoppin Mallee	WA	Mallee to 5m	White	From the town of Burracoppin in south-west WA, where the species is found
Eucalyptus cadens J.D.Briggs & Crisp	1989	Tumble-down Swamp Gum	Vic	Tree to 25m	White	Latin *cadens* = falling; referring to drooping branches

TABLE 3: EUCALYPTUS

Name and Author	Date Desc.	Common Name	Where it Occurs	Tree Form and Size	Flower Colour	Name Meaning
Eucalyptus caesia Benth. subsp. *caesia*	1867	Caesia	WA	Mallee to 10m	Pink	Latin *caesius* = lavender blue; referring to the colour of the branchlets, buds and gumnuts
Eucalyptus caesia subsp. *magna* Brooker & Hopper	1982	Silver Princess	WA	Mallee to 15m	Red/pink	Latin *magnus* = large, great; referring to the greater size of the buds and gumnuts
Eucalyptus calcareana Boomsma	1979	Nundroo Mallee	SA/WA	Tree/mallee to 8m	Creamy white	Latin *calcareus* = limy; referring to the soil where this species is found
Eucalyptus calcicola Brooker subsp. *calcicola*	1974	Boranup Mallee	WA	Mallee to 4m	White	Latin *calci-* = lime, *-cola* = dwelling; referring to the habitat of this species
Eucalyptus calcicola subsp. *unita* D.Nicolle	2002		WA	Mallee to 6m	White	Latin *unitus* = join together; referring to this subspecies as link between *E. ligulata* and ssp. *calcicola*
Eucalyptus caleyi Maiden subsp. *caleyi*	1906	Caley's Ironbark	Qld/NSW	Tree to 30m	Creamy white	Honours George Caley (1770–1829), botanical collector financed by Sir Joseph Banks
Eucalyptus caleyi subsp. *ovendenii* L.A.S.Johnson & K.D.Hill	1991	Ovenden's Ironbark	NSW	Tree to 15m	White	Honours Peter John Ovenden (1929–97), forester who first recognised this subspecies
Eucalyptus caliginosa Blakely & McKie	1934	Broad-leaved Stringybark	Qld/NSW	Tree to 35m	White	Latin *caliginosus* = full of darkness; possibly referring to its spreading crown, which offers ample shade
Eucalyptus calycogona Turcz. subsp. *calycogona*	1852	Gooseberry Mallee	SA/WA	Mallee to 5m	White/pink	Greek *kalyx* = calyx, *-gonia* = angled; referring to the 4-sided buds and gumnuts
Eucalyptus calycogona Turcz. subsp. *miracula* D.Nicolle & French	2009		WA	Mallee to 5m	White	Latin *miraculum* = marvel; referring to the location of the species at Marvel Loch
Eucalyptus calycogona subsp. *spaffordii* D.Nicolle	2000		SA	Mallee to 5m	White/pink	Honours Walter John Spafford (1884–1962), agricultural scientist from SA Dept of Agriculture
Eucalyptus calycogona subsp. *trachybasis* D.Nicolle	2000		NSW/Vic/SA	Mallee to 6m	White/pink	Greek *trachys* = rough, *basis* = base; referring to the rough bark of this subspecies
Eucalyptus calyerup McQuoid & Hopper	2002		WA	Tree to 10m	Cream/yellow	From the Nyoongar Aboriginal name of the area where this species was found, Calyerup Rocks
Eucalyptus camaldulensis Dehnh. subsp. *camaldulensis*	1832	River Red Gum	All mainland states	Tree to 45m	White	From Camaldoli, Italy, where the tree was growing and from which specimen the species was described
Eucalyptus camaldulensis subsp. *acuta* Brooker & M.W.McDonald	2009	River Red Gum	Qld/NSW	Tree to 30m	White	Latin *acutus* = sharpened; referring to shape of bud cap
Eucalyptus camaldulensis subsp. *arida* Brooker & M.W.McDonald	2009	River Red Gum	WA/NT/Qld/NSW/SA	Tree to 30m	White	Latin *aridus* = arid; referring to its arid zone occurrence
Eucalyptus camaldulensis subsp. *minima* Brooker & M.W.McDonald	2009	River Red Gum	Qld	Tree to 25m	White	Latin *minimus* = small; referring to the size of buds and gumnuts
Eucalyptus camaldulensis subsp. *obtusa* (Blakely) Brooker & M.W.McDonald	1934	River Red Gum	WA/NT/Qld/NSW/SA	Tree to 30m	White	Latin *obtusus* = obtuse; referring to the blunt end of the bud cap
Eucalyptus camaldulensis subsp. *refulgens* Brooker & M.W.McDonald	2009	River Red Gum	WA	Tree to 30m	White	Latin *refulgens* = reflecting light; referring to the shiny leaves
Eucalyptus camaldulensis subsp. *simulata* Brooker & Kleinig	1994	Red Gum	Qld	Tree to 35m	White	Latin *simulatus* = resembling; referring to the buds which are indistinguishable from *E. tereticornis*
Eucalyptus cambageana Maiden	1913	Dawson Gum	Qld	Tree to 25m	White	Honours Richard Hind Cambage (1859–1928), surveyor with a strong interest in botany
Eucalyptus cameronii Blakely & McKie	1934	Diehard Stringybark	Qld/NSW	Tree to 40m	White	Honours Rev. Archibald Peter Cameron (1869–1945), Presbyterian minister and plant collector
Eucalyptus camfieldii Maiden	1920	Camfield's Stringybark	NSW	Tree to 10m	White	Honours Julius Henry Camfield (1852–1916), gardener at Royal Botanic Gardens, Sydney
Eucalyptus campanulata R.T.Baker & H.G.Sm.	1912	New England Blackbutt	Qld/NSW	Tree to 35m	White	Latin *campanulatus* = bell-shaped; referring to the fruit
Eucalyptus campaspe S.Moore	1819	Silver Gimlet	WA	Mallet to 10m	Creamy white	After Campaspe, the mistress of Alexander the Great, who was renowned for her beauty
Eucalyptus camphora R.T.Baker subsp. *camphora*	1899	Swamp Gum	Qld/NSW	Tree/mallee to 10m	White	Refers to camphor in the essential oils of the foliage
Eucalyptus camphora subsp. *humeana* L.A.S.Johnson & K.D.Hill	1990	Mountain Swamp Gum	NSW/Vic	Tree/mallee to 25m	White	Honours Hamilton Hume (1797–1872), Australian explorer
Eucalyptus canaliculata Maiden	1920	Grey Gum	NSW	Tree to 30m	White	Latin *canaliculatus* = channelled; reference uncertain
Eucalyptus canescens D.Nicolle subsp. *canescens*	1997	Ooldea Range Mallee	SA	Mallee to 3m	Creamy white	Latin *canescens* = becoming grey; referring to the branchlets, buds and gumnuts
Eucalyptus canescens subsp. *beadellii* Nicolle	1997	Beadell's Mallee	SA	Mallee to 3m	Creamy white	Honours Len Beadell, surveyor of many desert roads, including the Gunbarrel Highway
Eucalyptus canobolensis (L.A.S.Johnson & K.D.Hill) J.T.Hunter	1997	Mt Canobolas Candlebark	NSW	Tree to 12m	White	Named after Mt Canobolas, where the species is found
Eucalyptus capillosa Brooker & Hopper subsp. *capillosa*	1991	Wheatbelt Wandoo	WA	Tree to 12m	White	Latin *capillosus* = hairy; referring to the seedlings
Eucalyptus capillosa subsp. *polyclada* Brooker & Hopper	1991	Mallee Wandoo	WA	Mallee to 12m	White	Greek *poly-* = many, *clados* = branch; referring to the mallee habit
Eucalyptus capitellata Sm.	1795	Brown Stringybark	NSW	Tree to 25m	White	Latin *capitellatus* = with a little head; possibly referring to the small fruit clusters
Eucalyptus captiosa Brooker & Hopper	1993		WA	Mallee/mallet to 4m	Cream/yellow	Latin *captiosus* = deceiving; referring to the conspicuously narrow-leaved crown unlike related species
Eucalyptus carnabyi Blakely & H.Steedman ex Blakely	1941	Carnaby's Mallee	WA	Mallee to 5m	Pale yellow-pink	Honours Ivan Clarence Carnaby (1908–74), WA naturalist
Eucalyptus carnea R.T.Baker	1906	Broad-leaved White Mahogany	Qld/NSW	Tree to 25m	White	Honours Walter Mervyn Carne (1885–1952), plant pathologist
Eucalyptus carnei C.A.Gardner	1928	Carne's Blackbutt	WA	Tree/mallee to 6m	Creamy white	Honours Walter Mervyn Carne (1885–1952), plant pathologist
Eucalyptus castrensis K.D.Hill	2002		NSW	Mallee to 8m	?	Latin *castra* = an encampment, *-ensis* = origin of species; noting its occurrence on Singleton Army Base

TABLE 3: EUCALYPTUS

Name and Author	Date Desc.	Common Name	Where it Occurs	Tree Form and Size	Flower Colour	Name Meaning
Eucalyptus celastroides Turcz. subsp. *celastroides*	1852	Snap and Rattle	WA	Tree/mallee to 8m	White	Greek *kelastros* = a genus of tree, *-oides* = resembling; probably referring to the similarity of the leaves
Eucalyptus celastroides subsp. *virella* Brooker	1986		WA	Tree/mallee to 10m	White	Latin *virellus* = becoming green; referring to the much greener appearance of the subspecies
Eucalyptus cephalocarpa Blakely	1934	Mealy Stringybark	NSW/Vic	Tree to 20m	White	Greek *cephalos* = head, *carpos* = fruit; referring to the crowded heads of gumnuts
Eucalyptus ceracea Brooker & Done	1986	Seppelt Range Yellowjacket	WA	Tree to 6m	Bright orange	Latin *cereus* = waxen; referring to the extreme waxiness of the plant
Eucalyptus cerasiformis Brooker & Blaxell	1978	Cherry-fruited Mallee	WA	Mallee to 3m	Pale yellow	Latin *cerasi-* = of cherries, *-formis* = form; referring to the pendulous bunches of buds
Eucalyptus ceratocorys (Blakely) L.A.S.Johnson & K.D.Hill	1988	Horn-capped Mallee	WA	Mallee to 6m	Cream/red	Greek *keros* = horn, *korys* = helmet; referring to the horn-shaped bud cap
Eucalyptus cernua Brooker & Hopper	2002	Red-flowered Moort	WA	Mallee/mallet to 5m	Cream to red	Latin *cernuus* = nodding; referring to the pendulous flowers
Eucalyptus chapmaniana Cameron	1947	Bogong Gum	NSW/Vic	Tree to 35m	White	Honours Wilfrid Dinsey Chapman (1891–1955), engineer with interest in botany and discoverer of this species
Eucalyptus chartaboma D.Nicolle	2000		Qld	Tree to 18m	Orange	Greek *charte* = paper, *bomos* = base; referring to the papery bark around the base of the tree
Eucalyptus chloroclada (Blakely) L.A.S.Johnson & K.D.Hill	1988	Red Gum	Qld/NSW	Tree to 20m	White	Greek *chloro-* = green, *clados* = branch or shoot; probably referring to the non-grey adult leaves
Eucalyptus chlorophylla Brooker & Done subsp. *chlorophylla*	1986		WA/NT/Qld	Tree/mallee to 18m	Creamy white	Greek *chloro-* = green, *phyllon* = leaf; referring to the crown of glossy green leaves
Eucalyptus chlorophylla subsp. Archer River (K.Hill+ 1771) Qld Herbarium			Qld			An undescribed subspecies from Archer River
Eucalyptus cinerea F.Muell. ex Benth. subsp. *cinerea*	1867	Argyle Apple	NSW	Tree to 15m	White	Latin *cinereus* = ashen; referring to the generally silvery grey appearance of all its parts
Eucalyptus cinerea subsp. Beechworth (J.D.Briggs 2607) Vic Herbarium			Vic			An undescribed subspecies from Beechworth, Vic
Eucalyptus cinerea subsp. *triplex* (L.A.S.Johnson & K.D.Hill) Brooker, Slee & J.D.Briggs	1995		NSW	Tree to 10m	White	Latin *triplex* = triple, three-fold; referring to the buds which are borne in threes
Eucalyptus cladocalyx F.Muell.	1853	Sugar Gum	SA	Tree to 35m	White	Greek *clados* = branch, shoot, *Kalyx* = calyx; referring to the leafless shoots bearing flowers
Eucalyptus clelandii (Maiden) Maiden	1912	Cleland's Blackbutt	WA	Mallet/mallee to 10m	White	Honours Sir John Burton Cleland (1878–1971), medical practitioner and plant collector
Eucalyptus clivicola Brooker & Hopper	1991	Green Mallet	WA	Mallet to 12m	Pale yellow	Latin *clivi-* = hill slope, *-cola* = dwelling; referring to the habitat of the species
Eucalyptus cloeziana F.Muell.	1878	Gympie Messmate	Qld	Tree to 55m (25m)	White	Honours Francois Stanislaus Cloez (1817–83), French analytical chemist interested in eucalypt oils
Eucalyptus cneorifolia DC.	1828	Kangaroo Island Narrow-leaved Mallee	SA	Tree/mallee to 10m	White	Referring to the likeness of the leaves to the genus *Cneorum*
Eucalyptus coccifera Hook.f.	1847	Tasmanian Snow Gum	Tas	Tree/mallee to 15m	White/pink	Latin *coccus* = grain, pill, *-fera* = bearing; referring to the scale insects that may infect some plants
Eucalyptus codonocarpa Blakely & McKie	1930		Qld/NSW	Mallee to 6m	White	Greek *codon* = bell, *carpos* = fruit; referring to the bell-shaped gumnuts
Eucalyptus comitae-vallis Maiden	1923	Comet Vale Mallee	WA	Mallee to 6m	Cream	Refers to its occurrence at Comet Vale, WA goldfields
Eucalyptus communalis Brooker & Hopper	1993		WA	Mallee to 4m	Creamy white	Latin *communalis* = communal; referring to the dense pure stands of the species
Eucalyptus concinna Maiden & Blakely	1929	Victoria Desert Mallee	SA/WA	Mallee to 6m	White	Latin *concinnus* = pretty, neat; probably referring to the general appearance of the species
Eucalyptus conferruminata D.J.Carr & S.G.M.Carr subsp. *conferruminata*	1980	Bald Island Mallee	WA	Mallee/shrub to 5m	Pale green	Latin *conferruminatus* = fused; referring to the fused buds and gumnuts
Eucalyptus conferruminata subsp. *recherche* D.Nicolle & M.E.French	2008		WA	Mallee/shrub to 5m	Pale green	Refers to its occurrence on the Recherche Archipelago
Eucalyptus confluens Maiden	1916	Kimberley Gum	WA/NT	Tree to 8m	White	Latin *con-* = together, *fluo* = to flow; referring to one of the leaf veins which joins the leaf margin
Eucalyptus conglobata (Benth.) Maiden subsp. *conglobata*	1922	Port Lincoln Mallee	SA/WA	Mallee to 5m	White	Latin *conglobatus* = like a ball; probably referring to cluster of stalkless buds
Eucalyptus conglobata subsp. *perata* Brooker & Slee	2004		WA	Mallee to 5m	White	Latin *peratus* = western; referring to its location compared with subspecies *conglobatus*
Eucalyptus conglomerata Maiden & Blakely	1929	Swamp Stringybark	Qld	Tree/mallee to 8m	White	Latin *con-* = together, *glomeratus* = form into a ball; referring to the clusters of gumnuts
Eucalyptus conica H.Deane & Maiden	1900	Fuzzy Box	Qld/NSW	Tree to 20m	White	Latin *conicus* = conical; referring to the shape of the gumnuts
Eucalyptus conjuncta L.A.S.Johnson & K.D.Hill	1990		NSW	Tree to 15m	White	Latin *conjunctus* = joined; referring to its link between *E. eugenioides* and *E. sparsifolia*
Eucalyptus consideniana Maiden	1904	Yertchuk	NSW/Vic	Tree to 30m	White	Honours Denis Considen (c. 1760–1815), Assistant Surgeon on *Scarborough* and founder of *Eucalyptus* oil industry
Eucalyptus conspicua L.A.S.Johnson & K.D.Hill	1991	Gippsland Swamp Box	NSW/Vic	Tree to 10m	White	Latin *conspicuus* = conspicuous; referring to the grey colour of the crown
Eucalyptus conveniens L.A.S.Johnson & K.D.Hill	1998		WA	Mallee to 2.5m	White	Latin *conveniens* = coming together; referring to its link between *E. pleurocarpa* and *E. gittinsii*
Eucalyptus coolabah Blakely & Jacobs	1934	Coolabah	WA/NT/Qld/NSW/SA	Tree to 10m	White	Aboriginal name for the tree
Eucalyptus cooperiana F.Muell.	1880	Many-flowered Mallee	WA	Mallee to 4m	Cream/yellow	Honours E. Cooper (1829–1918), American horticulturist who introduced many eucalypt species to USA
Eucalyptus copulans L.A.S.Johnson & K.D.Hill	1991		NSW	Tree to 6m	White	Latin *copulans* = joining; referring to its link between *E. moorei* and *E. stellulata*
Eucalyptus cordata Labill.	1806	Heart-leaved Silver Gum	Tas	Tree to 20m	White	Latin *cordatus* = heart-shaped; referring to the leaf shape

TABLE 3: EUCALYPTUS

Name and Author	Date Desc.	Common Name	Where it Occurs	Tree Form and Size	Flower Colour	Name Meaning
Eucalyptus cornuta Labill.	1800	Yate	WA	Tree to 20m	Yellowish	Latin cornutus = horned; referring to the bud cap
Eucalyptus coronata C.A.Gardner	1933	Crowned Mallee	WA	Mallee to 3m	?yellow	Latin coronatus = crowned; referring to the sculptured bud cap
Eucalyptus corrugata Luehm.	1897	Rib-fruited Mallee	WA	Mallee to 15m	White	Latin corrugatus = corrugated; referring to the ribbed bud cap
Eucalyptus corticosa L.A.S.Johnson	1962	Olinda Box	NSW	Tree to 8m	White	Latin corticosus = of the bark; distinguished from E. mannifera by its soft, rough, slightly tessellated bark
Eucalyptus corynodes A.R.Bean & Brooker	1994		Qld	Tree to 20m	White	Greek corynodes = club-shaped; referring to the shape of the buds
Eucalyptus cosmophylla F.Muell.	1855	Cup Gum	SA	Tree/mallee to 10m	White	Greek cosmos = order, form, ornament, phyllon = a leaf; probably referring to the attractive juvenile leaves
Eucalyptus costuligera L.A.S.Johnson & K.D.Hill	2000		WA	Tree to 10m	White	Latin costa = vein, rib, -ula = diminutive, -ger = bearing; referring to the finely ribbed gumnuts
Eucalyptus crebra F.Muell.	1859	Narrow-leaved Red Ironbark	Qld/NSW	Tree to 35m	White	Latin creber = frequent; referring to its abundance
Eucalyptus crenulata Blakely & Beuzev.	1939	Victorian Silver Gum	Vic	Tree to 12m	White	Latin crenulatus = minutely crenate; referring to the scalloped edges of the leaves
Eucalyptus creta L.A.S.Johnson & K.D.Hill	1991	Large-fruited Gimlet	WA	Tree to 10m	White	Latin cretus = grown bigger; referring to the buds and gumnuts compared with related species
Eucalyptus cretata P.J.Lang & Brooker	1990	Darke Peak Mallee	SA	Mallee to 4m	White	Latin cretatus = marked with chalk; referring to the greyish branchlets, buds and gumnuts
Eucalyptus crispata Brooker & Hopper	1991	Yandanooka Mallee	WA	Mallee to 8m	Cream	Latin crispatus = curled; referring to the loose rough bark
Eucalyptus croajingolensis L.A.S.Johnson & K.D.Hill	1990	Gippsland Peppermint	NSW/Vic	Tree to 30m	White	After the district Croajingalong in eastern Gippsland, Vic
Eucalyptus crucis Maiden subsp. crucis	1923	Southern Cross Silver Mallee	WA	Mallee to 15m	Cream	Latin crucis = of the cross; referring to the town of Southern Cross near where the species occurs
Eucalyptus crucis subsp. lanceolata Brooker & Hopper	1982		WA	Mallee to 15m	Cream	Latin lanceolatus = lance-shaped; referring to the leaf shape
Eucalyptus crucis subsp. praecipua Brooker & Hopper	1993		WA	Mallee to 15m	Cream	Latin praecipuus = special; referring to the different bark, leaves, buds and fruits of this subspecies
Eucalyptus cullenii Cambage	1920	Cullen's Ironbark	Qld	Tree to 15m	White	Honours Sir William Portus Cullen (1855–1935), who had a notable academic and political career
Eucalyptus cunninghamii Sweet	1830	Cliff Mallee Ash	NSW	Mallee to 2m	White	Honours Allan Cunningham (1791–1839), botanist, explorer and plant collector
Eucalyptus cuprea Brooker & Hopper	1993	Mallee Box	WA	Mallee to 6m	Creamy white	Latin cupreus = coppery; referring to the colour of the stems
Eucalyptus cupularis C.A.Gardner	1964	Hall's Creek White Gum	WA/NT	Tree to 8m	White	Latin cupula = a little cup; referring to the shape of the gumnut
Eucalyptus curtisii Blakely & C.T.White	1931	Plunkett Mallee	Qld	Tree/mallee to 7m	Creamy white	Honours Densil Curtis (1892–1973), farmer and naturalist who collected the first specimen
Eucalyptus cuspidata Turcz.	1849		WA	Mallee	?	Latin cuspidatus = cuspidate, tapering gradually to a rigid point; possibly referring to the bud cap
Eucalyptus cyanophylla Brooker	1977	Blue-leaved Mallee	Vic/SA	Mallee to 5m	White	Greek cyano- = blue, phyllon = a leaf; referring to the bluish appearance of the mallee
Eucalyptus cyclostoma Brooker	1981		WA	Mallee to 3m	White	Greek cyclo- = ring, stoma = a mouth; referring to the marked rim of the gumnuts
Eucalyptus cylindriflora Maiden & Blakely	1925	White Mallee	WA	Mallee to 4m	Creamy white	Latin cylindri- = cylindrical, flora = flower; referring to the cylindrical buds
Eucalyptus cylindrocarpa Blakely	1934		WA	Mallee to 6m	White	Latin cylindri- = cylindrical, Greek carpos = fruit; referring to the cylindrical gumnuts
Eucalyptus cypellocarpa L.A.S.Johnson	1962	Mountain Grey Gum	NSW/Vic	Tree to 65m	White	Greek cypellum = a cup, carpos = fruit; referring to the cup-like gumnuts
Eucalyptus dalrympleana Maiden subsp. dalrympleana	1920	Mountain Gum	NSW/Vic/Tas	Tree to 40m	White	Honours Richard Dalrymple Hay (1861–1943), who monitored forest conservation for Forests Dept NSW
Eucalyptus dalrympleana subsp. heptantha L.A.S.Johnson	1962	Mountain Gum	Qld/NSW	Tree to 40m	White	Greek heptanthos = 7-flowered; referring to the flower clusters
Eucalyptus dalrympleana subsp. Howmans Gap (N.G.Walsh 5293) Vic Herbarium						An undescribed subspecies
Eucalyptus dawsonii R.T.Baker	1899	Slaty Box	NSW	Tree to 20m	White	Honours James Dawson (flor. 1876–99), surveyor with an interest in native plants
Eucalyptus dealbata A.Cunn. ex Schauer	1943	Tumble-down Red Gum	Qld/NSW	Tree to 20m	White	Latin dealbatus = covered with whiteness; referring to the white wax on the buds and gumnuts
Eucalyptus deanei Maiden	1904	Round-leaved Gum	Qld/NSW	Tree to 65m	White	Honours Henry Deane (1847–1924), railway engineer and botanist
Eucalyptus decipiens Endl. subsp. decipiens	1837		WA	Tree/mallee to 5m	Creamy white	Latin decipiens = deceiving; reference obscure; possibly resembling another species
Eucalyptus decipiens subsp. adesmophloia Brooker & Hopper	1993		WA	Tree/mallee to 5m	Creamy white	Greek adesmo- = unfettered, phloios = bark; referring to the loose, paler ribbony rough bark
Eucalyptus decipiens subsp. chalara Brooker & Hopper	1993		WA	Tree/mallee to 5m	Creamy white	Greek chalaros = loose; referring to the loose bark, which is flaky rather than ribbony
Eucalyptus decolor A.R.Bean & Brooker	1989		Qld	Tree to 25m	White	Latin decolor = discoloured, faded; referring to the leaves, which are paler on the underside
Eucalyptus decorticans (F.M.Bailey) Maiden	1921	Gum-topped Ironbark	Qld	Tree to 40m	White	Latin decorticans = without bark; referring to the peeling bark on the medium and small branches
Eucalyptus decurva F.Muell.	1863	Slender Mallee	WA	Mallee to 3m	White	Latin decurvus = down curved; referring to the drooping flower clusters
Eucalyptus deflexa Brooker	1976	Lake King Mallee	WA	Mallee to 3m	Cream/pale pink	Latin deflexus = deflexed; referring to curved down flower clusters
Eucalyptus deglupta Blume	1849	Rainbow Gum	SE Asia	Tree to 60m	White	Meaning obscure
Eucalyptus delegatensis R.T.Baker subsp. delegatensis	1900	Alpine Ash	NSW/Vic	Tree to 60m	White	After the town of Delegate, southern NSW
Eucalyptus delegatensis subsp. tasmaniensis Boland	1985	Blue Leaf	Tas	Tree to 50m	White	After Tasmania, where the species is found
Eucalyptus delicata L.A.S.Johnson & K.D.Hill	1999		WA	Tree to 15m	Creamy white	Latin delicatus = dainty; referring to the small buds and gumnuts

TABLE 3: EUCALYPTUS

Name and Author	Date Desc.	Common Name	Where it Occurs	Tree Form and Size	Flower Colour	Name Meaning
Eucalyptus dendromorpha (Blakely) L.A.S.Johnson & Blaxell	1972	Budawang Ash	NSW	Tree to 30m	White	Greek dendros = tree, morphos = form; referring to habit compared with mallee form of related species
Eucalyptus densa Brooker & Hopper subsp. densa	1991		WA	Mallet to 10m	Pale yellow	Latin densus = dense; referring to the crown
Eucalyptus densa subsp. improcera Brooker & Hopper	1991	Dwarf Blue Mallee	WA	Mallee to 3m	Lemon	Latin improcerus = short; referring to the habit compared with the other subspecies
Eucalyptus denticulata I.O.Cook & Ladiges	1991	Shining Gum	NSW/Vic	Tree to 35m	White	Latin denticulatus = toothed; referring to the leaf edges
Eucalyptus depauperata L.A.S.Johnson & K.D.Hill	1992		WA	Mallee to 4m	Lemon/ pink	Latin depauperatus = depauperate; referring to habit, buds and gumnuts compared with related E. eremophila
Eucalyptus desmondensis Maiden & Blakely	1925	Desmond Mallee	WA	Mallee to 6m	Cream/ yellow	After Mt Desmond near Ravensthorpe, where the species is found
Eucalyptus deuaensis Boland & P.M.Gilmour	1986	Mongamulla Mallee	NSW	Mallee to 4m	White	After Deua National Park in south-eastern NSW, where the species is located
Eucalyptus dielsii C.A.Gardner	1927	Cap-fruited Mallet	WA	Mallet to 8m	Yellow/ green	Honours Frederick Ludwig Emil Diels (1874–1945), eminent German botanist who collected in Australia
Eucalyptus diminuta Brooker & Hopper	2002		WA	Mallee to 4m	Creamy white	Latin diminutus = diminished; referring to the habit, buds and gumnuts compared with related E. stowardii
Eucalyptus diptera C.R.P.Andrews	1904	Two-winged Gimlet	WA	Mallet to 10m	Cream/ green	Latin dipterus = 2-winged; referring to the small wings at the base of the buds and gumnuts
Eucalyptus discreta Brooker	1979		WA	Mallee to 5m	Creamy white	Latin discretus = separate; referring to the juvenile leaves which are not joined like the related E. uncinata
Eucalyptus dissimulata Brooker subsp. dissimulata	1988	Red-capped Mallee	WA	Mallee to 3m	Creamy white	Latin dissimulatus = hidden; referring to its long unrecognised occurrence in the southern wheatbelt
Eucalyptus dissimulata subsp. Truslove (M.I.H.Brooker 7499) NSW Herbarium						An undescribed subspecies
Eucalyptus distans Brooker, Boland & Kleinig	1980		NT/Qld	Tree to 7m	Creamy white	Latin distans = standing apart; referring to its differences from E. microtheca with which it was confused
Eucalyptus distuberosa D.Nicolle subsp. distuberosa	2009		WA	Mallet to 14m	White	Latin dis = not; tuberosus = full of lumps; referring to the lack of lignotuber
Eucalyptus distuberosa D.Nicolle subsp. aerata D.Nicolle	2009		WA	Mallet to 14m	White	Latin aeratus = covered with bronze; referring to its restricted occurrence at Bronzite Ridge
Eucalyptus diversicolor F.Muell.	1863	Karri	WA	Tree to 80m	White	Latin diversi- = diverse, -color = colour; referring to the leaves, which are paler on the underside
Eucalyptus diversifolia Bonpl. subsp. diversifolia	1814	Soap Mallee	SA/Vic	Mallee to 6m	White	Latin diversi- = diverse, folium = leaf; referring to the change of leaf shape at different growth stages
Eucalyptus diversifolia subsp. hesperia I.J.Wright & Ladiges	1997	Madura Mallee Ash	WA	Mallee to 4m	White	Greek hesperius = west; referring to the western distribution of this subspecies
Eucalyptus diversifolia subsp. megacarpa I.J.Wright & Ladiges	1997		Vic/SA	Mallee to 6m	White	Greek mega- = large, carpos = fruit; referring to the much larger gumnuts of this subspecies
Eucalyptus dives Schauer	1843	Broad-leaved Peppermint	NSW/Vic	Tree to 20m	White	Latin dives = rich; referring to the rich oil content of the leaves
Eucalyptus dolichocera L.A.S.Johnson & K.D.Hill	1999		WA	Mallee to 6m	Creamy white	Greek dolicho- = long, narrow, keros = horn; referring to long cap on the buds
Eucalyptus dolichorhyncha (Brooker) Brooker & Hopper	1993	Fuchsia Gum	WA	Mallet to 6m	Yellow	Greek dolicho- = long, narrow, rhynchos = nose; referring to the long cap on the buds
Eucalyptus dolorosa Brooker & Hopper	1993	Mt Misery Mallee	WA	Mallee to 1.5m	White	Latin dolorosus = sad; referring obliquely to the only locality where the species is found
Eucalyptus doratoxylon F.Muell.	1860	Spearwood	WA	Mallee/tree to 5m	Creamy white	Greek dorato- = spear, xylon = wood; referring to Aboriginal use for the stems
Eucalyptus dorrigoensis (Blakely) L.A.S.Johnson & K.D.Hill	1990	Dorrigo White Gum	NSW	Tree to 30m	White	After Dorrigo, where the species is found
Eucalyptus drummondii Benth. subsp. drummondii	1867	Drummond's Mallee	WA	Mallee to 4m	White	Honours James Drummond (1786–1863), energetic botanical collector
Eucalyptus drummondii subsp. Moora (D.Nicolle 1653) D.Nicolle						An undescribed species from Moora, WA
Eucalyptus drummondii subsp. York (D.Nicolle & M.French DN 3684) D.Nicolle						An undescribed species from York, WA
Eucalyptus dumosa A.Cunn. ex J.Oxley	1820	White Mallee	NSW/Vic/ SA	Mallee to 10m	White	Latin dumosus = shrubby; referring to its growth habit
Eucalyptus dundasii Maiden	1916	Dundas Blackbutt	WA	Tree to 15m	Creamy white	After Dundas, an early mining town near Lake Dundas, south of Norseman
Eucalyptus dunnii Maiden	1905	Dunn's White Gum	Qld/NSW	Tree to 50m	White	Honours William Dunn (1860–flor. 1921), forester and first collector of this species
Eucalyptus dura L.A.S.Johnson & K.D.Hill	1991		Qld	Tree to 25m	White	Latin durus = hard; referring to the bark
Eucalyptus dwyeri Maiden & Blakely	1915	Dwyer's Red Gum	NSW	Tree/mallee to 10m	White	Honours Joseph Wilfred Dwyer (1869–1939), priest and plant collector
Eucalyptus ebbanoensis Maiden subsp. ebbanoensis	1921	Sandplain Mallee	WA	Mallee to 6m	White	After Ebbano, a locality where the species occurs
Eucalyptus ebbanoensis subsp. glauciramula L.A.S.Johnson & K.D.Hill	1998		WA	Mallee to 6m	White	Latin glauci- = glaucous, grey, ramulus = branch; referring to the grey bloom on the branches
Eucalyptus ebbanoensis subsp. photina Brooker & Hopper	1993		WA	Mallee to 6m	White	Greek photeinos = shiny; referring to the shiny leaves of this subspecies
Eucalyptus educta L.A.S.Johnson & K.D.Hill	1992		WA	Mallee to 4m	Creamy white	Latin eductus = drawn out; referring to the bud cap
Eucalyptus effusa Brooker subsp. effusa	1976	Rough-barked Gimlet	WA	Mallee to 4m	White	Latin effusus = spread out, straggling; referring to the habit
Eucalyptus effusa subsp. exsul L.A.S.Johnson & K.D.Hill	1991		WA	Mallee to 4m	White	Latin exsul = an exile; referring to the remote location of this subspecies
Eucalyptus elaeophloia Chappill, Crisp & Prober	1990	Apple Jack, Nunniong Gum	Vic	Tree/mallee to 10m	White	Greek elaeo- = olive, phloios = bark; referring to the bark colour
Eucalyptus elata Dehnh.	1829	River Peppermint	NSW/Vic	Tree to 40m	White	Latin elatus = tall; referring to its habit

TABLE 3: EUCALYPTUS

Name and Author	Date Desc.	Common Name	Where it Occurs	Tree Form and Size	Flower Colour	Name Meaning
Eucalyptus elegans A.R.Bean	2005		Qld/NSW	Tree to 25m	White	Latin *elegans* = elegant; referring to the attractive habit
Eucalyptus elliptica (Blakely & McKie) L.A.S.Johnson & K.D.Hill	1990	Bendemeer White Gum	NSW	Tree to 20m	White	Latin *ellipticus* = elliptical; referring to the gumnut shape
Eucalyptus erectifolia Brooker & Hopper	1986	Stirling Range Mallee	WA	Mallee to 2.5m	White	Latin *erecti-* = erect, *folium* = leaf; referring to its characteristic crown
Eucalyptus eremicola Boomsma subsp. *eremicola*	1975		WA/SA	Mallee to 4m	White	Greek *eremi-* = desert, *-cola* = dweller; referring to its habitat
Eucalyptus eremicola subsp. *peeneri* (Blakely) D.Nicolle	2005		WA/SA	Mallee to 6m	White	After an Aboriginal name for this subspecies
Eucalyptus eremophila (Diels) Maiden subsp. *eremophila*	1920	Sand Mallee	WA	Mallee/mallet to 5m	Lemon/pink	Greek *eremi-* = desert, *philos* = lover; referring to its dry habitat
Eucalyptus eremophila subsp. *pterocarpa* (Blakely & H.Steedman) L.A.S.Johnson & Blaxell	1973		WA	Mallee/mallet to 5m	Lemon/pink	Greek *ptero-* = winged, *carpos* = fruit; referring to the ribbed fruit
Eucalyptus erosa A.R.Bean	2005		Qld	Tree to 30m	White	Latin *erosus* = irregularly toothed; referring to the leaf margins
Eucalyptus erythrocorys F.Muell.	1860	Illyarrie	WA	Tree/mallee to 8m	Yellow	Greek *erythro-* = red, *korys* = helmet; referring to the red bud caps
Eucalyptus erythronema Turcz. var. *erythronema*	1852	Red-flowered Mallee	WA	Tree/mallee to 6m	Red/yellow	Greek *erythro-* = red, *nemos* = thread; referring to the stamens
Eucalyptus erythronema var. *marginata* (Benth.) Domin	1913	Red-flowered Mallee	WA	Tree/mallee to 6m	Red/yellow	Latin *marginatus* = border; referring to the flange around the bud
Eucalyptus eudesmioides F.Muell. subsp. *eudesmioides*	1860		WA	Mallee to 6m	White	After the genus *Eudesmia*, which it resembles
Eucalyptus eudesmioides subsp. *pallida* L.A.S.Johnson & K.D.Hill ms.			WA	Mallee to 8m	White	Latin *pallidus* = pallid; referring to the pale leaves and gumnuts
Eucalyptus eudesmioides subsp. *selachiana* L.A.S.Johnson & K.D.Hill ms.			WA	Mallee to 3m	White	After the zoological group for sharks (*Selachii*); alluding to Shark Bay, where this subspecies occurs
Eucalyptus eugenioides Sieber ex Spreng.	1827	Thin-leaved Stringybark	Qld/NSW	Tree to 25m	White	After its supposed resemblance to the genus *Eugenia*
Eucalyptus ewartiana Maiden	1919		WA	Mallee to 7m	White	Honours Albert James Ewart (1872–1937), first Professor of Botany at Melbourne University
Eucalyptus exigua Brooker & Hopper	1993		WA	Mallee to 3m	White	Latin *exiguus* = little; referring to its habit compared with related *E. brachycorys*
Eucalyptus exilipes Brooker & A.R.Bean	1987	Fine-leaved Ironbark	Qld	Tree to 35m	White	Latin *exilis* = slender, *pes* = foot; referring to the very slender bud stalks
Eucalyptus exilis Brooker	1974	Boyagin Mallee	WA	Mallee to 4m	White	Latin *exilis* = slender; referring to the very slender stems
Eucalyptus exserta F.Muell.	1859	Queensland Peppermint	Qld/NSW	Tree to 20m	White	Latin *exsertus* = exserted; referring to the valves of the gumnuts
Eucalyptus extensa L.A.S.Johnson & K.D.Hill	1991		WA	Mallee to 12m	Yellow/green	Latin *extensus* = extended; referring to the long bud caps
Eucalyptus extrica D.Nicolle	2000	Eastern Tallerack	WA	Mallee to 4m	White	Latin *extrico* = disentangled; referring to the identity of this species being confused with *E. pleurocarpa*
Eucalyptus falcata subsp. Jerramungup (Canning CBG 038636) NSW Herb.			WA			An undescribed subspecies from Jerrimungup, WA
Eucalyptus falcata Turcz. subsp. *falcata*	1847	Silver Mallee	WA	Mallee to 5m	Cream/green	Latin *falcatus* = sickle-shaped; presumably describing the leaves, although not particularly appropriate
Eucalyptus falciformis (Newnham, Ladiges & Whiffin) K.Rule	2008	Grampians Peppermint	Vic	Tree to 15m	White	Latin *falciformis* = sickle-shaped; referring to the juvenile leaves
Eucalyptus famelica Brooker & Hopper	1989		WA	Mallee to 4m	Creamy white	Latin *famelica* = hungry; an oblique allusion to the nearby Starvation Boat Harbour
Eucalyptus farinosa K.D.Hill	1997		Qld	Tree to 9m	White	Latin *farinosus* = floury; referring to the greyish bloom on the leaves, buds and gumnuts
Eucalyptus fasciculosa F.Muell.	1855	Pink Gum	Vic/SA	Tree to 10m	White	Latin *fasciculosus* = cluster, bundle; referring to the conspicuous terminal flower clusters
Eucalyptus fastigata H.Deane & Maiden	1897	Brown Barrel	NSW/Vic	Tree to 60m	White	Latin *fastigatus* = high, exalted; referring to the habit of the tree
Eucalyptus fergusonii R.T.Baker	1917		NSW	Tree to 30m	White	Possibly honours William Hamilton Ferguson (1861–1957), geologist and plant collector
Eucalyptus fibrosa F.Muell. subsp. *fibrosa*	1859	Broad-leaved Red Ironbark	Qld/NSW	Tree to 35m	White	Latin *fibrosus* = fibrous; referring to the bark but seems inappropriate for an ironbark
Eucalyptus fibrosa subsp. *nubila* (Maiden & Blakely) L.A.S.Johnson	1962	Blue-leaved Ironbark	Qld/NSW	Tree to 35m	White	Latin *nubilus* = greyish blue; referring to the colour of the crown
Eucalyptus filiformis Rule	2004		Vic	Mallee to 6m	White	Latin *filum* = thread, *forma* = shape; referring to the extremely narrow juvenile leaves
Eucalyptus fitzgeraldii Blakely	1934	Paper-barked Box	WA	Tree to 12m	White	Honours W.V. Fitzgerald (1867–1929), forest botanist and explorer
Eucalyptus flavida Brooker & Hopper	1991	Yellow-flowered Mallee	WA	Mallee to 10m	Yellow	Latin *flavidus* = yellow; referring to the flower colour
Eucalyptus flindersii Boomsma	1980	South Australian Grey Mallee	SA	Mallee to 5m	White	Honours Matthew Flinders (1774–1814), who circumnavigated Australia with botanist Robert Brown
Eucalyptus flocktoniae (Maiden) Maiden subsp. *flocktoniae*	1916	Merrit	WA	Mallee to 8m	Creamy white	Honours Margaret Lilian Flockton (1861–1953), botanical artist with Royal Botanic Gardens, Sydney
Eucalyptus flocktoniae subsp. *hebes* D.Nicolle	1999		WA	Mallee to 8m	Creamy white	Latin *hebes* = dull; referring to the leaf colour compared with the other subspecies
Eucalyptus foecunda Schauer subsp. *foecunda*	1844	Fremantle Mallee	WA	Mallee to 3m	Creamy white	Latin *foecundus* = fecund; referring to the prolific production of flower buds
Eucalyptus foecunda subsp. Coolimba (M.I.H.Brooker 9556) WA Herbarium						An undescribed subspecies
Eucalyptus foelscheana F.Muell.	1882	Smooth-barked Bloodwood	WA/NT	Tree to 10m	White	Honours Paul Heinrich Foelsche (1831–1914), police inspector and photographer
Eucalyptus foliosa L.A.S.Johnson & K.D.Hill	1992		WA	Mallee to 3m	White	Latin *foliosus* = full of leaves; referring to the dense canopy
Eucalyptus formanii C.A.Gardner	1942	Die Hardy Mallee	WA	Tree/mallee to 10m	Creamy white	Honours Francis Gloster Forman (1904–80), Government Geologist, WA, and plant collector

Name and Author	Date Desc.	Common Name	Where it Occurs	Tree Form and Size	Flower Colour	Name Meaning
Eucalyptus forrestiana Diels	1904	Fuchsia Gum	WA	Mallet to 4m	Yellow	Honours Sir John Forrest (1847–1918), first Premier of WA and keen plant collector
Eucalyptus fracta K.D.Hill	1997		NSW	Tree/mallee to 8m	White	Latin *fractus* = broken; referring to its occurrence in the Broken Back Range
Eucalyptus fraseri (Brooker) Brooker subsp. *fraseri*	1976	Balladonia Gum	WA	Tree to 15m	White	Honours Sir Malcolm Fraser (1834–1900), Surveyor-General, WA
Eucalyptus fraseri subsp. *melanobasis* L.A.S.Johnson & K.D.Hill	2001	Fraser Range Blackbutt	WA	Tree to 15m	White	Greek *melano-* = black, *basis* = base; referring to the rough basal bark
Eucalyptus fraxinoides H.Deane & Maiden	1898	White Ash	NSW/Vic	Tree to 40m	White	Referring to some similarity to the genus *Fraxinus* (Ash)
Eucalyptus frenchiana D.Nicolle	2009		WA	Mallet to 14m	White	Honours Malolm E. French (b. 1947), collector who found this species
Eucalyptus froggattii Blakely	1934	Kamarooka Mallee	Vic	Tree/mallee to 10m	White	Honours Walter Wilson Froggatt (1858–1937), entomologist
Eucalyptus fruticosa Brooker	1979		WA	Mallee to 5m	Creamy white	Latin *fruticosus* = shrubby; referring to the habit
Eucalyptus fulgens K.Rule	1996		Vic	Tree to 20m	White	Latin *fulgens* = bright; referring to the shiny green leaves
Eucalyptus fusiformis Boland & Kleinig	1987	Nambucca Ironbark	Qld/NSW	Tree to 30m	White	Latin *fusiformis* = spindle-shaped; referring to the shape of the buds
Eucalyptus gamophylla F.Muell.	1978	Warilu	WA/NT/Qld/SA	Mallee to 8m	White	Greek *gamo-* = joined, *phyllon* = a leaf; referring to the juvenile leaves, which are joined around the stem
Eucalyptus gardneri Maiden subsp. *gardneri*	1924		WA	Mallet to 15m	Pale lemon	Honours Charles Austin Gardner (1896–1970), Government Botanist and Curator of WA Herbarium
Eucalyptus gardneri subsp. *ravensthorpensis* Brooker & Hopper	1991	Blue Mallet	WA	Mallet to 10m	Pale lemon	After Ravensthorpe, where the subspecies is located
Eucalyptus georgei Brooker & Blaxell subsp. *georgei*	1978		WA	Mallet to 12m	Creamy white	Honours Alexander Segger George (b. 1939), first Executive Editor of *Flora of Australia*
Eucalyptus georgei subsp. *fulgida* Brooker & Hopper	1993		WA	Mallet to 15m	Creamy white	Latin *fulgidus* = shining; referring to the leaves compared with the typical form
Eucalyptus gigantangion L.A.S.Johnson & K.D.Hill	1991	Kakadu Woolybutt	NT	Tree to 30m	Orange	Greek *gigant* = a giant, *aggeion* = a vessel; referring to the large fruit
Eucalyptus gillenii Ewart & L.R.Kerr	1926	Mallee Red Gum	WA/NT/SA	Mallee to 6m	White	Honours Francis James Gillen (1855–1912), Post and Telegraph Master, Alice Springs
Eucalyptus gillii Maiden	1912	Curly Mallee	NSW/SA	Mallee to 6m	Pale yellow	Honours Walter Gill (1851–1929), Conservator of Forests, SA
Eucalyptus gittinsii Brooker & Blaxell subsp. *gittinsii*	1978	Northern Sandplain Mallee	WA	Mallee to 5m	White	Honours Clifford Halliday Gittins (1904–95), engineer and plant collector
Eucalyptus gittinsii subsp. *illucida* D.Nicolle	2000		WA	Mallee to 4m	White	Latin *il-* = not, *lucidus* = shining; referring to the dull adult leaves of this subspecies
Eucalyptus glaucescens Maiden & Blakely	1929	Tingiringi Gum	NSW/Vic	Tree/mallee to 50m	White	Latin *glaucescens* = becoming grey; referring to the white wax on branchlets, buds and gumnuts
Eucalyptus glaucina (Blakely) L.A.S.Johnson	1962	Slaty Red Gum	NSW	Tree to 20m	White	Latin *glaucinus* = grey; referring to the white wax on the buds
Eucalyptus globoidea Blakely	1927	White Stringybark	NSW/Vic	Tree to 40m	White	Latin *globoideus* = globe-shaped; referring to the gumnuts
Eucalyptus globulus Labill. subsp. *globulus*	1800	Tasmanian Blue Gum	Vic/Tas	Tree to 70m	White	Latin *globulus* = a globe; referring to the shape of the gumnuts
Eucalyptus globulus subsp. *bicostata* (Maiden, Blakely & Simmonds) J.B.Kirkp.	1975	Southern Blue Gum, Eurabbie	NSW/Vic/SA	Tree to 45m	White	Latin *bicostatus* = 2-ribbed; referring to the fruit
Eucalyptus globulus subsp. *maidenii* (F.Muell.) J.B.Kirkp.	1975	Maiden's Gum	NSW/Vic	Tree to 50m	White	Honours Joseph Henry Maiden (1859–1925), Director Botanic Gardens, Sydney
Eucalyptus globulus subsp. *pseudoglobulus* (Naudin ex Maiden) J.B.Kirkp.	1975	Victorian Eurabbie	Vic	Tree to 45m	White	Latin *pseudo-* = false; referring to its similarity to *E. globulus* subsp. *globulus*
Eucalyptus glomericassis L.A.S.Johnson & K.D.Hill	2000	Scarp White Gum	NT	Tree to 10m	White	Latin *glomus* = a ball, *cassis* = a helmet; referring to the shape of the bud cap
Eucalyptus glomerosa Brooker & Hopper	1993	Jinjulu	WA/SA	Mallee to 5m	?	Latin *glomerosus* = like a ball; referring to the bud shape
Eucalyptus gomphocephala DC.	1828	Tuart	WA	Tree to 40m	White	Greek *gompho-* = club, *cephalos* = a head; referring to the bud shape
Eucalyptus gongylocarpa Blakely	1936	Baarla	WA/NT/SA	Tree to 16m	Creamy white	Greek *gongylo-* = ball-shaped, *carpos* = a fruit; referring to the gumnuts
Eucalyptus goniantha Turcz. subsp. *goniantha*	1847	Jerdacuttup Mallee	WA	Mallee to 7m	Creamy white	Greek *gonio-* = angled, *anthos* = flower; referring to the ribbed buds and gumnuts
Eucalyptus goniantha subsp. *notactites* L.A.S.Johnson & K.D.Hill	1992		WA	Mallee to 3m	Creamy white	Greek *notos* = southern, *aktites* = a watcher; referring to its southern coastal habitat
Eucalyptus goniocalyx F.Muell. ex Miq. subsp. *goniocalyx*	1856	Long-leaved Box	NSW/Vic/SA	Tree to 15m	White	Greek *gonio-* = angled; referring to the angles on the fruit
Eucalyptus goniocalyx subsp. *exposa* D.Nicolle	2000		SA	Mallee to 6m	White	English word referring to the exposed habitat in the Flinders Ranges
Eucalyptus goniocalyx subsp. Grampians (N.G.Walsh 4643) Vic Herbarium						An undescribed subspecies
Eucalyptus goniocarpa L.A.S.Johnson & K.D.Hill	1992		WA	Mallee to 7m	Creamy white	Greek *gonio-* = angled, *carpos* = fruit; referring to the ribbed gumnuts
Eucalyptus gracilis F.Muell.	1855	Yorrel	WA/SA/Vic/NSW	Mallee to 7m	White	Latin *gracilis* = slender; referring to the habit but not really applicable
Eucalyptus grandis W.Hill ex Maiden	1919	Flooded Gum	Qld/NSW	Tree to 60m	White	Latin *grandis* = great, large; referring to its size
Eucalyptus granitica L.A.S.Johnson & K.D.Hill	1991	Granite Ironbark	Qld	Tree to 20m	White	Latin *graniticus* = granite; referring to the soil type where this species occurs
Eucalyptus gregoriensis N.G.Walsh & Albr.	1998		NT	Tree/mallee to 8m	White	After Gregory National Park, where the species occurs, and A.C. Gregory, the first European to explore the area
Eucalyptus gregsoniana L.A.S.Johnson & Blaxell	1973	Wolgan Snow Gum	NSW	Mallee to 4m	White	Honours Edward Jesse Gregson (1882–1955) and father Jesse Gregson (1837–1919), both plant collectors
Eucalyptus griffithsii Maiden	1911		WA	Mallee to 10m	White	Honours John Moore Griffiths, friend of well-known botanist J.H. Maiden
Eucalyptus grisea L.A.S.Johnson & K.D.Hill	2000	Grey Gum	Qld	Tree to 28m	White	Latin *griseus* = grey; referring to the bark of the mature tree
Eucalyptus grossa F.Muell. ex Benth.	1867	Coarse-leaved Mallee	WA	Mallee to 3m	Yellow green	Latin *grossus* = thick, coarse; referring to the leaves, buds and gumnuts

TABLE 3: EUCALYPTUS

Name and Author	Date Desc.	Common Name	Where it Occurs	Tree Form and Size	Flower Colour	Name Meaning
Eucalyptus guilfoylei Maiden	1911	Yellow Tingle	WA	Tree to 40m	White	Honours William Robert Guilfoyle (c. 1840–1912) Director, Melbourne Botanic Gardens
Eucalyptus gunnii Hook.f.	1844	Cider Gum	Tas	Tree to 25m	White	Honours Ronald Campbell Gunn (1808–81), eminent Tasmanian botanist
Eucalyptus gypsophila D.Nicolle	1997	Kopi Mallee	WA/SA	Mallee to 6m	Creamy white	Latin *gypso-* = gypsum, *-phila* = loving; referring to the habitat
Eucalyptus haemastoma Sm.	1797	Scribbly Gum	NSW	Tree to 12m	White	Greek *haema* = blood, *stoma* = mouth; referring to the red disc at the mouth of the gumnut
Eucalyptus hallii Brooker	1975	Goodwood Gum	Qld	Tree to 20m	White	Honours Norman Hall (1906–2005), forester and botanical author
Eucalyptus halophila D.J.Carr & S.G.M.Carr	1980		WA	Mallee to 4m	White	Greek *halo-* = salt, *philos* = lover; referring to the habitat of this species
Eucalyptus hawkeri Rule	2004		Vic	Tree/mallee to 15m	White	Honours Peter Hawker, park ranger and plant collector
Eucalyptus hebetifolia Brooker & Hopper	1991		WA	Mallee to 8m	Creamy white	Latin *hebeti-* = dull, *folium* = leaf; referring to its appearance
Eucalyptus helidonica K.D.Hill	1999		Qld	Tree to 20m	White	After the town of Helidon, south-east Qld, where the species occurs
Eucalyptus herbertiana Maiden	1923	Kalumburu Gum	WA/NT	Tree/mallee to 10m	White	Honours Desmond Andrew Herbert (1898–1976), Professor of Botany, University of Qld
Eucalyptus histophylla Brooker & Hopper	1991		WA	Mallee to 6m	Pale yellow	Greek *histo-* = upright, *phyllon* = leaf; referring to the leaves of the crown
Eucalyptus horistes L.A.S.Johnson & K.D.Hill	1988		WA	Tree/mallee to 8m	Creamy white	Greek *horistes* = one who marks the boundaries; referring to occurrence at northern limit of SW Province
Eucalyptus houseana W.Fitzg. ex Maiden	1916	Kimberley White Gum	WA	Tree to 20m	White	Honours Dr Frederick Maurice House (1865–1936), government medical officer and explorer
Eucalyptus howittiana F.Muell.	1882	Howitt's Box	Qld	Tree to 20m	Creamy white	Honours Alfred William Howitt (1830–1908), explorer, botanist and geologist
Eucalyptus hypolaena L.A.S.Johnson & K.D.Hill	1999		WA	Tree/mallee to 15m	Pale yellow	Greek *hypo-* = under, *laena* = cloak; referring to unshed basal bark
Eucalyptus hypostomatica L.A.S.Johnson & K.D.Hill	1990	Pokolbin Box	NSW	Tree to 30m	White	Greek *hypo-* = under, *stoma* = mouth; referring to the stomates (pores) mostly on the underside of the leaf
Eucalyptus ignorabilis L.A.S.Johnson & K.D.Hill	1991		Vic	Tree to 20m	White	Latin *ignorabilis* = unknown; referring to its inadvertent earlier inclusion in *E. aromaphloia*
Eucalyptus imitans L.A.S.Johnson & K.D.Hill	1991	Illawarra Stringybark	NSW	Tree to 10m	White	Latin *imitans* = imitating; referring to its resemblance to *E. oblonga* (now included in *E. globoidea*)
Eucalyptus imlayensis Crisp & Brooker	1980	Mt Imlay Mallee	NSW	Mallee to 7m	White	After Mt Imlay, south-east NSW, where this species occurs
Eucalyptus impensa Brooker & Hopper	1993	Eneabba Mallee	WA	Mallee to 1.5m	Pink	Latin *impensus* = large; referring to the buds and gumnuts
Eucalyptus incerata Brooker & Hopper	2002	Mount Day Mallee	WA	Mallee to 5m	Yellow	Latin *inceratus* = covered with wax; referring to the buds and gumnuts
Eucalyptus incrassata Labill.	1806	Ridged-fruited Mallee	WA/SA/Vic/NSW	Mallee to 8m	Cream/pink	Latin *incrassatus* = thickened; referring to the leaves
Eucalyptus indurata Brooker & Hopper	1993	Ironbark	WA	Tree/mallee to 8m	Creamy white	Latin *induratus* = hard; referring to the rough bark
Eucalyptus infera A.R.Bean	1990	Durakai Mallee	Qld	Mallee to 8m	White	Latin *inferus* = inferior; referring to its occurrence as an understorey to other eucalypts
Eucalyptus insularis Brooker	1974	North Twin Peak Mallee	WA	Mallee to 3m	White	Latin *insularis* = of an island; referring to its occurrence on North Twin Peak Island off the Esperance coast
Eucalyptus interstans L.A.S.Johnson & K.D.Hill	1990		Qld/NSW	Tree to 20m	White	Latin *inter-* = between, *stans* = standing; referring to its botanical position between *E. prava* and *E. seeana*
Eucalyptus intertexta R.T.Baker	1900	Inland Red Box	WA/NT/Qld/NSW/SA	Tree to 20m	White	Latin *inter-* = between, *textus* = tissue; referring to the inter-weaving fibrous bark
Eucalyptus intrasilvatica L.A.S.Johnson & K.D.Hill	1999		WA	Mallee to 6m	White	Latin *intra-* = within, *silvaticus* = pertaining to woods; referring to its occurrence within the Jarrah forest
Eucalyptus jacksonii Maiden	1914	Red Tingle	WA	Tree to 65m	White	Honours Sydney William Jackson (1873–1946), commercial traveller and plant collector
Eucalyptus jensenii Maiden	1922	Wandi Ironbark	WA	Tree to 10m	Creamy white	Honours Dr Harald Ingemann Jensen (1879–1966), Government Geologist with an interest in plants
Eucalyptus jimberlanica L.A.S.Johnson & K.D.Hill	1991		WA	Tree/mallee to 10m	White	After Jimberlana Hill near Norseman, where the species was found
Eucalyptus johnsoniana Brooker & Blaxell	1978	Johnson's Mallee	WA	Mallee to 3m	Creamy white	Honours Lawrence Alexandra Sidney Johnson (1925–97), Director Royal Botanic Gardens, Sydney
Eucalyptus johnstonii Maiden	1922	Tasmanian Yellow Gum	Tas	Tree to 50m	White	Honours Robert MacKenzie Johnston (1845–1918), botanist and geologist
Eucalyptus jucunda C.A.Gardner	1964	Yuna Mallee	WA	Tree/mallee to 7m	Creamy white	Latin *jucundus* = pleasant; presumably referring to its appearance
Eucalyptus jutsonii Maiden subsp. *jutsonii*	1919	Jutson's Mallee	WA	Mallee to 6m	Cream	Honours John Thomas Jutson (1874–1959), geologist
Eucalyptus jutsonii Maiden subsp. *kobela* D.Nicolle & M.E.French	2007		WA	Mallee to 6m	Cream	Greek *kobele* = needle; referring to the needle-like leaves of this subspecies
Eucalyptus kabiana L.A.S.Johnson & K.D.Hill	1991	Mt Beerwah Mallee	Qld	Mallee to 5m	White	After the Kabi Aborigines who originally inhabited the area
Eucalyptus kartzoffiana L.A.S.Johnson & Blaxell	1973	Araluen Gum	NSW	Tree to 30m	White	Honours Michael Eugene Kartzoff (1908–87), seed collector and local government politician
Eucalyptus kenneallyi K.D.Hill & L.A.S.Johnson	2000	Keneally's White Gum	WA	Tree to 8m	White	Honours Kevin Francis Keneally (b. 1945), botanist, WA Herbarium
Eucalyptus kessellii Maiden & Blakely subsp. *kessellii*	1925	Jerdacuttup Mallee	WA	Tree/mallee to 10m	Creamy white	Honours Stephen Lackey Kessell (1897–1979), Conservator of Forests, WA
Eucalyptus kessellii subsp. *eugnosta* K.D.Hill & L.A.S.Johnson	1992		WA	Tree/mallee to 10m	Creamy white	Greek *eugnostos* = well known, familiar; referring to fact that this subspecies is more common than type
Eucalyptus kingsmillii (Maiden) Maiden & Blakely subsp. *kingsmillii*	1929	Kingsmill's Mallee	WA	Mallee to 7m	Yellow/pink	Honours Sir Walter Kingsmill (1864–1935), state politician, WA

Name and Author	Date Desc.	Common Name	Where it Occurs	Tree Form and Size	Flower Colour	Name Meaning
Eucalyptus kingsmillii subsp. *alatissima* Brooker & Hopper	1993		WA/SA	Mallee to 7m	Pink/red	Latin *alatissimus* = markedly winged; referring to the gumnuts
Eucalyptus kitsoniana Maiden	1917	Gippsland Mallee	Vic	Tree/mallee to 10m	White	Honours Sir Albert Ernest Kitson (1868–1937), geologist
Eucalyptus kochii Maiden & Blakely subsp. *kochii*	1929	Oil Mallee	WA	Mallee to 8m	White	Honours Max Koch (1854–1925), farmer and plant collector
Eucalyptus kochii subsp. *borealis* (C.A.Gardner) D.Nicolle	2005		WA	Mallee to 12m	White	Latin *borealis* = northern; referring to the northern distribution of this subspecies
Eucalyptus kochii subsp. *plenissima* (C.A.Gardner) Brooker	1988		WA	Mallee to 8m	White	Latin *plenissimus* = very full; referring to its excessive oil content
Eucalyptus kochii subsp. *yellowdinensis* D.Nicolle	2005		WA	Mallee to 8m	White	After the small town of Yellowdine, where this species occurs
Eucalyptus kondininensis Maiden & Blakely	1925	Kondinin Blackbutt	WA	Tree to 10m	White	After the town of Kondinin, near where this species is found
Eucalyptus koolpinensis Brooker & Dunlop	1978		NT	Tree to 5m	Creamy white	After Koolpin Creek, where this species is found
Eucalyptus kruseana F.Muell.	1895	Book-leaf Mallee	WA	Mallee/shrub to 3m	Greenish yellow	Honours John Kruse (1822–95), pharmacist
Eucalyptus kumarlensis Brooker	1988		WA	Tree to 10m	Creamy white	After Kumarl, a railway siding south of Norseman, near where the species occurs
Eucalyptus kybeanensis Maiden & Cambage	1915	Kybean Mallee Ash	NSW/Vic	Tree/mallee to 4m	White	After the town of Kybean, Vic., near where this species occurs
Eucalyptus lacrimans L.A.S.Johnson & K.D.Hill	1991	Weeping Snow Gum	NSW	Tree to 12m	White	Latin *lacrimans* = weeping; referring to the pendulous habit
Eucalyptus laeliae Podger & Chippend.	1969	Darling Range Ghost Gum	WA	Tree to 15m	Creamy white	After *Laelia*, a vestal virgin from ancient Rome, alluding to the smooth columnar trunk
Eucalyptus laevis L.A.S.Johnson & K.D.Hill	2001		WA	Tree/mallee to 10m	White	Latin *laevis* = smooth; referring to the smooth buds
Eucalyptus laevopinea R.T.Baker	1898	Silvertop Stringybark	Qld/NSW	Tree to 40m	White	Latin *laevo-* = left, *pinene* = a chemical term referring to the essential oil, laevo-rotatory pinene
Eucalyptus lane-poolei Maiden	1919	Salmon White Gum	WA	Tree/mallee to 10m	White	Honours Charles Edward Lane-Poole (1885–1970), Conservator of Forests, WA
Eucalyptus langleyi L.A.S.Johnson & Blaxell	1991	Green Mallee Ash	NSW	Mallee to 5m	White	Honours Laurence Joseph Langley (b. 1917), forester and commercial seed supplier
Eucalyptus lansdowneana F.Muell. & J.E.Br.	1891	Red-flowered Mallee Box	SA	Mallee to 6m	Red	Honours Thomas Lansdowne Browne (1860–1931), pastoralist and collector of the type specimen
Eucalyptus largeana Blakely	1934	Craven Grey Box	NSW	Tree to 40m	White	Honours Richard Large (b. 1882), forester who co-collected the type specimen
Eucalyptus largiflorens F.Muell.	1855	Black Box	Qld/NSW/Vic/SA	Tree to 20m	White	Latin *largus* = large, *florens* = flowering; referring to the large clusters of flowers
Eucalyptus latens Brooker	1988	Narrow-leaved Red Mallee	WA	Mallee to 5m	Creamy white	Latin *latens* = hidden; referring to its occurrence in the understorey of Jarrah forests
Eucalyptus lateritica Brooker & Hopper	1986	Laterite Mallee	WA	Mallee to 4m	White	Latin *lateriticus* = of bricks; referring to the brick-coloured laterite where the species occurs
Eucalyptus latisinensis K.D.Hill	1999	White Mahogany	Qld	Tree to 18m	White	Latin *latus* = wide, *-ensis* = inhabitant of; referring to the Wide Bay area where this species occurs
Eucalyptus lehmannii (Schauer) Benth. subsp. *lehmannii*	1867	Bushy Yate	WA	Mallee to 4m	Greenish yellow	Honours Johan Christian Lehmann (1792–1860), Director of Hamburg Botanic Gardens
Eucalyptus lehmannii subsp. Northern (M.French 425) WA Herbarium						An undescribed subspecies
Eucalyptus lehmannii subsp. *parallela* D.Nicolle & M.E.French	2008		WA	Mallee to 4m	Greenish yellow	Latin *parallelus* = parallel; referring to the narrower, more parallel-sided leaves compared with the type
Eucalyptus leprophloia Brooker & Hopper	1993	Scaly-butt Mallee	WA	Mallee to 5m	White	Greek *lepros* = scaly, *phloios* = bark; referring to the fibrous bark compared with the related *E. zopherophloia*
Eucalyptus leptocalyx Blakely subsp. *leptocalyx*	1934	Hopetoun Mallee	WA	Mallee to 5m	Creamy white	Greek *lepto-* = narrow, *kalyx* = calyx; referring to the bud shape
Eucalyptus leptocalyx subsp. *petilipes* L.A.S.Johnson & K.D.Hill	2001		WA	Mallee to 6m	Creamy white	Latin *petilis* = slender, *pes* = foot; referring to the slender flower stalk
Eucalyptus leptophleba F.Muell.	1859	Molloy Box	Qld	Tree to 20m	White	Greek *leptos* = fine, thin, *phlebos* = vein; referring to the fine veins of the leaves
Eucalyptus leptophylla F.Muell. ex Miq.	1856	Narrow-leaved Red Mallee	WA/SA/NSW/Vic	Mallee to 5m	Creamy white	Greek *leptos* = fine, thin, *phyllon* = leaf; referring to the narrow leaves
Eucalyptus leptopoda Benth. subsp. *leptopoda*	1867	Tammin Mallee	WA	Mallee to 5m	Cream	Greek *leptos* = fine, thin, *podos* = a foot; referring to the thin bud stalk
Eucalyptus leptopoda subsp. *arctata* L.A.S.Johnson & K.D.Hill	1992		WA	Mallee to 5m	Cream	Latin *arctatus* = narrowed; referring to the leaves
Eucalyptus leptopoda subsp. *elevata* L.A.S.Johnson & K.D.Hill	1992		WA/SA	Mallee to 5m	Cream	Latin *elevatus* = elevated; referring to the raised disc at the top of the gumnut
Eucalyptus leptopoda subsp. *subluta* L.A.S.Johnson & K.D.Hill	1992		WA	Mallee to 5m	Cream	Latin *sublutus* = washed beneath; referring to the pale waxiness of the branchlets
Eucalyptus lesouefii Maiden	1912	Goldfields Blackbutt	WA	Mallet to 15m	White	Honours Albert Sherbourne Le Souef (1877–1951), first Director, Taronga Park Zoological Gardens, NSW
Eucalyptus leucophloia Brooker subsp. *leucophloia*	1976	Snappy Gum	WA	Tree to 10m	White	Greek *leuco-* = white, *phloios* = bark; referring to the white bark
Eucalyptus leucophloia subsp. *euroa* L.A.S.Johnson & K.D.Hill	2000	Snappy Gum	NT/Qld	Tree to 6m	White	Latin *eurous* = eastern; referring to the location of this subspecies
Eucalyptus leucophylla Domin	1928	Cloncurry Box	Qld	Tree/mallee to 6m	White	Greek *leuco-* = white, *phyllon* = a leaf; referring to the grey-green leaves
Eucalyptus leucoxylon F.Muell. subsp *leucoxylon*	1855	Yellow Gum	Vic/SA	Tree to 25m	White/red/pink	Greek *leuco-* = white, *xylon* = wood; referring to the pale brown timber
Eucalyptus leucoxylon subsp. *bellarinensis* Rule	1998		Vic	Tree to 12m	White	After the Bellarine Peninsula, near Geelong, where this subspecies occurs
Eucalyptus leucoxylon subsp. *connata* Rule	1991		Vic	Tree to 20m	White	Latin *connatus* = joined; referring to the juvenile leaves, which are joined at the base
Eucalyptus leucoxylon subsp. *megalocarpa* Boland	1979	Large-fruited Yellow Gum	Vic/SA	Tree/mallee to 10m	White/red/pink	Greek *megalo-* = large, *carpos* = fruit; referring to the large gumnuts of this subspecies

Name and Author	Date Desc.	Common Name	Where it Occurs	Tree Form and Size	Flower Colour	Name Meaning
Eucalyptus leucoxylon subsp. *pruinosa* (F.Muell. ex Miq.) Boland	1979	Inland Blue Gum	NSW/Vic/SA	Tree to 25m	White	Latin *pruinosus* = white, like hoar frost; referring to the white wax on the buds and gumnuts
Eucalyptus leucoxylon subsp. *stephaniae* Rule	1991	Desert Blue Gum	Vic/SA	Tree/mallee to 15m	White/pink	Honours the author's daughter, Stephanie Rule, who accompanied him on field work
Eucalyptus ligulata Brooker subsp. *ligulata*	1974	Lucky Bay Mallee	WA	Mallee to 5m	White	Latin *ligulatus* = strap-like; referring to the bud stalks
Eucalyptus ligulata subsp. *stirlingica* D.Nicolle	2002		WA	Mallee to 3m	White	After the Stirling Range, where this species occurs
Eucalyptus ligustrina DC.	1828	Privet-leaved Stringybark	NSW	Mallee/tree to 7m	White	After the genus *Ligustrum* (privet); referring to the similarity of the leaves to that genus
Eucalyptus limitaris L.A.S.Johnson & K.D.Hill	2000		WA/NT	Mallee/tree to 8m	?	Latin *limitis* = border or boundary; referring to its distribution across the WA/NT border
Eucalyptus lirata W.Fitzg. ex Maiden	1921	Kimberley Yellowjacket	WA	Tree to 12m	Creamy white	Latin *liratus* = ridges between furrows; referring to one of its habitats
Eucalyptus litoralis Rule	2004	Anglesea Box	Vic	Tree to 18m	White	Latin *litoralis* = occurring on the shore; referring to its coastal habitat
Eucalyptus litorea Brooker & Hopper	1989		WA	Mallee to 6m	White	Latin *litoreus* = coastal; referring to its strictly coastal occurrence compared with related species
Eucalyptus livida Brooker & Hopper	1991	Mallee Wandoo	WA	Mallee to 5m	Creamy white	Latin *lividus* = bluish; referring to the leaves
Eucalyptus lockyeri Blaxell & K.D.Hill subsp. *lockyeri*	1991		Qld	Tree to 9m	White	Honours Michael Lockyer of Ravenshoe, who first drew attention to this species
Eucalyptus lockyeri subsp. *exuta* Brooker & Kleinig	1994		Qld	Tree to 12m	White	Latin *exutus* = outside; referring to the lack of greyness, which covers the buds and fruits of the type species
Eucalyptus longicornis (F.Muell.) F.Muell. ex Maiden	1919	Red Morrell	WA	Tree to 25m	White	Latin *longi-* = long, *-cornis* = horned; referring to the long-horned bud cap
Eucalyptus longifolia Link	1822	Woollybutt	NSW	Tree to 35m	White	Latin *longi-* = long, *folium* = a leaf; referring to the leaves which are up to 25cm long
Eucalyptus longirostrata (Blakely) L.A.S.Johnson & K.D.Hill	1988	Grey Gum	Qld	Tree to 30m	White	Latin *longi-* = long, *rostratus* = beaked; referring to the beaked bud cap
Eucalyptus longissima D.Nicolle	2005		WA	Mallee to 8m	White	Latin *longissimus* = longest; referring to the long juvenile leaf stalks and bud stalks
Eucalyptus loxophleba Benth. subsp. *loxophleba*	1867	York Gum	WA	Tree/mallee to 15m	White	Greek *loxos* = slanting, *phleps* = vein; referring to the slanting leaf veins
Eucalyptus loxophleba subsp. *gratiae* Brooker	1972		WA	Tree/mallee to 7m	White	Latinised form of grace; referring to Lake Grace, where the subspecies occurs
Eucalyptus loxophleba subsp. *lissophloia* L.A.S.Johnson & K.D.Hill	1992		WA	Mallee to 8m	White	Greek *lisso-* = smooth, *phloios* = bark; referring to the bark appearance
Eucalyptus loxophleba subsp. *supralaevis* L.A.S.Johnson & K.D.Hill	1992		WA	Tree to 13m	White	Latin *supra* = above, *laevis* = smooth; referring to the bark, which is rough at the base and smooth above
Eucalyptus lucasii Blakely	1934	Barlee Box	WA	Mallee to 10m	Creamy white	Honours Arthur Henry Shakespeare Lucas (1853–1936), teacher with an interest in marine algae
Eucalyptus lucens Brooker & Dunlop	1978		NT	Mallee to 5m	White	Latin *lucens* = shining; referring to the adult leaves
Eucalyptus luculenta L.A.S.Johnson & K.D.Hill	1999		WA	Mallee to 5m	Yellow/white	Latin *luculentus* = full of light; referring to the pronounced glossiness of the young gumnuts
Eucalyptus luehmanniana F.Muell.	1878	Yellow-top Mallee Ash	NSW	Mallee to 7m	White	Honours Johann Georg Luehmann (1843–1904), botanical assistant to Ferdinand von Mueller
Eucalyptus luteola Brooker & Hopper	1991		WA	Mallee to 3m	Lemon	Latin *luteolus* = pale yellow; referring to the flowers
Eucalyptus macarthurii H.Deane & Maiden	1899	Camden Woollybutt	NSW	Tree to 40m	White	Honours Sir William Macarthur (1800–82); horticulturist from the Camden area
Eucalyptus mackintii Kottek	1990	Orbost Stringybark	Vic	Tree to 30m	White	Honours James Andrew McKinty (1916–99), forester and first collector of this species
Eucalyptus macrandra F.Muell. ex Benth.	1867	River Yate	WA	Mallee to 4m	Yellow	Greek *macro-* = large, *andros* = male flower; referring to the long stamens
Eucalyptus macrocarpa Hook. subsp. *macrocarpa*	1842	Mottlecah	WA	Mallee to 3m	Red	Greek *macro-* = large, *carpos* = fruit; referring to the huge gumnuts
Eucalyptus macrocarpa subsp. *elachantha* Brooker & Hopper	1993	Mottlecah	WA	Mallee to 3m	Red	Greek *elach-* = small, *anthos* = flower; referring to the flowers that are smaller than the type subspecies
Eucalyptus macrorhyncha F.Muell. ex Benth. subsp. *macrorhyncha*	1867	Red Stringybark	NSW/Vic	Tree to 35m	White	Greek *macro-* = large, *rhynchos* = nose; referring to the long bud cap
Eucalyptus macrorhyncha subsp. *cannonii* (R.T.Baker) L.A.S.Johnson & Blaxell	1973	Capertee Stringybark	NSW	Tree to 13m	White	Honours David Cannon (c. 1868–1940), botanist and herbarium assistant, Museum of Applied Arts and Science
Eucalyptus magnificata L.A.S.Johnson & K.D.Hill	1990	Blue Box	Qld/NSW	Tree to 8m	White/lemon	Latin *magnificatus* = magnified; referring to the larger leaves than related species
Eucalyptus major (Maiden) Blakely	1934	Grey Gum	Qld	Tree to 20m	White	Latin *majus* = greater; referring to the coarser leaves, buds and gumnuts than the related *E. propinqua*
Eucalyptus malacoxylon Blakely	1934	Moonbi Apple Box	NSW	Tree to 20m	White	Greek *malacos* = soft, *xylon* = wood; referring to the soft timber
Eucalyptus mannensis Boomsma subsp. *mannensis*	1964	Mann Range Mallee	WA/NT/SA	Mallee to 10m	Creamy white	After the Mann Range in northern SA, where the species is found
Eucalyptus mannensis subsp. *vespertina* L.A.S.Johnson & K.D.Hill	1992		WA	Mallee to 10m	Creamy white	Latin *vesper* = western; referring to the far western distribution of this species
Eucalyptus mannifera Mudie subsp. *mannifera*	1834	Brittle Gum	NSW/Vic	Tree to 20m	White	Greek *manna* = manna, *-fera* = bearing; referring to the powdery white bark
Eucalyptus mannifera subsp. *gullickii* (R.T.Baker & H.G.Sm.) L.A.S.Johnson	1962	Mountain Spotted Gum	NSW	Tree to 20m	White	Honours William Applegate Gullick (1859–1922), government printer responsible for printing several botanical works
Eucalyptus mannifera subsp. *praecox* (Maiden) L.A.S.Johnson	1962	Brittle Gum	NSW	Tree to 10m	White	Latin *praecox* = precocious; referring to the production of flowers while juvenile leaves are present
Eucalyptus marginata D.Don ex Sm. subsp. *marginata*	1802	Jarrah	WA	Tree to 35m	Creamy white	Latin *marginatus* = with a margin; referring to the leaf edge—an obscure allusion
Eucalyptus marginata subsp. *thalassica* Brooker & Hopper	1993	Blue-leaved Jarrah	WA	Tree to 25m	Creamy white	Latin *thalassicus* = sea-water colour; referring to the leaves of the crown

Name and Author	Date Desc.	Common Name	Where it Occurs	Tree Form and Size	Flower Colour	Name Meaning
Eucalyptus mckieana Blakely	1930	McKie's Stringybark	NSW	Tree to 30m	White	Honours Rev. Ernest Norman McKie (1882–1948), amateur botanist with interest in eucalypts and grasses
Eucalyptus mcquoidii Brooker & Hopper	2002	Quoin Head Marlock	WA	Marlock/mallet to 3m	Greenish	Honours Nathan McQuoid (c. 1960), ecologist with an interest in eucalypts
Eucalyptus medialis Brooker & Hopper	1991		WA	Mallee to 5m	Creamy white	Latin *medialis* = median; referring to its taxonomic position between *E. xanthonema* and *E. melanophitra*
Eucalyptus mediocris L.A.S.Johnson & K.D.Hill	1999	Inland White Mahogany	Qld	Tree to 20m	Creamy white	Latin *mediocris* = middling; referring to the medium-sized tree habit of this species
Eucalyptus megacarpa F.Muell.	1860	Bullich	WA	Tree/mallee to 20m	White	Greek *mega-* = large, *carpos* = fruit; referring to the relatively large gumnuts
Eucalyptus megacornuta C.A.Gardner	1942	Warted Yate	WA	Mallet to 15m	Greenish yellow	Greek *mega-* = large, *cornutus* = horned; referring to the buds
Eucalyptus megasepala A.R.Bean	2006		Qld	Tree to 20m	White	Greek *mega-* = large, *sepalum* = sepal; referring to the sepals, which are larger than related *E. tetrodonta*
Eucalyptus melanoleuca S.T.Blake	1977		Qld	Tree to 30m	White	Greek *melanos* = black, *leukos* = white; referring to contrasting dark bark of trunk and white bark of branches
Eucalyptus melanophitra Brooker & Hopper	1991		WA	Mallet to 7m	Pale yellow	Greek *melanos* = black, *phitra* = trunk; referring to the dark, rough bark of the trunk
Eucalyptus melanophloia F.Muell. subsp. *melanophloia*	1859	Silver-leaved Ironbark	NT/Qld/NSW	Tree to 20m	White	Greek *melanos* = black, *phloios* = bark; referring to the dark bark
Eucalyptus melanophloia subsp. Dajarra (V.J.Neldner 1523) Qld Herbarium						An undescribed subspecies
Eucalyptus melanoxylon Maiden	1922	Black Morrell	WA	Tree to 15m	White	Greek *melanos* = black, *xylon* = wood; referring to the dark timber
Eucalyptus melliodora A.Cunn. ex Schauer	1843	Yellow Box	Qld/NSW/Vic/SA	Tree to 30m	White	Latin *melleus* = honey, *odora* = sweet smell; referring to the flowers
Eucalyptus merrickiae Maiden & Blakely	1925	Goblet Mallee	WA	Mallee to 4m	Creamy white	Honours Mary Merrick (b. 1897), librarian and stenographer, Botanic Gardens, Sydney (1921–c. 1927)
Eucalyptus michaeliana Blakely	1938	Hillgrove Gum	Qld/NSW	Tree to 30m	White	Honours Rev. Norman Michael (1884–1951), who first collected this species
Eucalyptus micranthera F.Muell. ex Benth.	1867	Milkshake Mallee	WA	Mallee to 4m	Creamy white	Greek *micro-* = small, *anthera* = anther; not an especially descriptive name for this species
Eucalyptus microcarpa (Maiden) Maiden	1923	Grey Box	Qld/NSW/Vic/SA	Tree to 25m	White	Greek *micro-* = small, *carpos* = fruit; referring to the tiny gumnuts
Eucalyptus microcorys F.Muell.	1860	Tallowwood	Qld/NSW	Tree to 60m	White to lemon	Greek *micro-* = small, *korys* = helmet; referring to the small bud caps
Eucalyptus microneura Maiden & Blakely	1925	Gilbert River Box	Qld	Tree to 10m	White	Greek *micro-* = small, *neuron* = nerve; referring to the inconspicuous veining of the leaf
Eucalyptus microschema Brooker & Hopper	1991		WA	Mallee to 3m	White	Greek *micro-* = small, *schema* = form; referring to its small stature
Eucalyptus microtheca F.Muell.	1859	Coolabah	WA/NT/Qld	Tree to 10m	White	Greek *micro-* = small, *thece* = a box; referring to the small gumnuts
Eucalyptus mimica Brooker & Hopper subsp. *mimica*	2002		WA	Mallet to 5m	?	Latin *mimicus* = mimicking; referring to its similarity to *E. steedmanii*
Eucalyptus mimica subsp. *continens* Brooker & Hopper	2002		WA	Mallet to 5m	?	Latin *continens* = remaining; referring to its persistent outer bud cap
Eucalyptus miniata A.Cunn. ex Schauer	1843	Darwin Woollybutt	WA/NT/Qld	Tree to 30m	Orange	Latin *miniatus* = flame-scarlet; referring to the colour of the flowers
Eucalyptus minniritchi D.Nicolle	2001		WA/NT/SA	Mallee to 3m	Creamy-yellow	After the bark type; minniritchi bark curls and peels and remains partially attached to the trunk
Eucalyptus misella L.A.S.Johnson & K.D.Hill	1992		WA	Mallee to 4m	White	Latin *misellus* = wretched; possibly an unwarranted reference to its low growth
Eucalyptus mitchelliana Cambage	?1919	Mt Buffalo Gum	Vic	Tree/mallee to 15m	White	Honours Major Sir Thomas Livingstone Mitchell (1792–1855), Surveyor-General NSW and plant collector
Eucalyptus moderata L.A.S.Johnson & K.D.Hill	1999		WA	Tree to 10m	Pale yellow	Latin *moderatus* = moderate; referring to the medium stature and parts compared with its closest relatives
Eucalyptus moluccana Roxb.	1832	Grey Box	Qld/NSW	Tree to 30m	White	After the Molucca islands of SE Asia; a misnomer as it does not occur outside Australia
Eucalyptus molyneuxii K.Rule	1999		Vic	Tree/Mallee to 5m	White	Honours W.M. Molyneux, nurseryman and plant collector
Eucalyptus mooreana W.Fitzg. ex Maiden	1914	King Leopold Range Mallee	WA	Tree/mallee to 6m	White	Honours Sir Newton James Moore (1870–1936), surveyor and politician, Premier of WA (1906)
Eucalyptus moorei Maiden & Cambage subsp. *moorei*	1905	Narrow-leaved Sally	NSW	Mallee to 7m	White	Honours Charles Moore (1820–1905), Director Royal Botanic Gardens, Sydney (1848–96)
Eucalyptus moorei subsp. *serpentinicola* (L.A.S.Johnson & Blaxell) Brooker & Kleinig	1999		NSW	Mallee to 3m	White	Latin *serpenticola* = occurring on serpentine rock
Eucalyptus morrisbyi Brett	1939	Morrisby's Gum	Tas	Tree to 16m	White	Honours John Robert Morrisby (1832–1923), farmer who collected seed of this species for cultivation
Eucalyptus morrisii R.T.Baker	1900	Grey Mallee	NSW	Tree/mallee to 4m	White	Honours Robert Newton Morris (1844–1921), clergyman and educationalist with interest in eucalypts
Eucalyptus muelleriana A.W.Howitt	1890	Yellow Stringybark	NSW/Vic	Tree to 40m	White	Honours Ferdinand von Mueller (1825–96), botanist and Director of Melbourne Botanic Gardens
Eucalyptus multicaulis Blakely	1927	Whipstick Mallee Ash	NSW	Mallee to 8m	White	Latin *multi-* = many, *caulis* = a stem; referring to the mallee habit
Eucalyptus myriadena Brooker	1981		WA	Tree/mallee to 10m	White	Greek *myri-* = many, *adena* = glands; referring to the high density of oil glands in the leaf
Eucalyptus nandewarica L.A.S.Johnson & K.D.Hill	1990	Mallee Red Gum	NSW	Tree/mallee to 10m	White	After the Nandewar Range, where this species occurs
Eucalyptus neglecta Maiden	1904	Omeo Gum	Vic	Tree/mallee to 7m	White	Latin *neglectus* = neglected; referring to the fact that this species was not recognised as distinct
Eucalyptus neutra D.Nicolle	1999		WA	Mallee to 6m	Yellow/white	Latin *neutra* = middle; referring to its similarity between *E. flocktoniae* and *E. transcontinentalis*

TABLE 3: EUCALYPTUS

Name and Author	Date Desc.	Common Name	Where it Occurs	Tree Form and Size	Flower Colour	Name Meaning
Eucalyptus newbeyi D.J.Carr & S.G.M.Carr	1980	Beaufort Inlet Mallet	WA	Mallet to 8m	Yellow-green	Honours Ken Newbey (1936–88), farmer and plant collector who first found this species
Eucalyptus nicholii Maiden & Blakely	1929	Narrow-leaved Black Peppermint	NSW	Tree to 15m	White	Honours Richard Nichol (1866–1947), herbarium assistant Royal Botanic Gardens, Sydney
Eucalyptus nigrifunda Brooker & Hopper	1991	Desert Wandoo	WA	Tree to 10m	White	Latin *nigri-* = black, *fundus* = base; referring to the dark basal bark
Eucalyptus nitens (H.Deane & Maiden) Maiden	1913	Shining Gum	NSW/Vic	Tree to 70m	White	Latin *nitens* = shining; referring to the shiny leaves, buds, gumnuts and bark
Eucalyptus nobilis L.A.S.Johnson & K.D.Hill	1990	Giant White Gum	Qld/NSW	Tree to 70m	White	Latin *nobilis* = noble; referring to the tall, straight habit
Eucalyptus normantonensis Maiden & Cambage	1919		WA/NT/Qld	Mallee to 5m	White	After Normanton, Qld, where the type specimen was collected
Eucalyptus nortonii (Blakely) L.A.S.Johnson	1962	Long-leaved Box	NSW/Vic	Tree to 15m	White	Honours Alfred Ernest Norton (c. 1881–1962), beekeeper with an interest in eucalypts
Eucalyptus notabilis Maiden	1920	Blue Mountains Mahogany	Qld/NSW	Tree to 30m	White	Latin *notabilis* = noteworthy; allusion obscure
Eucalyptus nova-anglica H.Deane & Maiden	1900	New England Peppermint	Qld/NSW	Tree to 15m	White	Latin *nova* = new, *anglica* = England; referring to New England district in northern NSW
Eucalyptus nudicaulis A.R.Bean	1991		Qld	Mallee to 6m	White	Latin *nudus* = bare, *caulis* = stem; referring to the smooth bark on the stems
Eucalyptus nutans F.Muell.	1863	Red-flowered Moort	WA	Marlock to 3m	Red	Latin *nutans* = nodding; referring to the down-turned flowers
Eucalyptus obconica Brooker & Kleinig	1994		WA	Tree/mallee to 8m	White	Latin *obconicus* = obconical; referring to the shape of the gumnuts
Eucalyptus obesa Brooker & Hopper	1993		WA	Mallee to 4m	Creamy white	Latin *obesus* = fat; referring to the plump gumnuts
Eucalyptus obliqua L'Her.	1792	Messmate Stringybark	Qld/NSW/Vic/SA/Tas	Tree to 90m	White	Latin *obliquus* = oblique; referring to the asymmetrical shape of the leaves
Eucalyptus obtusiflora DC. subsp. *obtusiflora*	1828	Dongarra Mallee	WA	Mallee to 4m	Creamy white	Latin *obtusus* = obtuse, *florum* = flower; referring to the bluntness of the bud cap
Eucalyptus obtusiflora subsp. *cowcowensis* L.A.S.Johnson & K.D.Hill	2001		WA	Tree/mallee to 4m	Creamy white	After the district Cowcowing, where this subspecies occurs
Eucalyptus obtusiflora subsp. *dongarraensis* (Maiden & Blakely) L.A.S.Johnson & K.D.Hill	2001	Dongarra Mallee	WA	Mallee to 4m	Creamy white	After Dongarra, where this subspecies occurs
Eucalyptus occidentalis Endl.	1837	Swamp Yate	WA	Tree to 20m	Lemon to cream	Latin *occidentalis* = western; referring to its distribution
Eucalyptus ochrophloia F.Muell.	1878	Yapunyah	Qld/NSW	Tree to 15m	White	Greek *ochro-* = yellow, *phloios* = bark; referring to the upper smooth bark
Eucalyptus odontocarpa F.Muell.	1859	Sturt Creek Mallee	WA/NT/Qld	Mallee to 4m	Whitish	Greek *odontos* = tooth, *carpos* = fruit; referring to the four teeth on the rim of the gumnut
Eucalyptus odorata Behr	1847	Peppermint Box	SA	Tree/mallee to 7m	White	Latin *odoratus* = having a smell; referring to the crushed leaves
Eucalyptus oldfieldii F.Muell. subsp. *oldfieldii*	1860	Oldfield's Mallee	WA	Tree/mallee to 5m	White	Honours Augustus Frederick Oldfield (1820–87), botanist and plant collector with an interest in eucalypts
Eucalyptus oldfieldii subsp. Millar Range (M.French 303) WA Herbarium			WA	Mallee to 3m	White	An undescribed subspecies from Millar Range
Eucalyptus oleosa F.Muell. ex Miq. subsp. *oleosa*	1856	Red Morrell	WA/SA/NSW/Vic	Mallee to 8m	White	Latin *oleosus* = bearing oil; referring to the conspicuous oil glands in the leaves
Eucalyptus oleosa subsp. *ampliata* L.A.S.Johnson & K.D.Hill	1999		SA	Mallee to 8m		Latin *ampliatus* = increased; referring to the larger leaves, buds and gumnuts compared with the type
Eucalyptus oleosa subsp. *corvina* L.A.S.Johnson & K.D.Hill	1999		WA	Mallee to 8m	White	Latin *corvinus* = of ravens; referring to the occurrence near Ravensthorpe
Eucalyptus oleosa subsp. *cylindroidea* L.A.S.Johnson & K.D.Hill	1999		WA	Tree/mallee to 8m	White	Latin *cylindroideus* = cylinder; referring to the more or less cylindrical shape of the gumnut
Eucalyptus olida L.A.S.Johnson & K.D.Hill	1990	Strawberry Gum	NSW	Tree to 30m	White	Latin *olidus* = smelling; referring to the unusual smell of the crushed leaves
Eucalyptus oligantha Schauer subsp. *oligantha*	1843	Broadleaf Box	WA/NT	Tree to 12m	Creamy yellow	Greek *oligis* = few, *anthos* = flower; referring to the small number of flowers in the clusters
Eucalyptus oligantha subsp. *modica* L.A.S.Johnson & K.D.Hill	2000		WA	Tree to 12m	Creamy yellow	Latin *modicus* = moderate-sized; referring to smaller size of leaves, buds and gumnuts compared with type
Eucalyptus olivina Brooker & Hopper	1993		WA	Tree/mallee to 5m	Creamy white	Latin *olivinus* = olive green; referring to the leaves
Eucalyptus olsenii L.A.S.Johnson & Blaxell	1980	Woila Gum	NSW	Tree to 12m	White	Honours Ian Sinclair Olsen (b. 1943), landscape designer, Royal Botanic Gardens, Sydney
Eucalyptus ophitica L.A.S.Johnson & K.D.Hill	1990	Serpentine Ironbark	NSW	Tree to 10m	White	Greek *opites* = serpentine rock; referring to the substrate where the species is found
Eucalyptus optima L.A.S.Johnson & K.D.Hill	1999		WA	Tree/mallet to 20m	Pale yellow	Latin *optimus* = best; referring to the fact that this species is the largest of its related species
Eucalyptus oraria L.A.S.Johnson	1962	Ooragmandee	WA	Mallee to 7m	White	Latin *orarius* = coastal; referring to its main occurrence
Eucalyptus orbifolia F.Muell.	1865	Round-leaved Mallee	WA/NT/SA	Mallee to 5m	Yellow	Latin *orbi-* = round, *folium* = leaf; referring to the shape of the adult leaves
Eucalyptus ordiana Dunlop & Done	1992		WA	Tree/mallee to 6m	White	After the Ord River locality, where the species is found
Eucalyptus oreades R.T.Baker	1900	Blue Mountains Ash	Qld/NSW	Tree to 40m	White	Greek *Oreades* = mountain nymphs; referring to its mountain habitat
Eucalyptus orgadophila Maiden & Blakely	1928	Mountain Coolabah	Qld	Tree to 20m	White	Greek *orgados* = meadow or well-watered spot, *philos* = loving; referring to its habitat
Eucalyptus ornata Crisp	1985	Silver Mallet	WA	Mallet to 10m	Creamy white	Latin *ornatus* = ornate; referring to the sculptured buds
Eucalyptus orophila L.D.Pryor	1995		Timor	Tree to 14m	White	Latin *orophila* = mountain-loving; referring to its habitat

TABLE 3: EUCALYPTUS

Name and Author	Date Desc.	Common Name	Where it Occurs	Tree Form and Size	Flower Colour	Name Meaning
Eucalyptus orthostemon D.Nicolle & Brooker	2005		WA	Mallee to 7m	Creamy white	Greek *ortho-* = straight, *stemon* = thread; referring to its straight stamens compared with related *E. vegrandis*
Eucalyptus ovata Labill. var. *ovata*	1806	Swamp Gum	NSW/Vic/SA	Tree to 20m	White	Latin *ovatus* = ovate; referring to the shape of the gumnuts
Eucalyptus ovata var. *grandiflora* Maiden	1916	Large-flowered Swamp Gum	SA	Tree to 15m	White	Latin *grandi-* = big, *florum* = flower; referring to the flowers, which are larger than the type species
Eucalyptus ovularis Maiden & Blakely	1925	Small-fruited Mallee	WA	Tree/mallee to 12m	White	Latin *ovularis* = egg-shaped; referring to the shape of the buds
Eucalyptus oxymitra Blakely	1936	Sharp-capped Mallee	WA/NT/SA	Mallee to 4m	Pale yellow	Greek *oxy-* = sharp, *mitra* = headdress; referring to the pointed bud cap
Eucalyptus pachycalyx Maiden & Blakely subsp. *pachycalyx*	1929	Shiny-barked Gum	Qld	Tree to 14m	White	Greek *pachy-* = thick, *kalyx* = calyx; referring to the thick-walled gumnuts
Eucalyptus pachycalyx subsp. *waajensis* L.A.S.Johnson & K.D.Hill	1991	Pumpkin Gum	Qld/NSW	Tree to 15m	White	After Waaje in the Barakula State Forest, Qld, where this species was first found
Eucalyptus pachyloma Benth.	1867	Kalgan Plains Mallee	WA	Mallee to 4m	White	Greek *pachy-* = thick, *loma* = border, referring to the thick rim of the gumnut
Eucalyptus pachyphylla F.Muell.	1859	Red Bull Mallee	WA/NT/Qld	Mallee to 5m	Cream	Greek *pachy-* = thick, *phyllon* = a leaf; referring to the thickly textured leaves
Eucalyptus paedoglauca L.A.S.Johnson & Blaxell	1991	Mt Stuart Ironbark	Qld	Tree to 10m	White	Greek *paidos* = a child, *glaukos* = grey; referring to the grey juvenile leaves
Eucalyptus paliformis L.A.S.Johnson & Blaxell	1973	Wadbilliga Ash	NSW	Tree to 12m	White	Latin *paliformis* = stake-like; referring to the slim, erect trunks
Eucalyptus paludicola D.Nicolle	1995	Fleurieu Swamp Gum	SA	Tree/mallee to 12m	White	Latin *paludicola* = swamp-dwelling; referring to its habitat
Eucalyptus panda S.T.Blake	1958	Yetman Ironbark	Qld/NSW	Tree to 20m	White	Latin *panda* = crooked; referring to its habit
Eucalyptus paniculata Sm.	1797	Grey Ironbark	NSW	Tree to 30m	White	Latin *paniculatus* = paniculate; referring to the form of the flower clusters
Eucalyptus pantoleuca L.A.S.Johnson & K.D.Hill	2000	Round-leaved Gum	WA	Tree to 6m	White	Greek *panto-* = entirely, *leukos* = white; referring to the generally white appearance of the tree
Eucalyptus paralimnetica L.A.S.Johnson & K.D.Hill	2001		WA	Tree to 10m	White	Greek *para-* = beside, *limneticos* = relating to lakes; referring to its occurrence near salt lakes
Eucalyptus parramattensis E.C.Hall subsp. *parramattensis*	1913		NSW	Tree to 15m	White	After Parramatta, the general region of the type collection locality
Eucalyptus parramattensis subsp. *decadens* L.A.S.Johnson & Blaxell	1991		NSW	Tree to 10m	White	Latin *decadens* = falling down; referring to the tumble-down habit of the tree
Eucalyptus parramattensis var. *sphaerocalyx* Blakely	1934	Parramatta Red Gum	NSW	Tree to 10m	White	Greek *sphaera* = a ball, *kalyx* = calyx; referring to the shape of the bud cap
Eucalyptus parvula L.A.S.Johnson & K.D.Hill	1991	Small-leaved Gum	NSW	Tree to 10m	White	Latin *parvulus* = little; referring to the tree size and the leaves
Eucalyptus patellaris F.Muell.	1859	Weeping Box	NT	Tree to 15m	White	Latin *patella* = knee cap; referring erroneously to the shape of the bud cap (it is conical or beaked)
Eucalyptus patens Benth.	1867	Blackbutt	WA	Tree to 40m	White	Latin *patens* = spreading; referring to the habit, but not particularly relevant
Eucalyptus pauciflora Sieber ex Spreng. subsp. *pauciflora*	1827	Snow Gum	Qld/NSW/Vic/Tas/SA	Tree/mallee to 30m	White	Latin *pauci-* = few, *florum* = flower; a misnomer as the tree is usually floriferous
Eucalyptus pauciflora subsp. *acerina* Rule	1994	Snow Gum	Vic	Tree/mallee to 12m	White	Latin *acerinus* = lacking wax; referring to the green branchlets, buds and gumnuts
Eucalyptus pauciflora subsp. *debeuzevillei* (Maiden) L.A.S.Johnson & Blaxell	1973	Jounama Snow Gum	NSW	Tree/mallee to 10m	White	Honours Wilfred Alexander Watt de Beuzeville (1884–1954), forester with an interest in eucalypts
Eucalyptus pauciflora subsp. *hedraia* Rule	1994	Snow Gum	Vic	Tree/mallee to 10m	White	Greek *hedraios* = sessile; referring to the stalkless buds and gumnuts
Eucalyptus pauciflora subsp. *niphophila* (Maiden & Blakely) L.A.S.Johnson & Blaxell	1973	Snow Gum	NSW/Vic	Tree/mallee to 7m	White	Greek *niphophilos* = snow-loving; referring to its alpine habitat
Eucalyptus pauciflora subsp. *parvifructa* Rule	1994	Snow Gum	Vic	Tree/mallee to 5m	White	Latin *parvi-* = small, *fructus* = fruit; referring to the gumnuts, which are smaller than the other subspecies
Eucalyptus pellita F.Muell.	1864	Large-fruited Red Mahogany	Qld/PNG	Tree to 40m	White	Latin *pellitus* = covered with skin; probably referring to leaves which Mueller described as thick and leathery
Eucalyptus pendens Brooker	1972	Badgingarra Weeping Mallee	WA	Mallee to 4m	White	Latin *pendens* = pendulous; referring to the habit of the species
Eucalyptus peninsularis D.Nicolle	1999	Cummins Mallee	SA	Mallee to 6m	Pale yellow	Latin *peninsularis* = of a peninsula; referring to its occurrence on Eyre Peninsula
Eucalyptus perangusta Brooker	1988	Fine-leaved Mallee	WA	Mallee to 4m	Creamy white	Latin *per-* = very, *angustus* = narrow; referring to the leaves
Eucalyptus percostata Brooker & P.J.Lang	1990	Devil's Peak Mallee	SA	Mallee to 10m	White	Latin *per-* = very, *costatus* = ribbed; referring to the bud cap
Eucalyptus perriniana F.Muell. ex Rodway	1893	Spinning Gum	NSW/Vic	Tree/mallee to 7m	White	Honours George Samuel Perrin (1849–1900), forester
Eucalyptus persistens L.A.S.Johnson & K.D.Hill	1991		Qld	Tree to 12m	White	Latin *persistens* = persisting; referring to the bud cap, which remains until flowering, and persistent bark
Eucalyptus petiolaris (Boland) Rule	1992	Water Gum	SA	Tree to 15m	White to red	Latin *petiolaris* = having a leaf stalk; referring to the seedlings and juvenile leaves
Eucalyptus petraea D.J.Carr & S.G.M.Carr	1983	Granite Rock Box	WA	Tree/mallee to 5m	Creamy white	Latin *petraeus* = rocks; referring to its habitat
Eucalyptus petrensis Brooker & Hopper	1993		WA	Mallee to 3m	Creamy white	Latin *petrensis* = of rocks; referring to its habitat
Eucalyptus phaenophylla Brooker & Hopper subsp. *phaenophylla*	1991		WA	Mallee to 5m	Pale lemon	Greek *phaeno-* = shiny, *phyllon* = a leaf; referring to its shiny leaves
Eucalyptus phaenophylla subsp. *interjacens* Brooker & Hopper	1991		WA	Mallee to 5m	Pale lemon	Latin *interjacens* = coming between; referring to its geographical position between the type and *E. tumida*

Name and Author	Date Desc.	Common Name	Where it Occurs	Tree Form and Size	Flower Colour	Name Meaning
Eucalyptus phenax Brooker & Slee subsp. *phenax*	1996	Green Dumosa Mallee	WA/SA/Vic	Mallee to 7m	White	Greek *phenax* = impostor; referring to the fact that it was identified wrongly as *E. anceps* for many years
Eucalyptus phenax subsp. *compressa* D.Nicolle	2000	Kangaroo Island Mallee	SA	Mallee/shrub to 8m	Creamy white	Latin *compressus* = compressed; referring to the clusters of gumnuts
Eucalyptus phoenicea F.Muell.	1859	Scarlet Gum	WA/NT/Qld	Tree to 12m	Orange	After the phoenix, mythical Arabian bird with brilliant scarlet feathers
Eucalyptus phylacis L.A.S.Johnson & K.D.Hill	1992	Meelup Mallee	WA	Tree/mallee to 5m	Creamy white	Greek *phylax* = guard; referring to its location overlooking a nearby bay
Eucalyptus pilbarensis Brooker & Edgecombe	1986		WA	Mallee to 3m	White	After the Pilbara district where the species occurs
Eucalyptus pileata Blakely	1934	Capped Mallee	WA	Tree/mallee to 6m	White	Latin *pileatus* = cap-shaped; referring to the bud cap
Eucalyptus pilularis Sm.	1797	Blackbutt	Qld/NSW	Tree to 70m	White	Latin *pilularis* = a small pill; referring to the gumnuts
Eucalyptus pimpiniana Maiden	1912	Pimpin Mallee	WA/SA	Mallee to 2m	Yellow	After *pimpin*, the Aboriginal name for the plant
Eucalyptus piperita Sm. subsp. *piperita*	1790	Sydney Peppermint	NSW	Tree to 20m	White	Latin *piperitus* = pepper-like; probably referring to the peppermint aroma from the leaves
Eucalyptus piperita subsp. *urceolaris* (Maiden & Blakely) L.A.S.Johnson & Blaxell	1973	Sydney Peppermint	NSW	Tree to 20m	White	Latin *urceolaris* = urn-shaped; referring to the shape of the gumnut
Eucalyptus placita L.A.S.Johnson & K.D.Hill	1990	Ironbark	NSW	Tree to 30m	White	Latin *placitus* = pleasing; referring to its bright green foliage
Eucalyptus planchoniana F.Muell.	1878	Needlebark Stringybark	Qld/NSW	Tree to 20m	White	Honours Jules Emile Planchon (1823–88), Assistant Herbarium Curator, Kew, UK
Eucalyptus planipes L.A.S.Johnson & K.D.Hill	2001		WA	Mallee to 8m	White	Latin *planus* = flat, *pes* = foot; referring to the flattened flower stalk
Eucalyptus platycorys Maiden & Blakely	1929	Boorabin Mallee	WA	Mallee to 8m	Creamy white	Greek *platy-* = flat, *korys* = helmet; referring to the bud cap
Eucalyptus platydisca L.A.S.Johnson & K.D.Hill ex D.Nicolle & Brooker	2006	Jimberlana Mallee Ash	WA	Mallee to 5m	White	Greek *platy-* = broad, *discus* = a circular plate; referring to the broad rim on the gumnut
Eucalyptus platyphylla F.Muell.	1859	White Gum	Qld	Tree to 20m	White	Greek *platy-* = broad, *phyllon* = a leaf; referring to the broad leaves
Eucalyptus platypus Hook. subsp. *platypus*	1851	Moort	WA	Mallet/marlock to 8m	Creamy green	Greek *platy-* = broad, *-pus* = footed; referring to the broad flower stalk
Eucalyptus platypus subsp. *congregata* Brooker & Hopper	2002	Moort	WA	Mallet/marlock to 8m	Pale yellow	Latin *congregatus* = to flock together; referring to the pure stands of this subspecies
Eucalyptus pleurocarpa Schauer	1844	Tallerack	WA	Mallee to 5m	Whitish	Greek *pleura* = rib, *carpos* = fruit; referring to the angular gumnut
Eucalyptus pleurocorys L.A.S.Johnson & K.D.Hill	2001		WA	Mallee to 5m	White	Greek *pleura* = rib, *korys* = helmet; referring to the bud cap
Eucalyptus pluricaulis Brooker & Hopper subsp. *pluricaulis*	1991		WA	Mallee to 5m	Lemon	Latin *pluri-* = many, *caulis* = stem; referring to its difference from the related mallet *E. gardneri*
Eucalyptus pluricaulis subsp. *porphyrea* Brooker & Hopper	1991	Purple-leaved Mallee	WA	Mallee to 3m	Lemon	Latin *porphyreus* = purple; referring to the leaves
Eucalyptus polita Brooker & Hopper	1993		WA	Mallet to 15m	White	Latin *politus* = smooth; referring to the bark
Eucalyptus polyanthemos Schauer subsp. *polyanthemos*	1843	Red Box	NSW	Tree to 20m	White	Greek *poly-* = many, *anthemos* = flower; referring to each flower cluster
Eucalyptus polyanthemos subsp. *longior* Brooker, Connors & Slee	1996	Red Box	Vic	Tree to 25m	White	Latin *longior* = longer; referring to the leaves, which are longer than other subspecies
Eucalyptus polyanthemos subsp. *marginalis* Rule	2004	Red Box	Vic	Tree to 12m	White	Latin *marginalis* = edge; referring to the distribution, which is at the edge of the red box complex
Eucalyptus polyanthemos subsp. *vestita* L.A.S.Johnson & K.D.Hill	1990	Red Box	NSW/Vic	Tree to 20m	White	Latin *vestitus* = clothed; referring to the rough bark
Eucalyptus polybractea R.T.Baker	1901	Blue-leaved Mallee, Blue Mallee	NSW/Vic/SA	Mallee to 8m	White	Greek *poly-* = many, *bracteus* = bract; referring to the bracts, which appear in young flower clusters
Eucalyptus populnea F.Muell.	1859	Poplar Box, Bimble Box	Qld/NSW	Tree to 20m	White	Latin *populneus* = poplar-like; referring to the leaves
Eucalyptus porosa F.Muell. ex Miq.	1856	South Australian Mallee Box	NSW/Vic/SA	Tree/mallee to 12m	White	Latin *porosa* = with pores; referring to the opening of the anthers
Eucalyptus praetermissa Brooker & Hopper	1991		WA	Mallet to 10m	Pale yellow	Latin *praetermissus* = overlooked; referring to the late discovery of this species
Eucalyptus prava L.A.S.Johnson & K.D.Hill	1990	Orange Gum	Qld/NSW	Tree to 15m	White	Latin *pravus* = crooked; referring to the habit
Eucalyptus preissiana Schauer subsp. *preissiana*	1844	Bell-fruited Mallee	WA	Mallee to 2.5m	Yellow	Honours Johann August Preiss (1811–83), botanist and enthusiastic plant collector
Eucalyptus preissiana subsp. *lobata* Brooker & Slee	1995	Quagi Beach Mallee	WA	Shrub to 1m	Yellow	Latin *lobatus* = lobed; referring to the lobes at the mouth of the gumnut
Eucalyptus prolixa D.Nicolle	2000	Square-fruited Mallet	WA	Mallet to 10m	Creamy white	Latin *prolixus* = stretched out; referring to elongated gumnuts and the slender mallet habit
Eucalyptus prominens Brooker	1976		WA	Mallee to 3m	White	Latin *prominens* = prominent; referring to the prominent valves on the gumnut compared with related species
Eucalyptus propinqua H.Deane & Maiden	1896	Grey Gum	Qld/NSW	Tree to 40m	White	Latin *propinquus* = near; referring to its similarity to *E. punctata*
Eucalyptus protensa L.A.S.Johnson & K.D.Hill	1991		WA	Mallet to 10m	Yellow-green	Latin *protensus* = stretched out; referring to the long bud cap
Eucalyptus provecta A.R.Bean	2000		Qld	Tree to 12m	White	Latin *provectus* = extended; referring to the rough bark extending throughout
Eucalyptus proxima D.Nicolle & Brooker	2005		WA	Mallee to 5m	Cream/yellow	Latin *proximus* = nearest; referring to its relationship with *E. cernua*
Eucalyptus pruiniramis L.A.S.Johnson & K.D.Hill	1992	Jingymia Gum	WA	Mallee/tree to 4m	White	Latin *pruina-* = covered in frost, *ramus* = branch; referring to the white wax covering the branches
Eucalyptus pruinosa Schauer subsp. *pruinosa*	1843	Silver Box	WA/NT/Qld	Tree/mallee to 10m	Creamy white	Latin *pruina-* = covered in frost; referring to the waxy nature of the foliage and buds
Eucalyptus pruinosa subsp. *tenuata* L.A.S.Johnson & K.D.Hill	2000	Silver Box	WA/NT	Tree/mallee to 10m	Creamy white	Latin *tenuatus* = slender; referring to the stems of the buds and flower clusters compared with the type
Eucalyptus psammitica L.A.S.Johnson & K.D.Hill	1990	White Mahogany	Qld/NSW	Tree to 15m	White	Greek *psammos* = sand; referring to its sandstone habitat
Eucalyptus pterocarpa C.A.Gardner ex P.J.Lang	1988		WA	Mallet to 10m	White	Greek *ptero-* = winged, *carpos* = fruit; referring to the ribbed gumnuts
Eucalyptus pulchella Desf.	1829	White Peppermint	Tas	Tree to 20m	White	Latin *pulchellus* = beautiful; referring to its general appearance

TABLE 3: EUCALYPTUS

Name and Author	Date Desc.	Common Name	Where it Occurs	Tree Form and Size	Flower Colour	Name Meaning
Eucalyptus pulverulenta Sims	1819	Silver-leaved Mountain Gum	NSW	Tree/mallee to 10m	White	Latin *pulverulentus* = powdered; referring to the white wax on the leaves, buds and gumnuts
Eucalyptus pumila Cambage	1919	Pokolbin Mallee	NSW	Mallee to 5m	White	Latin *pumilus* = dwarf; referring to its habit
Eucalyptus punctata DC.	1828	Grey Gum	Qld/NSW	Tree to 35m	White	Latin *punctatus* = spotted; referring to the oil glands in the leaves
Eucalyptus purpurata D.Nicolle	2002	Bandelup Silver Mallet	WA	Mallet to 10m	Creamy white	Latin *purpuratus* = purple; referring to the purplish new growth of leaves, branchlets and buds
Eucalyptus pyrenea Rule	2004		Vic	Tree to 18m	White	After the Pyrenees Range of west-central Vic
Eucalyptus pyriformis Turcz.	1849	Dowerin Rose	WA	Mallee to 5m	Red or yellow	Latin *pyriformis* = pear-shaped; referring to the buds
Eucalyptus pyrocarpa L.A.S.Johnson & Blaxell	1973	Large-fruited Blackbutt	NSW	Tree to 30m	White	Latin *pyrus* = pear, *carpos* = fruit; referring to the gumnut shape
Eucalyptus quadrangulata H.Deane & Maiden	1899	White-topped Box	Qld/NSW	Tree to 50m	White	Latin *quadrangulatus* = 4-angled; referring to the cross-section of the branchlets
Eucalyptus quadrans Brooker & Hopper	1993		WA	Mallee to 5m	White	Latin *quadra* = square; referring to the 4-sided base of the gumnut
Eucalyptus quadricostata Brooker	1985	Square-fruited Ironbark	Qld	Tree to 10m	White	Latin *quadri-* = 4, *costatus* = ribbed; referring to the 4 ribs on the buds and gumnuts
Eucalyptus quaerenda (L.A.S.Johnson & K.D.Hill) Byrne	2004		WA	Mallee to 4m	White	Latin *quaerendus* = to search; referring to the early searches for this species
Eucalyptus quinniorum J.T.Hunter & J.J.Bruhl	1999		NSW	Mallee/tree to 12m	White	Honours brothers Chris and Francis Quinn of the University of New England
Eucalyptus racemosa Cav.	1797	Scribbly Gum	Qld/NSW	Tree to 20m	White	Latin *racemosus* = in a raceme; referring to the flower clusters (allusion obscure)
Eucalyptus radiata Sieber ex DC. subsp. *radiata*	1828	Narrow-leaved Peppermint	NSW/Vic/Tas	Tree to 40m	White	Latin *radiatus* = radiating; referring to the flower clusters
Eucalyptus radiata subsp. *robertsonii* (Blakely) L.A.S.Johnson & Blaxell	1973	Narrow-leaved Peppermint	NSW/Vic	Tree to 50m	White	Honours Colin Charles Robertson (late 1870s– 1946), forester with special interest in eucalypts
Eucalyptus radiata subsp. *sejuncta* L.A.S.Johnson & K.D.Hill	1990	New England Narrow-leaved Peppermint	Qld/NSW	Tree to 30m	White	Latin *sejunctus* = separated; referring to its disjunct distribution compared with other subspecies
Eucalyptus rameliana F.Muell.	1876		WA	Mallee to 3m	Yellow	Honours Prospero Ramel (flor. 1877), responsible for introducing eucalypts into Algeria and southern France
Eucalyptus raveretiana F.Muell.	1877	Black Ironbox	Qld	Tree to 30m	White	Honours C. Raveret-Wattel, active in introducing eucalypts into southern France
Eucalyptus ravida L.A.S.Johnson & K.D.Hill	1991		WA	Mallet to 10m	White	Latin *ravidus* = greyish; referring to the new growth of the crown
Eucalyptus recta L.A.S.Johnson & K.D.Hill	1992	Silver Mallet	WA	Mallet to 15m	Creamy white	Latin *rectus* = straight; referring to the trunks
Eucalyptus recurva Crisp	1988	Mongarlowe Mallee	NSW	Mallee to 4m	White	Latin *recurvus* = recurved; referring to the downturned tip of the leaves
Eucalyptus redimiculifera L.A.S.Johnson & K.D.Hill	2001		WA	Tree to 10m	White	Latin *redimiculum* = a band, *-fera* = bearing; referring to the bracelet of shed bark around small branches
Eucalyptus redunca Schauer	1844	Black Marlock	WA	Mallee to 2m	Lemon	Latin *reduncus* = bent backwards; referring to the bud cap, but it is not always evident
Eucalyptus regnans F.Muell.	1870–71	Mountain Ash	Vic/Tas	Tree to 90m	White	Latin *regnans* = ruling; referring to the dominance of the trees
Eucalyptus relicta Hopper & Wardell-Johnson	2004		WA	Tree to 12m	?	Latin *relictus* = left behind; referring to the species being a relict of wetter times
Eucalyptus remota Blakely	1934	Kangaroo Island Ash	SA	Tree/mallee to 12m	White	Latin *remotus* = remote; referring to its remoteness from related species
Eucalyptus repullulans D.Nicolle	1997		WA	Mallee to 5m	?	Latin *repullulans* = sprouting again; referring to the presence of a lignotuber
Eucalyptus resinifera Sm. subsp. *resinifera*	1790	Red Mahogany	Qld/NSW	Tree to 45m	White	Latin *resiniferus* = resin-bearing; referring to the bark
Eucalyptus resinifera subsp. *hemilampra* (F.Muell.) L.A.S.Johnson & K.D.Hill	1990	Red Mahogany	Qld/NSW	Tree to 45m	White	Greek *hemi-* = half, *lampra* = shining; referring to the leaves, which are shiny on the top side
Eucalyptus retinens L.A.S.Johnson & K.D.Hill	1990	Hillgrove Box	NSW	Tree to 25m	White	Latin *retinens* = retaining; referring to the unshed rough bark
Eucalyptus retusa D.Nicolle & M.E.French	2008		WA	Mallee to 4m	Yellow-green	Latin *retusus* = blunt or rounded; referring to the adult leaves
Eucalyptus rhodantha Blakely & H.Steedman var. *rhodantha*	1938	Rose Mallee	WA	Mallee to 3m	Red	Greek *rhodo-* = red, *anthos* = flower; referring to the red flowers
Eucalyptus rhodantha var. *X petiolaris* Blakely	2005		WA	Mallee to 3m	Red	Latin *petiolaris* = having a leaf stalk; this plant is considered to be a hybrid with *E. pyriformis*
Eucalyptus rhombica A.R.Bean & Brooker	1994		Qld	Tree to 20m	White	Latin *rhombus* = rhomboid; referring to the diamond-shaped buds
Eucalyptus rhomboidea D.Nicolle & Hopper	2007		WA	Mallet to 18m	Creamy yellow	Latin *rhombus* = rhomboid; referring to the diamond-shaped buds
Eucalyptus rigens Brooker & Hopper	1989	Salt Lake Mallee	WA	Mallee to 4m	Creamy white	Latin *rigens* = stiff; referring to the leaves
Eucalyptus rigidula Maiden	1928	Stiff-leaved Mallee	WA	Mallee to 4m	Creamy white	Latin *rigidulus* = somewhat rigid; referring to the leaves
Eucalyptus risdonii Hook.f.	1847	Risdon Peppermint	Tas	Tree to 8m	White	After the locality of Risdon, where it grows
Eucalyptus robusta Sm.	1795	Swamp Mahogany	Qld/NSW	Tree to 30m	White	Latin *robustus* = robust; referring to the appearance of the tree
Eucalyptus rodwayi R.T.Baker & H.G.Sm.	1912	Swamp Peppermint	Tas	Tree to 20m	White	Honours Leonard Rodway (1853–1936), Honorary Government Botanist for Tasmania
Eucalyptus rosacea L.A.S.Johnson & K.D.Hill	1992		WA	Mallee to 4m	Pink	Latin *rosaceus* = pink; referring to the flower colour
Eucalyptus rossii R.T.Baker & H.G.Sm.	1902	Scribbly Gum	NSW	Tree to 15m	White	Honours William John Clunies Ross (1850–1914), lecturer Sydney Technical College
Eucalyptus roycei S.G.M.Carr, D.J.Carr & A.S.George	1970	Shark Bay Mallee	WA	Tree/mallee to 6m	Cream	Honours Robert Dunlop Royce (b. 1914), Curator WA Herbarium and botanical writer
Eucalyptus rubida H.Deane & Maiden subsp. *rubida*	1899	Candlebark	NSW/Vic/Tas	Tree to 20m	White	Latin *rubidus* = red; referring to the seasonally red bark

TABLE 3: EUCALYPTUS

Name and Author	Date Desc.	Common Name	Where it Occurs	Tree Form and Size	Flower Colour	Name Meaning
Eucalyptus rubida subsp. *barbigerorum* L.A.S.Johnson & K.D.Hill	1991	Blackbutt Candlebark	NSW	Tree to 15m	White	Latin *barbigerorum* = of the beard-bearing ones; referring to the bearded pioneers of the district
Eucalyptus rubiginosa Brooker	1984		Qld	Tree to 15m	White	Latin *rubiginosus* = rusty; referring to the red-brown fibrous bark
Eucalyptus rudderi Maiden	1904	Rudder's Box	NSW	Tree to 30m	White	Honours Augustus Rudder (1828–1904), forester and plant collector
Eucalyptus rudis Endl. subsp. *rudis*	1837	Flooded Gum	WA	Tree to 20m	White	Latin *rudis* = rough; probably referring to the apparently worthless timber
Eucalyptus rudis subsp. *cratyantha* Brooker & Hopper	1993	Flooded Gum	WA	Tree to 25m	White	Greek *craty-* = strong, *anthos* = flower; referring to the larger buds of this subspecies
Eucalyptus rugosa Blakely	1934	Kingscote Mallee	SA	Mallee to 10m	White	Latin *rugosus* = wrinkled; possibly referring to the buds and gumnuts
Eucalyptus rugulata D.Nicolle	2002		WA	Mallet to 15m	Creamy white	Latin *rugulus* = wrinkled; referring to the buds and gumnuts and the rugged sites where it occurs
Eucalyptus rummeryi Maiden	1923	Steel Box	NSW	Tree to 40m	White	Honours George Edward Rummery (1877–1958), forester with good knowledge of NSW north coast forests
Eucalyptus rupestris Brooker & Done	1986	Prince Regent Gum	WA	Tree to 5m	White	Latin *rupestris* = rock-growing; referring to its habitat
Eucalyptus sabulosa Rule	1996		Vic	Tree to 12m	White	Latin *sabulosus* = of the sand; referring to its habitat
Eucalyptus salicola Brooker	1988	Salt Gum	WA	Tree to 15m	Creamy white	Latin *sali-* = salt, *-cola* = dweller; referring to the saline habitat
Eucalyptus saligna Sm.	1797	Sydney Blue Gum	Qld/NSW	Tree to 55m	White	Latin *salignus* = willow-like; allusion obscure
Eucalyptus salmonophloia F.Muell.	1878	Salmon Gum	WA	Tree to 25m	Creamy white	Latin *salmoneus* = salmon-coloured, Greek *phloios* = bark; referring to the bark colour
Eucalyptus salubris F.Muell.	1876	Gimlet	WA	Tree to 15m	White	Latin *salubris* = healthful, wholesome; allusion obscure
Eucalyptus sargentii Maiden subsp. *sargentii*	1924	Salt River Gum	WA	Tree/mallee to 11m	Pale lemon	Honours Oswald Hewlett Sargent (1880–1952), pharmacist with an interest in botany
Eucalyptus sargentii subsp. *onesia* D.Nicolle	2005		WA	Mallee to 6m	Pale lemon	Greek *onesis* = use; referring to the potential value of this subspecies for reclamation of saline areas
Eucalyptus saxatilis J.B.Kirkp. & Brooker	1977	Suggan Buggan Mallee	NSW/Vic	Tree/mallee to 5m	White	Latin *saxatilis* = rock-dwelling; referring to its habitat
Eucalyptus scias L.A.S.Johnson & K.D.Hill subsp. *scias*	1990	Red Mahogany	NSW	Tree to 20m	White	Greek *skias* = shade; referring to its spreading crown
Eucalyptus scias subsp. *apoda* L.A.S.Johnson & K.D.Hill	1990	Tenterfield Red Mahogany	NSW	Tree to 10m	White	Greek *apoda* = without a foot; referring to the stalkless buds
Eucalyptus scoparia Maiden	1905	Wallangarra White Gum	Qld/NSW	Tree to 15m	White	Latin *scoparius* = broom-like; allusion obscure
Eucalyptus scopulorum K.D.Hill	1997		NSW	Tree to 8m	White	Latin *scopulus* = a cliff; referring to the habitat
Eucalyptus scyphocalyx (F.Muell. ex Benth.) Maiden & Blakely subsp. *scyphocalyx*	1929	Goblet Mallee	WA	Mallee to 5m	Creamy white	Greek *scypho-* = cup, *kalyx* = calyx; referring to the shape of the gumnut
Eucalyptus scyphocalyx subsp. *triadica* L.A.S.Johnson & K.D.Hill	2001		WA	Mallee to 5m	Creamy white	Latin *triad* = group of three; referring to the arrangement of the buds
Eucalyptus seeana Maiden	1904	Narrow-leaved Red Gum	Qld/NSW	Tree to 18m	White	After Sir John See (1844–1907), Premier of NSW (1901–04)
Eucalyptus semiglobosa (Brooker) L.A.S.Johnson & K.D.Hill	1992		WA	Mallee to 4m	White	Latin *semi-* = half, *globosus* = globular; referring to the shape of the gumnut
Eucalyptus semota C.J.Macpherson & Grayling	1996		WA	Tree/mallee to 8m	White	Latin *semotus* = remote; referring to the distance of this species from its close relatives
Eucalyptus sepulcralis F.Muell.	1882	Weeping Mallee	WA	Tree/mallee to 7m	Pale yellow	Latin *sepulcralis* = pertaining to a grave or sepulchre; referring to its weeping habit
Eucalyptus serraensis Ladiges & Whiffin	1993	Grampians Stringybark	Vic	Tree/mallee to 5m	White	After the Serra Range, where the species occurs
Eucalyptus sessilis (Maiden) Blakely	1934	Red Bud Mallee	WA/NT	Mallee to 5m	Yellow	Latin *sessilis* = sitting; referring to the buds, which lack a stalk
Eucalyptus sheathiana Maiden	1916	Ribbon-barked Gum	WA	Tree/mallee to 10m	Creamy white	Honours Jeremiah Sheath (1850–1915), Superintendent, King's Park, Perth
Eucalyptus shirleyi Maiden	1923	Silver-leaved Ironbark	Qld	Tree to 7m	White	Honours John Shirley (1849–1922), educationalist with an interest in botany
Eucalyptus sicilifolia L.A.S.Johnson & K.D.Hill	1991		Qld	Tree to 10m	White	Latin *sicilis* = a sickle, *folium* = a leaf; referring to the leaf shape
Eucalyptus siderophloia Benth.	1867	Ironbark	Qld/NSW	Tree to 20m	White	Greek *sidero-* = iron, *phloios* = bark; referring to the hard bark
Eucalyptus sideroxylon A.Cunn. ex Woolls subsp. *sideroxylon*	1887	Red Ironbark, Mugga	Qld/NSW/Vic	Tree to 25m	White, cream to red	Greek *sidero-* = iron, *xylon* = wood; referring to the hard wood
Eucalyptus sideroxylon subsp. Waaje (N.B.Byrnes 3955) Qld Herbarium	2002		Qld			An undescribed subspecies
Eucalyptus sieberi L.A.S.Johnson	1962	Silvertop Ash	NSW/Vic/Tas	Tree to 35m	White	Honours Franz Wilhelm Sieber (1789–1844), Czech botanist who worked in Australia
Eucalyptus silvestris Rule	1994		Vic/SA	Tree/mallee to 12m	White	Latin *silvestris* = pertaining to woods; referring to its woodland habitat
Eucalyptus similis Maiden	1913	Queensland Yellowjacket	Qld	Tree to 12m	Creamy white	Latin *similis* = similar to; referring to its similarity to *E. baileyana*
Eucalyptus singularis L.A.S.Johnson & Blaxell	2001		WA	Mallet to 6m	Pale yellow	Latin *singularis* = alone, solitary; referring to its single-stemmed mallet habit
Eucalyptus sinuosa D.Nicolle & M.E.French	2008		WA	Mallee to 4m	Yellow-green	Latin *sinuosus* = winding; referring to the distinctive twisting bud caps
Eucalyptus smithii R.T.Baker	1899	Gully Gum	NSW/Vic	Tree to 45m	White	Honours Henry George Smith (1852–1924), chemist who investigated the essential oils of eucalypts
Eucalyptus socialis F.Muell. ex Miq. subsp. *socialis*	1856	Red Mallee	NSW/Vic/SA	Mallee to 10m	Creamy white	Latin *socialis* = friendly; referring to occurrence with several other species
Eucalyptus socialis subsp. *eucentrica* (L.A.S.Johnson & K.D.Hill) D.Nicolle	2005	Red Mallee	WA/NT/Qld/SA	Mallee to 12m	Pale yellow	Greek *eu-* = well, *kentrikos* = of the centre; referring to its wide occurrence in the interior of Australia
Eucalyptus socialis subsp. *victoriensis* D.Nicolle	2005	Red Mallee	WA/SA	Mallee to 7m	Cream to yellow	After the Victoria Desert, where this species is found

Name and Author	Date Desc.	Common Name	Where it Occurs	Tree Form and Size	Flower Colour	Name Meaning
Eucalyptus socialis subsp. *viridans* D.Nicolle	2005	Red Mallee	Vic/SA	Mallee to 5m	Creamy white	Latin *viridans* = green; referring to the seedling and adult leaf colour
Eucalyptus sp. Badgingarra (D.Nicolle & M.French DN 3515) D.Nicolle						An undescribed species from Badgingarra, WA
Eucalyptus sp. Castlemaine (K.Rule 8203) Vic Herbarium						An undescribed species from Castlemaine, Vic
Eucalyptus sp. Consuelo Tableland (M.I.H.Broooker B4884) Qld Herbarium						An undescribed species from Consuelo Tableland, Qld
Eucalyptus sp. Esperance (M.E.French 1579) NSW Herbarium						An undescribed species from Esperance, WA
Eucalyptus sp. Eyre (K.Hill & L.A.S Johnson KH 2170) WA Herbarium				Mallee to 3m		An undescribed species from the Eyre district, WA
Eucalyptus sp. Flinders Ranges (D.Nicolle 562) D.Nicolle						An undescribed species from Flinders Ranges, SA
Eucalyptus sp. Fraser Range (D.Nicolle 2157) D.Nicolle				Mallee to 4m	Green	An undescribed species from Fraser Range, WA
Eucalyptus sp. Gippsland Lakes (H.I.Aston 1661) Vic Herbarium						An undescribed species from Gippsland Lakes area, Vic
Eucalyptus sp. Glasshouse Mountains (A.R.Bean 782) Qld Herbarium						An undescribed species from the Glasshouse Mountains, Qld
Eucalyptus sp. Great Victoria Desert (D.Nicolle & M.French DN 3877) D.Nicolle						An undescribed species from the Great Victoria Desert, WA
Eucalyptus sp. H Kimberley Flora (S.G.Forbes 2560) WA Herbarium				Tree to 7m	Creamy white	An undescribed species from the Kimberley, WA
Eucalyptus sp. Howes Swamp Creek (M.Doherty 26) NSW Herbarium						An undescribed species from Howes Swamp Creek, NSW
Eucalyptus sp. Kalbarri (M.I.H.Brooker 7937) Australian National Herbarium						An undescribed species from Kalbarri, WA
Eucalyptus sp. Kalkarindji (G.M.Wightman 6240) NT Herbarium						An undescribed species from NT
Eucalyptus sp. Killarney (C.R.Michell 2403) NT Herbarium						An undescribed species from NT
Eucalyptus sp. Lerderberg (K.Rule 7303) Vic Herbarium						An undescribed species
Eucalyptus sp. Little Sandy Desert (D.Nicolle & M.French DN 4304) D.Nicolle						An undescribed species from Little Sandy Desert, WA
Eucalyptus sp. Madura Beach (D.Nicolle 1570) D.Nicolle						An undescribed species from Madura Beach, WA
Eucalyptus sp. Montejinni Station (G.M.Chippendale 2171) NT Herbarium						An undescribed species from Montejinni Station, NT
Eucalyptus sp. Mornington Peninsula (K.Rule 210)						An undescribed species from Mornington Peninsula, Vic
Eucalyptus sp. Mt Garnet (D.J.Carr+ 1672B) Qld Herbarium						An undescribed species from Mt Garnet, Qld
Eucalyptus sp. Mt Hope Homestead (E.J.Thompson+ BUC175) Qld Herbarium						An undescribed species from Mt Hope Homestead, Qld
Eucalyptus sp. Mt King (S.van Leeuwen 3605) WA Herbarium						An undescribed species from Mt King, WA
Eucalyptus sp. Mt Nameless (D.Nicolle 1191) D.Nicolle				Mallee		An undescribed species from Mt Nameless, WA
Eucalyptus sp. Mulga Rock (K.D.Hill & L.A.S.Johnson KH 2668) NSW Herbarium						An undescribed species from Mulga Rock, NSW
Eucalyptus sp. Nhill (N.G.Walsh 6030) Vic Herbarium						An undescribed species from Nhill, Vic
Eucalyptus sp. North Balladonia (D.Nicolle & M.French DN 3620) D.Nicolle						An undescribed species from North Balladonia, WA
Eucalyptus sp. North Pilbara (D.Nicolle 4258) D.Nicolle						An undescribed species from north Pilbara, WA
Eucalyptus sp. Point Hillier (D.Nicolle & M.French DN 3759) D.Nicolle						An undescribed species from Point Hillier, WA
Eucalyptus sp. Ravensthorpe (A.S.George 616) NSW Herbarium				Mallee to 4m	White	An undescribed species from near Ravensthorpe, WA
Eucalyptus sp. Rudall River (D.Nicolle & M.French DN 4279) D.Nicolle				Mallee	White	An undescribed species from Rudall River area, WA
Eucalyptus sp. Tarin Rock (D.Nicolle & M.French DN 3759) D.Nicolle						An undescribed species from Tarin Rock, WA
Eucalyptus sp. Wagerup (L.Johnson 9127 & B.Briggs) WA Herbarium				Mallee to 4m		An undescribed species from Wagerup, WA
Eucalyptus sp. Yealering (D.Nicolle & M.French DN 3424) D.Nicolle						An undescribed species from Yealering, WA
Eucalyptus sparsa Boomsma	1979		WA/NT/SA	Mallee to 10m	White	Latin *sparsus* = sparse; referring to its distribution
Eucalyptus sparsifolia Blakely	1934	Narrow-leaved Stringybark	NSW	Tree to 20m	White	Latin *sparsifolius* = sparse-leaved; referring to the crown, but is probably a misnomer
Eucalyptus spathulata Hook. subsp. *spathulata*	1844	Swamp Mallet	WA	Mallet to 10m	White	Latin *spathulatus* = spatula-shaped; allusion obscure
Eucalyptus spathulata subsp. *salina* D.Nicolle & Brooker	2005		WA	Mallet to 10m	White	Latin *salinus* = saline; referring to its habitat
Eucalyptus sphaerocarpa L.A.S.Johnson & Blaxell	1972	Blackdown Stringybark	Qld	Tree to 45m	White	Greek *sphaero-* = sphere, *carpos* = fruit; referring to the spherical gumnuts
Eucalyptus splendens Rule	1996	Mt Richmond Apple-jack	Vic	Tree to 10m	White	Latin *splendens* = splendid; referring to the bright leaves
Eucalyptus sporadica Brooker & Hopper	2002		WA	Mallee to 4m	Greenish yellow	Latin *sporadicus* = sporadic; referring to the relatively wide and scattered distribution
Eucalyptus spreta L.A.S.Johnson & K.D.Hill	2001		WA	Mallet to 10m	White	Latin *spretus* = separated or removed; referring to its geographic isolation from the related *E. pileata*
Eucalyptus squamosa H.Deane & Maiden	1898	Scaly Bark	NSW	Tree to 15m	White	Latin *squamosus* = scaly; referring to the loose, rough bark

TABLE 3: EUCALYPTUS

Name and Author	Date Desc.	Common Name	Where it Occurs	Tree Form and Size	Flower Colour	Name Meaning
Eucalyptus staeri (Maiden) Kessell & C.A.Gardner	1924	Albany Blackbutt	WA	Tree/mallee to 10m	Creamy white	Honours John Staer (1850–1933), nurseryman who collected the type specimen
Eucalyptus staigeriana F.Muell. ex F.M.Bailey	1883	Lemon-scented Ironbark	Qld	Tree to 12m	White	Honours Karl Theodore Staiger (1833–88), chemist with an interest in the essential oils of eucalypts
Eucalyptus steedmanii C.A.Gardner	1933	Steedman's Mallet	WA	Mallet to 12m	White	Honours Henry Steedman (c. 1866–1953), gardener at Perth Zoo and later plant collector
Eucalyptus stellulata Sieber ex DC.	1828	Black Sally	NSW/Vic	Tree/mallee to 15m	White	Latin *stellulatus* = star-shaped; referring to the arrangement of the flower buds
Eucalyptus stenostoma L.A.S.Johnson & Blaxell	1972	Jillaga Ash	NSW	Tree to 25m	White	Greek *steno-* = narrow, *stoma* = opening; referring to the narrow opening at the mouth of the gumnut
Eucalyptus stoatei C.A.Gardner	1936	Scarlet Pear Gum	WA	Mallet to 6m	Yellow	Honours Theodore Norman Stoat (1895–1979), Conservator of Forests, WA
Eucalyptus stowardii Maiden	1917	Fluted-horn Mallee	WA	Mallee to 5m	Creamy white	Honours Frederick Stoward (1866–1931), wine maker, botanist and plant pathologist
Eucalyptus striaticalyx W.Fitzg. subsp. *striaticalyx*	1904	Cue York Gum	WA	Tree to 12m	White	Latin *striatus* = striated, *kalyx* = calyx; probably referring to the finely striped gumnut
Eucalyptus striaticalyx subsp. *delicata* D.Nicolle	1997		WA	Tree to 12m	White	Latin *delicatus* = delicate, soft; referring to pendulous crown of narrow leaves and smaller buds and gumnuts
Eucalyptus stricklandii Maiden	1911	Strickland's Gum	WA	Tree to 9m	Yellow	Honours Sir Gerald Strickland (1861–1940), successive governor of Tas, WA and SA
Eucalyptus stricta Sieber ex Spreng.	1827	Blue Mountains Mallee Ash	NSW	Mallee to 7m	White	Latin *strictus* = upright, straight; referring to the many stems
Eucalyptus strzeleckii Rule	1992	Wax Tip	Vic	Tree to 30m	White	Honours Sir Paul Edmund de Strzeleckii (1797–1873), explorer with an interest in the environment
Eucalyptus sturgissiana L.A.S.Johnson & Blaxell	1972	Ettrema Mallee	NSW	Mallee to 5m	White	Honours James H. Sturgiss (1890–1983), pastoralist and discoverer of this species
Eucalyptus subangusta (Blakely) Brooker & Hopper subsp. *subangusta*	1991		WA	Mallee to 5m	White	Latin *subangustus* = somewhat narrow; referring to the leaves
Eucalyptus subangusta subsp. *cerina* Brooker & Hopper	1991		WA	Mallee to 5m	White	Latin *cerinus* = waxy; referring to the greyish branchlets
Eucalyptus subangusta subsp. *pusilla* Brooker & Hopper	1991		WA	Mallet/mallee to 7m	White	Latin *pusillus* = very small; referring to the buds and gumnuts, which are the smallest of the species
Eucalyptus subangusta subsp. *virescens* Brooker & Hopper	1991		WA	Mallet/mallee to 5m	White	Latin *virescens* = becoming green; referring to the glossy, green leaves
Eucalyptus subcrenulata Maiden & Blakely	1929	Tasmanian Alpine Yellow Gum	Tas	Tree to 20m	White	Latin *sub-* = somewhat, *crenulatus* = crenulate; referring to the slightly toothed leaves
Eucalyptus suberea Brooker & Hopper	1986	Mt Leseuer Mallee	WA	Tree/mallee to 3m	White	Latin *subereus* = corky; referring to the rough bark
Eucalyptus subtilis Brooker & Hopper	1991	Narrow-leaved Mallee	WA	Mallee to 3m	Cream	Latin *subtilis* = subtle or delicate; referring to the narrow leaves
Eucalyptus suffulgens L.A.S.Johnson & K.D.Hill	1991		Qld	Tree to 25m	White	Latin *sub-* = somewhat, *fulgens* = shining; referring to the somewhat glossy adult leaves
Eucalyptus suggrandis L.A.S.Johnson & K.D.Hill subsp. *suggrandis*	1992		WA	Mallee to 5m	Creamy white/ red	Latin *sub-* = somewhat, *grandis* = large; referring to the rather large buds and gumnuts compared with related species
Eucalyptus suggrandis subsp. *promiscua* D.Nicolle & Brooker	2005		WA	Mallee to 5m	Creamy white/ red	Latin *promiscuus* = mixed; referring to its apparent similar characteristics to other species
Eucalyptus surgens Brooker & Hopper	1993		WA	Mallee to 2m	Creamy white	Latin *surgens* = rising; referring to the more or less vertical scar on the rim of the gumnut
Eucalyptus sweedmaniana Hopper & McQuoid	2009		WA	Mallee to 1m	Pink	Honours Luke Sweedman (b. 1958), Curator, WA Seed Technology Centre
Eucalyptus synandra Crisp	1982	Jingymia Mallee	WA	Mallee to 4m	White/ pink	Greek *synandra* = male parts joined; referring to the staminal threads
Eucalyptus talyuberlup D.J.Carr & S.G.M.Carr	1980		WA	Tree/mallee to 10m	Greenish yellow	After Mt Talyuberlup, Stirling Range, where the species was collected
Eucalyptus tardecidens (L.A.S.Johnson & K.D.Hill) A.R.Bean	2000		Qld	Tree/mallee to 7m	White	Latin *tarde-* = tardily, *cidens* = falling; referring to falling of the outer bud cap early in bud development
Eucalyptus taurina A.R.Bean & Brooker	1994	Helidon Ironbark	Qld	Tree to 22m	White	Latin *taurinus* = of bulls; referring to an encounter by the first author when he first saw this species
Eucalyptus tectifica F.Muell.	1859		WA/NT/ Qld	Tree to 15m	Creamy white	Latin *tectum* = roof, *facere* = to make; possibly referring to the Aboriginal use of the bark
Eucalyptus tenella L.A.S.Johnson & K.D.Hill	1991	Narrow-leaved Stringybark	NSW	Tree to 15m	White	Latin *tenellus* = delicate; referring to the narrow leaves
Eucalyptus tenera L.A.S.Johnson & K.D.Hill	1992	Sand Mallee	WA	Mallee to 5m	Lemon-yellow	Latin *tener* = delicate; referring to the smaller buds and gumnuts compared with the related *E. eremophila*
Eucalyptus tenuipes (Maiden & Blakely) Blakely & C.T.White	1931	Narrow-leaved White Mahogany	Qld	Tree to 5m	White	Latin *tenuis* = thin, *pes* = foot; referring to the slender bud stalk
Eucalyptus tenuiramis Miq.	1856	Silver Peppermint	Tas	Tree to 25m	White	Latin *tenuis* = thin, *ramus* = branch; presumably the author considered that the branches were slender
Eucalyptus tenuis Brooker & Hopper	1993		WA	Mallee/mallet to 10m	?	Latin *tenuis* = thin; referring to the slender trunks
Eucalyptus tephroclada L.A.S.Johnson & K.D.Hill	1992		WA	Mallee to 4m	Pale lemon-yellow	Greek *tephros* = ash-grey, *klados* = stem; referring to the greyish branchlets
Eucalyptus tephrodes L.A.S.Johnson & K.D.Hill	2000		WA	Tree to 12m	?	Greek *tephros* = ash-grey, *-odes* = resembling; referring to the conspicuous bluish-grey crown
Eucalyptus terebra L.A.S.Johnson & K.D.Hill	1991		WA	Mallet to 12m	Greenish yellow	Latin *terebrus* = borer, gimlet; referring to the common name of this group of trees
Eucalyptus tereticornis Sm. subsp. *tereticornis*	1795	Forest Red Gum	Qld/NSW	Tree to 50m	White	Latin *teres* = circular in cross-section, *cornus* = horn; referring to the shape of the bud cap

TABLE 3: EUCALYPTUS

Name and Author	Date Desc.	Common Name	Where it Occurs	Tree Form and Size	Flower Colour	Name Meaning
Eucalyptus tereticornis subsp. Bunya Mountains (P.V.Holzworth AQ397993) Qld Herbarium			Qld			An undescribed subspecies from the Bunya Mountains
Eucalyptus tereticornis subsp. Consuelo Tableland (M.I.Brooker B4880) Qld Herbarium			Qld			An undescribed subspecies from Consuelo Tablelands
Eucalyptus tereticornis subsp. *mediana* Brooker & Slee	1999	Gippsland Red Gum	Vic	Tree to 20m	White	Latin *medianus* = median; referring to its similarity to *E. camaldulensis*
Eucalyptus terrica A.R.Bean	1991		Qld	Tree to 10m	White	After Terrica Station, where the species was collected
Eucalyptus tetrapleura L.A.S.Johnson	1962	Square-fruited Ironbark	NSW	Tree to 30m	White	Greek *tetra-* = 4, *pleura* = rib; referring to the shape of the gumnut
Eucalyptus tetraptera Turcz.	1849	Square-fruited Mallee	WA	Mallee to 4m	Red	Greek *tetra-* = 4, *pteron* = wing; referring to the square gumnuts
Eucalyptus tetrodonta F.Muell.	1859	Darwin Stringybark	WA/NT/ Qld	Tree to 25m	White	Greek *tetra-* = 4, *odontos* = teeth; referring to the 4 teeth on the rim of the gumnut
Eucalyptus thamnoides Brooker & Hopper subsp. *thamnoides*	2002		WA	Mallee to 4m	Cream	Greek *thamnos* = shrub, *-oides* = similar to; referring to its mallee (not mallet) habit
Eucalyptus thamnoides subsp. *megista* Brooker & Hopper	2002		WA	Mallee to 4m	Cream	Greek *megistos* = largest; referring to the gumnuts compared with the type species
Eucalyptus tholiformis A.R.Bean & Brooker	1994		Qld	Tree to 15m	White	Latin *tholiformis* = dome-shaped; referring to the top of the gumnut
Eucalyptus thozetiana F.Muell. ex R.T.Baker	1906	Mountain Yapunyah	NT/Qld	Tree to 17m	White	Honours Anthelme Thozet (1826–78), French botanist who collected in Qld
Eucalyptus tindaliae Blakely	1929	Tindal's Stringybark	Qld/NSW	Tree to 30m	White	Honours Anne Grant Tindal (1859–1928), member of pastoral family who was interested in the local flora
Eucalyptus tintinnans (Blakely & Jacobs) L.A.S.Johnson & K.D.Hill	1988	Ringing Gum	NT	Tree to 15m	White	Latin *tintinnus* = a bell; referring to the ringing sound that hollow trees give out when struck with an axe
Eucalyptus todtiana F.Muell.	1882	Prickly Bark	WA	Tree to 5m	White	Honours Emil Todt (c. 1810–1900), sculptor and artist who made drawings for F. Mueller
Eucalyptus torquata Luehm.	1897	Coral Gum	WA	Tree to 12m	Pink	Latin *torquatus* = adorned with a necklace; referring to the ribbing at the base of the buds and gumnuts
Eucalyptus tortilis L.A.S.Johnson & K.D.Hill	1991	Gimlet	WA	Mallet to 8m	White	Latin *tortilis* = twisted; referring to the gimlet type trunk
Eucalyptus transcontinentalis Maiden	1919	Redwood	WA	Tree/mallet to 12m	Pale yellow	After the Transcontinental Railway, which passes through its distribution
Eucalyptus tricarpa (L.A.S.Johnson) L.A.S.Johnson & K.D.Hill subsp. *tricarpa*	1991	Red Ironbark	NSW/Vic	Tree to 35m	White/pale pink	Greek *tri-* = 3, *carpos* = fruit; referring to the gumnuts, which are borne in threes
Eucalyptus tricarpa subsp. *decora* Rule	2004		Vic	Tree to 15m	White/pale pink	Latin *decorus* = beautiful; referring to the general appearance of the tree
Eucalyptus triflora (Maiden) Blakely	1934	Pigeon House Ash	NSW	Tree to 12m	White	Latin *tri-* = 3, *florum* = flower; referring to the flowers which are in threes
Eucalyptus trivalva Blakely	1936	Desert Mallee	WA/NT/ SA	Tree/mallee to 5m	White	Latin *tri-* = 3, *valvis* = valve; referring to the 3 openings at the top of the gumnut
Eucalyptus tumida Brooker & Hopper	1991		WA	Mallee to 3m	White/pale yellow	Latin *tumidus* = swollen; referring to the buds, which are the largest in this group of eucalypts
Eucalyptus ultima L.A.S.Johnson & K.D.Hill	1999		WA	Mallee to 4m	White	Latin *ultimus* = most distant; referring to its occurrence at the extreme of the range of related species
Eucalyptus umbra R.T.Baker	1901	Broad-leaved White Mahogany	NSW	Tree to 25m	White	Latin *umbra* = shade; referring to the shade offered by the tree
Eucalyptus umbrawarrensis Maiden	1922	Umbrawarra Gum	NT	Tree to 18m	White	After the locality of Umbrawarra, where the species occurs
Eucalyptus uncinata Turcz.	1849	Hook-leaved Mallee	WA	Mallee to 4m	Creamy white	Latin *uncinatus* = uncinate; botanical term referring to the curved tip of the leaf
Eucalyptus urna D.Nicolle	1999	Merrit	WA	Mallet to 16m	Creamy white	Latin *urnus* = pitcher, urn; referring to the shape of the gumnut
Eucalyptus urnigera Hook.f.	1847	Urn Gum	Tas	Tree to 15m	White	Latin *urni-* = urn, *-igera* = bearing; referring to the shape of the gumnut
Eucalyptus urophylla S.T.Blake	1977	Timor Mountain Gum	Timor/ PNG	Tree to 45m	White	Greek *uro-* = with an elongated appendage, *phyllon* = a leaf; referring to the extended leaf tip
Eucalyptus utilis Brooker & Hopper	2002		WA	Mallet/mallee to 7m	Creamy white	Latin *utilis* = useful; referring to its common use on farms and in street planting
Eucalyptus valens L.A.S.Johnson & K.D.Hill	2001		WA	Mallet to 10m	?	Latin *valens* = strong; referring to its robust habit compared with related species
Eucalyptus varia Brooker & Hopper subsp. *varia*	1991		WA	Mallee to 7m	Yellow	Latin *varius* = varying; referring to its variable stature, bark and adult leaf width
Eucalyptus varia subsp. *salsuginosa* Brooker & Hopper	1991		WA	Mallee to 4m	Lemon	Latin *salsuginosus* = in brackish places; referring to its habitat
Eucalyptus vegrandis L.A.S.Johnson & K.D.Hill subsp. *vegrandis*	1992		WA	Mallee to 6m	Creamy white	Latin *vegrandis* = not very large; referring to small stature and because it was confused with *E. suggrandis*
Eucalyptus vegrandis subsp. Fine leaf (P.J.White 452) WA Herbarium			WA	Mallee to 5m	Creamy white	An undescribed subspecies
Eucalyptus vegrandis subsp. *recondita* D.Nicolle & Brooker	2005		WA	Tree/mallee to 5m	Creamy white	Latin *reconditus* = not easily seen; referring to the fact that this subspecies was not easily recognised
Eucalyptus vernicosa Hook.f.	1847	Varnished Gum	Tas	Shrub to 4m	White	Latin *vernicosus* = varnished; referring to the shiny appearance of the leaves
Eucalyptus verrucata Ladiges & Whiffin	1995	Mt Abrupt Stringybark	Vic	Shrub/tree to 5m	White	Latin *verrucatus* = warty; referring to the buds
Eucalyptus vesiculosa Brooker & Hopper	2002	Corackerup Marlock	WA	Marlock to 3m	Red	Latin *vesiculosus* = with vesicles (small blisters); referring to the warty bud cap
Eucalyptus vicina L.A.S.Johnson & K.D.Hill	1991	Manara Hills Red Gum	NSW	Tree/mallee to 8m	White	Latin *vicinus* = near; referring to its resemblance to *E. dwyeri*
Eucalyptus victoriana Ladiges & Whiffin	1995		Vic	Tree to 20m	White	After the Victoria Range, where it is endemic
Eucalyptus victrix L.A.S.Johnson & K.D.Hill	1994	Smooth-barked Coolabah	WA/NT	Tree to 15m	Creamy white	Latin *victrix* = one who conquers; referring to its success in a difficult climate
Eucalyptus viminalis Labill. subsp. *viminalis*	1806	Manna Gum, Ribbon Gum	NSW/Vic/ Tas/SA	Tree to 90m	White	Latin *viminalis* = bearing shoots or ribbons for wicker-work; referring to the long pieces of peeling bark

TABLE 3: EUCALYPTUS

Name and Author	Date Desc.	Common Name	Where it Occurs	Tree Form and Size	Flower Colour	Name Meaning
Eucalyptus viminalis subsp. *cygnetensis* Boomsma	1980	Rough-barked Manna Gum	Vic/SA	Tree/mallee to 10m	White	After the Cygnet River, Kangaroo Island, from where the type specimen was collected
Eucalyptus viminalis subsp. *hentyensis* Brooker & Slee	2006	Western Tasmanian Sand Gum	Tas	Tree to 6m	White	After the Henty River, near where the species grows
Eucalyptus viminalis subsp. *pryoriana* (L.A.S.Johnson) Brooker & Slee	1996	Gippsland Manna Gum	Vic	Tree to 15m	White	Honours Lindsay Dixon Pryor (1915–98), Professor of Botany, ANU, and renowned eucalyptologist
Eucalyptus virens Brooker & A.R.Bean	1986		Qld	Tree to 25m	White	Latin *virens* = green; referring to the bright green adult leaves
Eucalyptus virginea Hopper & Wardell-Johnson	2004		WA	Tree to 20m	White	Latin *virgineus* = pure white; referring to the bark but also to the original collector, forester Barney White
Eucalyptus viridis R.T.Baker	1900	Green Mallee	Qld/NSW/Vic/SA	Tree/mallee to 8m	White	Latin *viridis* = green; referring to the leaves
Eucalyptus vittata D.Nicolle	2009		WA	Mallet to 14m	White	Latin *vittatus* = bound with ribbon; referring to the bark, which is shed in long ribbons
Eucalyptus vokesensis D.Nicolle & L.A.S.Johnson	1999		SA	Mallee to 7m	Pale yellow	After Vokes Hill, Great Victoria Desert, where this species was first found
Eucalyptus volcanica L.A.S.Johnson & K.D.Hill	1990		NSW	Tree to 25m	Creamy white	Latin *volcanicus* = volcanic; referring to the area where the species was found
Eucalyptus walshii Rule	2004		Vic	Tree to 9m	White	Honours Neville Walsh, Senior Conservation Botanist, Melbourne Botanic Gardens
Eucalyptus wandoo Blakely subsp. *wandoo*	1934	Wandoo	WA	Tree to 18m	White	After Wandoo, the Aboriginal name for the tree
Eucalyptus wandoo subsp. *pulverea* Brooker & Hopper	1991	Wandoo	WA	Tree to 15m	White	Latin *pulvereus* = powdery; referring to the bark
Eucalyptus websteriana Maiden subsp. *websteriana*	1916	Webster's Mallee	WA	Mallee to 5m	Cream/pale lemon	Honours Leonard Clarke Webster (1870–1942), pharmacist and medical doctor who collected the type specimen
Eucalyptus websteriana subsp. *norsemanica* L.A.S.Johnson & K.D.Hill	1992		WA	Mallee to 5m	Cream/pale lemon	After the town of Norseman, near where this species occurs
Eucalyptus wetarensis L.D.Pryor	1995		Wetar Island	Tree to 17m	White	After Wetar Island, near Timor, where the plant is found
Eucalyptus whitei Maiden & Blakely	1925	White's Ironbark	Qld	Tree to 15m	White	Honours Cyril Tenison White (1890–1950), Qld Government Botanist
Eucalyptus wilcoxii Boland & Kleinig	1983	Deua Gum	NSW	Tree mallee to 10m	White	Honours Michael David Wilcox (b. 1940), NZ forester who first collected this species
Eucalyptus williamsiana L.A.S.Johnson & K.D.Hill	1990	Large-leaved Stringybark	Qld/NSW	Tree to 20m	White	Honours John Beaumont Williams (1932–2005), botanist, University of New England
Eucalyptus willisii Ladiges, Humphries & Brooker	1983	Peppermint	Vic/?Tas	Tree to 15m	White	Honours James Hamlyn Willis (1910–95), Victorian Government Botanist
Eucalyptus wimmerensis Rule subsp. *wimmerensis*	1990		Vic	Mallee to 4m	White	After the Wimmera district in north-west Vic where the species occurs
Eucalyptus wimmerensis subsp. Mt Arapiles (N.G.Walsh 4644) Vic Herbarium			Vic			An undescribed species from Mt Arapiles, Vic
Eucalyptus woodwardii Maiden	1910	Lemon-flowered Gum	WA	Mallet to 10m	Bright yellow	Honours Bernard Henry Woodward (c. 1846–1916), Director, WA Museum
Eucalyptus woollsiana R.T. Baker	1900	Narrow-leaved Grey Box	Qld/NSW	Tree to 25m	White	Honours William Woolls, clergyman and botanist
Eucalyptus wubinensis L.A.S.Johnson & K.D.Hill	2001		WA	Mallee to 8m	White	After the Wubin district, where the species occurs
Eucalyptus wyolensis Boomsma	1988		SA	Mallee to 7m	Yellow	After Lake Wyola, near the only occurrence of the species
Eucalyptus x bennettiae D.J.Carr & S.G.M.Carr	1980		WA	Mallee	Green/cream	Reputed hybrid between *E. lehmannii* and *E. sporadica*
Eucalyptus x chillagoensis K.D.Hill & L.A.S.Johnson						An undescribed hybrid from Chillago, Qld
Eucalyptus x erythrandra Blakely & H.Steedman	1938		WA	Mallee to 5m	Cream/red	Greek *erythro-* = red, *andros* = male; referring to the red stamens
Eucalyptus x missilis Brooker & Hopper	2002	Bullet Bush	WA	Mallee to 3m	Pale yellow	Latin *missilis* = that which may be thrown; referring to the bullet-shaped buds ('x' refers to its hybrid status)
Eucalyptus x stoataptera E.M.Benn.	1995		WA	Tree to 4m	Apricot	A hybrid between *E. stoatei* and *E. tetraptera*
Eucalyptus xanthonema Turcz. subsp. *xanthonema*	1847	Yellow-flowered Mallee	WA	Mallee to 4m	White/pale lemon	Greek *xantho-* = yellow, *nema* = thread; referring to the colour of the flowers
Eucalyptus xanthonema subsp. *apposita* Brooker & Hopper	1991		WA	Mallee to 3m	White/pale lemon	Latin *appositus* = side by side; referring to the closeness of the two subspecies
Eucalyptus xerothermica L.A.S.Johnson & K.D.Hill	2000		WA	Tree/mallee to 6m	Creamy white	Greek *xeros* = dry, *thermos* = hot; referring to the climate of the Pilbara, where the species occurs
Eucalyptus yalatensis Boomsma	1975	Yalata Mallee	WA/SA	Mallee to 4m	Creamy white	After Yalata, a settlement in far western SA, where the species occurs
Eucalyptus yarraensis Maiden & Cambage	1922	Yarra Gum	Vic	Tree to 15m	White	After the Yarra area, where the species occurs
Eucalyptus yilgarnensis (Maiden) Brooker	1986	Yorrel	WA	Tree/mallee to 10m	White	After the Yilgarn district, where the species occurs
Eucalyptus youmanii Blakely & McKie	1930	Youman's Stringybark	Qld/NSW	Tree to 20m	White	Honours Thomas Youman (1874–1962), farmer with an interest in the local flora
Eucalyptus youngiana F.Muell.	1876	Yarldarlba	WA/SA	Mallee to 8m	Red/pink/yellow	Honours Jess Young (?–1880), who accompanied Ernest Giles on the crossing of Australia in 1875
Eucalyptus yumbarrana Boomsma	1979	Yumbarra Mallee	SA	Mallee to 6m	Creamy white	After Yumbarra, the locality where the species occurs
Eucalyptus zopherophloia Brooker & Hopper	1993	Blackbutt Mallee	WA	Mallee to 4m	White	Greek *zophero-* = dusky, *phloios* = bark; referring to the dark rough bark

758 species plus 151 subspecies

Index

References in **bold** refer to illustrations

40 Australian Eucalypts in Colour 264, 265
Aboriginal use of eucalypts 77–89
Aborigines of Victoria, The 81
Ada Tree 217
*Adventures of Snugglepot and Cuddlepie and Little Ragged
    Blossom, The* 290
advertising 274–7
Africa 234, **234**, 235, **235**
agriculture and eucalypts 98–100
Allosyncarpia ternata 3, **4**
America, North 236
Amyema melaleucae 47
Amyema pendula **47**
Andrade, Edmundo Navarro de 151, 152, 231
Angophora vi, 3, 53, 257
Angophora bakeri 65
Angophora cordifolia see Angophora hispida
Angophora costata 16, 16, **23**, **24**, 138, 142, **142**, **256**
Angophora hispida 53, 55, **55**, **257**, 257, 279
Angophora robur 55
Angophora, number of species 53, 313
Anoplognathus sp. **126**
anther structure **70**, 71
ants attending lerps **40**
APC (Australian Plant Census) 63, 64, 313
Apis mellifera 165
APNI (Australian Plant Name Index) 63
Apple 15, 55, 300
Apple Jack 191
Apple, Argyle 20, **179**, 185, **300**, 300
Apple, Dwarf 55, **55**
applied art 267–73
Arillastrum 3
Arillastrum gummiferum **2**
Armillaria luteobubalina 128, **128**
Armillaria mellea 128
artist craftmen 162
Arve Big Tree 217
Ash, Alpine **29**, 114, **124**, 156
    Australian 158
    Moreton Bay 18, **19**, **25**
    Mountain 15, 28, 30, **96**, **97**, 113, **115**, 156, **156**, 161, **214**,
        215, **251**, 276, **276**, 281
    Victorian 158
    White 281
Associated Paper and Pulp Mills Ltd 114
Australia Beautiful: The Home Pictorial Annual 1929 **252**,
    255
Australia: 300 Years of Botanical Illustration 257
Australia: The Tallest Trees in the British Empire 275, **276**
Australian Cultivar Registration Authority 131, 132
Australian Encyclopaedia 227
Australian Humanitarian Overseas Service Medal **119**
Australian Labor Party 201, 224
*Australian Landscape with Cattle: The artist's property
    Patterdale* 246, **246**
Australian National Botanic Gardens 138, 148, **148**
Australian Plant Census 63, 313
Australian Plant Name Index 63
Australian Tree Portraits 255
Australian Wildflower Fairies 296
Australian Wildflower Magic 297
Australiana and collectables 279–85

Baeuerlen, William 66
Bail, Murray 291, 302
Baker, Richard T. 65, **65**, 188, 267, 268
Baker, Terry 163

Bakewell Brothers Ltd 270
Banks, Joseph vi, 53, 187, 257
bark for dwellings **94**, **95**
bark form 16–19
Barrett, H. 262
Barton, Professor Alan 195
Basedow, Herbert 80, 287
Battarbee, Rex 248
Bauer, Ferdinand 258
Bayliss, Charles 82
Beale, Bob 220
Bean, Tony 60
bedding plants 139, **140**
bee hives **164**
bee, honey 165
bee, Ligurian 167
bee, Australian native **36**, 167, **167**
beetle, Christmas **126**, 178, 188
beetle, ladybird 128
beetle, paropsis 128, 178
Bell Miners 127
Bell, G.W. 104
Bentham, George 63, 64, **64**
Bentham, Jeremy 64
Bettong, Brush-tailed 112
Big Ash One **214**
Big Fella Gum 217
Bigfoot 217
biology of eucalypts 3–51
bio-oil 195
bird nests 42
Bird Tree 217
Blackbutt 104, 138, 156, **158**, 162, 220
Blackbutt, Kondinin 136
Blackwood 266
Blades, Mary 269
Blakella 56, 200
Blakely, William 22, 66, **66**, **71**
Blaxell, Don 68
Blinky Bill 296
Bliss 291, 302
Blogg, John Kendrick 268
Bloodwood
    Bristle-leaved 59, **60**, 142
    Desert, **77**
    Long-fruited **22**, 81
    Pink 57
    Red 56, **57**, 132, **279**, 296
    Swamp 132, **133**, 173
    Twin-leaved 142
    Yellow 18, **122**, 296
bloodwoods 56, 88, **89**
Blue Gum 248
Blue Gum Romance 290
Boldrewood, Rolf 299
Bonwick, James 293
bonsai eucalypts 142, **142**
Boschen, Janet 281
Bosisto, Joseph 187
Botany Bay 299
Botany-bay Flowers 298
Bowes, Arthur 91
Box, Apple **28**, 135, 167, 171
    Badgingarra **210**, 211
    Brush 37, 39
    Coast Grey 103
    Grey **19**
    Mallee 211

Narrow-leaved Grey 38
Poplar 18, 38, 92, 135, **135**
Red **139**
Red-flowered Mallee 213, **213**
Silver **73**, 142
Tropical Red 23
White 104, 166, 282
Yellow **19**, 38, **46**, **79**, **88**, 88,135, 141, 142, 167, **168**, 288
box bark 18
Brazil 191, **228**, 231
bridges 101–3, **102**, **103**
Brooker, Ian 56, 60, **68**, 68
Brooks, Albert 227
Brown Barrel **38**
Brown, Robert 63
bullock team **108**, 109
bullroarer 287
Bunce, Daniel 79
Bungendore Wood Works Gallery 162
Bunjil's Spear 217
Bunyip Bluegum 296
Burke and Wills expedition 222
burls 162, **163**
Burning Bush: A Fire History of Australia 31
Burrendong Botanic Garden and Arboretum 151, **151**
bush coconuts **77**, 78
Butchart, Eva 182, 184
Butterfly, Xerces Blue 236

Cadaghi 138, **139**
Caesia 16, **144**
Caire, Nicholas J. 96, 251
Campbell, Archibald J. 250, 252
Candlebark 16
canoe tree **83**
canoes, Aboriginal 82–5, **82**, **85**, **86**
caoutchouc 20
Carbeen **25**
carbon dioxide as growth promoter 32
cards, collecting **279**
Carey, Peter 291, 302
Carman, Jean 183, 184
Carr, Dennis J. 67, **67**
Carr, Stella G. Maisie 67, **67**
carvings, Aboriginal 87, **87**, **88**
Cassytha 48
Cassytha melantha 48, **48**
Cavanilles, Antonio José 53, 257
Cazneaux, Harold 225, 252, 255
Cazneaux Tree, The **225**, **253**
Centurion 115, 217, 218
Cherry, Native 49, **49**
children and eucalypts 292–7
China 232
Chippendale, George 264
Christensen, Lisa 281
Christmas Tree, Western Australian 49, **49**
cinema 290, 291, **291**
cineole 188, 191 ,235
citronellal 188
clapsticks 287
Clark, Marcus 299
Clarke, John 290
Clarke, William B. 93
Classification of the Eucalypts, A 67
classifying eucalypts 53–73
Clearing, Early Morning, The 248, **249**
Cloez, F.S. 187

Coburn, John 275
Cockatoo, Gang-gang **37**
cochineal scale insects 183
Cohn, Ola 224, 225, **225**
Collins, Tom 300
Combe, Peter and Carolyn 290
Conabere, Betty 280
Considen, Dennis 187
Cook, Captain James vi, 107
Coolabah 5, 78, **198**, 199, 222, 235
Cope, Walter 288, 289
Corymbia vi, 56
   meaning of 56
   number of species 53, 316
Corymbia aparrerinja 61, 200, **201**
   arafurica 200
   aspera 200, 201
   bella 200, **201**, 201
   bloxsomei **24**
   cadophora 142
   calophylla **56**, 113, 131, 156, 280, 296
   citriodora 38, 39, 138, **138**, 156, **188**, 193, **232**
   citriodora 'Marion' 132
   disjuncta 7
   dunlopiana 59, **60**, 142
   'Dwarf Crimson' 133
   'Dwarf Orange' 133
   eximia 18, **122**, 281, 296
   ficifolia 132, 133, 138, **139**, **143**, 173, **268**, **273**, 280, 281
   ficifolia 'Vermillion Blaze' 132
   gummifera 56, **57**, 132, 143, **256**, **279**, 281, 296
   henryi 156
   intermedia 57
   latifolia 7
   maculata 16, **17**, 39, 104, 131, 156, 161, **161**
   novaguiniensis 7
   papuana 7, 200
   peltata 63
   polycarpa **22**, 81
   ptychocarpa 132, **133**, 143, 173
   ptychocarpa subsp. *aptycha* 133
   serendipita 61
   setosa 60
   'Summer Beauty' **130**, 132, 142
   'Summer Glory' 132
   'Summer Red' **131**, 132, 142, **312**
   'Summer Snow' 132
   terminalis **77**, 78
   tessellaris 18, **19**, 25, 131
   torelliana 138, **139**
   watsoniana 18, **19**
craft work 161
Crafts Council of Australia 162
Critical Revision of the Genus Eucalyptus, A 66, 71, 262, 264
Crowe, Russell 291
cultivation of eucalypts 125
cultivar, definition of 131
Cumming, Gordon 269
Curdie, Daniel 93
Currency Creek Arboretum 69, **146**, 147
Curtis's Botanical Magazine 257
Cuscuta 48

D'Arcy, Eamon 290
Dalrymple Hay, R. 111
Damocles 217
Darejo 217
Darwin, Charles vi, 246
Daum, Jean 272, 273
Davies, Thomas 96, 97
De Fructibus et Seminibus Plantarum **256**, 257
Deane, Henry 66
deciduous eucalypts 32, **33**
Dee, David 270
Dehnhardt, Frederick 84

Dendroglyphs or 'Carved Trees' of New South Wales, The **87**
Dicaeum hirundinaceum 45, **45**
Dick, John 222
Dick, Thomas 86, 87
didgeridoo 181, **286**, 287, **287**
dieback 127, 128, **128**
Dig Tree, The **222**, 222
Dipodium spp. 49
Discover Australia with Shell 279, **280**
distribution of eucalypts 5–7
Djin Djin 289
dodders 48, **48**
Dombrovskis, Peter 255
Don Shiel Collection **283**
Donn, James 60
Doritifera vulnerans **38**
Dot and the Kangaroo 294
Double 'D' Eucalyptus Oil 189, **190**
Douglas, Norman 301
Doulton & Co. 270
Dowerin Rose 173, **175**, 176, **264**, 281
drop log construction 95, **96**
drought 31, **32**
'Drover's Wife, The' 300
Dunlop, John 59
Dyemaking with Eucalypts **184**
dyes from eucalypts 183–5, **183**

Eagle Tree 217
Earle, Augustus 242, 244
Eaton, John Bertram 252
eco-prints 184, **185**
Ednie Brown, John 262
Egerton, Mark 291
endangered eucalypts 207–13
Endangered Species: Eucalypts 207
Environment Protection and Biodiversity Conservation Act 1999 174, 207
epicormic buds, shoots 15, **20**, **27**, **28**
Eriococcus confusus **129**
Eriococcus coriaceus 41, 128
Erythrophleum chlorostachys 88
ethanol production 195
Etheridge, R. 87
Eucalypti Waltzes, The 288, **289**
Eucalyptographia: A Descriptive Atlas of Eucalypts of Australia and Adjoining Islands 64, 262, 263
Eucalyptolima maideni 39
eucalypts, cold tolerant 141
eucalypts overseas 229–39
Eucalypts of South Australia 69, 147
Eucalypts of Victoria and Tasmania 69
Eucalypts Volume II 264
Eucalyptopsis 4
Eucalyptus absita **210**, 211
   accedens 16, **17**
   agglomerata 38
   aggregata **25**, 109
   alba 13
   alba var. *alba* 5, 6, 7
   alba var. *australasica* 5, 6, **7**, 32
   albens 104, 166, 282
   amplifolia 24
   Amygdalina Regnans **251**
   amygdalina 186, **256**
   angulosa 24
   aperrerinja 224, **248**, 254, 281
   archeri 141
   astringens 24
   'Augusta Wonder' 133
   bakeri 65
   balanites 211
   bancroftii 38
   banksii **20**
   baxteri **30**, 38

beardiana 211, **213**
benthamii 64
bigalerita 7, 32
blakelyi **12**, 67
bosistoana 103
botryoides 131
brachyandra 23
brassiana 7
brevipes 211
bridgesiana **28**, 135, 141, 167, 171
brookeriana 68
burdettiana 211
burracoppinensis **60**
caesia 16, 63, **144**, 280
caesia subsp. *magna* 142, 144, 173
calophylla 176, 280
camaldulensis vii, 5, **6**, 12, 35, 37, 38, 79, 82, **83**, **84**, 96, 109, **111**, 117, 131, 142, **156**, 157, 161, **163**, 166, 191, 217, 221, **234**, **238**, **249**, 255, **274**, 280
camaldulensis hybrids 84
camaldulensis 'Dale Chapman' 132
camaldulensis x *E. globulus* 136, 231
camaldulensis x *E. grandis* 136, **137**, 231
campaspe 202
ceracea 174
chloroclada 38
cinerea 20, 141, 171, **179**, 185, **300**, 300
cinerea subsp. *triplex* 179
cladocalyx **24**, 133, 167, **233**, 235
cladocalyx 'Vintage Red' **132**, 133, 233
cladocalyx var. *nana* 233
cloeziana 188
cneorifolia 191
coccifera 141, 203, 204
comitae-vallis 281
conferruminata 235, **258**
confertifolia 13
conglomerata 211
consideniana 187
coolabah 5, 78, **198**, 199, 217, 222
copulans 5, 208
cordata 172
cornuta 79
corymbosa see *Corymbia gummifera*
cosmophylla **122**, 167
crebra 18, 131
crenulata 141, 172, 208, **209**
creta 202
crucis 16, **16**, 172
crucis subsp. *praecipua* 211
cuprea 211
curtisii 142, **144**
cylindriflora 167
cypellocarpa 38
dalrympleana 141
dalrympleana subsp. *dalrympleana* 223
deglupta 5, 6, **6**, 7, 10, 124
delegatensis **29**, 114, **124**, 156, 158
delegatensis subsp. *tasmaniensis* 141
denticulata 217
diptera 202
diversicolor vii, 15, **21**, 103, 111, 156, 219, 226, 281
diversifolia **259**
diversifolia subsp. *hesperia* **13**
dives 189, 191
dolichorhyncha 15, 138, 173, 280, **285**
dolorosa 60, 209
dumosa **14**, 81, 167, 191
dunnii **18**
effusa 202
elaeophora 191
elliptica 141
eremophila **265**
erythrocorys 173, **178**, **263**
erythronema 132, 133
exserta 232

Eucalyptus (cont.)
  fastigata **38**
  fibrosa 38
  ficifolia see Corymbia ficifolia
  flocktoniae **66**
  forrestiana 173, 280, **285**
  fraxinoides 281
  gamophylla 78
  gillii 172
  globoidea 38, 42
  globulus **23**, 31, 84, 114, 131, 139, **140**, **141**, 157, 167, 172,
      185, 187, 191, 217, 219, **237**, **239**, **260**, **272**, **280**, 280,
      281, **282**
  globulus subsp. bicostata 237, **237**, **248**
  globulus subsp. maidenii 66, 237
  globulus subsp. pseudoglobulus 237
  gomphocephala 103, 235
  grandis 84, 110, 127, 131, 156, **157**, 217, 236
  grandis x E. urophylla 129
  gregsoniana 141, 203, 204
  grossa 281
  gunnii 79, 139, **140**, 141, 142, 172, **263**
  gunnii subsp. divaricata 211
  haemastoma 16, 39, 87, 202, 203, 281, **282**, **297**
  halophila 9
  imlayensis 208, **208**
  impensa 209
  insularis 211, **213**
  johnsoniana 68
  kartzoffiana **17**
  kingsmillii **176**, 176
  kondininensis 136
  kruseana 172, **180**
  kybeanensis 141
  lacrimans **17**, 203, 204, **205**
  lansdowneana 213, **213**
  lehmannii 23, **24**
  leprophloia 211
  leucophloia **79**, 79
  leucoxylon 22, **81**, 191
  longifolia 38, 59
  luehmanniana **62**, 142, 281
  macarthuri 141, 193
  macrocarpa 23, **24**, 173, **180**, 209, **262**, 262
  macrocarpa subsp. elachantha **180**
  macrorhyncha 18, 42, **94**, 184, 231, **302**
  maidenii see E. globulus subsp. maidenii
  mannifera 11, **27**, **76**, 138, **139**
  marginata 15, 28, 31, **31**, 39, 60, 103, 111, **112**, 156, **156**,
      160, 161, **163**, **250**
  marginata subsp. elegantella 112
  marginata subsp. thalassica 112
  melanoxylon **12**
  melliodora **19**, 38, **46**, **79**, **88**, 88, 135, 141, 142, 167, **168**,
      288
  microcorys 37, 38, 104, 156, **156**, **158**
  microtheca 199, **200**
  miniata 173, **181**
  moluccana **19**
  moorei 208
  morrisbyi 141, 211, **212**
  muelleriana 38, 64
  nandewarica **127**
  neglecta 141
  nicholii 38, **145**
  nicholii as bonsai 142, **142**
  nitens 114, 139, 141
  nobilis 217
  nova-anglica 141
  obliqua **10**, **11**, 38, 53, **54**, 85, 109, 114, 156, 158, 162, 257,
      258, 282
  occidentalis 136
  oleosa 191
  olida 193, **193**
  orbifolia 142
  orophila 5, 6, 7

  ovata 209
  pachycalyx subsp. banyabba 211
  pachyphylla **170**, 173
  paludicola 211
  paniculata 109
  papuana see Corymbia papuana
  parramattensis 38
  patentinervis 230
  pauciflora 39, **39**, 141, 142, 167, 203, 281
  pauciflora subsp. acerina 203
  pauciflora subsp. debeuzevillei 203
  pauciflora subsp. hedraia 203
  pauciflora subsp. niphophila 204, **205**
  pauciflora subsp. pauciflora 203, **204**
  pellita 7
  pendens 153
  perriniana 171, **175**, 177
  petiolaris **52**
  phoenicea **118**, 173, **174**, 180
  phylacis 5, 210, **210**
  pilularis 104, 138, 156, **158**, 162, 217, 220
  piperita 187
  platypus 16
  pleurocarpa **29**, 172, **172**
  polyanthemos **139**
  polybractea 191, **192**, 194
  populnea 18, 38, 92, 135, **135**
  praetermissa 60
  preissiana 15, **21**, 141, 173
  preissiana subsp. lobata 21
  propinqua 37, 38, 127
  pruiniramis 211
  pruinosa **73**, 142
  pulchella **247**
  pulverulenta 171
  punctata 37, 38
  pyriformis 173, **175**, **264**, 281
  racemosa 16, 37, 38, 39, 202, **203**, 203
  radiata 127, 131, 187, 191, 282
  ravida 202
  recurva 5, **6**, **206**, **207**, 207
  regnans 15, 28, 30, **96**, **97**, 113, **113**, **115**, 156, **156**, 158,
      161, **214**, 215, 217, **218**, **251**, **276**, 281
  resinifera 38, 109
  rhodantha 173, 180, 209
  robusta 9, 38, 109, 131, 139, **140**, 230, 232, **232**
  rodwayi 141
  rossii 39, 202, **203**, 203
  roycei 67
  rubida 16, 141
  salicola **8**, 9, 136
  saligna **24**, 32, 109, **110**, 127, **154**, 156, 157
  salmonophloia 30, 100, **101**
  salubris 100, **101**, 201, **202**, **235**
  sargentii subsp. onesia 136
  scoparia 'Golden Crown' 132
  sepulcralis 153
  siderophloia 38
  sideroxylon **19**, 22, **81**, 131, 141, **166**, 167, **169**, 173, 191
  smithii 191, 235
  socialis 15, **78**
  sp. Howe's Swamp Creek 211
  spathulata **136**
  spathulata subsp. salina 136
  staigeriana 193, 231
  stellulata 141, 208, 281
  stricklandii 132
  subcrenulata 141
  synandra 22, **22**
  taurina 60
  terebra 202
  tereticornis 7, 37, 38, 131, 139, 229, **230**
  tereticornis subsp. mediana 230
  tessellaris 18, **19**
  tetragona see E. pleurocarpa
  tetraptera **24**, 142, **145**

  tetrodonta **12**, 79, 80, 81, **81**, 85, **88**, 88, **89**, 287
  tindaliae **18**, 38
  torquata 133, 138, **173**, 173, 176, **261**
  tortilis 202
  'Torwood' 133, 138, 176
  tricarpa 103, 169
  'Urrbrae Gem' 132
  uncinata **58**, 59
  urna **12**
  urnigera 141
  urophylla 5, **5**, 6, 7, 232, 236
  utilis 136
  viminalis 16, **28**, 35, 37, 38, 43, **43**, **59**, 78, 282
  viminalis subsp. cygnetensis 43
  viminalis subsp. hentyensis 43
  viminalis subsp. pryoriana 43
  viridis 191
  wandoo 30, 111, **111**
  wetarensis 5, 6, 7
  woodwardii 133, 138, 144, 173, **176**
  youmanii 231
  youngiana **36**, 173
eucalyptus oil 100, 186–95, **186**, **190**, **192**
Eucalyptus Blues 290
Eucalyptus Discovery Centre 149, **152**
Eucalyptus Mallee Company 188
Eucalyptus, the novel vii, 291
Eucalyptus, number of species 53, 337
Eucalyptus, type species of **54**
EUCLID 68, **72**, **73**, 313
Eudesmia 56
Eurabbie 237
European early use of eucalypts 90–105
Eustice, Alfred 282
Evans, Ted 88
*Evening Shadows, Backwater of the Murray, South
    Australia* 248, **249**
evolution of eucalypts 3–4
Exocarpos cupressiformis 49, **49**
Exotic Botany 257
Explorer's Tree, The **220**
Eyre, Edward J. 82

Fairies' Tree, The 224, **224**, **225**
farms **134**, 135, **135**
Farrer, William 93
Felton, Alfred 188
Felton, Grimwade and Bosisto Pty Ltd 187
Ferguson Tree 216
Fergusonina sp. 41
Field Guide to the Eucalypts Vols 1–3 68
Field, Barron 244, 298
fire and eucalypts 26–31, **26**
First Fruits of Australian Poetry 298
Fiveash, Rosa 262, 263, 270
Flint, India 184
Flockton, Margaret 66, 262, 264
flooring **154**
Flora Australiensis 64
Florilegium, The 257
florist trade 171–81
flower painters and illustrators 257–65
flowers and fruits 22
flowers, cut 173
foliage for florist trade 171, 177, **177**, 178
For the Term of His Natural Life 299
Forest Flora of South Australia 262, 263
forestry, a brief history of 107–15
forestry in New South Wales 109
forestry in Tasmania 114
forestry in Victoria 113
forestry in Western Australia 111
fossils 4, **4**
Francis, Peter 149
Frankel, Sir Otto 303
Franklin, Miles 300, 301

Fringe of Leaves, A 289
funeral, Aboriginal ceremonies 88, **89**
fungus, honey 128
fungus, leaf-spotting 179
Furphy, Joseph 300

Gaertner, Joseph 53, 256, 257
galls on eucalypts **40**, 41, 128
gardens, private 141
Gaubaea 56
General Sherman 217
George, Alex 67
geranyl acetate 188
'Getting Back to My Roots and Other Suckers' 289
'Ghost Gum, The' **254**
Giant Gum Tree, The **216**
Giant of the Arid North, A 225
Giant Trees of Victoria, The 216, 251
Gibbs, May 57, 117, 280, 281, 284, 294, 296, 297
Gill, S.T. 108
Gill, Walter 252
Gimlet, Large-fruited 202
    Rough-barked 202
    Silver 202
    Two-winged 202
gimlets 100, **101**, 201, 202, **235**
'Give Me a Home Among the Gum Trees' 289
Glaucopsyche xerces 236
Gloucester Tree, The 21, **226**, 226
Glover, John 246
gluing eucalypt wood 161, 162
Glycaspis sp. **40**
Golden Gleams **ii**, **252**
Golden Gum logo **277**
Gondwana, fragmentation of **3**, 9
Gordon, Adam Lindsay 299
grafting eucalypts 124
Grandfather, The 219
Grandis, The 217
grasshoppers 128
Gray, Alan 68
Gregory, A.C. 64
Grey, Zane 288
Grimwade, Frederick 188
Groom, Arthur 227
growth characteristics 15–25
Guilfoyle, William 139
Gum, Araluen **17**
    Bancroft's Red 38
    Black **25**, 109
    Blakely's Red **12**, **67**
    Blue 109
    Brittle **11**, **27**, **76**, 138, **139**
    Brooker's 68
    Bushy Sugar 233
    Buxton 208
    Cabbage **24**
    Camden White 64
    Cider 79, 139, **140**, 142, 172, **263**
    Coral 138, **173**, 173, **261**
    Cup **122**, 167
    Dunn's White **18**
    Dwarf Sugar 233
    Fleurieu Swamp 211
    Flooded 84, 110, 127, 131, 156, **157**, 231, 235, 236
    Forest Red 37, 38, 139, 229, **230**, 235
    Fuchsia 15, 138, 173, **285**
    Ghost 56, 61, 200, **201**, 224, **248**, 281
    Grey 37, 38, 127, 235
    Gully 191, 235
    Heart-leaved Silver 172
    Jingymia 211
    Jounama Snow 203
    Large-leaved Spotted 156
    Lemon 138
    Lemon-flowered 173, **176**

    Lemon-scented 38, 39, 138, **138**, 156, **188**, 193, 231, 232, **232**, 238
    Maiden's 66
    Mallee Red **127**
    Manna 16, 35, 37, 38, 43, **43**, 78
    Morrisby's 211, **212**
    Mountain 223
    Mountain Grey 38
    Mysore 231
    Northern Salmon 7, 32
    Parramatta Red 38
    Rainbow 6, **6**, 10
    Red 38
    Red Flowering 132, 133, 138, **139**, 141, 142, **143**, 173, **182**, 184, **273**
    Ribbon 16, 43, **43**, 282
    River Red vii, 5, **6**, 12, 35, 37, 38, 79, 82, **83**, **84**, 85, 96, 103, 109, **111**, 114, 117, 118, 131, 142, **156**, 157, 161, **163**, 166, 167, 191, 221, 224, 225, 231, 232, **234**, 235, 238, 248, **249**, 255, 274, 280
    Rough-leaved Ghost 201
    Salmon 30, 100, **101**
    Salt **8**, 9, 136
    Scarlet **118**
    Scarlet 173, **174**
    Scribbly 16, **17**, 37, 38, 87, 202, 299, 281, **282**, **297**
    Seppelt Range 174
    Shining 114, 139, 141
    Silver Dollar 171, 179
    Silver-leaved Mountain 171
    Snappy **79**, 79
    Snow 16, 39, **39**, 141, 142, 167, 203, 281
    Southern Blue **248**
    Spinning 171, **175**, 177
    Spotted 16, **17**, 39, 104, 132, 156, 161, **161**
    Strawberry 193, **193**
    Strickland's 132, 133
    Sugar **24**, 133, 167, **233**, 235
    Swamp 209
    Sydney Blue **24**, 32, **110**, 127, 156, 157
    Sydney Blue as flooring **154**
    Sydney Red 16, **16**, **23**, **24**, 138, 142, **142**
    Tasmanian Blue **23**, 31, 84, 114, 131, 139, **140**, 157, 167, 172, 185, 187, 191, 219, 231, 232, 235, 236, **237**, **239**, **141**, **260**, **272**, **280**, 281, **281**, **282**
    Tasmanian Snow 204
    Timor 232
    Timor Mountain 6, 236
    Victorian Silver 172, 208
    Water 39, **52**
    Weeping Snow **17**, 204, **205**
    White 6, 7, 32
    Wolgan Snow 204
    Yellow 22, **81**, 191
Gum Flowers and Love **260**
Gum Leaves **294**
Gum Tree Brownie and Other Faërie Folk of the Never-Never **294**
'Gum, The' 301
gum-leaf band **288**, **288**
Gum-Nut Babies and Gum-Blossom Babies 296
Gumnut Teahouse, Austraflora Nursery **276**
gumnuts 22, 176
Gungurru 144
Gunn's Plantation Ltd 114
Gunther, Bob 227
Guthridge, Ian 161

Hall, Edwin 65
Hall, Ken 288, 291
Hall, Norman 71
Handbook for Eucalyptus Planters, A 236
Harding, Matthew 163
haustorium 46, 47, **48**
Havens, Frank 236
Hawkins, Reg 270

hedges from eucalypts 141, **141**
Heer, Rolf de 85
Heliopolis Sporting Club **119**
Helms, Richard 144
Henry, Lucien 267, 273
Herbig Tree 221, **222**
Herbig, Friedrich 96, 221
Hewson, Helen 257
Heysen, Hans 248, 249, 255, 268, 280
Hill, Ken 56, 59, 68, **68**
'His Country After All' 300
historic eucalypts 219
Hogbin, Stephen 162
hollows as habitat **34**, 35, **35**
honey production 164–70, **165**
Hopper, Steve 60
How Does a Tree Grow? Or Botany for Young Australians 293
Howie, Laurence 117, 118, 268, 270
Howitt, Alfred 64
Humphries, Barry 289, **290**
hybrid, definition of 131
hybrids and cultivars 131–3
Hyperion 215, 217

Icarus Dream 217, **218**
Icones et Descriptiones Plantarum **257**
identifying eucalypts 71–3
Idiogenes 56
If Trees Could Speak 220
Illyarrie 173, **178**, **263**
India 229
Ingamells, Rex 301
Ingham, George 161
International Code of Botanical Nomenclature 59
International Code of Nomenclature for Cultivated Plants 131
Introduction to Botany Teachings at the Schools of Victoria 293
'In the Valley Where the Gum Trees Grow' 288
invertebrates in eucalypts 39
Ironbark, Broad-leaved 38
    Grey 38, 109
    Lemon-scented 193, 231
    Narrow-leaved 18
    Red **19**, 22, **81**, 103, 141, **166**, 167, **169**, 173, 191
Ironbarks 18
Ironwood 88

Jack Gardner's stable **96**
Jarrah 15, 28, 31, **31**, 39, 60, 103, 111, **112**, 113, 156, **156**, **160**, 161, **163**, 250
Jarrah Leafminer 39
jewellery 282, **283**
jetties 103
Jindyworobak movement 301
John, Alan 290
Johnson, Lawrence 56, 59, 67, **67**
Johnston, Don 71
Johnston, George 302
Johnstone, Henry James 248
Johnstone, Robert 264
Joyce, Helen 283
Jundiai Forest Garden 151
June Park, Van Dieman's Land, the general appearance of the country in its natural state **242**, 246
juvenile foliage 20, 28, **28**

Kamminga, Johan 81
Kangaroo 301
Karri vii, 15, **21**, 103, 111, 113, 156, 219, 226, 235, 281
Karri Knight 219
Kauffmann, John ii, 252, 255
Kelly Tree, The **223**
Kelly, Ned 223
Kelly, Stan 264, **264**, 265

Key to the Eucalypts, A 66, 71, **71**
Kidman, Nicole 291
King's Park, Perth **138**
kino, 79, **79**, **168**
koala food trees 38
koalas 37, **37**
Kurrajongs 4

L'Héritier de Brutelles, Charles Louis 53, 257
Labillardière, Jaques J.H. de 59
'Land of Contradictions, The' 298
Landcare programs 135, **136**
Lang, John 299
Lantana camara 127
Last Muster of the Aborigines at Risdon, The 246, **247**
Latz, Peter 78
Laurasia 3
Lawrence, D.H. 301
Lawrence, Ray 291
Lawson, Henry 299, 300
leaf form 20
Lefebvre, Charles 272, 273
Lerp, Spotted Gum 39
lerps 39, **40**, **76**, **127**
Liberty Silk Company 273
Lights of Adelaide from the Mount Lofty Ranges, The **274**
lignotubers 28, **99**
Lindsay, Norman 296
Linnaeus, Carl 69
literature, eucalypts in 298–303
Lone Hand, The **295**, 296
Lophostemon confertus 37
Lord, Lieutenant Edward 91
Lorrain, Claude 243
Luehmann, Johann Georg 63
Lycett, Joseph 245

MacDonnell Range 248
McKean's Eucalyptus Works **190**
'Magic Button, The' 296
Magic Pudding, The 296
Magnol, Pierre 69
Mahogany, Swamp 9, 38, 109, 139, 161, **140**, 230, 232, **232**, 235
Maiden, Joseph 20, 65, **65**, 66, 71, 184, 187, 262, 264, 267
Mallee, Baker's 65
   Beard's 211, **213**
   Bell-fruited 15, **21**, 141, 173
   Blue 191, **192**, 194
   Book-leaf 172, 176, **180**
   Burracoppin **60**
   Cadda Road 211
   Coarse-leaved 281
   Comet Vale 281
   Curly 172, 176
   Dandaragan 209
   Eneabba 209
   Green 191
   Hook-leaved **58**, 59
   Imlay 208
   Jingymia 22, **22**
   Johnson's 68
   Kangaroo Island Narrow-leaved 191
   Kingsmill's **176**, 176
   Meelup 5, 210, **210**
   Mongarlowe **6**, **206**, **207**, 207
   Mt Misery 60, 209
   Mukinbudin 211
   North Twin Peak 211, **213**
   Pear-fruited 175
   Plunkett 142, **144**
   Red **15**, **78**
   Red Bull **170**, 173, 176
   Red-flowered 132
   Ridge-fruited **24**
   Rose 173, 176, 180, 209

Round-leaved 142
Sand **265**
Scaly-butt 211
Soap **259**
Southern Cross 172
Southern Cross Silver 16, **16**
Square-fruited **24**, 142, **145**
Weeping **153**
White **14**, 81, 167, 191
Mallee Ash, Madura **13**
Mallee Ash, Yellow-top **62**, 63, 142, 281
'Mallee Boy' 289
Mallee Brand logo, The **277**
mallee, definition of 15
'Mallee Root Song, The' 289
mallee roots 98, **99**
mallet, definition of 15
Mallet, Brown **24**
   Swamp **136**
Manley, F.D. 280
manna 43, **43**, 78
Marlock, Bald Island 235, **258**
marlock, definition of 15
Marri **56**, 113, 156, 176, 296
Martens, Conrad 246, 248
Mass, Nuri 296
Melaleuca quinquenervia 129
Melbourne Botanic Gardens 139
menthol 191
Meredith, Louisa A. 99, 258, 260
Merrit **12**, **66**
Merton, D.V. 270
Meslee, Edmund la 94
Messmate 53, 85, 114, 162, 282
Messmate, Gympie 188
methyl cinnamate 193
Metrosideros 53, 256
mildew, powdery 129
Mills, Richard 290
Milson, Alfred Mrs 255
mining industry 100–1
minnirichi bark **16**, 144
mistletoe **44**, 45, **46**, 46, 47, **47**
Mistletoebird 45, **45**, 46
Mitchell, Thomas 87, 219
Monacalyptus 56
money 281, **281**, 282, **282**
Monkira Monster, The 217, **227**
Moort 16
mordant, definition of 183
Morrell, Black **12**
Morrell, Red 191
Mort, Eirene 271
moth, cup **38**
moth, Emperor Gum 39
moth, scribbly gum 39, **39**
Mottlecah 23, **24**, 173, 176, **180**, 209, **262**, 262
Mount Annan Botanic Gardens **150**
Mount Tree 217
Mountain, Adrien 104
Mountford, Charles P. 255
Mueller, Ferdinand von 23, 63, 64, **65**, 66, 69, 139, 144, 187, 215, 229, 262, 293
Mugga **169**
Muellerina celastroides **44**
Mulga 162, **166**, 167, 168, 173
'Municipal Gum' 303
Museu de Eucalipto 151, **152**
music 286–9
My Brilliant Career 300, 301
My Brother Jack 302
Mycosphaerella sp. 179
myrticolorin 184

Namatjira, Albert vii, 200, 248, 255, 281
naming eucalypts 58–61, **61**, 69

National Collection of Eucalypts, Royal Horticultural
   Society's 139
National Trust logo **275**
National Vegetation Information System 10
nectar 36
Nelson, David 53, 54
nematodes 41
New Zealand 141, **141**, 142, **142**, 300
Nicolle, Dean **68**, 69, 146, 147
Noble Tree 217
Nock, Olive 273
Noisy Miners 127
North, Alexander 269
North, Marianne 262
Notes and Sketches of New South Wales 99
Nuytsia floribunda 49, **49**

O Avó de Chavín 219
Oak, American Black 184
Oak, Tasmanian 158, 162
Ogmograptis sp. 16, 39, **39**, 202
oil glands 20
Oil Mallee Association 195
Oil Mallee Company 136
Old Calabria 301
'Old Gum Tree, The' 289, **289**
Old Tales of a Young Country 299
'On Myrticolorin, the Yellow Dye Material of Eucalyptus
   Leaves' 184
On Our Selection 300
Oodgeroo Noonuccal 303
Opuntia sp. 183
Orchid, Hyacinth 49
'Our Gum Trees' 299
Our Island Home: A Tasmanian Sketch Book 258
Outhwaite, Ida Rentoul 294
Oxley, John 55, 219

painting gum trees 243–9
Papa Zig **218**
parasite, definition of 45
parasites of eucalypts 44–9
Pardalote, Striated **34**
Parkinson, Sydney 257
Parrot Brand Eucalyptus Oil 187, **187**
Paterson, Banjo 299
Patten, Herbert **288**
Payne, Ellen N. 268
Pedley, Ethel 294
Peirce, J. Duncan 216, 251
Penfold, A.R. 188
Peppermint, Broad-leaved **189**, 191
Peppermint, Narrow-leaved 38, 127, 187, 191, 282
   Narrow-leaved Black **145**
   Narrow-leaved Black as bonsai 142, **142**
   Queensland 232
   Sydney 187
pests and diseases 127–9
Peter Francis Points Arboretum **149**, 152
phellandrene 188, 191
Phillip, Captain Arthur 107, 139
Phillips, Ernest John 271
phosphorous acid 128
photographing gum trees 250–5
Phytophthora cinnamomi 112, 113, 127, 128, 141, 156, 208
Pine, Stephen 31
piperitone 188, 191
Plant Breeder's Rights 131
planting technique 125, **125**
plough, stump-jump 98, **99**
Possum, Western Pygmy 36
postage stamps **278**, 280
postcards 116, **116**, 117, **117**, 118, 282, **283**
Poussin, Nicolas 243
Premier Pottery 270
Preston, Walter 90

Prima Hosiery logo **277**
Proclamation Tree, The 221, **221**, 280
propagation and cultivation 123–6
Pryor, Lindsay 56, 67, 138, 139, 207
psyllid 39, 43, **76**, 127, 178
Puccinia psidii 129, **129**
pukumani poles 88, **89**
punch cards for identification 71, **72**

Quandongs 49
Quercus velutina 184
Quin, Tarella 294
Quoll, Western 112

railways and tramways 102, 103, **103**, **111**
Rangle River 288
Redheads matchbox 280
Redouté, Pierre J. 54, 257, 259
Redwood, Coast 215
Remued ware 270, **270**
Research on the Eucalypts, Especially in Regard to Their Essential Oils, A 65
Rhysobius ventralis 128
Rhytidoponera tasmaniensis 40
ringbarking **92**, 93, **93**
road paving 104, **104**, **105**
Robbery Under Arms 299
Roberts, Tom 255
root parasites 49
root system **31**
rootstock 132, 143
Rosa, Salvator 243
Rose, D. 280
Rowan, Ellis 258, 260, 270, 271
Royal Botanic Gardens, Sydney 138
Royal Worcester Porcelain Company 270, 271
Royle, Bert 289
Rudd, Steele 300
Rullah Longatyle 217
Rushton, Gertrude 266, 267, 268
Rust, Guava 129, **129**
rutin 231

St Paul's Church of England, Stanthorpe, Qld **95**
Sally, Black 208, 281
  Narrow-leaved 208
Salt Pan Plain, Van Diemen's Land 244, **245**
salt-tolerant eucalypts 136
salinity, combating 136, **136**, **137**
Santalum spp. 49
sawfly larva 128, **129**
sawpits 107
scale, gum tree 41, 128
scale insects 178
Scott, Harriet and Helena 258
Scouts Australia logo **275**
Sculthorpe, Peter 287, 289
seed, eucalypt **25**, 36
seed, propagation 122, 123, **123**
Separation Tree, The 221, **221**
Sequoia sempervirens 215, 217
Sequoiadendron giganteum 217
Sertum Anglicum 54
Seven Little Australians 293
shelters, Aboriginal **80**, **81**
shields, Aboriginal **81**
shingles 96, **96**, **97**
Siegesbeck, Johann G. 69
Silver Princess 142, 144, 173, 176
Sinclair, Marion 297

Smith, Doug 139
Smith, H.G. 188
Smith, Henry 65, 184
Smith, J.E. 257
Smyth, Brough 81
Snugglepot and Cuddlepie 280
Snugglepot and Cuddlepie **297**
Snugglepot and Cuddlepie ballet **290**
Solander, Daniel 53
Sons of Gwalia mine **101**
Sorghum 12, 13
Souter, David Henry 294
South Australian School of Design 269
South Coast Wood Works Gallery 162
South View of Sydney-Cove taken from the General Spring nigh the Eastern entrance to Pitt's Row **244**
souvenirs and memorabilia 282
Spielvogel, Nathan 299
Spirit of Endurance, The 225, **253**, 255
Splitters **108**
Squatter's Daughter, The 288
Stathmopoda melanochra 128
Still Sorrow 217
Stockwellia quadrifida 3
street tree planting 138, 139, **139**
stringybark 18, 109, 302, **302**
Stringybark, Blue-leaved 38
  Brown **30**, 38
  Darwin **12**, 79, 80, 81, **81**, 85, **88**, 88, **89**, 287
  Messmate **10**, **11**, 38, 156
  Red 18, 38, 42, **94**, 184, 231, **302**
  Swamp 211
  Tindal's **18**, 38
  White 38, 42
  Yellow 38, 64
  Youman's 231
Sturt School for Wood 162
Symphyomyrtus 56
Syncarpia glomulifera 104

Table Looms and Some Australian Dyes as Home Crafts 184
Tahune Airwalk 115
Tall Timber 291, **291**
Tall Timbers 291, **291**
Tallarack **29**, 172, **172**, 176
Tallowwood 37, 38, 104, 156, **156**, **159**
Tasman, Abel 78
Tate, Ralph 144
taxon, meaning of 61
Ten Canoes 85, **85**
termites 41, **41**
Thailand **238**
theatre 289, 290, **290**
Themeda 12
Thiele, Colin 301
Thornhill, D. 280
timber crafts 161–4
timber industry, economics of 155
timber names 158
timber production 155–9
tissue culture of eucalypts 124
Tjuta 78
Tooth's 'KB' Lager **277**
Tree of Knowledge, The 201, 224, **224**
Tree of Man, The 302
Tree Wonders of Australia 227
Triodia 12, 13, 80
Tristaniopsis laurina 39

Trompf, Percy 274, 276
Tropical eucalypt woodland/grassland **12**, 13
Truchanas, Olegas 255
Tuart 103, 235
Turner, Ethel 292, 293, 294, 296
Turpentine 104
Two Towers 217, **218**
type species, meaning of 53, 59

urban landscaping 137–41
Useful Native Plants of Australia 184

vegetation, classification of 10–13
Veitch, John G. 91
View of Part of the Town of Parramatta, in New South Wales 90
View of Salt Pan Plain—Van Diemen's Land 244, **245**
Views in Australia 244, 245
Vincent Tree 217
vine thickets 10
Viscum 48
Voyage of the Beagle, The vi

Wadsworth, S. 283
Waite Arboretum **150**
Walker, Kath 303
Walker, W.C. 236
Wall, Dorothy 296
'Waltzing Matilda' 299
Wandoo 30, 111, **111**
Wandoo, Powder-bark 16, **17**
war and eucalypts 116–19, **119**
Warilu 78
Waterman, Robert H. 236
Watling, Thomas 244
Watson, Jack 226
wattle and daub huts 95
Webb, Duncan 291
wharves 103
'White Gum' **292**
White, Patrick 289, 302
wildlife habitat 35
Wilkes, Charles 91
Williamson, J.C. 289
Williamson, John 289
Willis, Jim 227
Willoughby, Howard 92
Wills, W.D. & H.O. 279
Winds of Jarrah, The 291
wood pellets 195
woodblocks 104–5
Woodman, Tom 277
wood-turning 162
Woolls, William 220
Woollybutt 38, 59
Woollybutt, Camden 193
  Darwin 173, **181**
  Tenterfield **20**
Worgan, George 91
wreath of eucalypt leaves **119**
Wright, Judith 303

Yarldarlba **36**, 173
Yate 79
Yate, Bushy 23, **24**
  Swamp 136
Yellowjacket **24**
Yellowjacket, Large-fruited 18, **19**
Yuranigh 87, 88
Yuruga Nursery 136, **137**

This edition published in 2012
First published in 2010

Allen & Unwin
Sydney, Melbourne, Auckland, London

83 Alexander Street
Crows Nest NSW 2065
Australia
Phone: (61 2) 8425 0100
Email: info@allenandunwin.com
Web: www.allenandunwin.com

Cataloguing-in-Publication details are available
from the National Library of Australia
www.trove.nla.gov.au

ISBN 978 1 74331 080 9

Internal design by Liz Seymour
Photographs by the authors (unless otherwise attributed)
Printed in China by 1010 Printing Limited

10 9 8 7 6 5 4 3 2

Heading motif: *Eucalyptus meliodora*, from a woodblock engraving published by
Ferdinand von Mueller in 1877.